Eurographics Workshop
on
Sketch-Based Interfaces and Modeling
2006

Vienna, Austria
September 3 – 4, 2006

Workshop Chair
Joaquim Armando Pires Jorge, Technical University of Lisbon, Portugal

Program Co-Chairs
Thomas Stahovich, University of California Riverside, USA
Mario Costa Sousa, University of Calgary, Canada

Local Organizer
Stefan Jeschke, Vienna University of Technology, Austria

Proceedings Production Editors
Dieter Fellner (Graz University of Technology, Austria)
Stephen Spencer (The University of Washington, USA)

Co-sponsored by ACM SIGGRAPH and EUROGRAPHICS Association

Dieter W. Fellner, Werner Hansmann, Werner Purgathofer, François Sillion
Series Editors

Published by the Eurographics Association
-PO Box 16, CH-1288 Aire-la-Ville, Switzerland-
in cooperation with
Institute of Computer Graphics & Knowledge Visualization at Graz University of Technology
and
Institute of Scientific Computing at Technical University Brunswick.

Printed in Germany

Cover design by Stefanie Behnke

ISBN 3-905673-39-8
ISSN 1812-3503

The electronic version of the proceedings is available from the Eurographics Digital Library at
`http://diglib.eg.org`

Table of Contents

Sketch and Symbol Recognition

Content Interpretation

3D Design

Interfaces

Table of Contents

Applications

System Evaluation

Preface

The mouse and keyboard have defined user interfaces for the nearly forty years since the former was invented, yet interfaces based on this hardware often leave much to be desired. For example, while computers are indispensable aids in engineering and architectural design tasks, they have yet to become the preferred tools in the very early stages of design, where pencil and paper still reign. This is because current user interfaces are too cumbersome for rapid exploration of the design space. Sketch-based interfaces are emerging as an approach to address this, since they provide flexible, informal interaction between computers and users in a way that that does not hinder creativity. These interfaces are becoming increasingly practical because of the many recent advances in pen input devices, especially tablet computers.

The 2006 Eurographics Workshop on Sketch-based Interfaces and Modeling, held in conjunction with the 2006 Eurographics Conference, brings together an international community of researchers working to advance the state of the art in sketch-based interfaces and their applications. The workshop is intended to provide an opportunity for these researchers to share lessons learned, present new results, and discuss open issues. The workshop also includes two invited presentations. In the first of these, Eric Saund of the Palo Alto Research Center presents one possible view of a "killer application" for pen-based interfaces - games. In the second, Marc Alexa from the Technical University of Berlin presents exciting new work in sketch-based 3D surface design.

After a careful reviewing process, we selected 19 papers out of 29 submissions for presentation at the workshop and inclusion in this volume. These cover a wide range of cutting-edge research topics. Some papers present fundamental advances in sketch understanding and user interface design. Others explore the use of pen-based interfaces for creating natural, easy-to-use modeling tools, including 3D geometric modelers, texture creation engines, and tools for modeling biological structures. Yet others present new applications, such as shape search, visualization of 3D medical data, and animation. Finally, there are several studies on the effectiveness of pen-based interfaces that provide insights that will help shape the future directions of the field.

We would like to thank all those who have contributed to making this workshop a success, including the participants, the program committee for contributing their time and expertise to the paper review process, the invited speakers, Stefan Jeschke for his indefatigable work on local arrangements and Stefanie Behnke for her invaluable help with the proceedings. We would also like to extend a special thanks to Nokia, who graciously sponsored this workshop.

Joaquim Armando Pires Jorge, Technical University of Lisbon, Portugal
Mario Costa Sousa, University of Calgary, Canada
Thomas Stahovich, University of California, Riverside, USA

Sponsors

Eurographics Association

Keynote

Games: The Killer App for Pen Computing?

Eric Saund (saund@parc.com)

Perceptual Document Analysis Area
Intelligent Systems Laboratory
Palo Alto Research Center

Abstract

Because of the lack of compelling applications, relatively few people are attracted to pen computing hardware. And without sufficient hardware adoption rates, few application vendors are investing heavily in applications that take full advantage of the drawing, writing, and direct manipulation affordances of the electronic stylus on a screen.

The question arises, "What will be the killer app for pen computing?"

One possible answer is a hit game. Poker, Monopoly, Scrabble, Pong, Pictionary, Tetris, Rubik's Cube, the Sims, were (are) all phenomena in their time. The Playstation, XBox, and Gamecube prove that games drag specialized and expensive hardware. Games can come from out of the blue to strike it big. New platforms are rare opportunities. This talk will discuss the new possibilities that pen computing offers for games, and suggest criteria that must be met to create a "killer app" game compelling enough to drive adoption of pen computing hardware so that all the rest of our neat applications will have a place to go. I will demonstrate a few example games that may be cute but are not good enough. The audience will be challenged to do better.

Biographical Note

Eric Saund is manager of the Perceptual Document Analysis area in the Intelligent Systems Laboratory at the Palo Alto Research Center. His research is in the field of computational vision, specializing in perceptual organization in the domain of document images. Applications of this work include ubiquitous document imaging, diagrammatic user interfaces, and perceptually-supported image editing, as well as classical document recognition. Dr. Saund received a B.S. in Engineering and Applied Science from the California Institute of Technology and a Ph.D. in Cognitive Science from the Massachusetts Institute of Technology. He has been granted twenty-three patents to date, and has received Best Conference Paper awards for his work in perceptually supported image editing and inference from opponent betting behavior in poker.

Keynote

Editing Surface Meshes by View-Dependent Sketching

Marc Alexa (marc@cs.tu-berlin.de)

Faculty of Electrical Engineering and Computer Science
Technical University of Berlin

Abstract

I present a method for the intuitive editing of surface meshes by means of view-dependent sketching. In most existing shape deformation work, editing is carried out by selecting and moving a handle, usually a set of vertices. Our system lets the user easily determine the handle, either by silhouette selection and cropping, or by sketching directly onto the surface. Subsequently, an edit is carried out by sketching a new, view-dependent handle position or by indirectly influencing differential properties along the sketch. Combined, these editing and handle metaphors greatly simplify otherwise complex shape modeling tasks.

The editing approach makes use of Laplacian surface modeling techniques. The main computation involved in all operations is the solution of a sparse linear system, which can be done at interactive rates.

Biographical Note

Marc Alexa is a Professor in the Faculty of Electrical Engineering and Computer Science at the Technical University of Berlin and heads the Computer Graphics group. He is primarily interested in representing shapes and their deformation, using point sampled geometry, implicit surfaces, explicit representations, and linear spaces of base shapes. For his earlier work on morphing he received a PhD in Computer Science from Darmstadt University of Technology. He has presented and lectured on topics related to shape representations at SIGGRAPH and other conferences. Marc Alexa has been a co-chair and has served as a member of several committees of major graphics conferences.

EUROGRAPHICS Workshop on Sketch-Based Interfaces and Modeling (2006)
Thomas Stahovich and Mario Costa Sousa (Editors)

An Efficient Graph-Based Symbol Recognizer

WeeSan Lee,[1] Levent Burak Kara,[2] and Thomas F. Stahovich[3]

[1]Department of Computer Science, University of California, Riverside, CA 92521
[2]Mechanical Engineering Department, Carnegie Mellon University, Pittsburgh, PA 15213
[3]Mechanical Engineering Department, University of California, Riverside, CA 92521

Abstract
We describe a trainable symbol recognizer for pen-based user interfaces. Symbols are represented internally as attributed relational graphs that describe both the geometry and topology of the symbols. Symbol recognition reduces to the task of finding the definition symbol whose attributed relational graph best matches that of the unknown symbol. One challenge addressed in the current work is how to perform this graph matching in an efficient fashion so as to achieve interactive performance. We present four approximate graph matching techniques: Stochastic Matching, which is based on stochastic search; Error-driven Matching, which uses local matching errors to drive the solution to an optimal match; Greedy Matching, which uses greedy search; and Sort Matching, which relies on geometric information to accelerate the matching. Finally, we present promising results of initial user studies, and discuss the tradeoffs between the various matching techniques.

Categories and Subject Descriptors (according to ACM CCS): I.5.2 [Pattern Recognition]: Classifier Design and Evaluation

1. Introduction

Researchers have developed a variety of approaches for recognizing hand-drawn shapes and symbols. However, many of the current approaches have important limitations. For example, some methods are limited to single-stroke shapes drawn in preferred orientations [Rub91]. Others consider only aggregate properties of a shape and can confuse dissimilar shapes that have similar aggregate properties [FPJ02]. Other approaches require shapes to be drawn with a consistent pen stroke order [SD05].

Our work is aimed at overcoming some of these limitations. Our goal is to create an efficient, trainable, multi-stroke symbol recognizer that is insensitive to orientation, scaling, and drawing order. This is achieved via a graphical representation. Specifically, a symbol is represented with an attributed relational graph (ARG) describing its geometry and topology. The nodes in the graph represent the geometric primitives, and the edges represent the geometric relationships between them. Representing a symbol in terms of its topology allows us to achieve invariance to rotation and scaling, including non-uniform scaling. Because of the later capability, our approach is particularly tolerant of large variations in the shape of a hand-drawn symbol.

With our approach, symbol recognition reduces to the task of graph matching. During recognition, the ARG of the unknown symbol is matched against the ARG of each definition symbol to find the best match. The unknown is classified by whichever definition matches best. Graph matching, or sub-graph isomorphism [Ull76, DPZ01], is known to be NP-complete [GJ79]. Here, the problem is made more difficult because of noise. Noise comes from variations in how the symbols are drawn as well as from processing errors. For example, it is not uncommon for a symbol to have extra or missing geometric primitives, and thus extra or missing nodes in its ARG.

There has been considerable research in developing efficient graph matching techniques for a variety of applications [CFSV04]. Here we present and evaluate four new techniques specifically designed for recognizing hand-drawn shapes. These techniques are designed to be efficient enough for interactive performance, and to be tolerant of the noise inherent in hand-drawn symbols.

Our recognizer assumes that the individual symbols in a sketch have been located prior to recognition. In other work, we have developed sketch parsers for locating the symbols in a sketch [KS04, GKSS05].

The next section places this work in context by describing related work. This is followed by the details of our approach. Finally, results of a user study and conclusions are presented.

2. Related Work

Symbol recognition is an active area of research. An extensive overview of the literature can be found in [LVSM02]. Here, we present a representative sample of the literature.

Lee [Lee92] developed a graph-based recognizer in which the graph represents the precise geometry of the object. The approach is suitable for precisely drawn symbols with uniform scaling. For example, the approach has been used to recognize machine drawn symbols, symbols drawn using templates, and precise hand-drawn symbols. Lee's approach requires manual selection of key vertices during training.

Calhoun *et al.* [CSKK02] developed an approach in which the graph encodes topology, rather than geometry, so as to be more tolerant of variations in hand-drawn sketches. When learning definitions, thresholds are used to decide when a continuous property, such as intersection angle, should be included in the graph. If a property is included in the graph, it is represented by a single numerical value. In our work, attributes are described statistically, making our approach significantly more robust to pen stroke segmentation errors and drawing variations. Furthermore, to achieve interactive performance, Calhoun's approach requires the user to maintain a consistent drawing order. The system does have a mode that allows for variable drawing order. In that case, however, best-first search, which is computationally expensive, is used to do matching. The graph matching techniques we present are significantly more efficient. Likewise, Calhoun's approach requires the training examples to have a consistent drawing order, but this is not required for our approach.

In addition to symbol recognition, graph-based techniques have been used for a variety of other pattern recognition problems. Conte *et al.* [CFSV04] provides an extensive overview of graph matching techniques and their applications. According to the taxonomy presented there, our stochastic, error-driven, and greedy matching techniques can be considered approximate matching techniques based on continuous optimization.

Many existing approaches to symbol recognition rely on feature-based representations. Fonseca *et al.* [FPJ02] use features such as the smallest convex hull that can be circumscribed around the shape, the largest triangle that can be inscribed in the hull, and the largest quadrilateral that can be inscribed. Because their classification relies on aggregate features of the pen strokes, it might be difficult to differentiate between similar shapes. Rubine [Rub91] describes a trainable gesture recognizer designed for gesture-based interfaces. The recognizer is applicable only to single-stroke symbols, and is sensitive to the drawing direction and orientation. Pereira *et al.* [PBS*04] have extended Rubine's method to multi-stroke symbols. However, such symbols

must be drawn with a consistent set of strokes. Additionally, they have developed a graph-based symbol recognizer, but it is not trainable. Matsakis [Mat99] describes a system for converting handwritten mathematical expressions into a machine-interpretable typesetting command language. Each symbol requires a multitude of training examples, where each example must to be preprocessed to eliminate variations in drawing directions and stroke orderings. However, the preprocessing makes their approach sensitive to rotations. Gennari *et al.* [GKSS05] describe a trainable recognizer that uses nine geometric features to construct concise probabilistic models of input symbols. The approach is suitable for multi-stroke symbols with arbitrary drawing orders and orientations. The features are an abstraction of the topology, thus is possible for shapes with different topologies to have the same features. Hse and Newton [HN04] developed a recognizer based on Zernike moments. The method is insensitive to rotation and uniform scaling. However, because the moments are essentially properties of a bitmap, the method is intolerant of non-uniform scaling.

In addition to graph-based and feature-based methods, researchers have also explored a variety of other representations and approaches. For example, Sezgin and Davis [SD05] present a technique based on hidden markov models. The approach requires shapes to be drawn with a consistent pen stroke ordering. Hammond and Davis [HD04] developed a recognizer that relies on hand-coded shape descriptions. Their representation is similar to ours in that both contain topological information. However, their descriptions are hand-coded while ours are learned from training examples. Gross' [Gro94] approach relies on a 3x3 grid inscribed in the symbol's bounding box. The sequence of grid cells visited by the pen distinguishes each symbol. Because of the coarse resolution of a 3x3 grid, this approach may not be able to handle symbols with small features. Kara and Stahovich [KS05] developed a recognizer based on a bitmap representation. One advantage of the approach is that it is tolerant of over-stroking and variations in line styles. However, the approach is sensitive to non-uniform scaling.

Parametric methods such as polygon, B-spline, and Bezier curve fitting techniques have also been considered in shape representation and classification [HC96, RVR02]. A benefit of these approaches is that there is no need to segment the pen stroke into geometric primitives such as lines and arcs. Additionally, since only a few parameters are needed for shape description, these methods are computationally efficient. Similar to the Rubine's method, however, these methods are primarily applicable to single-stroke symbols or gestural commands.

3. Representation

We represent a symbol with an attributed relational graph (ARG) describing its geometry and topology. The nodes in the graph represent the geometric primitives, and the edges represent the geometric relationships between them.

Each node is characterized by the type of the primitive – line or arc – and its relative length. The primitives are obtained from the raw pen strokes via a speed-based segmenter [Sta04]. The relative length of a primitive is defined as the ratio of its length (in pixels) to the total length of the primitives comprising the symbol. For example, each of the four line segments in a perfect square would have a relative length of 0.25. Defining length on a relative basis results in a scale-independent recognizer.

The edges in a graph represent the geometric relationships between the primitives. Each pair of primitives is characterized by the number of intersections between them; the relative locations of the intersections; and for lines, the angle of intersection. When extracting intersections from a sketch, a tolerance of 10% of the length of the segments is used to allow for cases in which an intersection was intended but one of the segments was a little too short. Intersection locations are measured relative to the lengths of the two primitives. For example, if the beginning of one line segment intersects the middle of another, the location is described by the coordinates (0%, 50%). The intersection angle is defined as the acute angle between two line segments. It is defined for both intersecting and non-intersecting line segments. Defining an intersection angle for non-intersecting segments allows the program to represent the topology of disconnected symbols, such as the dashpot in Figure 5. Intersection angle is not defined for an intersection between an arc and another segment.

Figure 1 shows an example of an ARG for an ideal square. Each side of the square has a relative length of 0.25 and intersects two other sides with an intersection angle of 90°. Because of the drawing directions used, all intersections are located at the end of one segment and the beginning of another.

A definition for a symbol is created by constructing an "average" ARG from a set of training examples. (Additional details of the training process are described in Section 6.) Each node in the average ARG is assigned the primitive type that occurred most frequently for that node in the training data. The number of intersections assigned to a pair of primitives is determined in an analogous fashion. A pair of primitives is assigned two intersections if at least 70% of the examples had two. If less than 70% had two intersections, but there was at least one intersection 70% of the time, the pair is assigned one. Otherwise, the pair is assigned zero intersections. The remaining properties of the ARG – relative length, intersection angle, and intersection location – are continuous valued properties. These are characterized by the means and standard deviations of the values from the training examples.

4. Measuring Similarity

During recognition, it is necessary to compare the ARG of the unknown symbol to the ARG of each definition symbol to find the best match. The unknown is classified by whichever definition matches best. The match between an

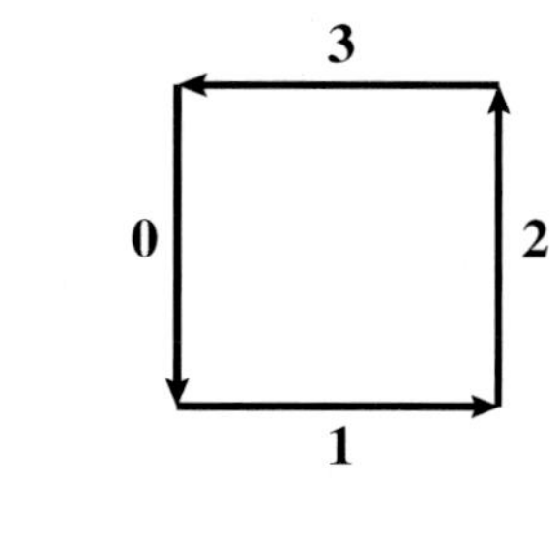

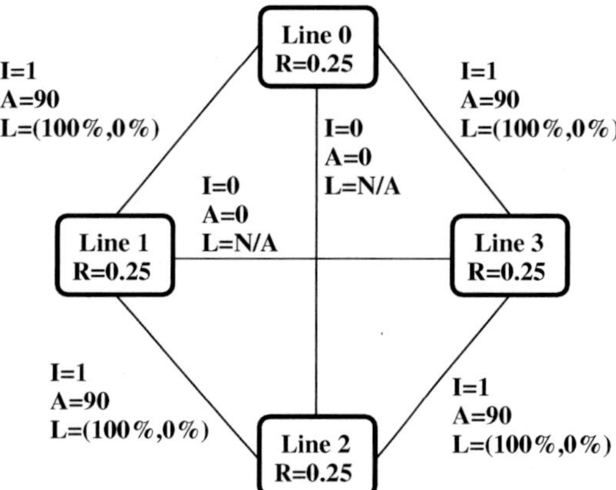

Figure 1: *Top: An ideal square drawn with a single, counterclockwise pen stroke. Arrows show the direction of drawing. Bottom: The corresponding ARG. I = number of intersections, A = intersection angle, L = intersection location, R = relative length.*

Error Metrics (E_i)	**Weight** (w_i)
E_1: Primitive count error	20%
E_2: Primitive type error	20%
E_3: Relative length error	20%
E_4: Number of intersections error	15%
E_5: Intersection angle error	15%
E_6: Intersection location error	10%

Table 1: *Error metrics and corresponding weights.*

unknown and a definition is quantified in terms of a dissimilarity score, which is computed using an ensemble of error metrics. These metrics consider both the intrinsic properties of the geometric primitives and the relationships between them. The former are encoded in the nodes of the ARG, the latter in the edges.

Table 1 lists our six error metrics and the weights applied to them when computing the dissimilarity score. The weights, which are based on empirical studies, reflect the relative importance of the various error metrics for discriminating between symbols. For the purposes of recognition, the dissimilarity score is converted to a *Similarity Score* as follows:

$$Similarity\ Score = 1 - \sum_{i=1}^{6} w_i E_i \qquad (1)$$

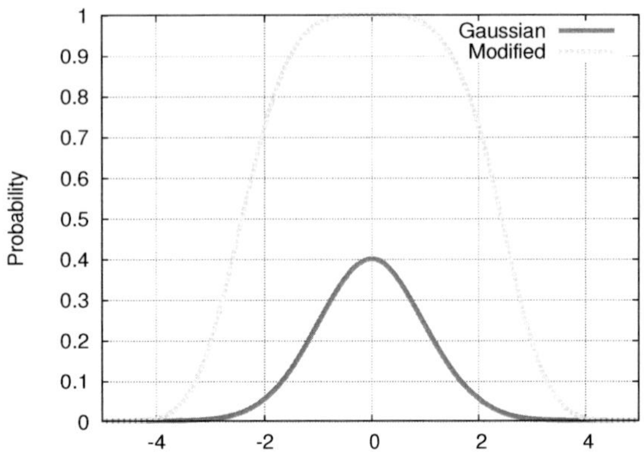

Figure 2: *Gaussian Probability Density Function and Modified Probability Density Function for $\mu = 0$ and $\sigma = 1$.*

where the E_i are the error metrics, and the w_i are the weights listed in Table 1.

The error metrics for relative length, intersection angle, and intersection location involve comparing properties of the unknown to distributions of those properties encoded in a definition. For example, it is necessary to compare the relative length of each primitive in the unknown to the mean and standard deviation of the relative length of the corresponding primitive in the definition. Ordinarily, this is done with a Gaussian probability density function. As an alternative, we have developed a modified probability density function (MPDF) that is better suited to our recognition task:

$$P(x) = exp[-\frac{1}{50.0} \cdot \frac{(x-\mu)^4}{\sigma^4}] \qquad (2)$$

Here μ and σ are the mean and standard deviation of the observed features learned from the training examples. This function was designed empirically such that its top is flatter than the Gaussian probability density function with the same μ and σ. This makes it easier to detect matches that are in the "vicinity." Additionally, we have found that the Gaussian distribution dies off too quickly towards its tails, which decreases its usefulness for recognition. For comparison, Figure 2 shows both the Gaussian probability density function and our modified probability density function for $\mu = 0$ and $\sigma = 1$.

The six error metrics used for computing the similarity score are described in the following sections. Here we use the term "unknown" to refer to the symbol to be recognized, or equivalently, the ARG of that symbol. Likewise, the term "definition" refers to the ARG of a definition symbol. Note also that each metric is normalized to the range [0, 1] so that the weights in Table 1 have predictable influences.

4.1. Primitive Count Error

This metric compares the number of nodes in the unknown to the number in the definition. The error is defined as:

$$E_1 = min(1.0, \frac{|N_U - N_D|}{N_{min}}) \qquad (3)$$

where N_U and N_D are the numbers of nodes in the unknown and the definition ARGs, respectively, and N_{min} is the minimum of N_U and N_D.

4.2. Primitive Type Error

This error metric accounts for differences between the primitive types of the corresponding nodes in the two ARGs. The error is defined as:

$$E_2 = \frac{N_{min} - \sum_{i=1}^{N_{min}} \delta(Type(U_i), Type(D_i))}{N_{min}} \qquad (4)$$

where U_i is a node from the unknown, D_i is the corresponding node from the definition, $Type(X)$ is a function that returns the primitive type (arc or line) of node X, and $\delta(p, q)$ is one when $p = q$, and zero otherwise.

4.3. Relative Length Error

This error metric compares the relative lengths of the primitives of the unknown to those of the definition. Corresponding primitives should have similar relative lengths. If not, an error is assigned. Here, similarity is measured using the MPDF defined in Equation 2. The error is computed as:

$$E_3 = \frac{\sum_{i=1}^{N_{min}} [1 - P(U_R^i)]}{N_{min}} \qquad (5)$$

where U_R^i represents the relative length encoded in the ith node of the unknown ARG. $P(x)$ is evaluated using the mean and standard deviation from the corresponding node in the definition.

4.4. Number of Intersections Error

This error metric compares the intersections of the unknown with those of the definition. A pair of primitives in the unknown should have the same number of intersections as the corresponding pair in the definition. If not, an error is assigned. The total error is computed as:

$$E_4' = \frac{\sum_{i=1}^{N_{min}} \sum_{j=i+1}^{N_{min}} |I(U_i, U_j) - I(D_i, D_j)|}{min(M_U, M_D)} \qquad (6)$$

where $I(X,Y)$ returns the number of intersections between the primitives in nodes X and Y, and M_U and M_D are the numbers of edges in the unknown and definition ARGs, respectively. A pair of primitives can intersect as many as two times. E_4' thus has a range of $[0, 2]$. So that all error metrics have the same range of $[0, 1]$, the value of E_4' is "squashed" with the following function:

$$S(x) = \frac{1}{1 + exp[6(1 - x)]} \tag{7}$$

As a result, the "Number of Intersections Error" is defined as:

$$E_4 = S(E_4') \tag{8}$$

4.5. Intersection Angle Error

This error metric compares the intersection angles of the unknown with those of the definition. The intersection angle of a pair of lines in the unknown should be similar to that of the corresponding pair of lines in the definition. (Intersection angle is defined only for pairs of lines.) If not, an error is assigned. Here, similarity is again measured using the MPDF defined in Equation 2. The total error is computed as:

$$E_5 = \frac{\sum_{i=1}^{N_{min}} \sum_{j=i+1}^{N_{min}} [1 - P(A_{ij})]}{\sum_{i=1}^{N_{min}} \sum_{j=i+1}^{N_{min}} T(Line(U_i, U_j), Line(D_i, D_j))} \tag{9}$$

where A_{ij} is the angle at which the primitive from node i of the unknown intersects the primitive from node j of the unknown. $P(A_{ij})$ is evaluated using the mean and standard deviation from the corresponding pair of primitives from the definition. Note that if the two primitives are not lines, A_{ij} is undefined and $P(A_{ij})$ is taken to be one. $Line(X,Y)$ is one when the nodes X and Y are both lines, and zero otherwise. $T(p,q)$ equals one if p and q are both one, and zero otherwise (i.e., T is the logical "and" operator). The numerator normalizes the error by the total number of intersections.

4.6. Intersection Location Error

This error metric compares the intersection locations of the unknown with those of the definition. The locations of the intersections between a pair of primitives from the unknown should be similar to those of the corresponding pair of primitives in the definition. If not, an error is assigned. Here, similarity is again measured using the MPDF defined in Equation 2. Because intersection location is defined by two coordinates, the MPDF is applied twice for each intersection. The total error is computed as:

$$E_6 = \frac{\sum_{i=1}^{N_{min}} \sum_{j=i+1}^{N_{min}} \sum_{k=1}^{I(D_i,D_j)} ([1 - P(L_i^k)] + [1 - P(L_j^k)])}{\sum_{i=1}^{N_{min}} \sum_{j=i+1}^{N_{min}} 2 \cdot I(D_i, D_j)} \tag{10}$$

where (L_i^k, L_j^k) is the coordinates of the kth intersection between the primitives from nodes i and j of the unknown. $I(D_i, D_j)$ is the number of intersections between the primitives from nodes i and j of the definition. In cases where a pair of primitives intersect in the unknown but not in the definition, or vice versa, both $P(L_i^k)$ and $P(L_j^k)$ are set to zero.

5. Graph Matching

The previous section described how to compute the similarity between two graphs. This assumed that each node in the unknown ARG was assigned to a specific node in the definition ARG. This section describes how these assignments are obtained. This is a graph matching, or graph isomorphism problem. If the user always draws each symbol with a consistent number of segments and a consistent drawing order, the graph matching problem is trivial. In that case, drawing order would directly provide the correct node-pair assignments. In practice, however, users do not always maintain a consistent drawing order. Furthermore, the problem is made more difficult because of noise. Noise comes from variations in how the symbols are drawn as well as from processing errors. For example, it is not uncommon for there to be extra or missing nodes in the unknown (i.e., extra or missing geometric primitives). Likewise, a segment that was intended to be a line can be misinterpreted, either through ambiguity or processing errors, as an arc, or vice versa.

We have developed four efficient, approximate matching techniques to find the best match between two ARGs. These are: Stochastic Matching, Error-driven Matching, Greedy Matching, and Sort Matching. The first three methods are based on search. The fourth method avoids search by assuming a consistent orientation.

The search-based methods make initial node-pair assignments based on drawing order. Assignments are then swapped until the best match is obtained. The quality of the match at each iteration is determined using the similarity score defined in the previous section. Our three search-based approaches differ in the way they select the assignments to swap at each iteration.

If the two graphs being matched do not have the same number of nodes, the smaller one is "padded" with empty nodes. This ensures that every node in one graph has a match with a unique node in the other, and hence that every node is considered by the swapping process. When evaluating the error metrics, a pairing with an empty node produces the maximum possible local error. For example, the addition of empty nodes does not reduce the primitive count error, E_1.

Figure 3 illustrates the typical search-based process. For ease of explanation, the figure shows hypothetical symbols rather than ARGs. Finding the correct node-pair assignments is equivalent to finding the correct assignment of the segments of the unknown to the segments of the definition. Here, the segments of the definition symbol are numbered

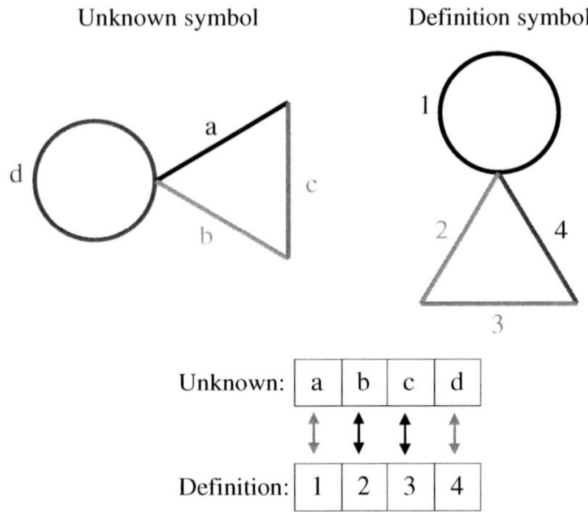

Figure 3: *Graph matching: assignments **b-2** and **c-3** are correct, while **a-1** and **d-4** are not.*

according to a typical drawing order. Likewise, the segments of the unknown are labeled with letters indicating the order in which they were actually drawn. Based on drawing order, segment **a** of the unknown is initially assigned to segment **1** of the definition, **b** is assigned to **2**, and so on. It is clear that assignments **b-2** and **c-3** are correct, while **a-1** and **d-4** are not. Swapping the latter to produce the assignments **d-1** and **a-4** is what is needed. The success of this swap can be measured by the resulting increase in the similarity score.

The following sections describe our four matching techniques in detail.

5.1. Stochastic Matching

This approach is based on stochastic search. To begin, the initial node-pair assignments are saved as the current best. Then, three node-pair assignments, which we will call A, B, and C, are randomly selected. A and B are swapped producing assignments A' and B'. B' is then swapped with C. If the new similarity score is better than the current best score, the new assignments are saved as the new current best. This process is repeated 100 times, and the current best node-pair assignments are returned as the best match. As this method is applied for a fixed number of iterations, the only cost that varies with problem size is the cost of evaluating the similarity score. This cost is $O(n^2)$, where n is the number of nodes.

5.2. Error-Driven Matching

With this approach, a local matching error determines the probability that a node-pair assignment will be selected to be swapped. For example, if a node from the unknown was a line primitive, and the corresponding node from the definition was an arc, there would be a relatively high local matching error, and correspondingly high probability that the node-pair would be selected for swapping. The local

matching error of a node-pair is defined as the portion of the dissimilarity score related to that node-pair. This includes all intersection angle, intersection number, and intersection location errors involving the primitives in that node-pair. Likewise, the local error also includes segment type and relative length errors.

At each iteration, the local error of each node-pair is computed and selection probabilities are assigned. Based on these probabilities, two node-pairs are selected and swapped. If the similarity score improves, the new assignments are kept. Otherwise, the swap is rejected. This continues until there are 20 consecutive iterations with no improvement, or until 100 iterations have been performed. The computational complexity of this approach is similar to that of the Stochastic Matching approach, but this approach typically takes fewer iterations, and thus has lower cost.

5.3. Greedy Matching

This approach uses greedy search to find good node-pair assignments. The program first considers the best assignment for the first node of the unknown. If there are n nodes, the program considers all $n-1$ cases in which the first node-pair is swapped with another. Whichever assignment produces the best similarity score is selected for the first node, and this node-pair is removed from further consideration. This is repeated for the second node-pair and so on. In all, $O(n^2)$ sets of node-pair assignments are considered. For symbols with less than about 10 nodes, this approach is less expensive than the previous two.

5.4. Sort Matching

This approach does not rely on search. Instead, the nodes are sorted based on the locations of their primitives. Each line segment is characterized by its minimum x and y-coordinates. Each arc is characterized by the coordinates of its center. The primitives are then sorted in ascending order of their x-values. Ties are broken using the y-values. The sorted order of the nodes determines the node-pair assignments.

This approach is useful only when the drawing orientation is fixed. Likewise, variations in drawing can result in different sorted orders. Nevertheless, as Section 7 describes, the approach often works reasonably well in practice. Additionally, because this approach is particularly efficient, it is suitable for devices with little computational power, such as PDAs.

6. Training

The recognizer is trained by providing a set of training examples for each symbol class. As described in Section 3, the program constructs an "average" ARG for each class. This entails another graph matching problem. To learn a definition, the program must match the ARGs of the various training examples to one another. This task is different from the previous matching problem because a similarity score cannot yet be computed. For example, the primitive type error cannot yet be determined because the expected primitive type of each node is yet to be determined.

We have explored two solutions to this problem. The first is to require the training examples to be drawn with a consistent drawing order. In this case, the matching problem is avoided as the drawing order uniquely identifies the nodes in an ARG. The second approach requires the user to draw symbols with a consistent orientation. In this case, geometric information is used for the matching. The training examples are scaled to have unit bounding boxes. The scaled symbols are then overlayed on top of one another. Finally, geometric proximity of the primitives is used to determine correspondence of the nodes. In particular, when two symbols are overlayed, each line or arc in one symbol is matched to the nearest line or arc in the other.

7. Results

We conducted a user study to evaluate the performance of our four matching techniques. The study involved nine participants. Each was asked to provide 15 examples of each of the 23 symbol classes shown in Figure 4. Data was collected using a Tablet PC. Figure 5 shows typical examples of the symbols drawn by the study participants.

	Stochastic	Error-driven	Greedy	Sort
Time (ms)	67.8	48.3	13.4	2.0
Top 1 (%)	93.7	93.5	92.3	78.5
Top 3 (%)	97.9	98.8	96.7	93.0

Table 2: *Results of user study: average time to classify a symbol and the top-one and top-three accuracies.*

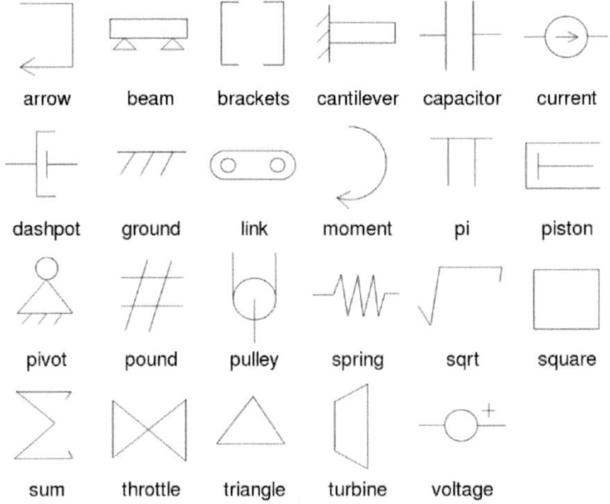

Figure 4: *Symbols used in the user study.*

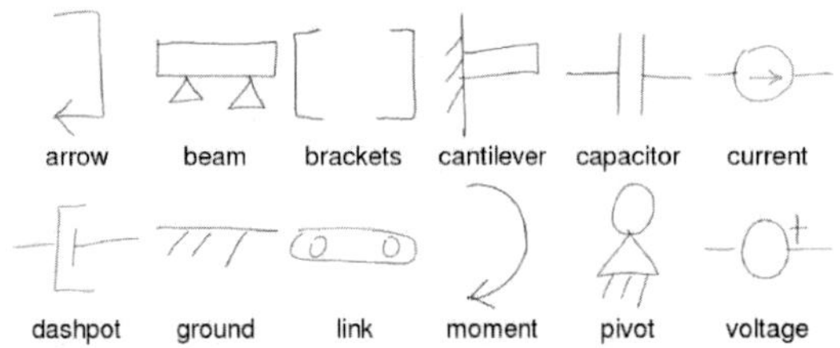

Figure 5: *Typical examples of symbols drawn in the user study.*

After the data was collected, recognition accuracy was determined offline. The participants received no feedback about the program's performance. To provide a good test of the matching ability of the four methods, the drawing order of each example was randomized after the data was collected. The system was tested in a user-dependent setting. For each experiment, the training and testing data were selected from a particular user. The results were then averaged across all users. Table 2 shows the recognition results when 14 examples were used for training. The training examples were randomly selected from the 15 examples provided by the particular user. This was repeated 10 times, using a cross-validation approach. The results in Table 2 are thus an average across 9 participants and 10 iterations of cross-validation.

The Stochastic, Error-driven, and Greedy methods all achieved similar performance of about 92% for top-one accuracy, and about 97% for top-three accuracy. Top-one accuracy is the rate at which the symbols were correctly classified. Top-three accuracy is the rate at which the correct class was one of the three highest ranked classes. The Error-driven approach took about 28% less time to recognize a symbol than the Stochastic approach. This is a result of using local matching error to guide the search to the best match. The Greedy approach worked well and took about 80% less time to recognize a symbol than the Stochastic approach. We expected that this approach would suffer from local maxima, but the results suggested otherwise. The Sort method achieved less accuracy than the other methods, but was significantly faster. This method worked reasonably well in these experiments because the participants drew the examples with a consistent orientation.

8. Conclusion

We have presented a trainable symbol recognizer for pen-based user interfaces. Symbols are represented internally as attributed relational graphs that describe both the geometry and topology of the symbols. Symbol recognition reduces to the task of finding the definition symbol whose attributed relational graph best matches that of the unknown symbol. One challenge addressed in the current work is how to perform this graph matching in an efficient fashion so as to achieve interactive performance. We presented four approximate graph matching techniques: Stochastic Matching, which is based on stochastic search; Error-driven Matching, which uses local matching errors to drive the solution to an optimal match; Greedy Matching, which uses greedy search; and Sort Matching, which relies on geometric information to accelerate the matching.

Our initial experiments provided promising results. The Stochastic, Error-driven, and Greedy graph matching techniques all achieved at least 92% accuracy in a user-dependent setting with only 14 training examples. The top-three accuracy under the same conditions was 97%. While all three methods achieved similar accuracy, the Greedy approach was significantly faster than the others. The Sort Matching technique is less accurate than the others, and requires consistent drawing orientation. However, this technique is an order of magnitude faster than the others.

While more testing is needed to understand all of the tradeoffs between these approaches, our initial results suggest that Greedy Matching provides the best combination of speed and accuracy. However, when computational resources are constrained, such as with a PDA, Sort Matching is a good solution.

References

[CFSV04]   CONTE D., FOGGIA P., SANSONE C., VENTO M.: Thirty years of graph matching in pattern recognition. *IJPRAI 18*, 3 (2004), 265–298.

[CSKK02]   CALHOUN C., STAHOVICH T. F., KURTOGLU T., KARA L. B.: Recognizing multi-stroke symbols. In *AAAI Spring Symposium on Sketch Understanding* (2002), pp. 15–23.

[DPZ01]   DICKINSON S., PELILLO M., ZABIH R.: Introduction to the special section on graph algorithms in computer science. *IEEE Transactions on Pattern Analysis and Machine Intelligence 23*, 10 (2001), 1049–1052.

[FPJ02]   FONSECA M. J., PIMENTEL C., JORGE J. A.: CALI- an online scribble recognizer for calligraphic interfaces. In *AAAI Spring Symposium on Sketch Understanding* (2002), pp. 51–58.

[GJ79]   GAREY M., JOHNSON D.: *Computers and Intractability: A guide to the Theory of NP-Completeness.* Freeman and Company, 1979.

[GKSS05]   GENNARI L., KARA L. B., STAHOVICH T. F., SHIMADA K.: Combining geometry and domain knowledge to interpret hand-drawn diagrams. *Computers & Graphics 29*, 4 (2005), 547–562.

[Gro94]   GROSS M. D.: Recognizing and interpreting diagrams in design. In *ACM Conference on Advanced Visual Interfaces.* (1994), pp. 88–94.

[HC96]   HUANG Z., COHEN F.: Affine-invariant b-spline moments for curve matching. *IEEE Transactions on Image Processing. 5*, 10 (1996), 1473–1480.

[HD04]   HAMMOND T., DAVIS R.: Automatically transforming symbolic shape descriptions for use in sketch recognition. In *AAAI-2004* (2004).

[HN04]   HSE H., NEWTON A. R.: Sketched symbol recognition using zernike moments. *icpr 01* (2004), 367–370.

[KS04]   KARA L. B., STAHOVICH T. F.: Hierarchical parsing and recognition of hand-sketched diagrams. In *UIST* (2004), pp. 13–22.

[KS05]   KARA L. B., STAHOVICH T. F.: An image-based, trainable symbol recognizer for hand-drawn sketches. *Computers & Graphics 29*, 4 (2005), 501–517.

[Lee92]   LEE S.-W.: Recognizing hand-drawn electrical circuit symbols with attributed graph matching. In *Structured Document Image Analysis*, Baird H. S., Bunke H., Yamamoto K., (Eds.). Springer-Verlag, 1992, pp. 340–358.

[LVSM02]   LLADÓS J., VALVENY E., SÁNCHEZ G., MARTÍ E.: Symbol recognition: Current advances and perspectives. In *GREC '01: Selected Papers from the Fourth International Workshop on Graphics Recognition Algorithms and Applications* (London, UK, 2002), Springer-Verlag, pp. 104–127.

[Mat99]   MATSAKIS N. E.: *Recognition of Handwritten Mathematical Expressions.* Master thesis, MIT, 1999.

[PBS*04]   PEREIRA J. P., BRANCO V. A., SILVA N. F., CARDOSO T. D., FERREIRA F. N.: Cascading recognizers for ambiguous calligraphic interaction. pp. 63–72.

[Rub91]   RUBINE D.: Specifying gestures by example. *Computer Graphics 25* (1991), 329–337.

[RVR02]   RAYMAEKERS C., VANSICHEM G., REETH F. V.: Improving sketching by utilizing haptic feedback. In *AAAI Spring Symposium on Sketch Understanding* (2002), AAAI Press, pp. 113–117.

[SD05]   SEZGIN T. M., DAVIS R.: HMM-based efficient sketch recognition. In *International Conference on Intelligent User Interfaces (IUI'05).* (New York, 2005).

[Sta04]   STAHOVICH T. F.: Segmentation of pen strokes using pen speed. *AAAI 2004 Fall Symposium: Making Pen-Based Interaction Intelligent and Natural* (2004).

[Ull76]   ULLMANN J. R.: An algorithm for subgraph isomorphism. *Journal of the ACM 23*, 1 (1976), 31–42.

EUROGRAPHICS Workshop on Sketch-Based Interfaces and Modeling (2006)
Thomas Stahovich and Mario Costa Sousa (Editors)

Constellation Models for Sketch Recognition

D. Sharon and M. van de Panne

University of British Columbia[†]

Abstract

Sketch-based modeling shares many of the difficulties of the branch of computer vision that deals with single image interpretation. Most obviously, they must both identify the parts observed in a given 2D drawing or image. We draw on constellation models first proposed in the computer vision literature to develop probabilistic models for object sketches, based on multiple example drawings. These models are then applied to estimate the most-likely labels for a new sketch. A multi-pass branch-and-bound algorithm allows well-formed sketches to be quickly labelled, while still supporting the recognition of more ambiguous sketches. Results are presented for five classes of objects.

1. Introduction

A large-class of sketch-based modeling systems, specifically those involving drawings of objects, diagrams, or maps, must solve a recognition problem. What did the user draw and what does each stroke correspond to? In many cases, this is solved with the help of domain knowledge, such as knowing that a sailboat has a mast and a hull. This recognition problem has a strong parallel with the goals of single-image interpretation in computer vision, an area which has seen significant progress over the past few years.

We apply a constellation or 'pictorial structure' model to the recognition of strokes in sketches of particular classes of objects. The model is designed to capture the structure of a particular class of object and is based on local features, such as the shape or size of a stroke, and pairwise features, such as distances to other known parts. We learn a probabilistic model from example sketches with known stroke labelings. The recognition algorithm determines a maximum-likelihood labeling for an unlabelled sketch by searching through the space of possible label assignments using a multi-pass branch and bound algorithm. Our technique supports flexible object structure by allowing for optional parts. By applying a recognition threshold, extraneous strokes can also be readily identified.

Figure 8 shows an example result for the recognition of parts in face sketches. A subset of the training examples are shown, along with a set of successfully labeled free-form sketches and trace-over sketches. A specific contribution of our method is to cope with objects that exhibit considerable variability in the way they are drawn and that allow a variable number of part instantiations.

The output of our algorithm is a set of labels assigned to the strokes. This can then be utilized by a variety of applications. Labelled strokes can be used to construct parameterized 3D models as in [YSvdP05]. Furthermore, they can help to instance models in a 2D or 3D scene, or serve as a partial interpretation of a larger sketched diagram. Sketches can also be used to retrieve images or 3D models from a database and can, in general, provide an intuitive alternative interface to models with complex internal parameterizations such as faces [fac].

Our system makes two particularly strong assumptions. First, it assumes that similar parts are drawn with similar strokes. For example, a flowerpot that is drawn with four separate strokes instead of one stroke is not easily modelled as part of the same object class. Second, object parts which are deemed mandatory in a sketch must have exactly one instance in the sketch. Optional parts may have multiple instances in a given sketch.

The remainder of the paper is organized as follows. Section 2 gives an overview of related work. Section 3 describes the details of the probabilistic constellation model. Section 4 then describes our algorithms for finding maximum-likelihood interpretations of images using the model. Results are presented and discussed in Section 5, including various

---

[†] email: dsharon,van@cs.ubc.ca

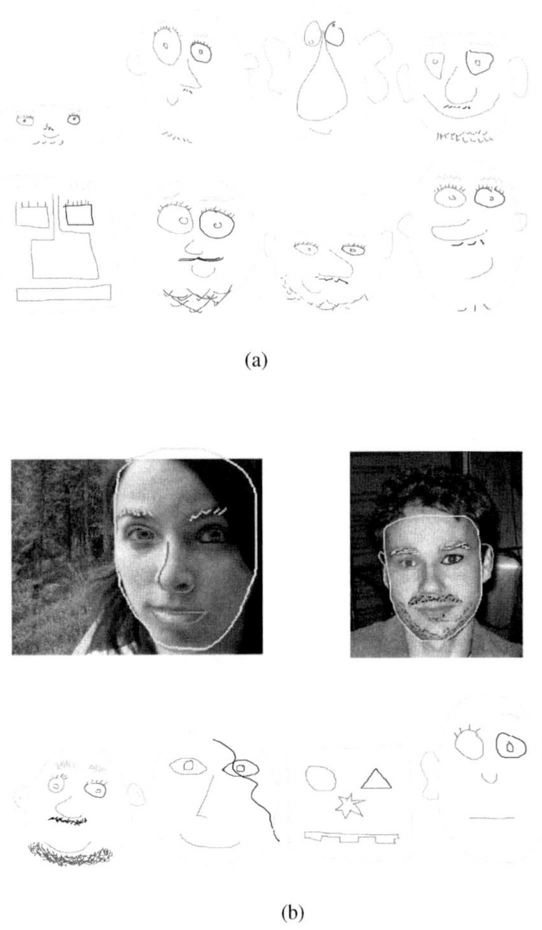

(a)

(b)

Figure 1: *(a) Face sketch training examples. The mandatory labels are* head, left-eye, right-eye, mouth, nose*; the optional labels are* left-pupil, right-pupil, left-ear, right-ear, left-eyebrow, right-eyebrow, left-eyelash, right-eyelash, moustache, beard. (b) Face sketches recognized using our system..

modes of use and examples of failure cases. Lastly, Section 6 provides conclusions and future work.

2. Related Work

In this paper we address the problem of understanding completed sketches with a known stroke structure and an unknown stroke ordering. Stroke information is assumed to be collected at the time of drawing creation or it can be extracted using image analysis of a raster drawing using morphology methods (erosion/dilation) and smooth continuation methods.

Recognizing single strokes in isolation is perhaps the sim-

plest version of sketch understanding and can be used to support interfaces that use pen gestures as commands [Rub91]. Recognizing multi-stroke visual structure is significantly more complex, given that the interpretation of strokes is dependant on its local context. Many algorithms use some type of 'parse tree' to search through the space of possible stroke labelings in order to find the most consistent interpretation of a given set of strokes. For applications that involve diagram interpretation, the search is often anchored by first finding well-defined symbols, such as drawn characters or electrical component symbols [KS04]. The search is then further constrained by exploiting the known structure of the given application domain or object classes.

Matching can be treated as a graph isomorphism problem [MF02], where it is applied to the recognition of human stick figures using a known model of connectivity. The work of [YSvdP05] applies a flexible form of hierarchical graph matching. For example, it first looks for the best subgraph representing a cup body before then proceeding to look for optional parts such as cup handles. Curve shape feature vectors are used to quantify the best match and stochastic search is used to explore the space of possible matches. Both of these graph-based models rely heavily on connectivity between parts. They are thus weak at recognizing drawings with disjoint parts, such as a nose or an airplane window.

A probabilistic approach to sketch stroke interpretation is proposed in [AD04]. This uses domain-specific libraries of 'Bayesian network fragments' that describe shapes and domain patterns. Several mechanisms to control the size of the space of hypotheses are presented, and the technique is applied to the domain of electrical circuit diagram recognition. [QSM05] proposes the use of conditional random fields for labeling box-and-line diagrams for particularly difficult ambiguous examples where constraints must propagate in order to find the most-likely interpretation. Perceptually-based shape descriptions are used to help infer the the recognition of image structure in [SMF*02]. Our work looks at recognition problems that do not require connectivity between parts and considers object sketches that can exhibit considerable variability.

Image-based techniques can also be used to help identify sketches or parts of sketches. Shape contexts [BM02] can be used to match sketch images to a fixed set of prototype template images. Image-based classifiers are applied in [SV04] in order to determine likely interpretations for subsets of strokes. An A* search procedure is used to search among the space of possible subset of strokes in order to find a maximum-likelihood interpretation for the image. This is applied to a graphic symbol set of 13 symbols.

Constellation models, also known as pictorial structure models, are composed of a set of local parts, each of which has an appearance model, and a geometry model that defines preferred relative locations or distances of the parts [FE73]. They are well suited to applications such as face recognition, where features such as the nose, eyes, and mouth have particular local features and also have relatively well-defined distances to each other. The model is further developed in [FH05], where it is applied to identify both faces and body configurations from images. The model continues to be extended, with an emphasis on learning pictorial structure models automatically from example images of object classes. More generally, this can be viewed as an example of *statistical relational learning*.

An agent-based approach is presented in [MA03], although this relies on a predefined grammar for the description of the components. The work of [KLP05] is similar to ours in that it uses a constellation-type model and a probabilistic framework. Our work differs in a number of respects, including application to a different domain, using different and larger individual and pairwise feature sets, supporting flexible object classes with optional parts, and a staged search strategy.

Our approach for sketch recognition is uniquely characterized by: (a) support for model definitions derived directly from a set of drawn training examples; (b) a probabilistic framework; (c) support for optional parts; (d) a constellation model with features specifically suited for sketch recognition; and (e) an efficient multi-stage search strategy. We demonstrate our approach on five classes of objects and multiple modes of use (drawing and tracing).

3. The Constellation Model

We represent an object using a constellation model, consisting of features of individual object parts, as well as features of pairs of parts. Individual features capture shape and global positions of parts, whereas pairwise features summarize relative positions of parts. An example constellation model of a face object is shown in Figure 2.

We define a four-element feature vector for individual object parts: $\mathcal{F} = [x\ y\ d\ \beta]$ where (x, y) are the location of the center of the axis-aligned bounding-box (AABB) of a stroke, as measured in image coordinates normalized to $x, y \in [0, 1]$; d is the normalized-coordinate length of the AABB diagonal; and $\beta = cos(\phi)$, with ϕ being the angle of the AABB diagonal with respect to the x-axis.

Similarly, we choose a four-element feature vector for part pairs defined by $\mathcal{G}_{ab} = [\Delta x_{ab}\ \Delta y_{ab}\ D_{ab}\ D_{ba}]$, where $\Delta x = x_a - x_b$ and $\Delta y = y_a - y_b$ define the relative positions of the AABB centers of strokes a and b in normalized coordinates, D_{ab} is the minimum distance between the endpoints of stroke a and any point on stroke b, and D_{ba} is the minimum distance between the endpoints of stroke b and any point on stroke a. In general, $\mathcal{G}_{ab} \neq \mathcal{G}_{ba}$.

Full constellation models do not scale well with the number of parts, n, since they result in $O(n^2)$ pairwise features. We choose to alleviate this by characterizing each label as

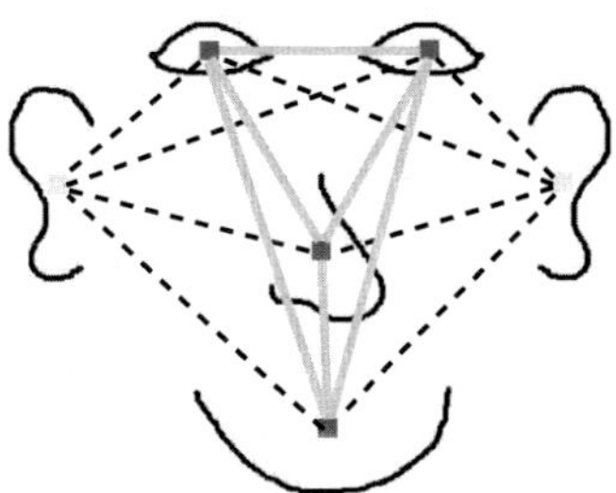

Figure 2: *Example constellation model for a sketched face, showing the pairwise interactions. In this example, the left-eye, right-eye, mouth, and nose are mandatory and thus have complete pairwise interactions. The left-ear and right-ear are optional and thus have pairwise interactions with all mandatory parts but not with each other.*

mandatory or optional. Individual features are computed for both mandatory and optional parts. However, pairwise features are only computed if one or both of the labels in the pair corresponds to a mandatory part. We note that it may be possible to further reduce the number of pairwise features by searching for subsets that yield good recognition performance [CFH05].

The sketch recognition process has two phases, the first which searches the space of possible mandatory label assignments, and the second which searches for optional labels for the remaining unlabelled strokes. In this way the mandatory labels provide contextual location information necessary for assigning appropriate labels to the potentially large number of optional parts. We describe the search algorithm in the following section.

3.1. Learning the Model

An object class model is represented using a probability distribution over features in object constellation models. This function is learned from a set of example labelled sketches. A straightforward choice of object class model is to use multivariate Gaussian distributions. However, in order to support recognition from a small number of training examples, we opt for a diagonal covariance matrix. Thus we independently compute the mean and covariance of each element of the feature vectors $\mathcal{F}$ and $\mathcal{G}$ for the set of labelled sketches that serve as training data. More explicitly, the probabilistic model for the fth element in the feature vector of a label ℓ is given by θ_ℓ^f and consists of the mean value for the feature element, μ_ℓ^f, as well as the standard deviation, σ_ℓ^f. Similarly, a pair feature model, $\theta_{\ell j}^f$, is given by $< \mu_{\ell j}^f, \sigma_{\ell j}^f >$.

3.2. Labeling Likelihood

The quality of a particular matching between labels and strokes is scored using a cost function. In early constellation models, the match quality is defined in terms of an energy that is a function of both the individual feature matches and the pairwise feature match. As in other recent work [CFH05], we cast the problem in a probabilistic framework and search for the most likely interpretation. The probability of a given labeling L is given by the product of the individual stroke labeling likelihoods, further multiplied by the product of all labelled stroke pair likelihoods. This can be expressed as:

$$P(L|\theta) = \prod_{i=1}^{N} \prod_{\ell=1}^{M} P(\mathcal{F}_i|\theta_\ell)^{\delta_{i\ell}} \prod_{j=1}^{m} \prod_{k=1}^{N} P(\mathcal{G}_{ik}|\theta_{\ell j})^{\delta_{kj}} \qquad (1)$$

In the above expression, the interior of the first term, $P(\mathcal{F}_i|\theta_\ell)^{\delta_{i\ell}}$, represents the probability of stroke i having label ℓ. This is computed for all strokes, as given by the outside product. The inside product is a notational convenience for expressing the stroke-label assignment.

The interior of the second term, $P(\mathcal{G}_{ik}|\theta_{\ell j})^{\delta_{kj}}$, represents the probability of stroke i in relation to all the mandatory parts, as measured by the pairwise feature vectors. Thus if a stroke is labelled as right ear but it is located below the mouth, then it is this term that will give that labeling a low likelihood. Pairwise relations are computed with respect to all mandatory parts, as given by the outside product. The inside product is a notational convenience for expressing the stroke-label assignment for the mandatory strokes.

The assignment of strokes to labels is modelled as a label-assignment matrix δ, with $\delta_{i\ell} = 1$ if stroke i is assigned label ℓ, and $\delta_{i\ell} = 0$ otherwise. The exponentiation using the δ values is a notational convenience for compactly representing stroke-label assignments. All terms having an exponent of $\delta = 0$ evaluate to 1 and thus effectively drop out of the likelihood computation. The label-assignment matrix has imposed upon it the appropriate restriction that each stroke can be assigned only one label, and that mandatory labels should map to a unique stroke. N is the number of strokes, M is the number of labels, and m is the number of mandatory labels. $P(\mathcal{F}_i|\theta_\ell)$ models the likelihood of stroke i having label ℓ. Similarly, $P(\mathcal{G}_{ik}|\theta_{\ell j})$ models the likelihood of the stroke pair (i,k) having the labeling (ℓ, j). The above omits the normalizing constant $P(\theta)$, which does not affect the ML solution. We assume a uniform prior on the likelihood of parts appearing in a sketch.

4. Maximum Likelihood Search

A maximum likelihood (ML) search procedure finds the most plausible labelling for all strokes that appear in the image. For a simple application of a constellation model having n strokes and m independent object part labels, there are m^n possible assignments that could in principle be explored, and each assignment configuration requires evaluating $O(n^2)$ pairwise interactions. Further complications arise because some strokes may not have plausible labels, and some object parts (i.e., labels) may not be found in a given sketch, or may have multiple instances. In order to allow for these complications, and to alleviate the computational cost associated with the exponential number of matches, the search over possible label assignments has two phases.

The first search phase involves labelling strokes that correspond only to the mandatory object parts and then commiting to those labels. This is followed by a linear search through the optional labels for the recognition of the remaining unlabelled strokes. Both search phases use the same objective function, namely the likelihood as described in the previous section.

The search over possible label assignments is carried out using a branch-and-bound search tree. Each node in the search tree represents a partial labeling of the sketch. A node at depth i in the tree has found corresponding strokes for labels 1 through i. Each node in the tree has a current assigned likelihood which is determined from the product of individual stroke-label likelihoods for the i assigned labels, as well as all the pairwise interaction likelihoods among all labelled parts.

To advance the search, a node is extended by evaluating all possible assignments of mandatory label $i + 1$ to unlabelled strokes. During the search, the algorithm tracks the cost of the best (most likely) known complete assignment of mandatory labels. The cost is used to bound branches of the search. Each completed search branch can potentially result in a better bound to restrict the remaining search.

Branches of the search tree can only be bounded once a complete assignment of mandatory labels is found. If the number of strokes or mandatory labels is high, finding complete assignments is prohibitively slow. We employ two approaches to further constrain the search: multipass thresholding and hard constraints.

With multipass thresholding, we bound branches of the search before encountering a full labelling. If a node's likelihood, as computed by its current partial set of label assignments, is lower than a specified threshold α, that search branch is terminated. We use multiple passes, beginning with an optimistic threshold. That is, at first, we assume all feature likelihoods in a match will be very high. This can result in an overly restrictive search that may lead to no complete labelings being found. However, this is quick to compute in comparison to a full search, or a search with a more pessimistic bound.

Upon failure to find a successful complete label assignment, each successive pass of the branch-and-bound search uses a progressively more pessimistic assumption until complete solutions are found. The first complete solutions found are then used as a good bound for a final search pass wherein the threshold can be as pessimistic as is desired. We begin with a threshold corresponding to $P(\mu + 1.3\sigma)$ for each feature element likelihood, and on each successive pass we scale this by $2/3$. Multi-pass thresholding makes the search feasible for a large number of strokes and mandatory labels and also results in fast labeling for 'good' sketches while supporting more extensive searches through the hypothesis space for assigning labels to more ambiguous sketches.

In lieu of a threshold based on the likelihood-to-date for the partial assignments, an alternative that we have found to be equally successful is to threshold based on individual part and pair likelihoods. Thus, a branch is terminated when it involves any individual likelihood that falls below a threshold β. For the examples shown in the paper, this is the type of multi-pass thresholding that we apply.

Hard constraints can be seen as a variant on the type of thresholding just described. For a particular object class, it may be the case that one feature label should always satisfy a particular relation with respect to another. For example, the nose could be required to always be located above the mouth in a face sketch. For our implementation, we infer *above, below, left,* and *right* relationships from the example sketches wherever they can be found. Thus, if the nose AABB center appears above the mouth AABB center in all the example sketches, this will be added as a hard constraint. An object class may have many such constraints between labelled parts.

5. Results and Discussion

We have tested the method on the 5 classes of objects listed in Table 1. These have 7–15 labels and have been tested on drawings having 3–200 strokes. We use on the order of 20-60 training examples for each class. Figures 8, 3, 4, 5, and 6 show training sketches and successful test sketches. The recognition time is typically 0.01-2.5s for the shown examples, with most of this time being spent on initialization. During initialization, a feature vector $\mathcal{F}$ is pre-computed for all strokes and another feature vector $\mathcal{G}$ for all stroke pairs of the input sketch. As an example, consider the bottom left face sketch in Figure 8, which contains 171 strokes. The recognition takes a total of 1.97 seconds, with 80% of the computation time spent on initialization, 18% on searching for mandatory labels, and 2% on finding labels for the optional parts. Spurious strokes can be rejected by placing a threshold on the fit of optional stroke labels.

The hard constraints discussed in Section 4 may significantly reduce recognition times. However, when they are automatically inferred from training data, the system may falsely register the existence of a hard constraint. For example, few training sketches may result in the system falsely believing that the left eye is always below a right eyelash. However, such a situation could easily occur in a cartoon-style

face sketch or a somewhat asymetric sketch. This could be viewed as an indication that more training data is required.

Figure 7 shows a set of failure examples, meaning that one or more strokes are mislabeled. Recognition can go wrong in several ways: (1) inability to find suitable mandatory strokes because of the hard constraints; (2) mislabeling of a mandatory stroke, leading to havoc with the remaining strokes; (3) mislabeling of optional strokes. In practice, errors of type (1) are rare and imply a lack of training data. Errors of type (2) can occur if unusual strokes occur that affect the overall bounding box and therefore result in atypical normalized coordinates. This might occur for adding overly long or bushy hair in face sketches, or certain atypical stems in flower sketches. Errors of type (3) most commonly occur when there are few mandatory strokes, such as for the sailboats or flowers. The model does not currently give any consideration to relationships between optional parts. Lastly, other mislabelings can be attributed to impoverished probability distribution models and inadequate feature vectors.

class	mandatory labels	optional labels
faces	5	10
flowers	2	5
sailboats	3	5
airplanes	3	4
characters	7	8

Table 1: *Object classes.*

In order to evaluate the utility of the multipass thresholding technique, we test the recognition of sketches with and without thresholding. Table 2 shows the results of this experiment. In all cases, the multipass thresholding results in significantly lower computation times. Most notable is a 103-stroke face sketch which took only 1.242 seconds to recognize with thresholding, yet without thresholding, failed to find a labeling within 9 hours.

class	num strokes	with multipass (s)	without multipass (s)
face	103	1.242	> 9 hours
flower	54	0.46	0.98
sailboat	8	0.02	0.03
airplane	21	0.08	0.1
character	18	0.12	126.69

Table 2: *Computation times for recognition algorithm with and without the multi-pass technique.*

Our system assumes a uniform prior for the a priori likelihood of optional parts. This decision stems in part from our expectation that a small number of training sketches will not necessarily reflect the probability of parts appearing in future sketches. Thus, the identity of parts depends solely on their shape and fit as modeled by the constellation model.

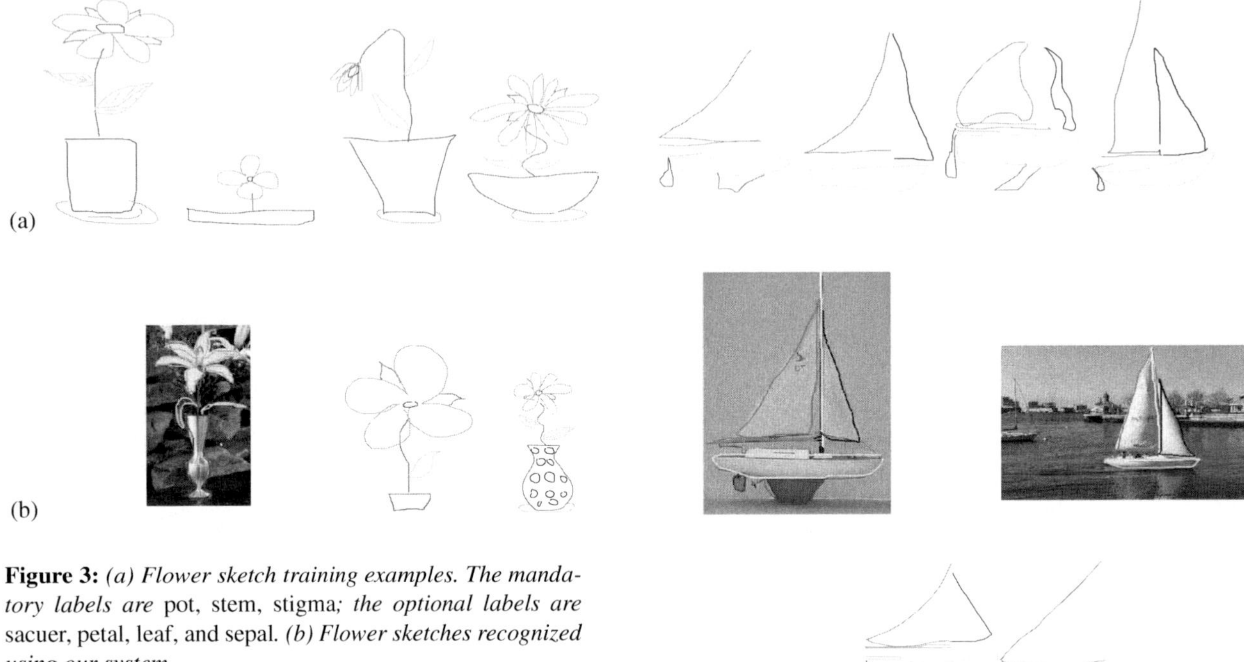

Figure 3: *(a) Flower sketch training examples. The mandatory labels are* pot, stem, stigma; *the optional labels are* sacuer, petal, leaf, and sepal. *(b) Flower sketches recognized using our system.*

Figure 4: *(a) Sailboat sketch training examples. The mandatory labels are* hull, main-sail, mast; *the optional labels are* jib, boom, keel, rudder, tiller.*(b) Sailboat sketches recognized using our system.*

We define the recognition of a sketch to be the labeling of the individual parts of a sketch that is of a known object class. If the class of the input sketch is unknown, the maximum likelihood fit could be determined for each of a list of object classes in order to provide information about the object class. The ML log-likelihoods that come from each class are not directly comparable, however, because object classes differ in their number of mandatory parts. Mandatory parts have fully-connected pairwise likelihoods while optional parts only have pairwise likelihoods in relation with mandatory parts. An appropriate normalization can be constructed to deal with this, although we have yet to investigate this. We believe that there are likely better discriminative object-classification methods that do not rely on complete part labeling.

It may be possible to further improve on the mean search time for the branch-and-bound algorithm by using variants of the A* algorithm. This involves expanding non-terminal nodes in the search in an order sorted by their cost-to-date. However, much of the leverage of A* comes from the ability to generate a suitable always-optimistic cost-to-go function. Unfortunately this provides little leverage given that it is possible that the remaining unlabelled strokes could perfectly match the mean features.

6. Conclusions

We have presented a system that adapts *constellation* or *pictorial structure* models from the computer vision literature for flexible sketch recognition. Adaptations include support for optional parts, the use of an efficient multi-pass branch and bound search for exploring the space of possible interpretations, and the construction of individual and pairwise features suitable for sketch recognition.

There remain a number of open directions for future work. The most significant limitation of the current system is the requirement to have one label per stroke. Thus, an eye or plane wing always needs to be drawing with a single stroke in our system. The ideas presented in [MA03] could be used to dynamically instantiate 'part hypotheses', which provide a path for top-down knowledge to help assemble multiple local strokes into a single primitive. Local stroke proximity information [SV04] may also be useful in determining likely groupings of strokes that represent a single part. It may also be possible to encode the most common stroke patterns used to construct a part into multiple part templates that are all associated with the same label. Lastly, a gestalt-based bottom-up grouping process may provide a significant speedup when assigning identical labels to large groups of strokes.

The current recognition process is largely top-down: the

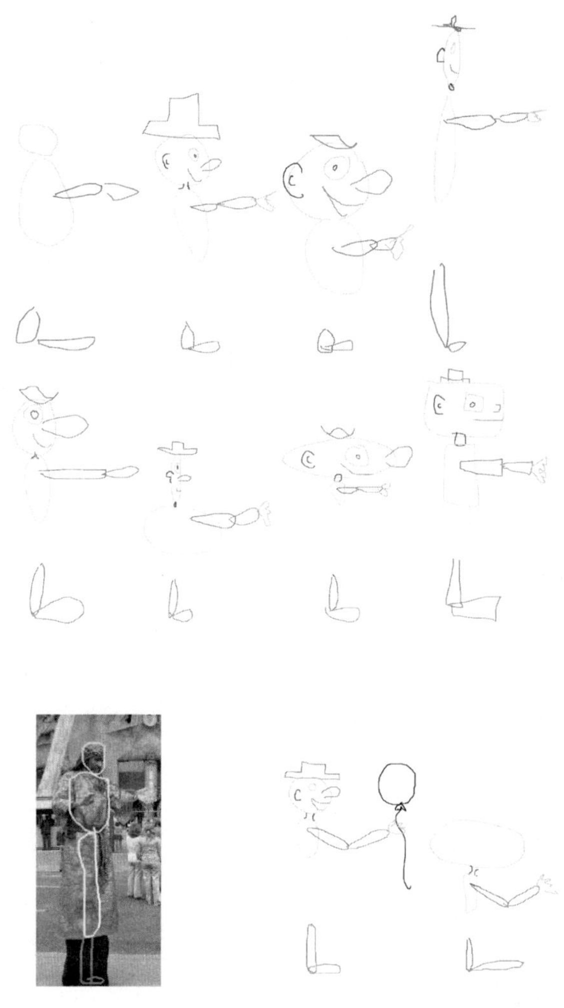

(b)

Figure 5: *Character sketch training examples. The mandatory labels are* head, torso, thigh, shin, foot, upper-arm, lower-arm; *the optional labels are* hat, neck, hand, nose, eye, pupil, mouth, ear. *(b) Character sketches recognized using our system.*

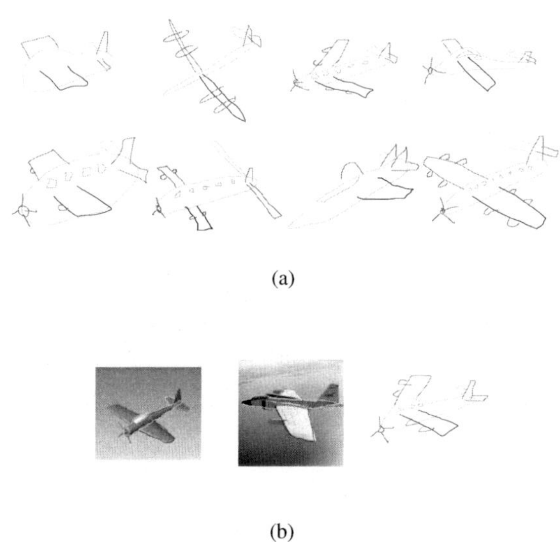

(a)

(b)

Figure 6: *(a) Airplane sketch examples. The mandatory labels are* fuselage, left-wing, right-wing; *the optional labels are* left-stabilizer, right-stabilizer, left-engine, right-engine, propellor, window, tail-fin. *(b) Airplane sketches recognized using our system.*

Figure 7: *Failure modes of our system. Mislabelling can be caused by lack of training sketches and inadequate features.*

diagram is searched for mandatory labels in a fixed order in order to construct the search tree. This ignores bottom-up information that could be used to reorder the search to begin with the strokes which have likely bindings to particular labels, thereby strongly constraining the search early on.

In the current system we have only experimented with a limited number of individual and pairwise features. It is likely that features other than those we have proposed will be useful in producing a more robust system. Given a large set of possible features and appropriate datasets, it should be possible to run an offline process that determines the k most informative features (individual and pairwise). How to best represent the probability distributions for a given set of features is a further open problem. Our model of independent, normally-distributed features is well suited for systems relying on only a small set of example labelled sketches. However, multi-variate Gaussian models or mixtures of Gaussians may provide better results for larger data sets, at the expense of requiring a larger number of labelled examples.

Acknowledgements

The authors would like to thank Kevin Murphy for early discussions related to this project, and the anonymous reviewers for useful suggestions for improving the paper.

References

[AD04] ALVARADO C., DAVIS R.: Sketchread: a multi-domain sketch recognition engine. In *UIST '04 ACM symposium on User interface software and technology* (2004), pp. 23–32.

[BM02] BELONGIE S., MALIK J.: Shape matching and object recognition using shape contexts. *IEEE Transactions on Pattern Analysis and Machine Intelligence 24*, 24 (April 2002), 509–522.

[CFH05] CRANDALL D., FELZENSZWALB P. F., HUTTENLOCHER D. P.: Spatial priors for part-based recognition using statistical models. In *Proceedings of CVPR* (2005), pp. 10–17.

[fac] Facegen. Singular Inversions Inc., http://www.facegen.com.

[FE73] FISCHLER M. A., ELSCHLAGER R. A.: The representation and matching of pictorial structures. *IEEE Transactions on Computers 22*, 1 (1973).

[FH05] FELZENSZWALB P. F., HUTTENLOCHER D. P.: Pictorial structures for object recognition. *Intl. Journal of Computer Vision 61*, 1 (January 2005), 55–79.

[KLP05] KAELBLING L., LOZANO-PEREZ T.: *Learning Three-Dimensional Shape Models for Sketch Recognition.* Tech. rep., MIT CSAIL, Jan 2005.

[KS04] KARA L. B., STAHOVICH T. F.: Hierarchical parsing and recognition of hand-sketched diagrams. In *Proceedings of UIST'04* (2004).

[MA03] MACKENZIE G., ALECHINA N.: Classifying sketches of animals using an agent-based system. In *Proceedings of the 10th International Conference CAIP, Springer Lecture Notes in Computer Science 2756* (2003), pp. 521 – 529.

[MF02] MAHONEY J. V., FROMHERZ M. P. J.: Three main concerns in sketch recognition and an approach to addressing them. In *AAAI Spring Symposium on Sketch Understanding* (2002).

[QSM05] QI Y., SZUMMER M., MINKA T. P.: Diagram structure recognition by bayesian conditional random fields. In *IEEE International Conference on Computer Vision and Pattern Recognition (CVPR)* (2005).

[Rub91] RUBINE D.: Specifying gestures by example. In *SIGGRAPH '91* (1991), pp. 329–337.

[SMF*02] SAUND E., MAHONEY J., FLEET D., LARNER D., LANK E.: Perceptual organization as a foundation for intelligent sketch editing. In *AAAI Spring Symposium on Sketch Understanding* (2002).

[SV04] SHILMAN M., VIOLA P.: Spatial recognition and grouping of text and graphics. In *Eurographics Workshop on Sketch-Based Interfaces and Modeling* (2004).

[YSvdP05] YANG C., SHARON D., VAN DE PANNE M.: Sketch-based modeling of parameterized objects. In *Eurographics Workshop on Sketch-Based Interfaces and Modeling* (2005).

EUROGRAPHICS Workshop on Sketch-Based Interfaces and Modeling (2006)
Thomas Stahovich and Mario Costa Sousa (Editors)

Automatic Learning of Symbol Descriptions Avoiding Topological Ambiguities

J. Mas [1] ,B. Lamiroy[2], G. Sanchez[1] and J. Llados[1]

[1]Computer Vision Center,Computer Science Dept. UAB, Spain
[2]INPL-LORIA,Ecole des Mines, Nancy CEDEX, France

Abstract

In this paper we address both automatic recognition of sketched symbols and the construction of the corresponding models from user drawn examples. Our approach is based on a two stage process. In a first phase we use an Adjacency Grammar to express topological properties of the symbol. In order to be able to further disambiguate topologically similar configurations on the rules of the grammar that are triggered by the recognition process produce a set of local geometric invariants is defined. The combination of both steps results in an efficient recognition method for user drawn sketches. Furthermore, we show that the same approach can easily be adapted for the generation of Adjacency Grammars from user provided and hand drawn examples.

Categories and Subject Descriptors (according to ACM CCS): I.5.1 [Computer Graphics]: Structural Model Generation based on sample users I.5.5 [Interactive systems]: Pen-Based Interfaces.

1. Introduction

Shape description is one of the important steps in symbol recognition. Depending on the primitives used to represent the shape, we may distinguish between two major categories on shape recognition, Contour-Based and Region-Based. The former bases the description on the contour or the edges of the image, while the latter is based on the whole image or on closed regions of the image. Inside these two categories we may distinguish between two methodologies: Structural and Global descriptors. Global descriptors calculate global features on the images. Inside this category we may find basic descriptors as: Area, Perimeter, Compactness, etc. and some other descriptors are based on moments and signal processing approaches like Zernike, Legendre, Fourier, *etc.* or based on grids as in Zoning.

On the contrary, Structural methods use features based on attributed primitives and the relations among them. As Structural methods we may find several different approaches as string-based methods, chain codes, polygonal approximation. Within this methodology we may further distinguish (among others) Syntactic methods. These methods are based on the representation of shapes applying techniques of formal language definition. In this paper, we focus more precisely on this last category of shape description. A review on shape description techniques is presented in [ZL04].

Although this techniques are widely used and deeply studied, one of the main problems and recurring difficulties of shape description is to cope with ambiguity. There always exist situations in which symbols cannot be disambiguated without addition of extra knowledge. This is most often due to the fact that all approaches need to be robust to noise and distortions on one hand, and need to be sufficiently discriminant on the other.

Some works presented in the literature try to describe sketches using an structural approach. Veselova in [VD04], captures the relevant characteristics describing a shape and formulate three heuristics to apply to this characteristics based on human perception. Using them they extract the constraints to create the final shape description based on a global threshold. Mankoff in [MHA00] presents a shape descriptor based on sketched GUI. It solve the problem of ambiguity by asking the user to chose among a set of possible models.

The work presented in this paper is based on a structural contour based descriptor, and more precisely on a syntactic approach defined by an Adjacency Grammar. An Adjacency grammar describes a symbol as a set of primitives and the relations among them. The description of each model is obtained by a learning process based on a set sketched instances. This allows us to infer the constraints forming the shape based on an adaptive learning instead of based on a global threshold as Veselova in [VD04].

The method therefore is able to cope with high distortion representations of the reality. Working with sketches introduces distortions on the relations among the primitives and also generates the difficulty of having to handle different chronological drawing of the strokes composing a symbol. Further more, as we shall further show in this paper, there are some intrinsic ambiguity problems related to the description method itself.

The purpose of the work is to improve the method presented in [MLSL06] with the capability to disambiguate between shapes. This method solve the ambiguity problem computing some invariants related to the constraints defining the shape, instead of asking the user as in the method presented by Mankoff in [MHA00]. On this paper we define two ambiguous shapes as topological identical. We consider two shapes being topological identical if they can be expressed with the same constraint set. Trying to disambiguate among shapes we we create a specific vector of invariants associated to any relation. This description contrary to the work presented by Veselova in [VD04], is rotated and scaled invariant.

The paper is organized as follows: In the next section we present the sketch based interface that has been used as environment for our experiments. Section 3 refers to the basis of the methodology used to learn the description of a symbol. Section 4 presents the method used to cope with the ambiguities, section 5 presents the experimental results and finally conclusions are presented on section 6.

2. Framework

The experiments described in this paper are developed under a sketch based environment. The application is named PVPC (Virtual Prototyping of Projects under Construction) and it is a sketch environment to design architectural floor plans. The user interacts with the system by means of drawings on a Wacom Tablet or a Tablet PC or using a digital pen & paper protocol (*e.g.* as the Digital IO Pen from Logitech [Log04]).

The application tries to recognize the different structural, furniture and services symbols that appears on it. More details on the application itself can be found in [SVL*04]. The method described in this paper is based on grammatical rules, expressed with respect to image primitives. However, before being able to manipulate the primitives that form a drawing, we need to extract them from the strokes of the user. Furthermore, when drawing, one single stroke may represent more than one primitive. We therefore pre-process the strokes with polygonal approximation as the presented in [TASD*00]. This approximation divides them by using

the high curvature points and also checks if the primitive is an arc or a segment. In this paper we restrict ourselves to segments although the method may be readily extended to arcs as well.

The method presented in this paper may be easily integrated in applications allowing users to define their own set of symbols to recognize. This may be a valuable add-on for applications in the architectural world, since there exists no standard in this area. The environment is also suitable for other kinds of applications like design of electrical circuits, physical blueprints, *etc.*

3. Adjacency Grammars

Adjacency grammars allow to describe 2D-shapes on a linear way, describing it in terms of a set of primitives and the relations among these primitives. Adjacency grammars were first introduced in [JG95]. The reader can also refer to [MSL05] for further details on the use of Adjacency Grammars for sketched symbol recognition.

3.1. Symbol Description Model

Figure 1: *From left to right:* incidence, adjacency, intersection

The main idea is to segment the sketch into primitives (*e.g.* line segments and curved arcs). For each pair of primitives (A, B), a number of constraints (as depicted in Figure 1) are evaluated using a normalized associated uncertainty degree $\delta = [0 \ldots 1]$ which measures the degree of distortion with regard to an ideal shape. Values close to 0 indicate that the constraint is satisfied, while values close to 1 mean that the constraint makes no sense. We currently associate the following constraints and functions:

- $Parallel(A, B) \rightarrow \frac{2}{\pi} \left| \widehat{A, B} \right|_{[0 \ldots \frac{\pi}{2}]}$
- $Perpendicular(A, B) \rightarrow 1 - \frac{2}{\pi} \left| \widehat{A, B} \right|_{[0 \ldots \frac{\pi}{2}]}$
- $Incident(A, B) \rightarrow$ min. distance between segments and endpoints
- $Adjacent(A, B) \rightarrow$ min. distance between endpoints
- $Intersects(A, B) \rightarrow$ min. distance between midpoints

This may then be used to describe symbols within the Adjacency Grammar. For instance, a rectangular triangle, made out of three line segments A, B and C, is described as follows:

$$Triangle(A, B, C) \begin{cases} Adjacent(A, B) \\ Adjacent(B, C) \\ Adjacent(A, C) \\ Perpendicular(A, C) \end{cases}$$

3.2. Automatical Model Generation

This approach is not only well suited for description and recognition, it can also be easily adapted to automatically infer and construct the models from sample sketches provided by the user.

Simply taking into account the constraints with the lowest associated cost may be sufficient to describe a symbol from a given sketch. However, notice that we work with sketched instances of symbols, which are rough expressions of the reality, containing a high degree of distortion with respect to an ideal model. Therefore, we need more than one single instance to correctly and automatically infer the ruleset of our adjacency grammar that describes the symbol. Not doing so would invariably lead to over- or underconstrained rulesets.

To correctly infer a sketched symbol we need several instances to cope with the possible distortions that may appear. To reach this description we build on the method presented in [MLSL06]. This method is divided into three steps:

- Ruleset Generation
- Ruleset Normalization and Primitives Alignment
- Factorization

The first step tries to keep those constraints which are sufficiently realistic sorting them by value. Fitting a normal distribution over the data allows to easily find the most appropriate and statistically salient features that compose the model.

The second step considers that drawing two instances of the same symbol not necessarily results in an identical numbering of primitives and that the resulting ruleset may contain different, but geometrically equivalent rules. This requires an explicit primitive alignment such that we obtain a correspondence among the primitives of different instances.

The last step is dedicated to levelling out differences between generated rulesets from different examples, occurring from drawing deformations. It constructs the final constraint set based on a majority voting scheme between all the instances of a model.

Table 1 represents the constraint set that was automatically inferred from the instance presented on Figure 2. Note that perpendicularity was deduced for primitives 4 and 5 (the crossing diagonals) for this particular instance, although the lines themselves aren't really perpendicular. Further samples may contribute to enforcing or rejecting this rule.

This method works well for several kinds of symbols. But, as we shall show in the next section, there exist some configurations where the generated rulesets are not precise enough to distinguish between configurations that are geometrically different, but share the same topology. Two of those configurations are shown in Figures 3 and 4. The next section presents a way to cope with this kind of ambiguities.

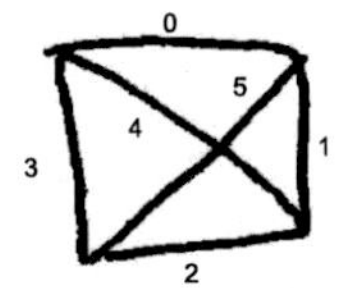

Figure 2: *Instance sample.*

Adjacent(primitive0, primitive5)
Adjacent(primitive0, primitive4)
Adjacent(primitive0, primitive3)
Adjacent(primitive0, primitive1)
Adjacent(primitive1, primitive2)
Adjacent(primitive1, primitive4)
Adjacent(primitive1, primitive5)
Adjacent(primitive2, primitive3)
Adjacent(primitive2, primitive5)
Adjacent(primitive2, primitive4)
Adjacent(primitive3, primitive4)
Adjacent(primitive3, primitive5)
Intersects(primitive4, primitive5)
Parallelism(primitive0, primitive2)
Parallelism(primitive1, primitive3)
Perpendicular(primitive0, primitive3)
Perpendicular(primitive0, primitive1)
Perpendicular(primitive1, primitive2)
Perpendicular(primitive2, primitive3)
Perpendicular(primitive4, primitive5)

Table 1: *Inferred Constraint Set for the instance of Figure 2*

4. Overcoming Topological Ambiguities

The previously described method fails to distinguish between topological similar configurations, simply because of the fact that the rules only embed very poor geometrical information (mainly parallelism and perpendicularity). On the other hand, these very loose geometric constraints make the method very well suited for recognizing and capturing hand written distortions. The main challenge therefore is to correctly distinguish between sufficiently different configurations, whilst maintaining robustness to deformations that are proper to sketch based interfaces. We use geometric invariants [GBB98] to solve this dilemma.

4.1. Geometric Invariants

Two forms are considered topologically equivalent if there exists a continuous deformation (possibly non-rigid) that projects the first in the second. Invariants such as connexity, incidence and holes are the only properties that are preserved in this case. Since purely topological descriptions are too poor to account for more or less subtle differences between forms (*e.g.* a square and a circle are topologically equivalent)

     J. Mas et al. / Automatic Learning of Symbol Descriptions Avoiding Topological Ambiguities

Figure 3: *A Plug, an Arrow and a Triangle, all three sharing the same ruleset*

Figure 4: *A square and a rectangle: topologically identical but geometrically different.*

it is imperative to embed more geometrical information into the symbol descriptions. Two forms are considered geometrically or rigidly equivalent, if there exists a rigid transform projecting the first into the second. The advantage of geometric transforms (translation, rotation, similarity, affinity, projective, ...) is that they very neatly enter in a completely computationally controlled mathematical framework. On the other hand, their great drawback is that they do not capture all deformations that occur in image analysis, and more particularly in sketched based environments.

Rather than searching for full rigid equivalence between forms, we propose to only use geometrical invariants on very local configurations. Furthermore, we restrict them to similarity transform invariant values (*i.e.* scale, rotation and translation invariant). Skew is rather considered as an artefact related to the hand drawn distortions.

4.2. Associating Invariants with Grammar Rules

We proceed by associating a vector of invariant measures to each rule in the ruleset of a symbol, based on either of the following:

- the length ratio between the primitives triggering the rule,
- the angle between the primitives,
- the relative normalized distance between the primitives.

Figure 5: *A T and a L Shapes.*

This classification lead us to define a set of specific invariants for each rule to cope with different configurations. For instance, as we see in Figure 5 the represented shapes differ by the position of their incidence point of one of the segments to the other, while the constraint set obtained from these two samples are the exposed on table 2.

It is noteworthy to mention here that we slightly differ from the approach in [MLSL06] and which we presented in the introduction, in the sense that we do not use the rule

Incident(P1,P2)	Incident(P1,P2)
Perpendicular(P1,P2)	Perpendicular(P1,P2)

Table 2: *Constraint Set corresponding the samples on Figure 5.*

of *Adjacency*. Adjacency is just seen as a particular case of incidence. Furthermore, not all invariants are computed for all kinds of rules. Some make more sense than others, and in some cases, the confidence measure of a rule already uses one of the mentioned invariants.

4.3. Length Ratio

The length ratio invariant is defined as the difference of length between the primitives forming the rule. Calculation is based on the following equation:

$$ratio = \min \left(\frac{length(P1)}{length(P2)}, \frac{length(P2)}{length(P1)} \right) \qquad (1)$$

The obtained value is guaranteed to be 0 and 1. This invariant is associated with all rules, and allows to distinguish between topological equivalent shapes as in Figure 4 : the square has a ratio near 1 among all its primitives ; on contrary, the rectangle has ratio near to 1 among the primitives that are parallel one to another, and it is different than 1 among the perpendicular ones.

4.4. Angle

The angle invariant only associated with the intersection and incidence rules. Since it is defined as the minimum angle between the primitives forming the rule, it is fairly useless to use it in the case of parallelism or perpendicularity. This angle is calculated taking one of the segments as reference and based on the cosines theorem such that the angle is always less or equal to π. This invariant allows to distinguish between topological equivalent shapes as in Figure 3.

4.5. Normalized Distances

According to the considered rule, two kinds of distances are measured. In the case of *Incidence*, we compute the relative position of the virtual incidence point with respect to the extreme of the segment, as shown in Figure 6. The relative distance of the two primitives is already accounted for in the uncertainty degree that is associated with the rule itself.

On the contrary, in case of a *Parallelism* rule, the previous measurement makes no sense, since there is no virtual incidence point between both primitives (or at best it's a badly conditioned one, prone to noise). Figure 6 shows how the distances are calculated in this case : *DX* represents distance

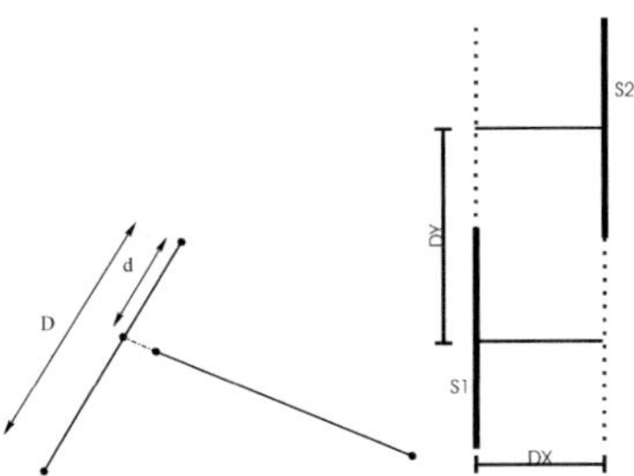

Figure 6: *Distances calculated between incident segments (left) and parallel segments (right)*

Constraint Plug	Ratio	Angle	Distance
Incident(0,1)	0.776	1.097	$1.229 * 10^{-13}$
Incident(1,2)	0.266	2.616	$3.714 * 10^{-14}$
Incident(0,2)	0.343	2.571	$4.771 * 10^{-13}$

Constraint Arrow	Ratio	Angle	Distance
Incident(0,1)	0.844	0.961	$2.942 * 10^{-15}$
Incident(1,2)	0.348	0.414	0.016
Incident(0,2)	0.412	0.546	0.017

Constraint Triangle	Ratio	Angle	Distance
Incident(0,1)	0.942	1.071	0.008
Incident(1,2)	0.939	1.010	0.036
Incident(0,2)	0.931	1.061	0.020

Table 3: *Constraints Sets corresponding to shapes of Fig. 3*

between the two lines supporting the segments, and *DY* represents the relative distance between their respective midpoints, measured following the direction of the segments.

All computed distances are normalized with respect to the length of the longest primitive, in order to remain invariant to scale.

Two special cases for this invariant are described in Figure 7(a) and (b). The particularity of Figure 7(a) is that there is a collinearity between the two segments. In this case the *DX* distance will be near 0. On the contrary, in Figure 7(b) the two segments are parallel and are aligned by their midpoints, the *DY* distance will be near 0 for this case.

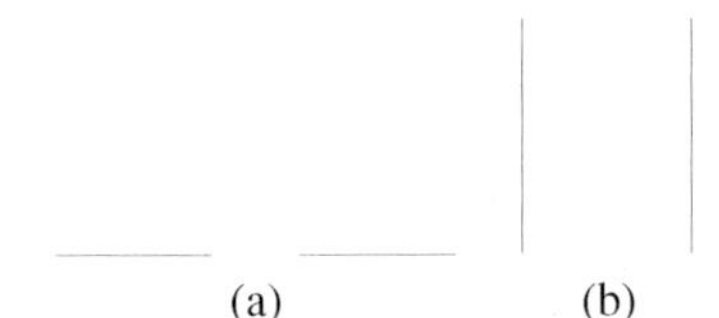

(a)   (b)

Figure 7: *Particularities on axis distances.*

4.6. Rules and Invariant Vectors

For any inferred constraint we can now define a specific vector with some of the previously mentioned invariants :

- the *Incidence* relation is associated with ratio, angle and the relative distance of the incidence point with respect of the extreme of the intersected segment.
- the *Parallelism* relation is defined by the ratio and the distances used for parallelism : *DX* and *DY*.
- *Perpendicular* is associated with the ratio and the distance.
- *Intersects* is defined by the angle between the primitives that form the rule.

The constraint set presented in table 3 shows the constraints with the corresponding parameters on *ratio*, *angle* and *distance*. We may observe as we explained before that in this case, the angle parameter, allows to distinguish between the topological equivalent samples.

4.7. Model Generation by Learning Invariants

Once we have defined how to avoid ambiguities between symbols which are topologically identical, we need to define a method or a way to learn the invariants from user provided samples.

Symbols are inferred from several instances, and the variability of their associated invariants is simply qualified by their average value and standard deviation. Average and standard deviation are computed on *ad hoc* models. From the experience we notice that the the angle invariant follows a normal distribution and that the ratio and the distance follow a χ^2-law.

4.8. Sketch Recognition

Once we have trained the system with the instances of the different symbols we want to recognize, we need a recognition process that, given an unidentified input, tells us what symbol that we have learnt is more similar. The process works as follows: given an input we calculate the value of the cumulated uncertainty degree, obtained by parsing the rules that are associated to our models. And we sort the resulting models by this value. Not all the rules are evaluated since we evaluate those rules that have the same number of primitives as the input. We then cross-verify the validity of the invariants in order to disambiguate among the rules that give very similar results. We select the model that minimizes both the cumulated uncertainty value of the rules and respects the invariants constraints.

5. Experiments

Experiments show how our approach improves the method presented in [MLSL06] and they show how it works when trying to describe two symbols with the same topology but being geometrically different. We also show that it is able to

Figure 8: *User Drawn Samples.*

differentiate between symbols that are made up out of disconnected parts.

As said in section 1, we consider that two symbols are topologically identical if they may be expressed with the same constraint set. *I.e.*, the shapes in Figure 3 are topologically identical and may be described with the constraint set presented on table 3. Figure 9 shows some other symbols that are difficult to differentiate due to this fact.

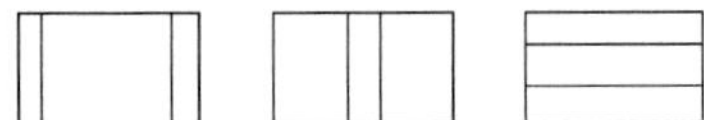

Figure 9: *Some samples of our experiment set*

For the first experiment we consider the three shapes of Figure 3 with 10 hand drawn instances for each shape. From the instances of the symbols we have calculated the expected value of the distribution and standard deviation for each invariant between the pairs of primitives. These expected and standard deviation values are showed on Figure 11 for each pair of primitives of the obtained ruleset (as shown also in Table 3). The big values on some of the standard deviations show that the user provided instances contained a high distortion level. Figure 10 shows some of the samples.

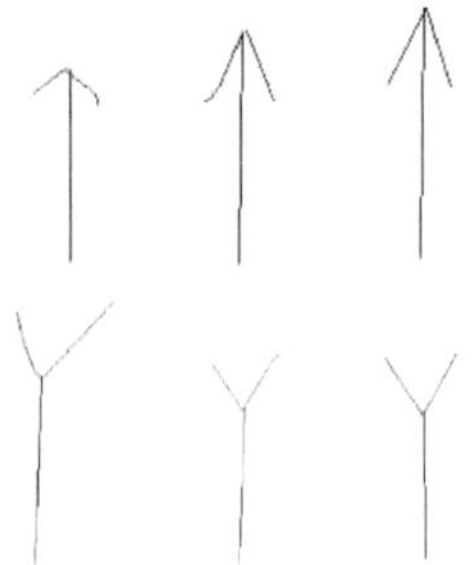

Figure 10: *Distorted samples on the experiment image set.*

The information to take into account is the one contributed by the invariants. If we look to the *ratio* invariant we may see that the shape representing the Triangle is easily discriminated from the other two by using this value. The ratio is near 1 on all the pair of primitives, while the Arrow and the Plug

have two primitives that have the same length but this length is approximatively $1/3$ of the length of the other primitive.

On the other hand, if we look to the angle invariant we may see that it is the most discriminating invariant of the three shapes. The shape representing meanwhile the Arrow have the angles among the primitives that have not the same length lesser than 90 degrees the Plug has the angles greater than 90 degrees. Referring to the triangle the three angles are approximatively the same. We may conclude that the angle invariant disambiguates among the shapes of Figure 3. The shapes with the corresponding primitive numbering are showed on fig. 12

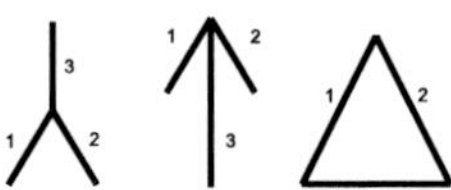

Figure 12: *Numbering of primitives for shapes: Plug, Arrow and Triangle.*

The second experiment tries to enforce the use of the invariant ratio. In order to enforce this invariant we have made the system to learn 2 shapes with 10 instances any representing and square and a rectangle.

The values obtained from the inference of the grammar are presented on Figure 13. As we may see we have presented the ratio and angle for any of the shapes. The values represented are the expected value of the distribution and standard deviation. Looking at the angle invariant we may observe that on both shapes are approximatively the same. We may observe two parallelism and four perpendiculars.

On contrary if we observe results on ratio invariant, we may distinguish between the two shapes in terms that the values on the shape representing the square, denoted as QUAD, are approximatively near 1 and the values on the other shape are near 0.4 between segments that are perpendicular and near 1 on segments that are parallel. Also if we take into account the ranks defined by the standard deviation we may seen that there not exists overlapping between the values accepted on by the ranks. This fact, take us to consider that the method will disambiguate between the two shapes.

Finally, the last experiment allows us to show if the method presented is able to distinguish between two shapes with disconnected parts as are the shapes of fig. 14. On Table 4 we may seen how the system will disambiguate between the two shapes taking into account the invariant distance.

If we look to the values on the ratio and angle invariant we may see that they are similar for the two shapes. The distance invariant on parallelism constraint calculated as we explained before let us to disambiguate between the two shapes. If we look the values for *Parallelism* constraint we observe that for *Parallelism(P1,P2)* the values

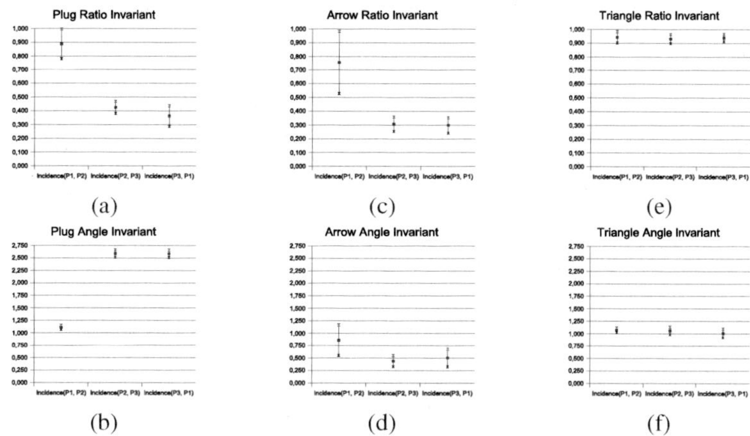

Figure 11: *Comparative among the ratio and the angle invariant for shapes: Plug, Arrow and Triangle.*

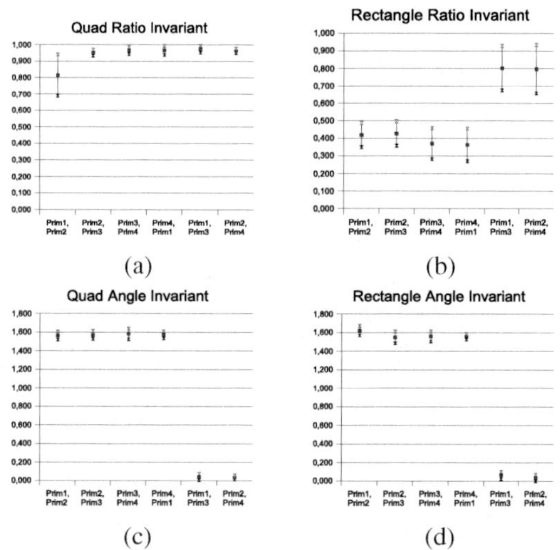

Figure 13: *Comparative among the ratio and the angle invariant for shapes: Quad and Rectangle.*

Constraint	Ratio	Angle	Distance1	Distance2
Incident(P0,P1)	0.813 ± 0.116	1.584 ± 0.045	$1.63 * 10^{-14} \pm 2.9 * 10^{-15}$	-
Incident(P2,P3)	0.905 ± 0.067	1.590 ± 0.079	$1.47 * 10^{-14} \pm 2.26 * 10^{-15}$	-
Parallelism(P1,P2)	0.887 ± 0.074	3.084 ± 0.050	0.129 ± 0.083	3.607 ± 0.643
Parallelism(P0,P3)	0.810 ± 0.106	0.030 ± 0.028	4.516 ± 0.545	0.186 ± 0.173

(a)

Constraint	Ratio	Angle	Distance1	Distance2
Incident(P0,P1)	0.920 ± 0.051	1.611 ± 0.067	0.0	-
Incident(P2,P3)	0.920 ± 0.041	1.604 ± 0.046	$4.98 * 10^{-15} \pm 1.47 * 10^{-15}$	-
Parallelism(P1,P2)	0.891 ± 0.066	3.090 ± 0.040	1.205 ± 0.264	3.809 ± 0.688
Parallelism(P0,P3)	0.838 ± 0.098	0.041 ± 0.028	4.705 ± 0.567	0.132 ± 0.081

(b)

Table 4: *Results related to the shapes of fig. 14 (a) Corresponds to fig. 14(a) and fig. 14 (b)*

Figure 14: *Special case: (a) Corners with collinear segments and (b) Corners without collinearity among segments.*

are 0.129 ± 0.083 and 3.607 ± 0.643 on table. 4(a), on contrary for the same constraint on table. 4(b) the values are 1.205 ± 0.264 and 3.809 ± 0.688. There exists a big difference between the two values what makes the system to reach its aim. The numbering of primitives follows the same configuration of fig. 14.

6. Conclusions

The aim of the method presented in this paper is to improve the description method presented in [MLSL06], allowing the differentiation among symbols which have the same topology although they are geometrically different. In order to achieve this, we have considered a set of invariants, based on the observation of the different confusions that we have observed. The Invariants that has been chosen are: *Ratio, Angle* and *Relative Distances*.

Results obtained from the conducted experiments show that the method is able to distinguish among topological identical but geometrically different symbols. Even when symbols contain disconnected parts the proposed method is able to distinguish them. This is the case for the symbols presented on Figure 14. The two corners in Figure 14(a) share collinear segments while in Figure 14(b) this collinearity does not exist.

We may observe that the description method based on two steps: a first step consisting in an *Automatic construction of a Constraint Set* [MLSL06], followed by a *Parametrization of the inferred constraints based on invariants* allows to describe forms, and construct models, avoiding the user to specify in a formal way the set of symbols she wants to use.

The use of additional attributes like *ratio, angle* and *distance* invariants also improves the alignment of primitives. This information helps to reduce the intrinsic complexity of the method.

Furthermore, the work is integrated in a sketch based framework, allowing the user to define the set of symbols it wants to use. These symbols may have or have not a functional background, *i.e.* the user can define a set of symbols that allows to interact with the framework by means of selecting, moving, rotating *etc.*

Future work will be related to define an on the fly recognition method that is able to recognize symbols while drawing (and possibly before completion). It will take into account the constraints forming the symbol and the invariants defined between any pair of primitives.

Acknowledgements

This work has been partially supported by the Spanish project CICYT TIC2003-09291.

References

[GBB98] GROS P., BOURNEZ O., BOYER E.: Using local planar geometric invariants to match and model images of line segments. *Computer Vision and Image understanding* 69, 2 (1998), 135–155.

[JG95] JORGE J., GLINERT E.: Online parsing of visual languages using adjacency grammars. In *Proceedings of the 11th International IEEE Symposium on Visual Languages* (1995), pp. 250–257.

[Log04] LOGITECH: IO digital pen, 2004. www.logitech.com.

[MHA00] MANKOFF J., HUDSON S. E., ABOWD G. D.: Providing integrated toolkit-level support for ambiguity in recognition-based interfaces. In *CHI* (2000), pp. 368–375.

[MLSL06] MAS J., LAMIROY B., SANCHEZ G., LLADOS J.: Automatic adjacency grammar generator from user drawn sketches. In *Proceedings of 18th International Conference on Pattern Recognition* (august 2006). Hong-Kong.

[MSL05] MAS J., SANCHEZ G., LLADOS J.: An adjacency grammar to recognize symbols and gestures in a digital pen framework. In *Proceedings of Second IBPRIA* (June 2005), pp. 115–122. Springer, Berlin.

[SVL*04] SÁNCHEZ G., VALVENY E., LLADÓS J., MAS J., LOZANO N.: A platform to extract knowledge from graphic documents. application to an architectural sketch understanding scenario. In *Document Analysis Systems VI*, Marinai S., Dengel A., (Eds.). World Scientific, 2004, pp. 349–365.

[TASD*00] TOMBRE K., AH-SOON C., DOSCH P., MASINI G., TABBONE S.: Stable and robust vectorization: How to make the right choices. In *Graphics Recognition: Recent Advances*, Chhabra A., Dori D., (Eds.). Springer-Verlag, Berlin, 2000, pp. 3–18. Vol. 1941 of LNCS.

[VD04] VESELOVA O., DAVIS R.: Perceptually based learning of shape descriptions for sketch recognition. In *AAAI* (2004), pp. 482–487.

[ZL04] ZHANG D., LU G.: Review of shape representation and description techniques. *Pattern Recognition 37*, 1 (January 2004), 1–19.

EUROGRAPHICS Workshop on Sketch-Based Interfaces and Modeling (2006)
Thomas Stahovich and Mario Costa Sousa (Editors)

Automatic interpretation of proofreading sketches

J.A. Rodríguez, G. Sánchez and J. Lladós

Computer Vision Center (Computer Science Department, Universitat Autonoma de Barcelona, Spain)

Abstract

We present a sketch-based system for proofreading documents. The gestures and words drawn by the proofreader on a document view are translated into high-level actions that represent editions such as replace, insert, delete and others. Our particular system is not restricted to a predefined alphabet of gestures. Instead, any symbol can be employed for striking out words or drawing inserts. This provides more flexibility and adaptability to the user. In contrast to other similar works, our interface integrates interpretation and recognition of handwritten words. The described system has been implemented for proofreading digital documents on screen but also for paper documents printed on Anoto paper and annotated using a digital pen.

Categories and subject descriptors: I.7.5 [Document capture]: Graphics recognition and interpretation, Document analysis.

1. Introduction

Despite the exponential increase of use of computers in many aspects of the daily life, there are still many usual situations in which the computer appears as a non-ergonomic and technically complex device. We still roll back to pen and paper in situations like fast sketching of an idea, taking notes or annotating documents.

Some digital devices exist that provide a natural pen interface not achievable by keyboard and other usual input peripherals. These devices such as palmtop and tablet computers, pen mice or digital pen and paper, allow systems accepting gestures [Rub91] and handwriting [PS00] as input. These devices open new possibilities such as document edition or proofreading based on sketches.

There are previous works that address this problem using various approaches. The automatic correction of printed documents was already addressed in [MB97] but from the image-based point of view. The advantage of this system is that the correction can be done with pen on paper, the most natural interface, but lacks of the on-line counterpart. The same authors have proposed an on-line version [BGM97] but it is based on menus and not on sketches. In [HKB93] a sketch-based system for on-line text editing is presented but it only supports delete, insert and move operations. Each of the actions is denoted by a specific gesture. This system only allows basic edition with restricted gestures. Another sketch-based proofreading system with a set of 11 gestures is reported in [AR99]. Even if the set of gestures is wider, there are a few items that break the naturality provided by hand movement: words must be inserted by typing and the user must click after finishing each gesture. Finally, a number of other pen-based system exist for annotating documents without or with little recognition capability, like [BM03, SW04], and even systems [Gui03] using emerging devices such as Anoto [Ano03] paper and digital pen .

In this paper we present a sketch-based system for proofreading documents. Our system interprets the sketched marks and words and translates them into high-level edition actions, such as replace, insert, delete, swap words, etc. It is possible, at the end of the process, to generate a new version of the document that is updated with the editions of the proofreader. Our system presents some advantages with respect to the discussed previous works. First, it is able to recognize handwritten input, determining the word label and associating it to the correct annotation. Second, our system has been implemented for tablet computers but also for proofreading documents printed on Anoto paper. The couple of Anoto paper and digital pen results in an emerging device that closes the loop between paper and digital documents. Finally, we let the user the possibility of striking out a word with any symbol rather than with a specific one. This makes the problem more complex but provides an open, usable and intuitive interface.

The rest of the paper is structured as follows. In Section 2 the sketch alphabet of our system is presented, which allows to formulate the problem formally in Section 3. Then, in Section 4 the designed system is described in detail. In Section 5 we discuss the results of some tests of performance. Finally, in Section 6 the conclusions are commented.

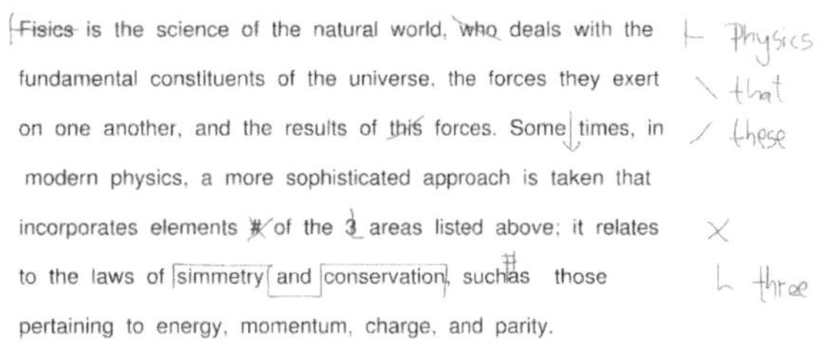

Figure 1: *Document excerpt annotated by a proofreader using a sketching interface*

2. Sketch alphabet

Our automatic proofreading interpreter accepts sketches drawn using the typographic conventions used by proofreading professionals. In Figure 1 a sample text fragment is shown. The proofreading sketches on this text follow the rules summarized in Figure 2. These rules provide gestures for the following actions: replace a text by another text, delete text, insert text, swap words, swap non-contiguous words, indent a line, merge two words and split a word in two.

REPLACE	this is a ~~sample~~ line in a document.	this is a text line in a document.
DELETE	this is a ~~sample~~ line in a document.	this is a line in a document.
INSERT	this is a sample line in a document	this is a sample line in a pdf document.
SWAP	text file	file text
BROKEN SWAP	text and file	file and text
INDENT	first line second line third line	first line 　　second line third line
MERGE	data set	dataset
SEPARATE	Harddisk	hard disk

Figure 2: *Proofreading notation used by the presented system.*

On the one hand, there is a set of actions (SWAP, BROKEN SWAP, INDENT, MERGE and SEPARATE) that we will call *direct* actions since they are directly encoded by a specific gesture. On the other hand, the actions REPLACE, DELETE and INSERT need annotations at the margin. For instance, to replace some word by another, the proofreader must strike out the word with a symbol. Then this symbol is repeated at the page margin (normally in reduced size) and finally the correct word is handwritten next to the repeated symbol. For deleting, the process is the same except that no text is written at the margin. Inserting works analogue to replace, with the obvious difference that instead of striking out a word, a symbol is placed at the position where the new text should be appended.

One novelty with respect to existing systems is the possibility of specifying these strike outs or insert symbols for REPLACE, DELETE and INSERT using any symbol. We take advantage from the fact that they appear in pairs to allow a more open and intuitive interface. The advantages of using an unrestricted alphabet of gestures for these cases are:

- The necessary previous knowledge of the particular system is reduced.
- The proofreader is more flexible to use preferred or improvised symbols.
- Different symbols can be used if the same edition action has to be repeated in a different part of the text, so that there is no possibility for confusion (in fact, this is a "best practice" in some proofreading conventions).

3. Formulation of the problem

From a formal viewpoint, proofreading consists of encoding a set of actions that affect the document contents into a set of sketches that can be either gestures or text. Let us denote the set of actions

$$A = \{A_k\} \tag{1}$$

with $k = 1 \ldots N_A$ where N_A is the number of actions. Each action A_k is an action from the following alphabet

$$A_k \in \{\text{REPLACE, DELETE, INSERT, SWAP BROKEN SWAP, INDENT, MERGE, SEPARATE}\} \tag{2}$$

The sketches on the document are represented by a set of strokes

$$S = \{S_i\}, i = 1 \ldots N_S \tag{3}$$

with N_S the number of strokes in S. Each stroke can be described by the set of points sampled by the sketching device between each pen down and pen up events:

$$S_i = \{\vec{p}_j\}, \vec{p}_j = (x_j, y_j), j = 1 \ldots N_{S_i} \tag{4}$$

or, alternatively, by the segments that link these points:

$$S_i = \{s_j\}, s_j = \text{seg}(\vec{p}_{j-1}, \vec{p}_j), j = 2, \ldots N_{S_i} \tag{5}$$

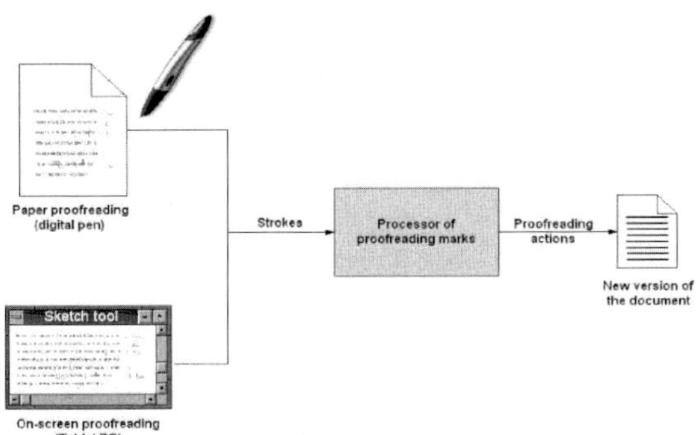

Figure 3: *System overview*

where N_{S_i} is the number of points sampled in stroke S_i and $\text{seg}(\vec{p}, \vec{q})$ designs the segment that starts at point $\vec{p}$ and ends at point $\vec{q}$. The automatic proofreading interpretation process can be formalized as finding the decoding f that converts S to A

$$A = f(S) \qquad (6)$$

As the document sketches are processed as a whole and not one by one, this decoding implies a coupling of the following problems:

- Symbol recognition
- Handwriting recognition
- Layout analysis

Of special interest is the problem of symbol recognition. As discussed in section 2, one can find two categories of symbols. On the one hand, there are the symbols that appear in pairs and that belong to an unrestricted alphabet that will be called W_u. On the other hand, there will be the symbols whose shape provides a direct meaning. These symbols are from a restricted symbol alphabet denoted W_r from now on.

Additionally, in the set of direct symbols there are symbols that have a fixed shape (SEPARATE, MERGE) and some others whose shape will vary depending on the words on which they act.

The specific details about the whole automatic proofreading system can be read in the following sections.

4. System architecture

Figure 3 shows an overview of the system. A user annotates either a printed document with digital pen or a PDF document on-screen, obeying the syntax explained in Section 2. A proofreading engine interprets the annotations and extracts all the contents affected by the corrections and the actions to apply to these contents. From this output it is possible to refactor the annotated document, obtaining an updated version where the output edition actions have been applied.

The system can be logically divided into input, processing and output blocks. The processing block can be further subdivided into a layout segmentation module, a symbol recognition module and a handwriting recognition module.

The system must be robust to multiple annotations in the same paragraph end even in the same line, and to multiple line text annotations; and must support the different symbols from W_u that the proofreader might write but at the same time it must permit sketching the actions with the same symbol class if they are clearly separated.

The implementation of the system has been developed with the Java programming language, supported by a Java platform for handling digital ink that has been programmed by the authors.

4.1. Input

The input of the system is the set of all strokes drawn by a corrector with a sketching device. As stated previously, we implemented the possibility of annotating using a digital pen on PDF documents printed on paper enabling Anoto functionality. And we also designed an on-screen editor which accepts mouse strokes. This possibility becomes useful for tablet computers or when using a pen mouse. In any case, the stroke format is unified and the coordinates refer to the document sheet. This is a device independent approach that allows future extension of the input possibilities.

4.2. Layout segmentation

The layout segmentation module is devoted to the analysis of the spatial information. Instead of trying to directly recognize symbols or groups of symbols and assigning them to one of the categories in Figure 2, one must take into account that the particular problem we are trying to solve is extremely context-dependent. So it is more interesting to first try to extract the highest possible amount of context information. Then, the recognition step will be conducted more effectively according to this context information (this can help e.g. in selecting the appropriate recognition method, discarding some classes, etc.)

As the context is encoded in the spatial information this step can be called layout segmentation. In this step, the strokes are grouped into symbols, they are then categorized into text and margin symbols and finally blocks of symbols that will be processed as a whole in subsequent modules are found.

The first step is to group the strokes into symbols using a connected component labelling. Two strokes S and S' are considered to be connected if

$$\exists i, j \text{ such that } \sqrt{(x_i - x'_j)^2 + (y_i - y'_j)^2} < d_{TC} \qquad (7)$$

where d_{TC} is a threshold distance that is empirically determined. For a more realistic connectivity determination, additional points were linearly interpolated for each stroke when evaluating the expression in Equation 7.

Once a symbol $\mathcal{S}$ has been obtained from a set of connected strokes, it is categorized into the group of symbols on the text and the group of symbols on the margin (shortly, text symbols and margin symbols) with the following criterion:

$$\mathcal{S} \in \left\{ \begin{array}{ll} \text{TEXT} & x_{min} < X_{MARGIN} \\ \text{MARGIN} & \text{otherwise} \end{array} \right. , x_{min} = \min_{(x_i, y_i) \in \mathcal{S}} x_i \tag{8}$$

where X_{MARGIN} is the x-coordinate on the document where the margin starts at.

The final step in the layout segmentation is to divide the paper vertically into blocks that contain annotations that are close to each other. We experienced that a high frequency of annotations in the same paper zone tends to produce blocks of margin symbols (shortly, margin blocks). If $(x_{BB}, y_{BB}), (x'_{BB}, y'_{BB})$ are the points defining the bounding box of a block, then the text zone with a vertical coordinate y such that $y_{BB} < y < y'_{BB}$ is called the influence zone of this block. In Figure 4 we present an example of a situation with two annotation blocks and their influence zones.

This figure illustrates how finding margin blocks and their influence zones simplifies the processing. On the one hand, if a text symbol $\mathcal{S}$ is not on any influence zone, we will consider that $\mathcal{S} \in W_p$. On the other hand, the the symbols $\mathcal{S}_a$ in a block such that $\mathcal{S}_a \in W_u$ must have a matching text symbol, which is expected to be in the influence zone.

The procedure to build blocks is also a connectivity labelling. Two symbols are considered to be connected if the vertical distance between their bounding box center is below a threshold d_{TB}. The influence zone of each symbol is determined as already explained.

Processing the annotation blocks separately rather than the whole document is advantageous since it reduces the number of matches to evaluate in further steps and thus the probability of confusion.

4.3. Symbol recognition

A number of elaborate techniques exist for recognizing symbols using different strategies [LVSM02]. However, with the layout already segmented, the sketches on the document can be decoded into actions taking much advantage of the available context, relying less on the symbol recognition itself. The strategy to follow is: first, from each influence zone the text symbols that match with the margin symbols are found. Then, the remaining symbols and the symbols that are not inside any influence zone are recognized using a particular symbol classifier.

Search for matching symbols

First, we subdivide each of the margin blocks into lines, using again a labelling of connected components. For this pur-

pose we consider that two symbols belong to the same line if their bounding box center is separated by a distance shorter than a threshold d_{TL}, where, obviously $d_{TS} < d_{TL} < d_{TB}$. This labelling results in a set of lines $L = L_1 \ldots L_{N_L}$ where each line L_i contains a set of symbols $L_i = \{\mathcal{S}_j\}$. From each line L_i, the symbol with smallest horizontal projection is extracted:

$$\mathcal{S}_i^{left} = \arg\min_{\forall j} x_{BB}(\mathcal{S}_j) \tag{9}$$

where $x_{BB}(\mathcal{S})$ stands for the x-coordinate of the $\mathcal{S}$-bounding box. Notice from Figure X. that each $\mathcal{S}_i^{left}$ can be either a symbol $\mathcal{S}_i^{left} \in W_u$ or $\mathcal{S}_i^{left} \in H$

Denote $\mathcal{S}_k$ the set of symbols on the influence zone of a block and $d(\mathcal{S}, \mathcal{S}')$ some distance measure between symbols $\mathcal{S}$ and $\mathcal{S}'$. Then a matrix D is built where each element is computed as

$$D_{ki} = d(\mathcal{S}_k, \mathcal{S}_i^{left}) \tag{10}$$

We search for the lowest distance value $D_{k'i'}$ in matrix D. The indices (k', i') are stored in a list and columns i and j are removed from matrix D. The process of finding the lowest distance is repeated until all remaining distance values in the matrix are below a threshold d_M, or until there are no more columns or rows in the matrix. At this moment we have a list of index pairs (k', i') that indicate a REPLACE, DELETE or INSERT action coded by $\mathcal{S}_k$ on the text and its pair $\mathcal{S}_i^{left}$ at the page margin.

The rest of the symbols in line L_i are considered to be words (or pieces of words). If in the consecutive following line L_{i+1} it happens that $\mathcal{S}_{i+1}^{left}$ had no match with any $\mathcal{S}_k$ then it is considered to be the continuation of text from the previous line, and so with every consecutive line. If the number of word symbols is greater than 0, we have decoded a REPLACE or an INSERT action. Both actions are distinguished from whether the involved symbol S_k intersects some printed words or not. In case that the number of words at the margin is 0, then we encounter a DELETE action. For each action, the complete set of words will be send to the handwriting recognition module preserving their spatial relations.

If a block only contains one line and its influence zone only contains one text symbol (lowest annotation in Figure 4), the correspondence is directly done and the matching process with matrix D is omitted.

Matching with Hausdorff distance

The symbol matching is performed using the line segment Hausdorff Distance [GL02]. This is a generalization of the Hausdorff distance between two point sets for computing distances between segment sets.

Let us define a distance between two segments s and s', which takes into account the angle between the segments,

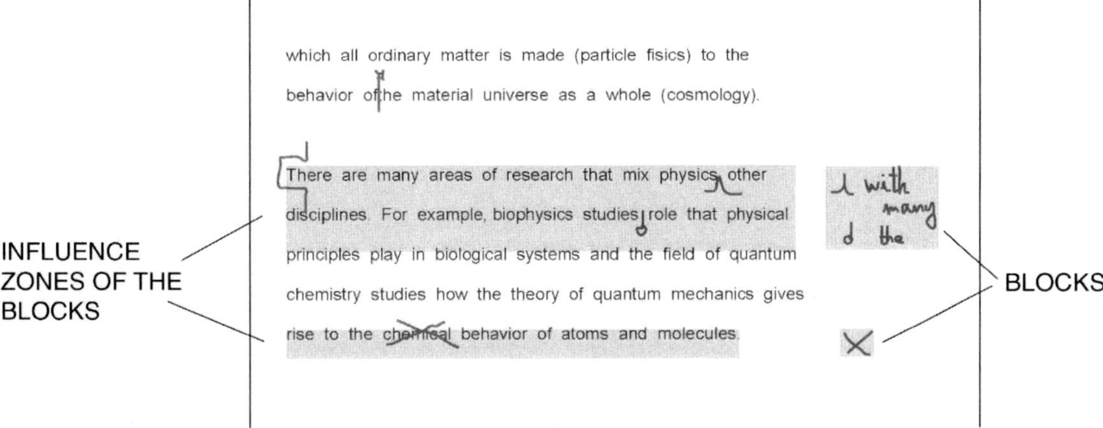

Figure 4: *Concept of annotation blocks. The symbols in the margin are clustered into blocks of similar position. The zone in the text overlapping each block represents the influence zone. The influence zone defines the region where the potential matches of the annotation symbols are.*

and the distance in horizontal and vertical projections:

$$d(s, s') = \sqrt{W^2 d_\theta(s, s')^2 + d_\parallel^2(s, s') + d_\perp^2(s, s')} \qquad (11)$$

where W is a parameter that is empirically determined, $d_\theta(s, s')$ is the tangent of the rotation angle for aligning the shortest segment with the longest one, and $d_\parallel$ and $d_\perp$ are the respective distances in parallel and normal direction with the shortest segment already aligned.

With this definition, the line segment Hausdorff distance between two sets of segments S and T is defined as

$$H(S, T) = max(h(S, T), h(T, S)) \qquad (12)$$

where

$$h(S, T) = \frac{1}{\sum_{s_i \in S} l_{s_i}} \sum_{s_i \in S} l_{s_i} \min_{t_j \in T} d(s_i, t_j) \qquad (13)$$

with l_{s_i} the length of segment s_i. Equation 13 is called directed distance and it is an improvement of the expression used in the classical Hausdorff distance.

A symbol is a set of strokes that can be represented as segments (Equation 5). If two symbols $\mathcal{S}$ and $\mathcal{T}$ are aligned, then $H(\mathcal{S}, \mathcal{T})$ can be interpreted as a dissimilarity measure. For computing the dissimilarity or, simply, distance between two symbols, first their coordinates will be scaled and shifted to a predefined bounding box and then equation 12 will be applied.

Predefined symbol recognition

Text symbols without matching margin annotations and text symbols outside influence zones of blocks are classified into the set W_p of predefined symbols using a two-stage symbol classifier.

First, note that the some segments of the SWAP and BROKEN SWAP symbols have different lengths as a function of the words they involve. Moreover, it is allowed that both symbols appear reflected. The selected strategy is first to try to classify a symbol using the directional information of the sketches to match predefined templates; and for imperfect or unrecognized symbols apply a secondary classifier based on the symbol shape.

In the first stage the strokes of the symbol to recognize are approximated to straight segments using the method described in [HN04]. The angles of the resulting segments are quantized in one of eight possible directions (N, NE, E, SE, S, SW, W, NW) and a chain is build from these direction codes. The direction codes are matched against predefined templates with a certain tolerance.

For the imperfect strokes that do not match the predefined templates, a Zernike moment descriptor classification using support vector machines is performed using library hhreco [HN04]. A previous training process is necessary for this classifier. One of the advantages of Zernike moments is that they are invariant to rotations and it is possible to detect the rotated versions of the SWAP symbols and even rotations of other symbols due to imperfect sketching.

The final Zernike moment classifier is also able to reject doubtful samples so that no proofreading decision is taken at all for very suspect symbols.

4.4. Handwritten word recognition

A handwriting recognition module is necessary to translate the words written by the proofreader at the margin. Several methods [PS00] as well as commercial engines are available. For this particular application a commercial module that supports on-line cursive handwriting has been used.

4.5. System output

A list of proofreading actions is generated as a result of the interpretation method. The actions include on which text to apply and, when necessary, which new text is attached. From this action list we can generate a new version of the document which includes all modifications that come from the proofreading interpretation. In the next section, some examples will be shown.

5. Experiments

The experiment sections shows both evaluation experiments used to design the system and evaluation of the system performance.

5.1. Evaluation of matching measures

In 4.3 the line Hausdorff distance was introduced. Our system uses this dissimilarity measure for the matching mechanism. The decision for the Hausdorff distance is taken after the study that we present now.

On a dataset of 700 samples from a single writer we have computed a modified Dunn's index [BP98] for different distances. The modified Dunn index gives an idea of the separability of classes given a distance measure between elements:

$$\nu = \min_{1 \leq s \leq c} \left\{ \min_{1 \leq t \leq c} \left\{ \frac{\delta(X_s, X_t)}{\max_{1 \leq k \leq c} \Delta(X_k)} \right\} \right\} \quad (14)$$

where $\delta(X_s, X_t)$ represents some distance between classes X_s and X_t and $\Delta(X_k)$ is a definition of the diameter of class X_k. We have taken

$$\delta(S, T) = \frac{1}{N_S N_T} \sum_{x \in S, y \in T} d(x, y) \quad (15)$$

and

$$\Delta(S) = \frac{1}{N_S(N_S - 1)} \sum_{x, y \in S, x \neq y} d(x, y) \quad (16)$$

where N_S is the number of elements in class S and d is the evaluated distance measure. Higher values of the modified Dunn index indicate more class separability for distance d.

In table 5.1 we present the Dunn index computed for different distance measures. As you can appreciate there, the measure with highest performance among the tested ones is the line segment Hausdorff distance.

The Line Segment Hausdorff distance appears as a very useful distance method between symbols, especially suited for on-line recognition as the extraction of the segments from the strokes is natural.

5.2. Performance of the automatic system

This section describes the experiments carried out to measure the performance of the automatic proofreading inter-

Distance	ν
Line segment Hausdorff distance (W=0.25)	1.73
ED between Geometric moments (L=1)	1.10
ED between Line moments [LN96] (L=1)	1.01
ED between Zernike moments (L=13)	0.87
ED between Line Legendre moments [LN96] (L=1)	0.74
ED between Legendre moments (L=1)	0.66

Table 1: *Modified Dunn indices computed for different distance measurements. ED stands for Euclidean distance. W is the parameter of the Hausdorff distance and L is the moment order. Only the best result for each distance among all the parameter variations is shown.*

Position	Action	Replaced text	New Text
0	REPLACE	Fisics	Physics
50	REPLACE	who	that
188	REPLACE	this (188)	these
203	MERGE		
316	DELETE	#	
386	REPLACE	simmetry	symmetry
492	DELETE	The	
546	REPLACE	phenomenons	phenomena
581	SWAP		
679	REPLACE	fisics	physics
711	SEPARATE		
721	INSERT		with
877	INSERT		the

Table 2: *List of actions obtained from the automatic proofreading interpreter for the previous sample. Position is an index for locating the word characters inside the document contents.*

preter. In these experiments, users were given a text document with some errors and were told to proofread it obeying the explained notation. The sketches of the users were done with digital pen. For this purpose, the PDF document to annotate was printed on digital paper enabling Anoto functionality. One of the samples is presented in figure 5. This benchmark resulted in a set of 33 documents filled out by 9 different proofreaders.

The most important point in our system is the association of annotations in the margin with their corresponding text symbol. It is clear that it is not the main target of this work to develop a symbol or a text recognizer. Therefore, we concentrate on measuring the degree of correctness with which the similar symbol pairs are matched and the annotation text correctly associated, and also the cases where this is not accomplished and for which reasons. Therefore, in each of the 33 outputs, we examine all annotations that have margin contents (REPLACE, DELETE and INSERT) and classify them in one of the following cases:

- Correct association: The text symbol has been associated

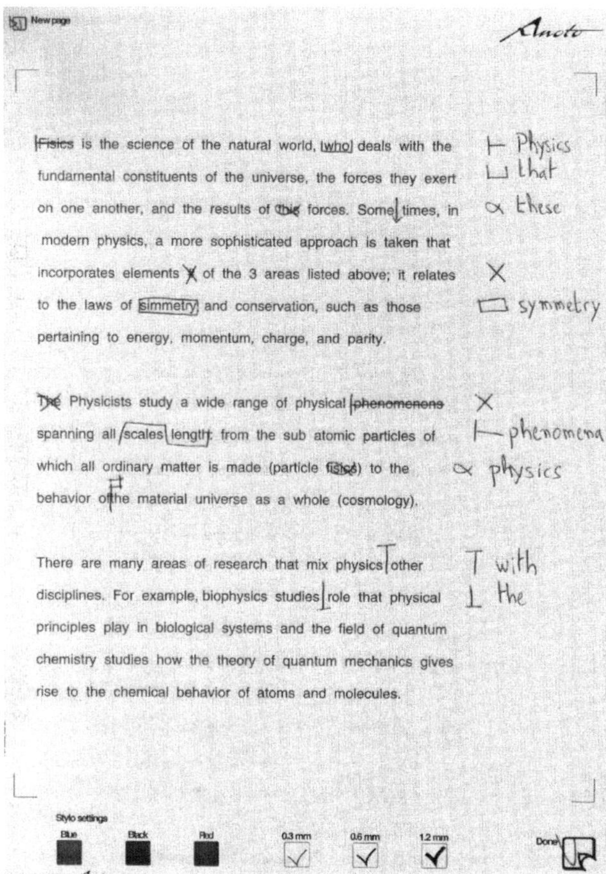

Figure 5: *Document annotated by a proofreader. The PDF document was printed on digital paper and the proofreading marks were sketched with digital pen.*

Correct associations	90.1 %
Incorrect associations	4.5 %
Missing associations	5.4 %
Number of documents with 100% correct actions	22

Table 3: *Results of the evaluation of correct association of annotations with text at the margin.*

with the corresponding margin symbol and the annotation text has been associated correctly.

- Incorrect association: The text symbol has been associated with a non-corresponding margin symbol, or the text has not been correctly association.
- Missing action: The text symbol is not associated with any symbol and has been processed as a symbol from W_p.

Results are summarized in table 3.

It can be observed that 90.1% of these annotations are correctly associated. Recall that for correctly associating annotations first a correct layout segmentation is necessary and then symbol pairs extraction from the set of all-with-all possible pairs, where additionally the symbol form is unrestricted, so that 90.1% is a good result for this first prototype. It should be noted that this 90.1% correctness is not a regular observation in most documents. On the contrary, it is due to few samples with unacceptable result. Observe in Table 3 that 22 out of the 33 documents had 100% correct associations (these are document containing an average of 6.5 annotations with margin, the smallest with 4 and the highest with 11 annotations with margin).

Regarding the reos of actions (direct actions), 83% of the symbols were correctly recognized, with 8.4% errors and 4.6% rejections. This not so high recognition rate may be due to the fact that the SVM classifier was trained with samples from a single writer. A recent experiment with the symbols extracted from the 33 documents, using the half for training and the half for test, increased the recognition rate to 95.0% with 5% error rate and 0% rejection rate.

From the analysis of the incorrect samples we observe that in most cases it happened that imperfect sketching increased the Hausdorff distance between symbols and prevented them from being matched correctly. At this point we believe that it would be of great help to have a method for discrimination between symbols and words. The additional information provided by this system for each symbol could help in the match search process and would increase the 90.1% accuracy.

6. Conclusions

We have presented a system that automatically interprets digital ink annotations that proofreaders sketch on documents. The system successfully recognizes the set of proposed gestures and recognizes the associated handwritten notes, something that is not usual in similar works. Moreover, a part of the actions can be specified using gestures from an unrestricted alphabet. With this, we have generalized the problem and have performed a step towards the ideal system that interprets any document annotation.

The Line Segment Hausdorff distance appears as a very useful dissimilarity measure between aligned sketched symbols. This distance behaves robustly to imperfect writing of the symbols.

For improving the performance of the automatic interpreter a text/symbol discriminator could be implemented for being applied to each of the symbols at the margin. This would provide supporting information just in the layer between layout segmentation and symbol recognition.

Under the performance conditions of such a system, a validation screen would be helpful for the proofreader to accept the interpreted actions. If the proofreader is also enabled to perform changes in the validation screen, this information could serve as new ground truth for retraining the processes involved in the refactoring.

Acknowledgements

This work has been partially supported by the Spanish project CICYT TIC2003-09291.

References

[Ano03] ANOTO: Development guide for services enabled by Anoto functionality, 2003.

[AR99] ANDRÉ J., RICHY H.: Paper-less editing and proofreading of electronic documents. In *EuroTeX '99 Proceedings* (1999).

[BGM97] BUNKE H., GONIN R., MOERI D.: A tool for versatile and user-friendly document correction. In *Proceedings of the 4th International Conference on Document Analysis and Recognition* (1997), IEEE Computer Society, pp. 433–438.

[BM03] BARGERON D., MOSCOVICH T.: Reflowing digital ink annotations. In *CHI '03: Proceedings of the SIGCHI conference on Human factors in computing systems* (2003), ACM Press, pp. 385–393.

[BP98] BEZDEK J. C., PAL N. R.: Some new indexes of cluster validity. *IEEE Transactions on Systems, Man and Cybernetics 28*, 3 (June 1998), 301–315.

[GL02] GAO Y., LEUNG M. K. H.: Line segment Hausdorff distance on face matching. *Pattern Recognition 35*, 2 (2002), 361–371.

[Gui03] GUIMBRETIÈRE F.: Paper augmented digital documents. In *UIST '03: Proceedings of the 16th annual ACM symposium on User interface software and technology* (2003), ACM Press, pp. 51–60.

[HKB93] HARDOCK G., KURTENBACH G., BUXTON W.: A marking based interface for collaborative writing. In *UIST '93: Proceedings of the 6th annual ACM symposium on User interface software and technology* (1993), ACM Press, pp. 259–266.

[HN04] HSE H., NEWTON A. R.: Sketched symbol recognition using Zernike moments. *Proceedings of the 17th international conference on pattern recognition (ICPR'04) 01* (2004), 367–370.

[LN96] LAMBERT G., NOLL J.: Discrimination properties of invariants using the line moments of vectorized contours. In *Proceedings of ICPR'96* (1996), pp. 735–739.

[LVSM02] LLADÓS J., VALVENY E., SÁNCHEZ G., MARTÍ E.: Symbol recognition: Current advances and perspectives. In *GREC '01: Selected Papers from the Fourth International Workshop on Graphics Recognition Algorithms and Applications* (2002), Springer-Verlag, pp. 104–127.

[MB97] MÖRI D., BUNKE H.: *Automatic interpretation and execution of manual corrections on text documents.* Handbook of Character Recognition and Document Image Analysis. World Scientific, 1997, pp. 679–702.

[PS00] PLAMONDON R., SRIHARI S. N.: On-line and off-line handwriting recognition: a comprehensive survey. *IEEE Transactions on Pattern Analysis and Machine Intelligence 22* (2000), 63–82.

[Rub91] RUBINE D.: Specifying gestures by example. In *SIGGRAPH '91: Proceedings of the 18th annual conference on Computer graphics and interactive techniques* (1991), ACM Press, pp. 329–337.

[SW04] SHILMAN M., WEI Z.: Recognizing freeform digital ink annotations. In *Document Analysis Systems* (2004), pp. 322–331.

EUROGRAPHICS Workshop on Sketch-Based Interfaces and Modeling (2006)
Thomas Stahovich and Mario Costa Sousa (Editors)

Parsing Ink Annotations on Heterogeneous Documents

Xin Wang[1] and Michael Shilman[2] and Sashi Raghupathy[1]

[1]Ink Parsing Team, TabletPC, Microsoft Corp, One Microsoft Way, RedMond, WA 98052, USA
[2]Microsoft Research, One Microsoft Way, Redmond, WA 98052, USA

Abstract

Annotation is an integral part of reading, comprehending, commenting, and authoring notes and documents. In this paper we present a system for recognizing annotations in a flexible digital notebook that may contain a variety of content ranging from text, to images, to handwritten notes. To accomplish the recognition task in real-time makes the complicated annotation parsing problem more difficult.

Our approach differs from previous approaches in several ways. First, our approach handles annotations on ink notes, which are significantly more ambiguous than annotations on printed documents and hence more difficult to recognize. Second, our approach is entirely learned from data, so it is easy to adapt to other scenarios. Third, our approach is more thoroughly evaluated than previous systems. On a test set of real user notes, the system has achieved an average recall of 0.9258 on all annotation types. Finally, the implementation of the approach will be commercially available as an API in the upcoming release of Windows® Vista® and Office 12®.

Categories and Subject Descriptors (according to ACM CCS): I.7.m [Computing Methodologies]: Document and Text Processing; I.5.4 [Computing Technology]: Pattern Recognition

1. Introduction

A Holy Grail of personal information management is a digital notebook application that simplifies storage, sharing, retrieval, and manipulation of a user's notes, diagrams, web clippings, and so on. This application should be able to flexibly incorporate a wide variety of data types and deal with them reasonably. One approach, as exemplified by Microsoft OneNote®, is to explicitly represent different data types in a single application, and let users capture and fluidly manipulate text, digital ink, and images in data type-specific ways. The application becomes more powerful when ink is intelligently interpreted and given appropriate behaviors according to the type. For instance, hierarchical lists in digital ink notes should be able to expand and collapse just like hierarchical lists in text-based note-taking tools.

Annotations are an important part of a user's interaction with both paper and digital documents, and can be used in numerous ways within the digital notebook. Users annotate documents for comprehension, authoring, editing, note-taking, author feedback, and so on.

When annotations are recognized, they become a form of structured content that semantically decorates any of the

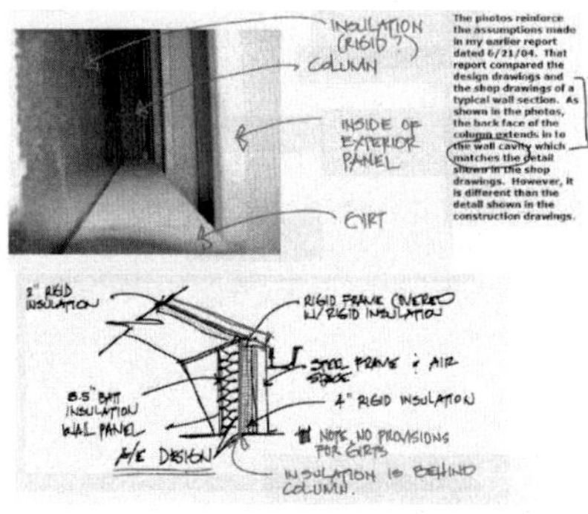

Figure 1: *A OneNote 12® file with a mixture of ink, text and images. The fist section of the file is a regular text region. The second section consists of two images with ink annotations. The last section is an ink-drawing with ink annotations surrounding it.*

other data types in a digital notebook. Recognized annotations can be anchored to document content, so that the annotations can be reflowed as the document layout changes. They can assist in information retrieval, marking places in the document of particular interest or importance. Editing marks such as deletion or insertion can be invoked as actions on the underlying document. Users annotate documents by habit; recognizing those annotations increases their value in the lifecycle of the digital document.

In this paper, we present a set of techniques for recognizing an assortment of digital ink annotations against a variety of underlying document content, including other digital notes and diagrams. Unlike previous work that heuristically recognizes, anchors, and reflows digital ink annotations against text documents [SW04], our approach works on document with heterogeneous content types. In particular, recognizing digital ink annotations in the context of other digital ink notes is highly ambiguous, and therefore extremely difficult. With the real–time requirement of an API to be integrated into commerical note taking softwares such as One Note, the problem is even more complicated.

Furthermore, our method is based entirely on learning from training data, so if new annotation types or new content types are added, the system can be retrained to incorporate these new types. This flexibility in the system design allows us to recognize more annotation types when moving from our Beta–1 version to Beta–2.

Finally, the technique we describe achieves reasonable accuracy on real user notes. It will be shipping with Windows Vista®[†] and OneNote® 2007[‡].

Recognizing ink annotations that occur in ink notes is significantly more difficult than in printed documents. On a printed document, every ink stroke must belong to an annotation of some type. For example, a strikethrough is identifiable if it is crosses through a printed line of text and aligns with its baseline. However, in an ink note it is not always clear which strokes should be grouped into lines, or, given a hypothesized line and a potential annotation stroke, whether the stroke is a strikethrough or perhaps merely a long crossing stroke on the letter "t". Numerous such problems make it difficult for the computer to accurately discriminate between the handwritten notes and the annotations that modify those notes.

In Section 2, we give an introduction to the terminology. We also introduce several important user scenarios of the annotation system as part of an introduction to the scope of the system. In Section 3, we describe the functional details of our ink annotation parsing system: its tasks, its architecture, and its integration with the rest of our ink parsing system. We also cover the algorithmic aspects of the system: its classification, segmentation, and annotation anchoring. In Section 5, we present the evaluation results of our system. In Section ??, we describe future work.

---

† `http://www.microsoft.com/windowsvista/`
‡ `http://office.microsoft.com/onenote/`

2. Definitions and User Scenarios

2.1. Annotation

An ink annotation on such a document consists of a group of semantically and spatially related ink strokes that annotate the main content of the document. They provide supplementary information to the main body and sometimes establish relationships between different parts of the document. In this paper, we will focus on annotations formed by drawing strokes, which do not group with the rest of the text the user has written.

As pointed out by [Mar97], there are many different types of annotation. Each serves a different type of marking or editing activity. There are two major classes of annotations:

- **Non-Actionable annotations:** annotations that just explain, summarize, emphasize or comment on the main content, see Figure 2;
- **Actionable annotations:** annotations that denote editorial actions such as insertion, deletion, transposition, and movement.

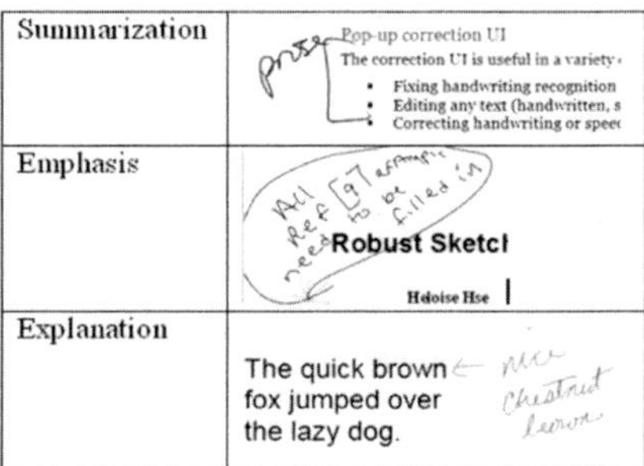

Figure 2: *Non-actionable annotations. Instead of specifying an special editorial actions on the main content, these annotations explain, summarize, emphasize, and comment on them.*

No matter whether it specifies an action or not, an annotation involves two types of information, the **geometric** information and the **semantic** information. In this paper, we use geometric information to refer to what kind of ink-strokes the annotation has, how the strokes form a geometric shape, and how the shape relates (both temporally and spatially) to other ink-strokes in the file. For all the annotation types supported by our system, we allow multiple-to-multiple mapping between the shapes of an annotation and their types. Without restricting the system to handle only the situation where a set of shapes are reserved for one annotation type only, this introduces additional difficulty into the parsing task.

We use semantic information to refer to the meaning or the function of the annotation, and how it relates to other semantic objects in the document—words, lines, and blocks of text, or images.

2.2. Supported Annotation Types

As shown in Figure 3, our system supports four categories and eight types of annotation according to both the semantic and the geometric information they carry.

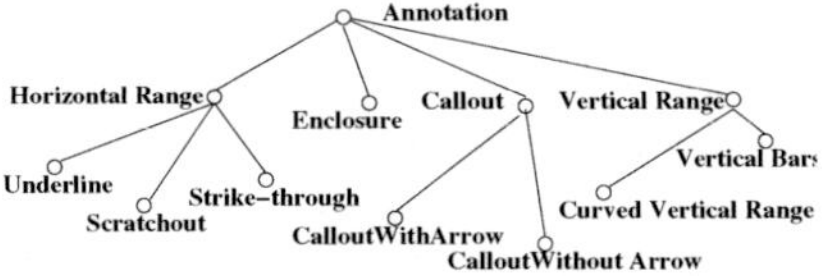

Figure 3: *Class hierarchy supported by our ink annotation system.*

The four categories we support are: horizontal ranges, vertical ranges, enclosures, and callouts. For horizontal ranges, we support three subtypes, underlines, strike-throughs, and scratch-outs of different shapes. For vertical ranges, to im-

Underline	*implement*
Strike-through	*Manual*
Scratch-out	*Accessible*
Vertical Range (brackets)	*thus providing default handling for what we don't handle.*
Vertical Bar	*→ catch WM_GETOBJECT → give it an IAccessible ptr. ↓ can we pass this on to*
Callout With Arrow	*my notes in ink*
Callout Without Arrow	*The quick brown fox jumped over the lazy dog. I'll bother when I see it!*
Enclosure	

Figure 4: *Samples for annotation types that are currently supported by the annotation parsing system. For each type, only one example of shape is shown, even though in our system they are not restricted to take only one shape.*

prove recognition accuracy, we divide the category into two subtypes, vertical range in general (brace, bracket, parantheses and etc), and vertical bar in particular (both single and double vertical bars).

For enclosure, we recognize blobs of different shapes: rectangle, ellipse, and other regular or irregular shapes. Our system can even recognize partial enclosures or enclosures that overlap more than once.

For callouts, we support both straight line callouts with or without arrowheads, curved callouts with or without arrowheads, and elbow callouts with or without arrowheads.

2.3. Anchoring

No matter what geometric shape it takes, an annotation always establishes a semantic relationship among parts of a document. The parts can be regions or *spans* in the document, such as part of a line, a paragraph, an ink or text region, or an image. The annotation can also denote a specific position in the document such as before or after a word, on top of an image and so on. We call these relationships anchors, and in addition to identifying the type of annotation for a set of strokes, the annotation parser must also identify its anchors.

3. Parsing System

3.1. System Overview

Our ink parsing system consists of a stack of engines as shown in 5. Each engine works on a specific semantic problem and enriches or improves upon the partial parsing results that are passed to it. For example, the writing-drawing classification engine classifies all the incoming ink strokes into writing or drawing [BSH04], and the line finding engine groups ink strokes into lines of writing [YSR*05]. The annotation engine is a new engine added to the end of the stack. It identifies groups of ink strokes that are annotations, their types, and their corresponding anchors.

Anybody who has tried to interpret full pages of ink notes from real user data knows that ink is locally ambiguous, and can only be accurately interpreted in a global context. Therefore it is not obvious how our feed-forward architecture can work on real notes. In some sense, each engine is responsible for its own task, plus some subset of the tasks before it in the stack. For example, the annotation engine will often second guess earlier writing-drawing decisions, examining writing strokes at the end of connectors to try to find arrowheads that have been misclassified. This increases the responsibility and reduces the modularity of each engine, but allows us to optimize each stage for accuracy and performance without resorting to a global optimization strategy which will be difficult to complete in real time on today's computers.

Our annotation parsing approach is an evolution of the annotation parser presented in [SW04] and the symbol grouping and classification approach of [SVC04]. [SW04] identified annotations and their anchors using a complex set of heuristics. [SVC04] simultaneously optimized over a set of segmentation and recognition hypotheses and was entirely learned from data. We first present an adaptation of [SVC04] to the problem of annotation parsing and anchoring. We then heuristically and greedily refine this adaptation to operate in close to real-time.

3.2. Optimal Annotation Parsing

The job of the annotation parser is to segment, recognize, and anchor ink strokes against a background document. We can perform all of these functions simultaneously using a variant of the technique described in [SVC04].

Assume a trained recognizer R, which, given a candidate set of strokes, anchors, and background, can reasonably hypothesize the candidate as an annotation of a specific type, or as garbage. Given such a recognizer, one merely needs to enumerate over a reasonable set of candidates. One method is to connect all of the strokes into a neighborhood graph. Two strokes are connected in the graph if the Euclidian distance between their convex hulls is less than a threshold, as shown in Figure Y. This threshold can be empirically determined based on the maximum distance between any two strokes that fall into the same labeled symbol in training data. Assuming some maximum number of strokes per symbol, K, [SVC04] presents an efficient way to enumerate connected subsets of this graph, which form symbol candidates.

Given the recognizer R, and a candidate enumeration method, it is possible to solve for an optimal grouping, recognition over all the strokes through dynamic programming on the recurrence equation in [SVC04].

Unfortunately, in consumer user interfaces we must often sacrifice optimality and simplicity for performance. Our entire stack of engines, including writing-drawing classification, line grouping, annotations parsing, and so on, must complete in approximately $1ms$ per stroke. If we budget 10% of this time for annotations parsing, this means our annotation engine must process a 500 stroke page, including segmentation and recognition, in $100ms$! Therefore, we employ a greedy optimization and a set of heuristics to approximate this optimization. In the next section, we describe the features and training procedure for R, and the heuristic accelerations of this optimization.

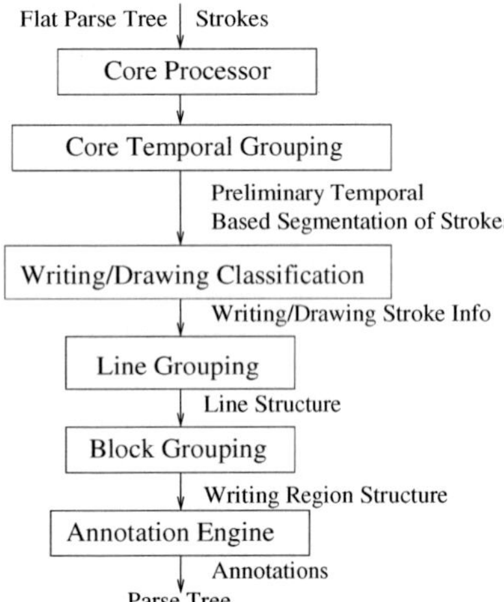

Figure 5: *The engine stack of ink parser. Partial parsing results, represented as parsing trees, are passed from one engine to another.*

3.3. Implementation

As one of the last engines at the engine stack in Fig. 5, in addition to the original ink, text and image information, it can also access the rich temporal and spatial information the other engines generated and their analysis results. For example, the annotation parser can use previous parsing results on ink type property of a stroke (writing/drawing). It can also use the previously parsed word, line, paragraph and block layout structure of the underlying document. As shown in

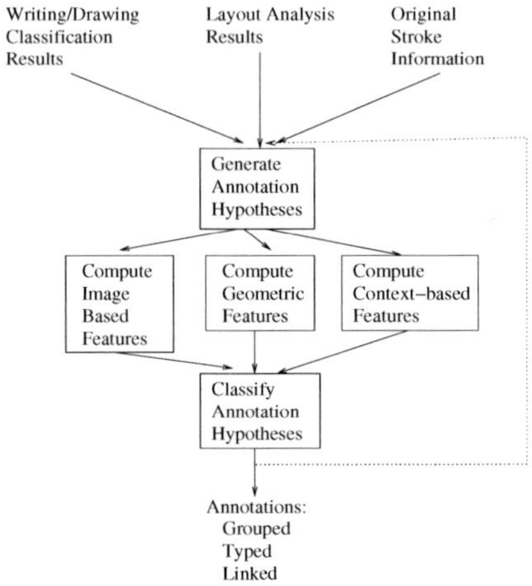

Figure 6: *Architecture of the annotation parser.*

Fig. 6, the annotation parser iterates through the following three steps: hypothesis generation, feature computation and hypothesis evaluation.

3.3.1. Generate Hypothesis

The first step is to generate hypothesis. Ideally, we want to generate a hypothesis for each possible stroke grouping, annotation type, and anchor set, but this is not feasible for a real-time system. Aggressive heuristic pruning has to be adopted to parse within the system's time limits. In practice, we found that spatial and temporal heuristics are not sufficient to achieve acceptable recognition results. Instead, it is necessary to use heuristics based on knowledge of previous parsing results.

For stroke grouping, we can prune the set of all possible annotation stroke group candidates greatly based on previous writing/drawing classification results. [§]

If we know the type of the underlying and surrouding regions of a stroke group candidate, we can limit its set of feasible annotation types to a subset of all annotation types supported by the system. For example, if we know a line segment goes from an image region to a text region, it is more

---

[§] Since the writing/drawing classification engine makes mistakes, we can not limit our choices to drawing strokes only.

likely to be a callout without arrow or a vertical range than a strike-through.

Similarly if we know the type of an annotation, we can also reduce the set of possible anchors. For a vertical range, its anchor can only be on its left or right side, and for an underline, its anchor can only be above it.

With carefully designed heurisitcs, we are able to significantly reduce the number of hypotheses generated.

3.4. Feature Computation

For each hypothesis we enumerate through, we compute a combined set of shape and context features. We use two types of shape features—the cheap image-based Viola-Jones filters and the more expensive features based on the geometric properties of its polyline and convex hull. For the geometric features, we use both features that are general enough to work across a variety of shapes and annotation types and features designed to discriminate two or more specific annotation types. More details can be found in Section 4.

3.5. Feature Selection and Hypothesis Evaluation

The annotation parser uses an *AdaBoost.M*1 [FS97] based classifier system to evaluate each hypothesis. If the hypothesis is accepted, it can be used to generate more annotation hypotheses, or to compute features for the classification other annotation hypotheses. By the end, the annotation parser produces annotations that are grouped, typed and anchored to its context.

4. Annotation Features

For each hypothesis, the annotation parser computes both shape features, and contextual features. We use two types of shape features. The first group consists of inexpensive image-based shape features as introduced by Viola and Jones in [VJ01]. The second group of features are similar to the carefully designed geometric feautures by Fonseca et al in [FPJ02]. The third group of features are the context-based features.

4.1. Geometric Features

All these geometric features are shape-related. Shape is an important clue to what the type of annotation could be. The following are examples of the geometric features used in the annotation engine:

1. **Aspect Ratio:** the aspect ratio of the minimal enclosed rectangle is used as a feature to estimate the "likelihood" of a shape being a line segement.
2. **Total Curvature:** the sum of curvature changes of the stroke(s) as it (they) forms the geometric shape.
3. **Total Turning Angle:** the sum of angle changes of the vertices in relinked polyline (in Radian).

4. **Curvature Profiles:** we divide the baseline (the major axis) of the geometric shape formed by the stroke into two or three buckets and compute the change of curvatures in each bucket.
5. **Horizontal Density:** The ratio between the *absolute horizontal movement* and the width of the minimal enclosed rectangle.
6. **Start-End Distance Ratio:** The ratio between the distance between the start and the end vertices and the width of the minimal enclosed rectangle–to measure the "closedness" of the shape.
7. **Shape Open Sided:** an heuristic binary feature, true when the polyline is open to a side (like for a paranthesis, a brace, or bracket)
8. **Open To Left Side:** a binary feature, heuristic, true when the polyline is open to the left side
9. **Side-Center Distance Ratio:** The distance between the mid-point of the open side and the center of the baseline, normalized by the width of the baseline.
10. **Maximal Inscribed Triangle Area Ratio:** Area of the maximal inscribed triangle of the convex hull of a stroke, divided by the area of its convex hull.

4.2. Context Features

As in [SW04], the annotation parser not only evaluates each hypothesis according to its geometric shape, but also according to its spatial context. However, unlike in [SW04], the context also contains ink strokes parsed from engines earlier in the stack. The ink context contains writing grouped into words, lines, and paragraphs that earlier engine has parsed with high confidence. It is the annotation parser's job to determine whether ambiguous strokes from the previous stages are actually annotations or are simply part of the notes.

All of the previous parsing results can be used to reduce the hypothesis space. For example, a straight line segment that is nowhere near a writing region is very unlikely to be a horizontal range. A straight line segment that is to the right and to the left of a writing region, and is perpenticular to its major axis, is very likely to a vertical bar than a horizontal range. In the annotation parser, these important contextual clues are captured through carefully designed contextual features, and fed into the classifier system, let it to determine the relative importance of each feature, and arbitrate between each hypothesis.

There are four different types of contextual feature. For each of the four categories of annotations we support, we designed a set of contextual features that are specific to the category. For example, if a stroke or a group of strokes form an enclosure, one important information is that how much "context" it contains. Since we have the structure of the underlying document, so we can search through the partial parse tree, and determine how many words, lines, or paragraphs in the tree fall into the polygon shape formed by the strokes.

As an illustration, Section 4.2.1 and Section 4.2.2 list the contextual features designed for horizontal ranges and vertical ranges respectively.

4.2.1. Context Features for Horizontal Ranges

For horizontal ranges, we use two different groups of contextual features, one group with respect to the line above the horizontal range, and one group with respect to the line lying under the horizontal ranges. For each group, we compute the following features:

1. **Existence of context line:** true if there is an anchor line—an underlying line or an above line, respectively.
2. **Angle Difference:** the angle difference between the baseline of theEnclosures anchor line, and the baseline of the annotation, rounded to $\left(-\frac{\pi}{2}, \frac{\pi}{2}\right]$.
3. **Anchor Line Center to Baseline Distance Ratio:** The distance between the center of the anchor line to the baseline of the annotation, normalized by the height of the anchor line.
4. **Baseline Center to Anchor Line Distance Ratio:** The distance between the center of the annotation's baseline to the baseline of the anchor line, normalized by the height of the anchor line.
5. **Anchor Line to Baseline Width Projection Ratio:** Project the baseline of the anchor line to the baseline of the annotation, and compute the ratio of the length between the projected line segment, and the length of the baseline it is projected to.
6. **BaseLine to Anchor Line Width Projection Ratio:** Same as above except the baseline of the annotation is projected to the baseline of the anchor line.

4.2.2. Context Features for Vertical Ranges

For common vertical ranges such as parantheses, braces and brackets, the shape itself is often a sufficient clue for determining its type. But for vertical bars as in Figure 4, it is very difficult to differentiate them from vertical dividers (as the vertical green line in Figure 7, without using context information such as which words, lines or paragraphs they refer to.

Frequently, a vertical range has lines of context on both sides. For vertical ranges such as braces, brackets, and parantheses, most of times, it is easy to determine which side is the open side, and which side is the back side, and thus which set of lines to anchor to. But for vertical bars, it is very difficult to determine which set to anchor to, without looking at context features that are computed with respect to both sets of lines.

1. **Number of Overlapped Lines:** Number of lines in the set that is vertically overlapped with the baseline of the vertical range
2. **Angle Difference with Anchor Block:** The angle difference between the baseline of vertical range and the vertical axis of the neighboring block

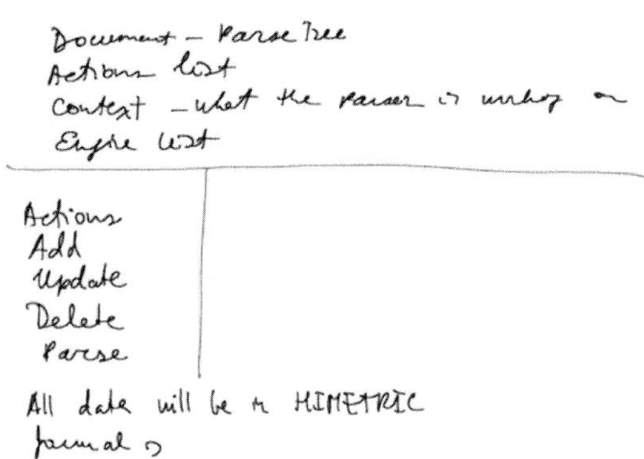

Figure 7: *With only "shape" information and no context information, it is very difficult to differentiate a vertical divider from a vertical bar.*

3. **Average Line Distance Ratio:** The average of distance from the start or end side of each vertically overlapped line in the set to the baseline of the vertical range.
4. **Sum of Vertical Overlap:** The sum of the vertical overlap of each neighboring line, normalized by the length of the baseline of the vertical range.

4.3. Context Feature Computation and Errors of Previous Engine

As shown in Section 4.2, the computation of context features utilizes parsing results of previous engines in the engine stack. But what if these engines make errors? Fed with the wrong values of the features, can the classifier still make the correct prediction? If we train our annotation parser with only the correctly labeled files, it is very likely for the classification system to produce poor results, since they have never seen these erratic configurations of feature values before.

The trick here is to train the annotation parser with partial parsing results from the previous engines instead of the correctly labeled files only. In fact, if we can predict the exact distribution of the annotation scenarios that the annotation parsing system will encounter when it is released to real world users, and if we have an unlimited amount of training data, it is better that we train with partial parsing results only. But since we do not know what the actual distribution will be, we train also with the labeled files, hopefully introducing a bias toward the more correct configurations of feature values.

5. Results

The annotation parsing system described here will be exposed through the Tablet PC Ink Analysis SDK for the development of ink applications for Tablet PC. It will be available with Windows Vista®. And in addition, it is also part of the entire ink parsing system that is used by the next version of OneNote$^{®}$ also to analyze ink and mixed ink and text documents.

5.1. Evaluation

To evaluate the system, we collected a large set of OneNote files from Microsoft employees who use OneNote as part of their day-to-day work. Many of these files contain annotations as described in this paper. To increase the size of our data set, we also had users create semi-natural annotations on documents. By semi-natural we mean that we asked them to perform natural tasks ("correct spelling errors in the third paragraph", "indicate that the author should move Figure 3 to the top of the page") without telling them exactly which annotations to use. Then for all these files, we labeled the annotations and their anchors to generate a ground truth data set of 1294 files. These files containing 6974 examples of annotations. Out of these examples, 1413 examples are set aside for cross-validation.

After training the engine, we tested its accuracy on another test set of 138 files. Parsing result of an actual file is shown in Fig 8.

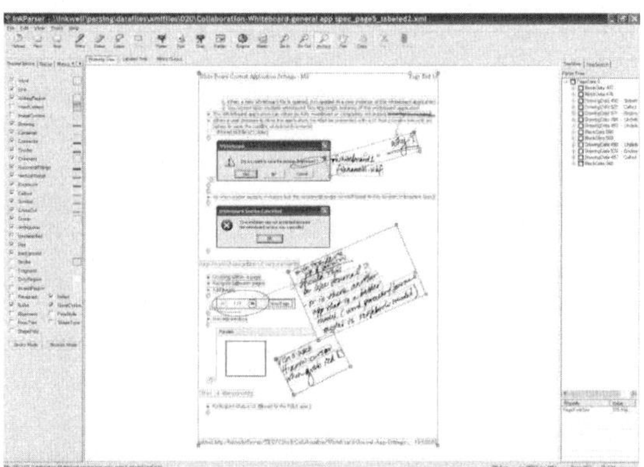

Figure 8: *Parsed Real World Example.*

To simplify the presentation of the results, we merge the results on vertical range and vertical bar together, and the results on callout with arrow and callout without arrow into one. The distribution of examples in this set is given as: $(22.08\%, 34.59\%, 4.57\%, 3.82\%, 5.15\%, 13.4\%, 16.39\%)$ for non-annotation drawings, underlines, strike-throughs, scratch-outs, enclosures, vertical ranges, and callouts respectively.

Table 2 shows the confusion matrix on the test set. The rows represent the labeled annotations, and the columns represent the parsed annotation results. For example, the cell $(1,1)$ shows the percentage of examples of non-annotation drawings correctly classified as non-annotation drawings.

Table 1: *Semantic Recall Results.*

File Type	Priority 1	Priority 2
Lightly Annotated	96.34	92.00
Highly Annotated	91.67	84.75
Mixed Ink and Text	91.30	76.87

The cell at $(2,3)$ shows the percentage of examples of underline misclassified as strike-through. The black-fonted number in each row is the recall number for that type of annotation. For example, the recall of underline is 98.02%.

On the average, the annotation parser has achieved an average recall of 0.9258 on all annotation types. Unlike many research findings in this area, which report accuracy numbers on a predefined set of pre-segmented symbols, these numbers are based on real user notes. Real users do not obey any fixed conventions when they take notes, and can be arbitrarily messy. Furthermore, the numbers reported here are a function not just of the annotation recognizer, but of the entire stack of engines that come before it. Given today's state of the art, a learning-based system that performs with 92.5% accuracy across a wide set of user notes is remarkable.

The errors shown here are not surprising. The largest number of misclassifications is between strike-through and scratch-out. Since both annotations indicate deletion, this error would actually not affect any user experience. The second largest confusion is underlines misrecognized as strikethroughs and vice versa. Such confusion is natural for a human reading an annotated paper, and is disambiguated using the underlying semantics of the document, or using higher-level context then we employ.

The worst-looking number in the confusion matrix is the 54% of drawing strokes that are misinterpreted as annotations. This number is poor but it is also misleading. Because only 4drawings, the actual number of errors is minor relative to the overall number of annotations processed.

6. Future Work

While we believe this system significantly advances the state of the art in processing handwritten annotations, it also opens new problems. On the recognition side, we would like to recognize increasingly more sophisticated annotation structures, including linkages between containers, callouts, ranges, and so on. By performing these linkages as part of the optimization strategy, we should be able to improve the system accuracy. We also believe that in the long-term, our feed-forward, greedy, multiple engine recognition strategy limits accuracy, but see no obvious ways to get around this without significantly reducing system performance. Another set of issues that we do not address in this paper is appropriate user interfaces for exposing and mediating the recognition results. In this work we present our best effort at provid-

Table 2: *Recognition Results on the Test Set.*

Labeled	*Drawing*	*Underline*	*Strike-through*	*Scratch-out*	*Enclosure*	*Vertical Range*	*Callout*
Underline	0.0099	**0.9802**	0.0035	0.0023	0.0006	0	0.0035
Strike-through	0.0176	0.0441	**0.8062**	0.1101	0.0132	0	0.0088
Scratch-out	0.0211	0.0053	0	**0.9474**	0.0053	0	0.0211
Enclosure	0.0078	0	0	0.0117	**0.9688**	0	0.0117
Vertical Range	0.0180	0	0.0015	0	0	**0.9099**	0.0706
Callout	0.0172	0.0147	0.0037	0.0025	0	0.0196	**0.9423**
Drawing	**0.4572**	0.1202	0.2996	0.0592	0.0082	0.0118	0.0437

ing a real-time recognition, but do not address the system's usability in the presence of errors.

Aknowledgement

The authors thank Dr. Paul Viola of MSR for many of his insightful discussions; Dr. Herry Sutanto, Dr. Ming Ye and Manoj Biswas for great discussions on the design and development of the system; Dr. Peter Slavik for discussion on Gestures; Benoit Jurion and Marie Millet for many discussions on the definition and user scenarios of annotations and their efforts on data collection; Forrest Oswald, Chengyang Li and especially Amber Pace for their efforts in setting up the testing sets and the manual and automatic testing of the annotation parser.

References

[AD05] ALVARADO C., DAVIS R.: Dynamically constructed bayes nets for multi-domain sketch understanding. In *Proceedings of IJCAI-05* (San Francisco, California, August 1 2005), pp. 1407–1412.

[AVK93] APTE A., VO V., KIMURA T. D.: Recognizing multistroke geometric shapes: An experimental evaluation. In *ACM Symposium on User Interface Software and Technology* (1993), pp. 121–128.

[BMP02] BELONGIE S., MALIK J., PUZICHA J.: Shape matching and object recognition using shape contexts. *IEEE Trans. Pattern Anal. Mach. Intell. 24*, 4 (2002), 509–522.

[BSH04] BISHOP C. M., SVENSEN M., HINTON G. E.: Distinguishing text from graphics in on-line handwritten ink. *iwfhr* (2004), 142–147.

[CSKK02] CALHOUN C., STAHOVICH T. F., KURTOGLU T., KARA L. B.: Recognizing multi-stroke symbols. In *AAAI Spring Symposium, Sketch Understanding* (2002), pp. 15–23.

[FPJ02] FONSECA M. J., PIMENTEL C., , JORGE J. A.: Cali: An online scribble recognizer for calligraphic interfaces. In *AAAI Spring Symposium, Sketch Understanding* (2002), pp. 51–58.

[FS97] FREUND Y., SCHAPIRE R. E.: A decision-theoretic generalization of on-line learning and an application to boosting. *J. Comput. Syst. Sci. 55*, 1 (1997), 119–139.

[HD03] HAMMOND T., DAVIS R.: LADDER: A language to describe drawing, display, and editing in sketch recognition. *Proceedings of the 2003 Internaltional Joint Conference on Artificial Intelligence (IJCAI)* (2003), 461–467.

[Kar04] KARA L. B.: *Automatic Parsing And Recognition Of Hand-Drawn Sketches For Pen-Based Computer Interfaces*. PhD thesis, Department of Mechanical Engineering, Carnegie Mellon University, Pittsburg, PA, 2004.

[Mar97] MARSHALL C.: Annotation: from paper books to the digital library. In *Proceedings of the ACM Digital Libraries Conference* (1997).

[ÖÖT*01] ÖZER Ö. F., ÖZÜN O., TÜZEL C. Ö., ATALAY V., ÇETIN A. E.: Vision-based single-stroke character recognition for wearable computing. *IEEE Intelligent Systems 16*, 3 (2001), 33–37.

[PdFJ02] PIMENTEL C. F., DA FONSECA M. J., JORGE J. A.: Experimental evaluation of a trainable scribble recognizer for calligraphic interfaces. In *Lecture Notes in Computer Science: Graphics Recognition, Algorithms and Applications : 4th International Workshop, GREC 2001*, (2002), vol. 2390, pp. 81–91.

[SV04] SHILMAN M., VIOLA P.: Spatial recognition and grouping of text and graphics. In *1st Eurographics Workshop on Sketch-Based Interfaces and Modeling* (2004).

[SVC04] SHILMAN M., VIOLA P., CHELLAPILLA K.: Recognition and grouping of handwritten text in diagrams and equations. In *Ninth International Workshop on Frontiers in Handwriting Recognition (IWFHR'04)* (2004), pp. 569–574.

[SW04] SHILMAN M., WEI Z.: Recognizing freeform digital ink annotations. In *Document Analysis Systems VI* (2004), pp. 322–331.

[SWR*03] SHILMAN M., WEI Z., RAGHUPATHY S., SIMARD P., JONES D.: Discerning structure from freeform handwritten notes. In *ICDAR* (2003), pp. 60–65.

[VJ01] VIOLA P. A., JONES M. J.: Robust real-time face detection. In *ICCV* (2001), p. 747.

[Wen03] WENYIN L.: On-line graphics recognition: State-of-the-art. In *GREC* (2003), pp. 291–304.

[YSR*05] YE M., SUTANTO H., RAGHUPATHY S., LI C., SHILMAN M.: Grouping text lines in freeform handwritten notes. In *ICDAR* (2005), pp. 367–373.

[YV04] YE M., VIOLA P.: Learning to parse hierarchical lists and outlines using conditional random fields. *iwfhr* (2004), 154–159.

EUROGRAPHICS Workshop on Sketch-Based Interfaces and Modeling (2006)
Thomas Stahovich and Mario Costa Sousa (Editors)

Producing Models From Drawings of Curved Surfaces

Matthew Kaplan[1] and Elaine Cohen[2]

[1] ARTIS, Inria Rhone-Alpes
[2] University of Utah

Abstract

We present a method for creating $2\frac{1}{2}D$ models from line drawings of opaque solid objects. We allow the artist to draw naturally, differing from many previous approaches. Our system allows both perspective and orthographic projection to be used and makes no a priori assumptions about the type of model to be produced (i.e. planar, curved, normalon) . The frontal geometry is reconstructed by placing constraints at the contours and solving a 2D variational system for the smoothest piecewise smooth surface. An analysis of line labelling allows us to determine what constraints are possible and/or required for each input line. However, because line labelling produces a combinatorial explosion of valid output geometries, we allow the user to guide the constraint selection and optimization with a simple user interface that abstracts the technical details away from the user. The system produces candidate reconstructions using different constraint values, from which the user selects the one that most closely approximates the model represented by the drawing. These choices allow the system to determine the constraints and reconstruct the model. The system runs at interactive speeds.

Categories and Subject Descriptors (according to ACM CCS): ([I]: .3.3)Computer GraphicsShape Modeling

1   Introduction

Few sketch based modeling systems allow the artist to draw naturally. Typically, designers are forced to learn a set of drawing operators that are used as an interface to an underlying CAD system. Alternatively, previous methods that analyze existing drawings typically limit the type of drawings/models that can be reconstructed to a subset of models useful in CAD. The goal of this research is to allow the artist to draw as naturally as possible, placing minimal restrictions on the structure and process of the input drawing and the form of the output model. The reconstructed model should be a close approximation of the artists intent. We briefly review how our system differs from previous work:

We allow the user to draw interactively, without having to learn any special rules, although we do limit the contours in our system to being representative of surface geometry of an opaque solid object. Since contours can be either straight or curved lines, we make no assumption about the type of model to be produced. Most previous research limited the type of models that could be represented to either polyhedral or normalon (all object faces parallel to one of the three coordinate axes), or CSG-tree style construction of curved mod-

els. Freedom in the ordering of the input strokes also yields an implicit construction method. This means that we place no limitation on the process by which the drawing is created whereas the CSG-tree process requires an explicit construction sequence. We relax the simplifying orthographic projection assumption that most previous research imposes because it does not correspond with how artists actually draw. We reconstruct from a single view for the same reason.

To use our system, the designer draws into the screen buffer. The system automatically locates constraints along curved and straight contours through analysis of line labeling techniques. Because line labeling yields a combinatorial explosion of valid constraints, we employ the user's perception to find a correct constraint set but abstract the constraint selection mechanism from the user, in order to minimize extra knowledge required to use the system. The system iteratively produces candidate reconstructions with different constraint possibilities. From these choices, the user selects the reconstruction that best approximates the desired output model. Successive user choices help to define a gradient through the system's constraint search space. The output is a piecewise smooth surface, created by applying constraints to a $2\frac{1}{2}D$ mesh embedded in the drawing plane.

2   Related Work

How to infer models from sketches has been extensively studied so we present only the most closely related work. To fully appreciate this technique, it helps to be familiar with the background material, especially line labeling, in [Mal87,LZS01,Var05].

2.1   Reconstruction Methods

Reconstruction methods create a model from an existing drawing. Most research in this area falls in the category of line labeling. See [CPM04] for a comprehensive overview.

The first successful attempts to catalogue types of line labels [Huf71,Clo71] were used to identify drawings that represented unrealizable scenes. The concept of gradient space was presented in [Mac73] to allow the labeling polyhedral scene drawings. The first method for producing labeling for curved line drawings was presented in [Tur74], while the first full theory of line labelings for piecewise smooth curved surfaces was developed in [Mal87]. Cases where three faces meet at a vertex were considered in [RH78], leading to a smaller junction catalogue. Another method for reconstructing drawings of curved objects was demonstrated in [VYJH04]. It required the user to create a line drawing of a polyhedral template corresponding to the curved drawing. Then the polyhedral template drawing would be inflated and used to guide reconstruction of the curved model. More recently, it was shown in [LB90] and [VM00,VSM04,VM02] that restricted classes of normalons and regular objects composed of planar faces can be interpreted. They argued strongly that the objects reconstructed under the assumption of regular angles are useful to engineers. A correlation based method, successful for polygonal objects, was presented in [LS02,LS96,Lip98], and extended with additional operators in [SC04].

2.2   Gestural Methods

Gestural methods use strokes to define input parameters to CAD operations. A CSG tree-like series of operations defines the model. Often, the user must select which operation each stroke should perform. This requires the user to learn the system conventions. Examples include Sketch [RCZ96] and Chateau [TI01].

Another class of algorithms assumes strokes are silhouettes and inflates the interiors of silhouette bounded regions. In [IMT99,dAJ03] the medial axis determines a polygonal height field for relative heights of shape interiors. In [KHR02] implicit surfaces are fitted to silhouette strokes, while in [TZF04,AGB04] implicit modes are formed by convolving implicit surfaces along stroke paths. They added complexity to the surfaces by composition and subtraction of implicit shapes. These systems require an explicit design order to model construction. Most steps extended, destroyed or altered previous detail. This removes one of the benefits of using drawings as input which is that there is no specific construction sequence.

2.3   Other Related Areas

The field of shape from shading analyzes image color or intensity gradients to determine the geometric properties of a scene. In [JJAR97] it is suggested that most of the interpretive process results from the use of previous experience with an object in order to classify it. This may be impractical for dealing with arbitrary input since it would be necessary to classify every possible object that a user *might* draw, matching under such general conditions would still be a hard problem, and this would not allow the user to draw new or imaginary items. The reader is referred to [Wil90,Wil91,Kan98,HAA97,OCDD01] for related, but not directly applicable, research in 3D shape recovery.

The research presented in [LZS01] on reconstructing surfaces by optimizing constraints defined from a single view is closely related and is examined more closely in Section 6.

3   Definitions

We use a simplified model of line drawings based only on the projection of depth and orientation (normal) discontinuities of an individual object in 3D space with no surroundings. As in [Mal87], an *object* is defined as a connected, bounded and regular subset of R^3 whose boundary is a piecewise smooth surface, where *regular* means that it is the closure of the interior. Each point within the object domain is the projection of a visible point on the object onto the 2D image plane. At each planar position (x,y), a height $f(x,y)$ and a normal $n(x,y)$, are defined. These functions are continuous at all points within the image except at lines, which represent discontinuities. The line drawing, then, is defined as the locus of these discontinuities. The locations at which two or more lines meet is called a *junction*. A surface incident to an line, is considered *attached* to that line if its depth is at least C^0 continuous with the line, or *detached*, if it is not.

4   Line Constraints

Line labeling is typically means classifying each image curve as corresponding to either a depth or orientation discontinuity in the scene and further subclassifying each type of discontinuity. Furthermore, a junction catalogue is defined that represents the possible configurations of labelings of each incoming stroke at a junction. A labeling of the drawing that corresponds to a projection of a realizeable scene is known as a *legal* labeling.

In a simplified labeling scheme, a line may be indicative of either a normal or depth discontinuity. Normal discontinuities are denoted by '+' for a convex edge,i.e., adjacent surfaces enclosing a filled volume corresponding to a dihedral angle less than π, or by '-' for a concave edge , i.e., adjacent surfaces enclose a filled volume corresponding to a dihedral angle greater than π. Depth discontinuities (silhouettes) are denoted '←' for an occluding convex edge or '←←' for a silhouette, though these two labels are often combined. The labelings for several different objects are shown in Figure 1. Most line labeling solutions involve backtracking (an example of the NP-complete constraint satisfaction problem) and

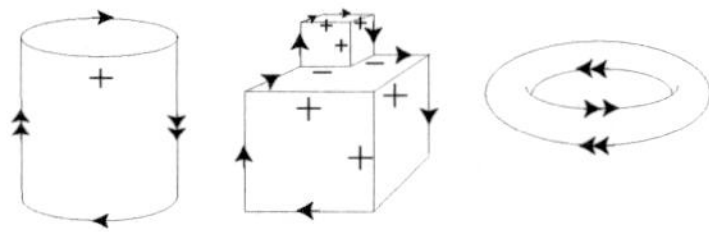

Figure 1: *Several models and their line labels.*

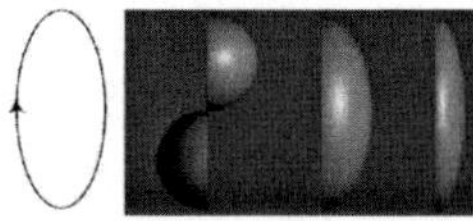

Figure 2: *A labeling for a drawing of an oval is shown at left. A reconstruction based on this labeling is not unique and can produce the three models whose profiles are shown at right.*

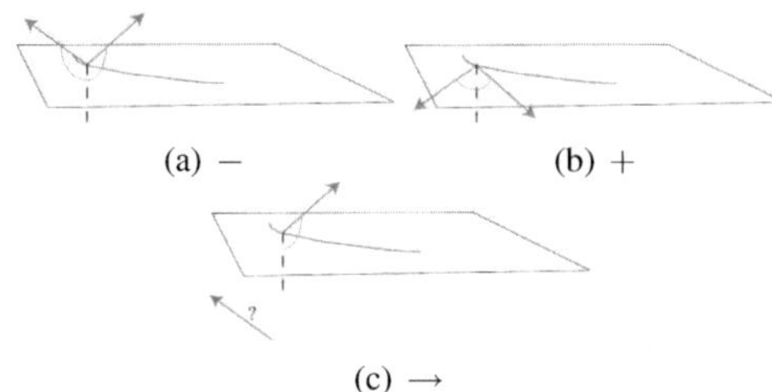

Figure 3: *The constraints formed by the line labels at an isolated point on the curve take the form of a) Concave b) Convex and c) Silhouette. The tangent to the incident surface is shown in green. The angle subtended by the local surfaces is shown in blue.*

produce numerous legal labelings. Once a legal labeling has been obtained, an optimization is performed to determine reasonable depth values, yielding a model. There is no way to know which legal labeling is the correct one, and even a correct labeling may yield a large number of output surfaces. An example of this is shown in Figure 2.

Line labeling produces constraints that are ambiguous. A contour is known to have normal and/or depth constraints, but the values that precisely define those constraints are unknown. We introduce a new method of classifying constraints for surfaces incident to a contour that allows identification of both the constraints and the parameters needed to fully specify a piecewise smooth output surface. Figure 3, which shows the type of constraints that may occur at each line.

- '+' A convex edge. The normal discontinuity that occurs along this edge represents the intersection of two smooth surfaces whose incident faces have surface normals with the angle in the span $[0, \pi)$.
- '-' A concave edge. The normal discontinuity that occurs along this edge represents the intersection of two smooth surfaces whose incident faces have surface normals with the angle in the span $[\pi, 2\pi)$.
- '→' A silhouette contour. The normal at the line satisfies the formula $N \cdot V = 0$, i.e., it is perpendicular to the view vector, or for convex occluders, $N \cdot V <= 0$. The attached surface has no constraint on its normal. The depth

across the contour is discontinuous, and the attached surface must lie above the occluded surface.

Though three labels are shown, contours have only depth (*silhouette*) and normal (*crease*)discontinuities. More importantly, certain constraints on incident surfaces must exist for each type of discontinuity. Constraints on the surfaces incident to each contour either specify the normal of the incident surface at each point on the contour, or specify the difference in depth between the attached and detached surfaces across a depth discontinuity. A normal discontinuity has two attached incident surfaces, so a surface normal constraint exists for each incident surface and is defined by a direction vector. A depth discontinuity has a surface normal constraint for its attached surface and a depth discontinuity for its detached surface and is defined by a scalar distance between the attached and detached surfaces. Although the detached surface must lie below the attached surface, no assumption is made as to whether the attached surface is raised or the detached surface depressed.

In conclusion, a frontal reconstruction of a piecewise smooth model can be obtained if, given that each line is parameterized by $0 \leq t \leq 1$, at each point on every line in the scene it is necessary to have 1) a position $z = f(t)$ that is C^0 continuous on each line but not at junctions, 2) a surface normal, $N_0(t)$ and/or $N_1(t)$, for each incident attached surface, and 3) a depth relation for each detached surface incident from a line, $D_0(t)$ or $D_1(t)$. This is a more stringent set of conditions than that required in [Mal87] and may be unobtainable in an arbitrary sense since it requires a full dense labeling (see Section 5).

5   Reducing the Dense Labeling Problem

In drawings of curved objects a label may transition along the contour, as shown in Figure 4, at *critical points*. A single label applied to each line yields a *sparse* labeling, whereas applying a label to every point on every line yields a *dense* labeling. Dense labeling is neccesary to fully consider all curved objects that *may* be produced by a drawing. Fortunately, instances where scenes project to drawings that can be represented *only* by dense labelings are rare, so one solution is to split lines at critical points and then use a sparse labeling to find the solution.

If critical points are overlooked by the system, the reconstruction may be incorrect. If too many critical points are identified, then the reconstruction will be more difficult to produce. There has been extensive research on identifying how viewers locate important landmarks in line drawings. In [Mal87] splitting contours at zeros of curvature is suggested while in [HR85] it is postulated that part boundaries occur at extremas of negative curvature. Our system splits contours at sharp bends, zeroes of curvature, and local maxima and minima of curvature. Then it combines split locations that are close to avoid the creation of degenerate lines that occupy few pixels.

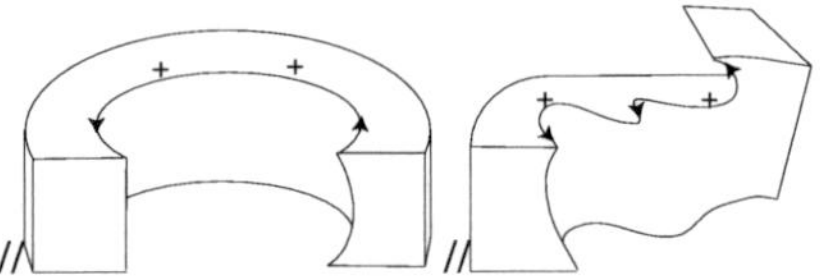

Figure 4: *Line labels may change at critical points (also known as* phantom junctions*) along contours.*

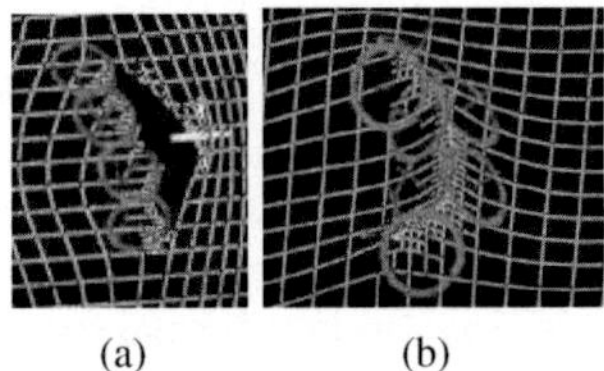

(a)   (b)

Figure 5: *a) Normal and depth constraints applied around a silhouette. b) Normal constraints applied around a crease.*

6 Solver

We require the system to allow constraints to be placed as presented in Section 4 in a mesh defined over the drawing plane, to be capable of producing both planar and curved output meshes, and to run at interactive rates. We use the method in [LZS01] and cast the model reconstruction problem as a constrained variational optimization problem. In [LZS01], they fit a piecewise continuous surface represented as an adaptive grid over the image plane and solve a large scale optimization with user defined constraints. This produces a smooth surface.

Our system places point constraints (normal and depth constraints) for incident surfaces and curve constraints (depth and normal discontinuity constraints) along contours. Constraints are automatically placed for all contours whose constraint types have been determined. Point constraints are placed every 5 pixels along a contour, several pixels away from the contour in the normal direction. If a contour has a detached surface, then a depth discontinuity constraint is placed. If a contour has two attached surfaces, then a normal discontinuity is placed. This specifies the location of the constraints in the image plane; Section 7 presents how to determine values for the normal vectors and depths.

While a human could place constraints manually and use [LZS01] to achieve a similar result, it would require a high degree of knowledge of their system to place proper constraints and would take far longer to do by hand. Indeed, even a simple scene with manual constraints placed mainly along very simple contours required 156 constraints in [LZS01], while for more complex scenes, they report requiring 264 or more constraints. Another other similar system [Koe98] required a constraint for every pixel. The reduction in human effort offered by our system is advantageous.

7 Finding Constraints with User Guidance

Since domain knowledge affects labeling and parameters, it may be impossible to choose them automatically. Therefore, we coopt the user's domain knowledge to determine correct constraints. By abstracting technical details from the artist

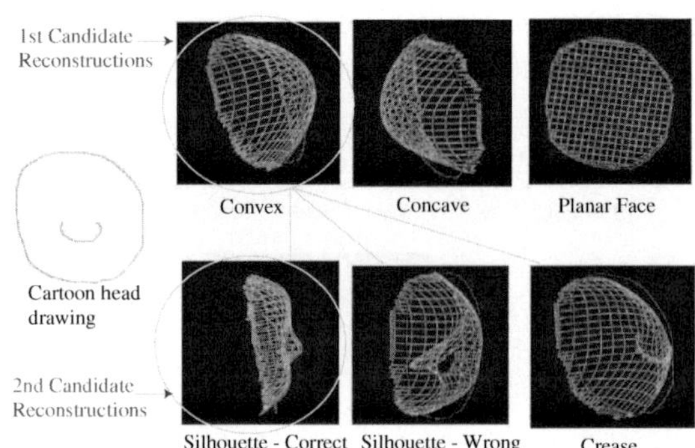

Figure 6: *A simple example: The PCG (Section 7.2) first produces constraints for the exterior silhouette. The convex case is most like the head, so the user chooses* Good *for it (its constraints descend to all future reconstructions), denoted by the green circle. Next, the PCG tests constraints for the interior contour as a crease and as a silhouette from either side. The crease case makes a small dent on the surface. One silhouette case actually places the nose behind the face, whereas the silhouette on the left places the nose correctly. The model is correspondingly as crude as the drawing.*

and allowing him to apply just perception, we hope to minimize the amount of specific system knowledge needed.

Our system iteratively presents the user with multiple candidate reconstructions, each constructed using different constraint values. Users choose, via a simple interaction mechanism, the reconstruction that best fits their concept of the model, gradually allowing the system to deduce correct constraints. The user never needs to know the details of the constraint selection mechanism. An overview of our system is shown in Figure 10. A simple demonstration of the process is shown in Figure 6.

Known capacities of viewer perception support the validity of this method. A series of papers on the topic of human perception of shape in 2D images and line drawings [Koe98,Koe84,KvDCL96,PTKK] that argue strongly that smooth surfaces generate a set of perceptually salient landmarks that are viewpoint invariant. They report that users are typically able to establish correspondence between surface normal and the projection of surface features with high accuracy,on average within a few degrees, over different orientations. Viewers are also able to establish surface depth but with slightly less accuracy. Techniques similar to ours have been previously demonstrated in other contexts [MAP 97].

7.1 User Interface

Each tentative reconstruction is viewed in its own window. We provide an interface where a user is able to indicate, at a very high level, the quality of each candidate surface reconstruction by applying their comparative perception to the surface meshes. The meaning of the five buttons provided as a selection mechanism is as follows:

- **Good** : This is good.
- **Bad** : Some portion is incorrect.

- **Refine** : This indicates that the the user desires more reconstructions like the current one.
- **Refine+** : A special case of the refine instance, this tells the system that the corrections needed are minor.
- **Refine-** : A special case of the refine instance, this tells the system that the corrections needed are large.

A history class records the type of constraint and parameters used for each line, and the user selected value in each candidate reconstruction. Selecting *Good* or *Refine* for any candidate reconstruction automatically closes all other currently shown reconstructions with a value of *Bad* in their history.

7.2 Finding the Right Constraint

We define a *Probable Constraint Generator* (PCG) that iteratively attempts to generate new, better sets of constraints based on a drawing and a history of attempted reconstructions. During any iteration, the PCG attempts to produce constraints for (in order of decreasing importance) : 1) a set of lines, 2) a set of faces, 3) an individual face or 4) an individual line. The PCG only attempts to generate constraints for one specific set of contours at a time, that is, though the PCG may produce several candidate reconstructions simultaneously, they will all be operating on the same contour(s). This restricts the search domain to simplify and speed the search.

The PCG first attempts to determine the appropriate type of each constraint and second, the value of the parameter for that constraint. In our system, a normal is defined by an angle in the range $[0, 2\pi]$. According to [Mal87] the surface normal at a contour should be perpendicular to that contour, so the angle simply specifies where the normal is within the unit circle lying in the normal plane at any given location on the contour. For a normal constraint representing a face, a hemisphere of directions must be considered. Depth constraints have an unbounded scalar domain, though in practice, this is bounded to near and far clipping planes.

In successive iterations, the PCG generates new candidate solutions either when no search has been initiated, or when a search is currently underway. In the first case, if there are contours with undefined constraints, a set of undefined contours are chosen and constraints are generated as discussed in Section 7.3. The first user selection of *Good* or *Refine* determines the correct constraint type for the contours being tested. Selecting *Bad* excludes the constraint type from the current search. The initial parameter value from case 1 then defines a start condition for a search of the parameter domain that is performed in case 2.

A simple search of the parameter domain, akin to a binary search, can be performed. The history set defines a gradient through the parameter domain, allowing the search to gradually approach a correct parameter value. For every parameter value being tested, a candidate reconstruction is created. If the user selects *Good* for a candidate, the constraint type and parameter are validated and the search is terminated. If *Refine* is selected, the PCG creates two new candidate reconstructions that bisect the remaining domain space surrounding the current parameter value. If *Refine+* is selected, the new parameter values move 75% in either direction in the surrounding domain, whereas a *Refine-* moves the parameter 25%.

Line drawing is a process, i.e., a given drawing may be a proper subset of the completed drawing. Therefore, successive lines may invalidate previously generated constraints. In these cases, some of the history set may need to be deleted.

Line labeling theory aids in making logical inferences about situations where certain constraints are required. This is done by analyzing the set of valid configurations of labels for incoming lines at a junctions. This defines a *junction catalogue*. We use the junction catalogue defined by Malik [Mal87], for curved surfaces. This is useful in determining many occlusion cases automatically, and can automatically determine many constraint types (especially for polyhedral models).

The PCG uses the junction catalogue to weight reconstruction attempts by keeping a record of how often each junction, constraint and parameter configuration occur. We give higher priority to reconstructions that abide by the catalogue rules and occur frequently. Because the catalogue does not consider surfaces that are not piecewise smooth, we do allow junction configurations that fall outside its rule set.

7.3 Generating Initial Constraints

A input contour can generate constraints in its immediate neighborhood or over a region occupied by a set of lines. Here, we define the situations in which both can occur and present methods to generate initial sets of constraints.

Single Contour. Initially, the junction catalogue is consulted to see if any cases can be automatically determined for a line. If not, the system produces three initial guesses for each contour added to the system (as specified in Section 4): a crease case and two silhouette cases (occluding on either side). A crease has normal constraints created for each incident surface. A silhouette has normal constraints created for the incident surface and depth constraints are created that specify that the attached surface lay above the detached surface.

Multiple Contours. A line can affect a region beyond its immediate neighborhood if it extends the surface area of the model, creates a face that defines either a hole or a bounded planar face or modifies an existing face. These situations cause new constraints to be generated simultaneously for multiple contours.

Surface extension occurs any time a loop of contours is created in which part of the loop falls outside the current model domain. This occurs automatically when the closure of the interior, or, the object's silhouette, is first defined. Silhouette constraints are automatically created for all contours that bound the object. Contours identified as silhouettes, but no longer on the boundary of the object domain after surface extension, have their constraints reset. A strong assumption [Var05] about silhouettes is that surfaces all locally fit

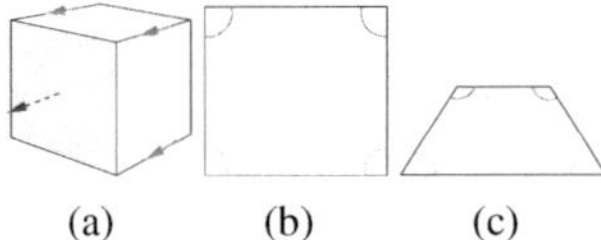

Figure 7: *a)The directions (red) of lines incident to the shaded face help approximate a normal for that face (blue). b) A regular polygon is shown perpendicular to the viewer. c) The interior angles converge to a limit of* $0°$ *(green) or* $180°$*(purple) under projection. Measuring how close the interior angles are to their limit allows determining how perpendicular a polygon is to the viewer.*

within an osculating curve (corresponding to surface inflation). This can be emulated by using convex normal constraints for all silhouettes. A weaker, opposite assumption may be made that all silhouette constraints are concave.

A *face* is a bounded closed loop of lines. In the case that faces are added, removed or divided, constraints may be generated for the set of lines that compose each new or altered face. In our system, faces may represent either holes or planar faces. In the case that a face represents a hole, all the lines that compose the face are marked as silhouettes and the interior of the face is removed from the model.

For faces composed of straight lines, the probability that the interior of the face is planar is so strong that most surface reconstruction methods consider *only* this case. A normal constraint is created, at the center of the face, that is used for each contour that bounds the face on the side attached to the face interior. The constraints on the other side are not defined by this method and must be determined later.

The junction catalogue defines certain restrictions on the interpretation of line drawings. Some suppositions may be made automatically, such as those relating to T-Junctions and depth discontinuities [Mal87]. We define a best guess method that attempts to determine if any lines are restricted to a single interpretation based on the junction catalogue. Many useful relationships can be deduced automatically this way. We created a probability density function that records how often each junction configuration occurs in practice, allowing us to make a best guess even for configurations that are not automatically determined by the catalogue.

Initial Normal Estimation. In order to make an initial guess about the normal direction and magnitude, we assume that the model is composed of all orthogonal, regular faces. We do not require our final reconstruction conform to this assumption. In practice, the method presented here yielded reasonable results even for models that do not have these properties. Since mutual orthogonality is assumed, both the normal and adjacent faces must be orthogonal to the current face, so the lines composing adjacent faces can be used to estimate the normal direction. Though perspective projection will distort the relationships of adjacent faces in the drawing, averaging all of the lines that connect to the current face accounts for this (excluding all lines whose directions are similar to lines composing the current face isolates the orthogonal direction). This yields a perspective correct esti-

mate of the direction vector, assuming all lines converge at a vanishing point.

Assuming that all faces are regular allows us to estimate the magnitude of the normal. In a drawing, all internal angles of a regular polygon that is perpendicular to the view vector are equal. As faces are tilted away from the view vector, their internal angles in the image plane converge to either $0°$ or $180°$. By calculating how far away from equal each internal angle is, we can estimate the perpendicularity of each face. We then scale the normal based on this measure.

8　Results

We tested our implementation on a variety of line drawings, shown in Figures 8- 12, of both curved and polyhedral models, some containing features known to be difficult. Shown are both the input drawings and the output models. Reference images used as textures are shown, where applicable.

Figure 8a-c shows a line drawing of a polygonal surface and its corresponding reconstruction. The reconstructed surface approximates the correct planar normals to within about 5 $15°$, which we consider acceptable. The lines do not follow the correct projection of straight lines, due to the fact that they are hand drawn, creating errors in the planarity near normal discontinuities. The more accurate the input drawing, the less apparent this error is. However, the polygonal reconstructions are correct in a coarse sense: the planar faces and connections between the polygons are all correct; only errors present in the input lines induce errors in the reconstruction.

Figure 9 shows several reconstructions from drawings of polyhedral objects. In these cases, the face normals are within a few degrees of the correct normals. For simple polyhedral models such as these, the junction catalogue is useful in determining the correct constraint types for each lines. If the initial parameter estimates are good, no user intervention is required to produce the output model. The constraints for all models shown in Figure 9 were determined automatically by the system. Our initial normal estimates were even reasonable for models without orthogonal faces such as Figure 9j. Figure 9p shows that traditional line labels can be deduced using our system.

Figure 8d-g shows a reconstruction of a two point perspective cube. All constraints were determined automatically. The planar normals for the three faces are mutually orthographic to within a few degrees.

Figure 8h-j shows an example of a line drawing with a well known problem corner containing two incoming lines that could be either occluding silhouettes or convex. Our system distinguishes between the two cases with user guidance producing silhouettes that create tears in the surface rather than a solid corner, as shown in Figure 8g. This reconstruction also handles contour splitting at critical points, switching from a crease to a silhouette in the contour interior. Critical points are outlined by blue rectangles in Figure 8e. Our contour splitting algorithm, while effective, was a bit overzealous in practice. Often, it made regular cases more difficult to process since some lines that could have been handled with a single label were split. It is possible that some further user guidance in this area would be of benefit for determining problem areas.

Figures 11- 12 show models reconstructed from drawings of curved surfaces. Each drawing is based at on a source image, which is subsequently used to texture the output model. For a simple drawing, such as Figure 11b, the junction catalogue can be used to determine the constraint type of every line automatically. Using our systems user interface, depth relationships and exact normals can be defined more precisely, but in this instance, our initial parameter estimates for normal and depth values are reasonable. It is impossible to make a claim that our values are correct since they are subject to the artists perception.

Figure 11j shows the use of a hole within the model domain (on the bears mouth) demonstrating that our system can handle topologically complex frontal geometry.

While the reconstruction of the head in Figure 12 is far from perfect, note that the input drawing is simplified and does not contain many of the discontinuities present on an actual human head. For commonplace objects, many discontinuities are *assumed* as opposed to expressed. The artist assumes that viewers know such discontinuities exist and does not include them. A drawing with some contours assumed in Figure 12b is shown in Figure 12l. In this case, the quality of the reconstruction is limited by the lack of relevant input data. There may be no practical solution to this since the system can not guess what data might be missing. In the worst case, users can be prompted for more detail if they are unhappy with the quality of the reconstruction.

Furthermore, many real world objects, such as the head, are not C^2 continuous within bounded surface elements and cannot be fully represented with piecewise smooth models. Strokes related to curvature are rarely addressed in previous research and we view the extension of this methodology to curvature discontinuities as future work. Yet despite these limitations, the features of the head model roughly correspond to the features of an actual human head. Therefore, we view this example as a success since the reconstruction method creates a good model despite its limitations.

The time complexity of our system scaled with the complexity of the input drawing and was limited only by the time taken by the solver to converge. Drawing operations occurred in real time and all non-solver related operations took neglible calculation time. The solver typically required 2-5 seconds to converge for a reconstruction with five or fewer contours. Average convergence time for a single reconstruction was about 5 seconds, though the gross differences between the reconstructions being compared was usually visible after a few seconds. Highly complex models required up to 10-20 seconds to converge but we gained a dramatic speedup by initializing new candidate reconstructions with the last known mesh selected as *Good*. This took computation time down to around 5-10 seconds for complex models. Typically, 2-3 candidate solutions were created simultaneously. All timings are for a 1.8 Ghz Pentium 4.

Simple models such as those shown in Figure 8 required under a minute to create. The models shown in Figure 9 had constraints that were automatically deduced by the system and required only the time for the solver to converge on the solution which was typically 10-15 seconds for the full model. The bear model took about 4 minutes to create. The head model shown in Figure 12 took about 6 minutes to create. This drawing was saved and running the algorithm on the completed drawing required about 3 minutes to recreate.

Users required very little time discerning which candidate reconstructions were appropriate for the scene at a high level. They did require convergence of the solver and several seconds for comparison when attempting to pinpoint exact normal and depth parameters, since candidates were similar at that scale. We found that users selection was more efficient when starting from a completed drawing. This may be because the PCG attempted to change large regions first on completed drawings, whereas interactively created drawings updated constraints one detail at a time.

9　Future Work

We have presented a method of generating constraints that asks for extensive user input for analysis and verification. It would be preferable to make those decisions without user input, where possible. We feel this area may be improved significantly in the future as the understanding of human vision and line drawing interpretation improves.

The simplified model of drawing we consider is not adequate to fully represent all drawings that occur in practice so extending our system to encompass other types of lines such as those generated by curvature, color, lighting, and texture is desirable. Many surface reconstruction methods use a beautification step to clean up the mesh after reconstruction, so we would like to explore this option to lessen the influence of hand-drawn errors in the output surface or as a pre-process in the input drawings.

Our ultimate target is to produce a system that automatically reconstructs models from drawings created by an artist that imposes no interference on the artistic process and requires no extra input or knowledge from the artist whatsoever. The presented system is a first step towards that goal.

References

[AGB04]　ALEXE I. A., GAILDRAT V., BARTHE L.: Interactive Modelling from Sketches using Spherical Implicit Functions. In *AFRIGRAPH* (03-05 novembre 2004), ACM.

[Clo71]　CLOWES M. B.: On seeing things. *Artificial Intelligence 2* (1971), 79–116.

[CPM04]　COMPANY P., PIQUER A., M.CONTERO: On the evolution of geometrical reconstruction as a core technology to sketch-based modeling. *EUROGRAPHICS Workshop on Sketch-Based Interfaces and Modeling* (2004).

[dAJ03]　DE ARAUJO B., JORGE J.: Blobmaker: Free form modelling with variational implicit surfaces. *Proceed-*

ings of 12th Encontro Português de Computação Gráfica (2003).

[HAA97]   HORRY Y., ANJYO K.-I., ARAI K.: Tour into the picture: using a spidery mesh interface to make animation from a single image. In *SIGGRAPH '97* (1997), pp. 225–232.

[HR85]   HOFFMAN D. D., RICHARDS W. A.: Parts of recognition. In *Visual Cognition*, Pinker S., (Ed.). MIT Press, London, 1985, pp. 65–96.

[Huf71]   HUFFMAN D.: Impossible objects as nonsense sentences. *Machine Intelligence 6* (1971), 295–323.

[IMT99]   IGARISHI T., MATSUOKA S., TANAKA H.: Teddy: A sketching interface for 3d freeform design. In *SIGGRAPH* (1999).

[JJAR97]   JOSEPH J. ATICK P. A. G., REDLICH N.: Statistical approach to shape from shading: Reconstructin of 3d face surfaces from single 2d images.

[Kan98]   KANG S.: Depth painting for image-based rendering applications, 1998.

[KHR02]   KARPENKO O., HUGHES J. F., RASKAR R.: Free-form sketching with variational implicit surfaces. *Computer Graphics Forum 21*, 3 (Sept. 2002), 585–594.

[Koe84]   KOENDERINK J. J.: What does the occluding contour tell us about solid shape?, 1984.

[Koe98]   KOENDERINK J. J.: Pictorial relief, 1998.

[KvDCL96]   KOENDERINK J. J., VAN DOORN A. J., CHRISTOU C. G., LAPPIN J. S.: Shape Constancy in Pictorial Relief. *Perception 25*, 2 (Feb. 1996), 155–164.

[LB90]   LAMB D., BANDOPADHAY A.: Interpreting a 3d object from a rough 2d line drawing. *Proceedings of Visualization90* (1990), 59–66.

[Lip98]   LIPSON H.: Computer aided 3d sketching for conceptual design, phd thesis, 1998.

[LS96]   LIPSON H., SHPITALNI M.: Optimization-based reconstruction of a 3D object from a single freehand line drawing. *Computer-aided Design 28*, 8 (1996), 651–663.

[LS02]   LIPSON H., SHPITALNI M.: Correlation-based reconstruction of a 3d object from a single freehand sketch, 2002.

[LZS01]   LI ZHANG GUILLAUME DUGAS-PHOCION J.-S. S., SEITZ S. M.: Single view modeling of free-form scenes. In *Proc. Computer Vision and Pattern Recognition* (2001).

[Mac73]   MACKWORTH A. K.: Interpreting pictures of polyhedral scenes. *Artif. Intell. 4*, 2 (1973), 121–137.

[Mal87]   MALIK J.: Interpreting line drawings of curved objects. *International Journal of Computer Vision* (1987), 73–103.

[MAP 97]   MARKS J., ANDALMAN B., P.A.BEARDSLEY, W.FREEMAN, S.GIBSON, J.HODGINS, T.KANG, B.MIRTICH, H.PFISTER, W.RUML, K.RYALL, J.SEIMS, S.SHIEBER: Design galleries:a general approach to setting parameters for computer graphics and animation. In *SIGGRAPH* (1997), pp. 389–400.

[OCDD01]   OH B. M., CHEN M., DORSEY J., DURAND F.: Image-based modeling and photo editing. In *SIGGRAPH 2001* (2001), pp. 433–442.

[PTKK]   PHILLIPS F., TODD J. T., KOENDERINK J. J., KAPPERS A. M. L.: Perceptual representation of visible surfaces.

[RCZ96]   ROBERT C. ZELEZNIK KENNETH P. HERNDON J. F. H.: Sketch: An interface for sketching 3d scenes.

[RH78]   R.SHAPIRA, H.FREEMAN: Computer description of bodies bounded by quadric surfaces from a set of imperfect projection, 1978.

[SC04]   SHESH A., CHEN B.: Smartpaper: An interactive and user friendly sketching system. *Comput. Graph. Forum 23*, 3 (2004), 301–310.

[TI01]   T. IGARISHI J. F. H.: A suggestive interface for 3d drawing. In *Symposium on User Interface Software and Technology* (2001).

[Tur74]   TURNER K.: Computer perception of curved objects using a television camera, 1974.

[TZF04]   TAI C.-L., ZHANG H., FONG J. C.-K.: Prototype Modeling from Sketched Silhouettes based on Convolution Surfaces. *Computer Graphics Forum 23* (2004).

[Var05]   VARLEY P. A. C.: The state of the art in line drawing interpretation, 2005. http://uk.geocities.com/pacvarley/StateOfTheArt.html.

[VM00]   VARLEY P. A. C., MARTIN R. R.: A system for constructing boundary representation solid models from a two-dimensional sketch. In *GMP* (2000), pp. 13–32.

[VM02]   VARLEY P. A. C., MARTIN R.: Estimating depth from line drawings. In *Proc. 7th ACM Symposium on Solid Modeling and Applications* (2002), pp. 180–191.

[VSM04]   VARLEY P. A. C., SUZUKI H., MARTIN R. R.: Making the most of using depth reasoning to label line drawings of engineering objects, 2004.

[VYJH04]   VARLEY P. A. C., Y.TAKAHASHI, J.MITANI, H.SUZUKI: A two-stage approach for interpreting line drawings of curved objects. In *EUROGRAPHICS Workshop on Sketch-Based Interfaces and Modeling* (2004).

[Wil90]   WILLIAMS L.: 3d paint. In *SI3D '90: Symposium on Interactive 3D graphics* (1990), pp. 225–233.

[Wil91]   WILLIAMS L.: Shading in two dimensions. In *Graphics Interface '91* (1991), ACM Press, pp. 143–151.

Construction and Modification of 3D Geometry Using a Sketch-based Interface

Levent Burak Kara[†1] and Kenji Shimada[‡1]

[1]Mechanical Engineering Department, Carnegie Mellon University, Pittsburgh, Pennsylvania 15213

Abstract

We present an interactive pen-based computer program for designing 3D objects through direct sketching. The proposed techniques are tailored toward the creation of free-form curves and surfaces, and are therefore particularly useful for styling design purposes. In our approach, the design process consists of two main steps. In the first step, the user designs a wireframe model by sketching its constituent curves in 3D. Using purely sketch-based operations, the initial curves can then be modified as desired. In the second step, the user constructs interpolating surfaces on the wireframe to obtain a solid model. Again, through sketch-based operations, the user can modify the initial surfaces, and specify the boundary conditions if necessary. In addition to the main modeling operations, a gesture-based command interface allows many of the frequently used commands to be input through pen strokes. The utility of our system is demonstrated with various examples.

Categories and Subject Descriptors (according to ACM CCS): H.5.2 [User Interfaces]: Graphical User Interfaces (GUI) Pen-based interaction; I.3.5 [Computational Geometry and Object Modeling]: Curve, surface, solid, and object representations, Physically based modeling.

1. Introduction

We describe a sketch-based design tool for the construction and modification of 3D geometry. Users of our system can design a variety of objects consisting of relatively complex edge and surface geometries. A key advantage of our system is that resulting geometry is directly dictated by input strokes thus making our system suitable for product styling design. This is in contrast to systems that use input strokes as gestures to modify primitives in certain directions, or those that use indirect manipulation methods based on handles or control lattices.

Our system supports a variety of pen-based operations both for modeling and command inputting. In a typical scenario, the user begins by constructing the wireframe of the design object. For this, the user simply sketches the constituent curves. Input strokes are first beautified into smooth curves in the image plane, and are then projected into 3D

to form the wireframe. Initially created curves can be later modified by simply sketching their new shapes. For curve modification, our program uses a physically-based deformation technique that modifies the original curve until it best conforms to the new shape dictated by input strokes. If desired, connectivity constraints between different curves can be set by simple pen operations. After the desired wireframe is obtained, the user constructs interpolating surfaces that cover the wireframe. Guided by sketch input, initial surfaces can then be smoothly modified to give them new shapes. Boundary conditions across different surfaces can also be specified through direct sketching of tangent planes. At any point during the design cycle, a trainable, gesture-based command interface allows frequently used commands to be specified with simple pen gestures.

2. Related Work

While most 3D modeling software traditionally evolved around a windows-mouse-menu-based interaction paradigm, recent advances in stylus-enabled tablet technology has made sketch-based interaction an appealing alternative. To

---

† e-mail: lkara@andrew.cmu.edu

‡ e-mail: shimada@cmu.edu

                    Levent Burak Kara & Kenji Shimada / Sketch-based Design of 3D Geometry

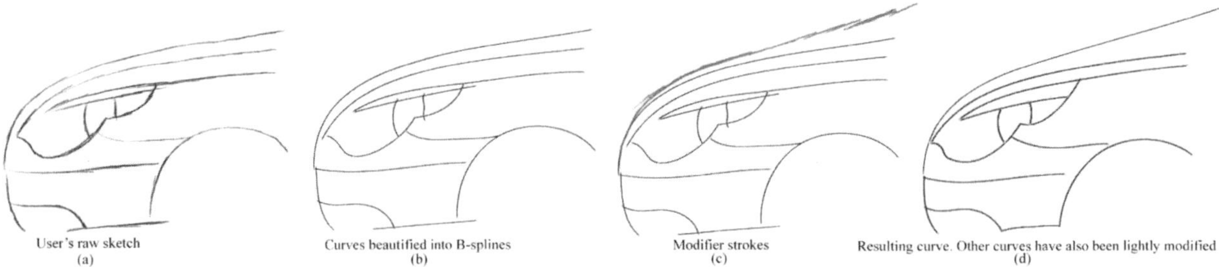

Figure 1: *Illustration of curve creation and modification in 2D. Curves are initially created by beautifying input strokes into B-splines. Once created, a curve can be modified by simply sketching its new shape near the original curve.*

date, researchers have developed a variety of sketch-based 3D modeling systems in various domains [ZHH96, IMT99, KHR02, TBSR04, BCCD04, DDGG05, MKL05]. In gesture-based approaches such as [ZHH96, EBE95, HQ03, DE03], designers' strokes are used primarily for geometric operations such as extrusion, bending, and primitive modification. Silhouette-based approaches [IMT99, KHR02, BCCD04, SWSJ05, CSSJ05] enable free-form surface generation. In these methods, users' strokes are used to form a 2D silhouette representing an outline or a cross-section, which is then extruded, inflated or swept to give 3D form. Systems such as [KG05, CCP*04, NSACO05] allow users to directly operate on existing surfaces to deform or add features lines using a digital pen. The key difference of these systems compared to gesture-based interfaces is that users' strokes are directly replicated in the resulting shape. However, these systems are most useful during later design stages where the main geometry is already available. Optimization-based algorithms such as [MKL05] produce the most plausible 3D shape from a 2D sketch of its wireframe. Line-labeling techniques have also been explored for 3D shape construction from 2D input. While many previous systems were limited to straight-edge models with planar surfaces, recent systems such as [PYJH04] have begun to extend these techniques to curved edges. Template based methods such as [MSK00, KDS06] allow the desired 3D form to be obtained by deforming an underlying 3D template.

3. Wireframe Creation and Modification

In the first step of the design process, the user creates a wireframe model by sketching the constituent curves in 3D. Users are allowed to sketch each curve using an arbitrary number of strokes, drawn in arbitrary directions and order. During curve construction, input strokes are first beautified into B-splines in the image plane using a curve fitting algorithm. The curves obtained in the image plane are then projected back into 3D to yield the final wireframe model. Once the initial curves are laid out, the user may modify each curve using a physically-based deformation algorithm. If desired, the user can specify connectivity constraints between individual curves. To facilitate discussion, we first describe our techniques in a 2D environment. We then describe how we extend the fundamental principles to 3D.

3.1. An Illustrative Example in 2D

Our curve creation and modification techniques are both purely sketch-based. Figure 1 illustrates the main steps involved in a typical design scenario. To begin, the user first sketches a rough outline of the design object. When creating a curve, users are free to use an arbitrary number of strokes, drawn in arbitrary directions and order. However, the user is asked to indicate the separation between the stroke groups that make up different curves. In Figure 1a, for instance, the user may draw the front hood using as many strokes as desired, but must inform the program (currently by tapping a button) when moving onto, say the wheel well.

Our program beautifies each stroke group into a cubic B-spline using a minimum least-squares curve fitting algorithm described in [PT97]. As shown in Figure 1b, resulting curves closely approximate the input strokes. After creating the initial curves, the user can set the system in 'modification' mode and modify each curve by simply sketching the curve's new shape. Figure 1c shows an example where the user has sketched several strokes above the hood. We call these strokes as *modifiers* as their purpose is to modify existing curves rather than to create new ones. After drawing the modifiers, the user invokes the 'process' command by gesturing a checkmark[†]. With this, our program first determines the curve that the user is intending to modify. This is done by identifying the curve that is closest to the modifiers, e.g., the hood in Figure 1. Next, our program uses an energy minimization algorithm based on active contours [KWT88] to deform the original curve until it best conforms to the modifiers. In this formulation, the original curve is treated as a physical spline that works to minimize both an internal energy term arising from stretching and bending, and an

---

[†] A detailed description of our gesture interface is given in Section 5.

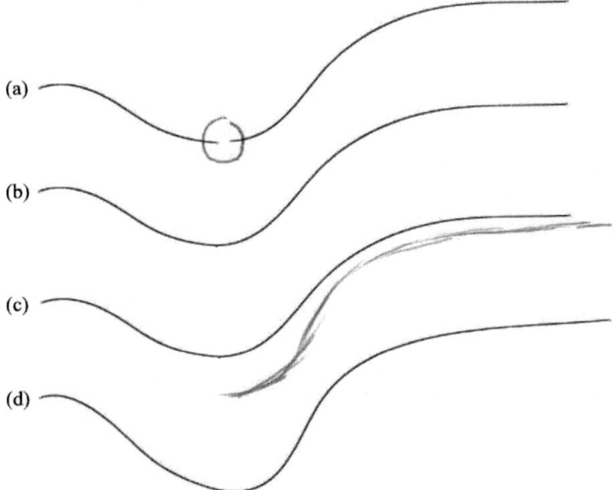

Figure 2: *Joining curves. (a-b) A counter clockwise 'o' gesture joins curves whose ends lie inside the gesture. (c-d) Once connected, subsequent modifications to one curve induce complying modifications in others in the group to preserve connectedness.*

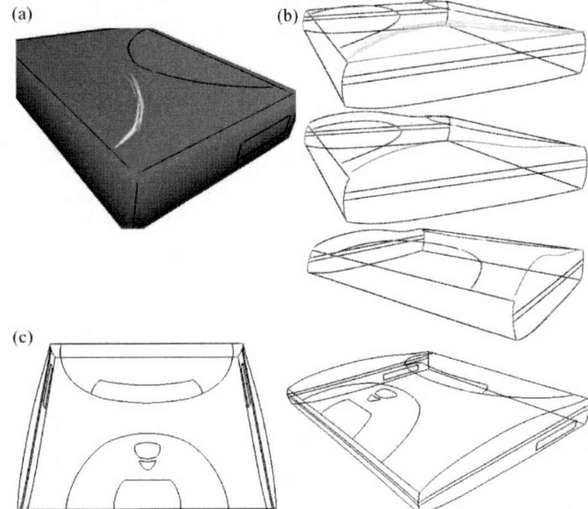

Figure 3: *Curve creation and modification in 3D. (a) An initial 3D template helps anchor input strokes in 3D. (b) A curve can modified by simply sketching its new shape. The optimal 3D configuration is determined by minimizing the deviation from the original curve in 3D, while closely approximating input strokes in 2D. (c) Final wireframe model.*

external energy term arising from the modifiers' presence. The internal energy forces the curve to evolve as a smooth curve. The external energy can be thought of a driving potential which decreases as the original curve approaches the modifiers. The balance between smoothness versus compliance of the final curve can be conveniently controlled by adjusting the corresponding weights in the energy functional. Figure 1d shows the hood modified in this way.

When desired, two or more curves can be joined at their ends with a counter clockwise 'o' gesture as shown in Figure 2. This operation applies a set of rotations and scalings to the curves until their ends meet at the same point. It also establishes the connectivity between the curves in that subsequent modifications to one curve induces modifications on the other curves to keep the group connected. When necessary the curves can be detached by a clockwise 'o' gesture.

3.2. Wireframe Creation in 3D

We use the same principles described above for 3D modeling. Users begin the design by sketching the curves of the wireframe. The main difference, however, is that we facilitate 3D modeling through the use of an underlying template model. This template acts as a platform that helps anchor users' initial strokes in 3D space, and is typically a very simplified model of the design object in question. For instance a thin rectangular prism serves as a suitable template for the design of a laptop computer as shown in Figure 3a.

With the presence of the template, the curves originally constructed in the image plane using B-spline fitting are uniquely projected into 3D using a standard ray intersection

algorithm. At the end, a set of 3D curves is obtained whose projections to the image plane match the input strokes. Since the curves obtained this way lie directly on the template, the initial wireframe constructed at the end of this step will usually possess a roughly correct geometry and relative proportions. This greatly lessens the work involved in the subsequent step of wireframe modification. Additionally the use of a template helps circumvent the well-known challenge of one-to-many mapping in 3D interpretation from 2D input.

3.3. Modification in 3D

Once the initial curves comprising the wireframe are constructed, the base 3D template is removed, leaving the user with a set of 3D curves. Next, through direct sketching, the user modifies the initially created curves to give them the precise desired shape. To modify a curve, the user simply sketches the modifier strokes that specify the new shape of the curve as it would occur from the current viewpoint. With this, our system modifies the curve in three steps. In the first step, the target curve is identified by projecting the existing 3D curves to the image plane, and determining the curve that lies spatially nearest to the modifiers. In the second step, our system uses the active-contour-based energy minimization algorithm described earlier to deform the projected curve in the image plane until it conforms to the modifiers. Finally, the newly obtained 2D curve is projected back into 3D resulting in the new 3D curve. Figure 3b shows an example. A key challenge here is that there are infinitely many such back-projections into 3D. We must therefore determine the best 3D configuration by constraining the problem. In our approach we use the following constraints:

- The 3D curve should appear right under the modifiers.
- If the modifier strokes appear precisely over the original target curve, i.e., the strokes do not alter the curve's 2D projection, the target curve should preserve its original 3D shape.
- If the curve is to change shape, it must maintain a reasonable 3D form. By "reasonable," we mean a solution that the designer would accept in many cases, while anticipating it in the worst case.

Based on these premises, we choose the optimal 3D configuration as the one that minimizes the spatial deviation from the original 3D curve. That is, among the 3D curves whose projections match the newly designed 2D curve, we choose the one that lies nearest to the original target curve. For this, a surface that originates from the current eye position, passes through the modifiers, and extends into the page, is first computed. Theoretically, all candidate solutions lie on this surface. The optimal 3D curve is then found by computing the minimum distance projection of the original curve onto this surface. Further details of our algorithm can be found in [KDS06].

By remaining proximate to the original curve, the new curve can be thought to be "least surprising" when viewed from a different viewpoint. One advantage of this is that curves can be modified incrementally, with predictable outcomes in each step. That is, as the curve desirably conforms to the input strokes in the current view, it still preserves most of its shape established in earlier steps as it deviates minimally from its previous configuration. This allows geometrically complex curves to be obtained by only a few successive modifications from different viewpoints.

4. Surface Creation and Modification

Once a wireframe model is obtained, the user constructs interpolating surfaces to obtain a solid model. Initially created surfaces can later be modified to the desired shape. The following paragraphs detail these processes.

4.1. Initial Surface Creation

Given the wireframe model, the goal in surfacing is to construct a surface geometry for each of the closed face loops of the wireframe. Figure 4 illustrates the process. For each surface to be created, the user first identifies the associated face loop by highlighting the constituent wireframe curves involved in that face loop (Figure 4a). With this, our system creates an interpolating surface in three steps. First, a vertex is created at the centroid of the boundary vertices. A set of initial triangles are then created that use the new vertex as the common apex, and have their bases at the boundary (Figure 4b). Finally, a series of edge swapping, face subdivision

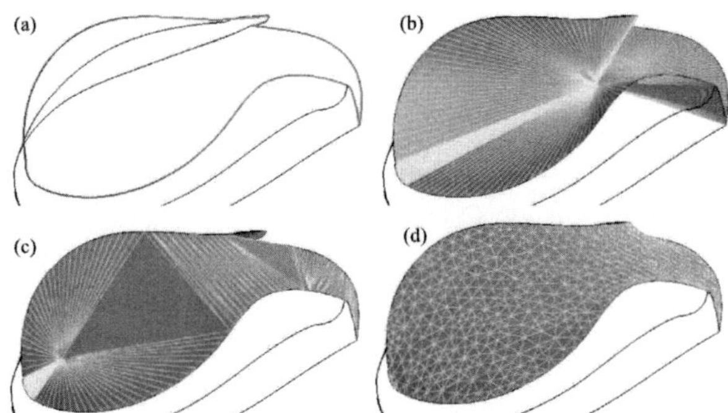

Figure 4: *Surface creation on a face loop. (a) Highlighted boundary curves, (b) Centroid vertex and associated initial triangulation, (c) An intermediate state during edge swapping, (d) Resulting surface after edge swapping, face subdivision and Laplacian smoothing.*

and Laplacian smoothing is applied until a sufficient number of uniformly distributed triangles are obtained (Figure 4d). The result is a smooth polygonal surface consisting of purely triangular elements. For a given face loop geometry, the resulting surface has the unique property of having the minimum surface area due to the nature of Laplacian smoothing.

4.2. Specifying Surface Deformations

Initially created surfaces can be modified to give them the desired shape. To deform a surface, the user first sketches a *reference curve* on it as shown in Figure 5a. This curve defines a region of interest in which the surface vertices closest to the reference curve are selected for subsequent deformation. Next, the user sketches a new curve that specifies the desired shape of the reference curve in 3D (Figure 5b). The 3D configuration of this new curve is computed by modifying the reference curve using the methods described in Section 3.3. Given the initially selected surface vertices and the new curve, our system invokes an optimization algorithm that deforms the surface until the selected surface vertices lie close to the target shape (Figure 5c). During deformation, the objective function we minimize is the Hausdorff distance [Ruc96] between the surface vertices, and the points comprising the target curve. The Hausdorff distance provides a convenient metric that reveals the spatial proximity between two point sets in the form of an upper bound: If the Hausdorff distance is d, all points in the first point set are at most distance d away from the other point set (and vice versa).

At the heart of our deformation mechanism is an intuitive method that simulates the effect of a pressure force on a thin membrane (see [KDS06] for details). This tool allows surfaces to be inflated or flattened in a predictable way. A key advantage of this technique is that surfaces can be deformed wholistically in a smooth way without generating

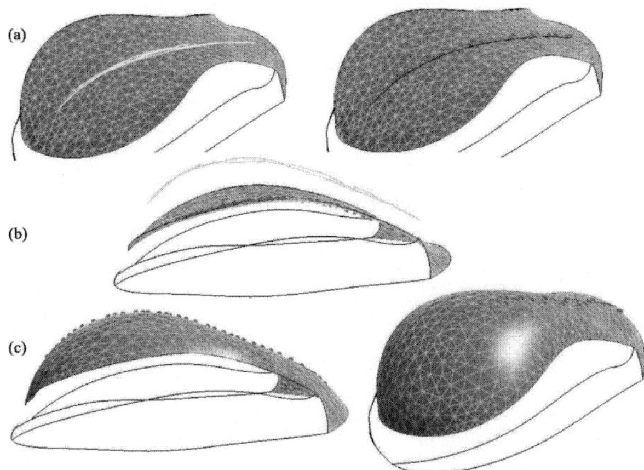

Figure 5: *Surface deformation. (a) A sketched reference curve and selected surface vertices, (b) The user sketches the new desired shape, (c) The surface is inflated using a pressure force until the surface closely approximates the new shape.*

unintended creases. The extent of the deformation depends on the magnitude of the pressure, whose optimal value is determined by our optimization algorithm. In other words, our algorithm seeks for the optimal pressure value which produces a deformation that minimizes the Hausdorff distance mentioned above. Figure 5c shows the result of a surface deformed using this technique.

4.3. Specifying Boundary Conditions

If desired, the user can also specify the boundary conditions along surface edges. Normally, it is assumed that the user wishes the surface boundaries to interpolate the wireframe edges, and hence position constraints are already implicit in the wireframe model. Since created surfaces automatically interpolate the boundary curves, position constraints are readily satisfied. The user, however, can specify tangent directions along various parts of the boundary by sketching the silhouettes of the tangent planes at desired points. Figure 6 shows an example. For this, the user first marks a boundary vertex, across which the tangent will be specified (Figure 6a). Next, after transforming to a suitable viewpoint, the user sketches the tangent plane as it would be seen from the side(Figure 6b). This defines a plane in 3D that passes through the input strokes, and extends into the page along the current viewpoint. The normal vector of this virtual plane is then set as the normal of the vertex under consideration (Figure 6c). Note that the normal of a vertex provides precisely the same information as the tangent plane through the vertex.

We only require the user to specify the normal directions (in the form of tangent planes) at a handful of discrete vertices. The normal directions at intermediate vertices along the boundary are identified using a weighted linear averaging function. For instance, the normal vector at an intermediate vertex q is computed as the weighted average of two surrounding vertices p and r as:

$$\mathbf{n}_q = (w)\mathbf{n}_p + (1-w)\mathbf{n}_r$$

where w is distance (along the boundary) between vertices q and r divided by the distance (along the boundary) between vertices p and r . With this formulation, normals at intermediate vertices will change smoothly between the normals of p and q. Figure 6d shows an example. If necessary, more control on the normal directions can be achieved by increasing the number of vertices for which the normals are explicitly specified. Once specified, these constraints are taken into account by both the surface creation and deformation tools described above, resulting in surfaces that conform to the constraints. Note that specification of the boundary normals naturally results in our surfaces to be G^1 continuous across the boundary edges.

5. Command Gestures

Besides the main modeling operations described so far, our system also provides a gesture-based command interface for inputting frequently used commands. The command interface is extensible and customizable in that new gestures can be trained, or existing gestures can be linked to different commands. Figure 7 shows the currently used gestures and their associated commands. Each gesture is a single stroke entity that is sensitive to orientation and drawing direction. Due to variation in drawing speeds, input raw strokes frequently consist of data points spaced non-uniformly along the stroke's trajectory (low pen speeds cause dense point clouds while high pen speeds cause large gaps between points), which adversely affect their recognition. To alleviate this difficulty, input strokes are first resampled using a linear interpolation function to obtain data points equally spaced along the stroke's trajectory.

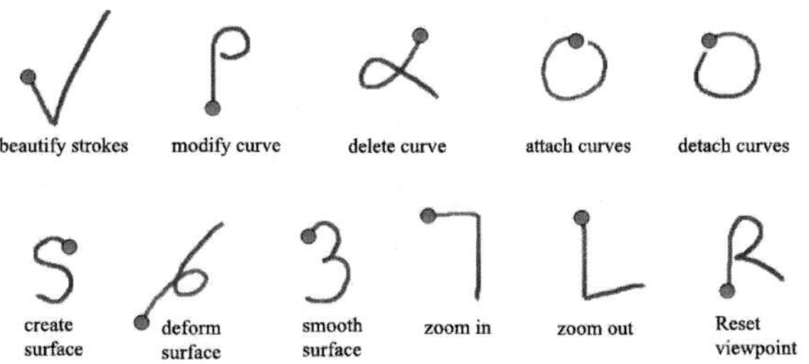

Figure 7: *Currently used gestures and their associated commands. Red dots indicate the starting points of the gestures.*

Our gesture recognizer employs neural networks to learn and classify gestures. For each gesture, a separate network is constructed. The networks in our approach use the angles

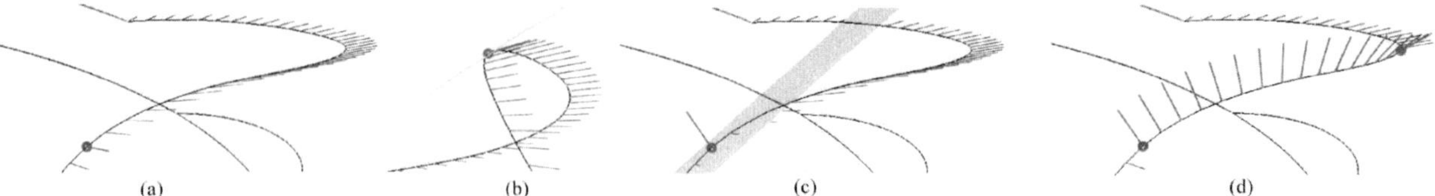

Figure 6: *Specifying boundary normals. (a) A selected boundary vertex and its default normal. (b) User sketches the tangent plane across this vertex from a suitable viewpoint. (c) New vertex normal. Notice that the new normal is the normal of the virtual plane generated in b. (d) The user has specified the normals of two vertices. The normals of intermediate vertices are interpolated smoothly between the two vertex normals.*

formed by the horizontal line, and the line segments connecting consecutive points as the input feature vector. Figure 8 shows these angles. The entries in this vector suitably range between $[-\pi,+\pi]$, thereby providing a congruent range to the input layer of the networks in all cases. The nature of this feature vector makes gesture recognition sensitive to orientation and drawing direction, but insensitive to scale. While additional geometric features could be considered to characterize a stroke more specifically, we have found the proposed angle information to be sufficiently discriminatory for our purposes.

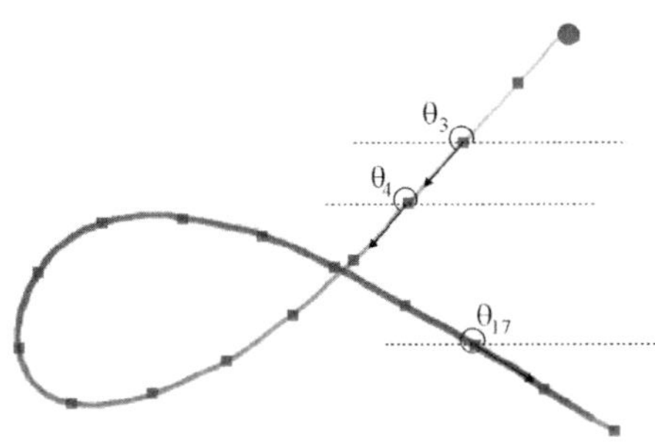

Figure 8: *The angles between the line segments in a gesture and the horizontal line form the feature vector for the neural network during gesture recognition.*

Each network in our command interface is designed as a fully-connected, feed-forward back propagation neural network with 18 inputs, 16 neurons in the first hidden layer, 6 neurons in the second hidden layer, and 1 output neuron. The inputs to the network are the entries of the feature vector described above[‡]. In each neuron, a tangent sigmoid ('tansig') function is used as the activation function. The output of the network is a single neuron which outputs a real number in the range [0,1]. For each gesture, the network is trained using around 200 positive and 200 negative examples. During training, a target value of 1.0 and 0.0 is assigned to positive

and negative examples respectively. During recognition, an unknown stroke is evaluated by each of the neural networks. The stroke is classified as the gesture whose network produces the highest real value at the output neuron. In actual use, the classification of a stroke by the ensemble of networks is almost instantaneous.

A key issue in gesture recognition however is that, prior to deciding *which* gesture a stroke represents, it is necessary to decide *if* the stroke is a gesture in the first place. This issue is discussed in detail in [SL03] on modeless input. The free-form sketching nature of our modeling operations makes this initial distinction a much challenging task, as the strokes used during modeling operations can be easily mistaken for a gesture and vice-versa. To avert this difficulty, we ask the user to hold a modifier button on the tablet or the keyboard when gesturing.

6. Examples

Figure 9 shows several models designed using our system. In each case, the user starts the design on a simple template. In the case of the laptop computer and the shaver, starting templates are simply rectangular prisms. For the mouse, it is a half-egg shape. Normally our system is only loosely dependent on the underlying template. Indeed, the template is only necessary to lay out a rough wireframe model containing a handful of characteristic curves. Once such a wireframe is obtained, its curves can be quickly modified resulting a simple but geometrically accurate wireframe. Next, this wireframe can be surfaced to obtain a set of initial surfaces that define the main style of the design object. Further curves and surfaces can thus be added later using this initial model as a convenient base platform. This is especially useful for adding small details such as buttons or impressions. In the examples shown above this strategy has been used extensively, and has proven to be quite effective. To further facilitate design, our program provides the option to preserve symmetry across one of the three principal Cartesian planes. This way, work performed on one side of the symmetry plane is automatically duplicated on the other side. The above examples take advantage of this feature.

All processes described in earlier sections are performed

[‡] Input strokes are thus resampled to 19 data points, which results in 18 angles that form the input vector.

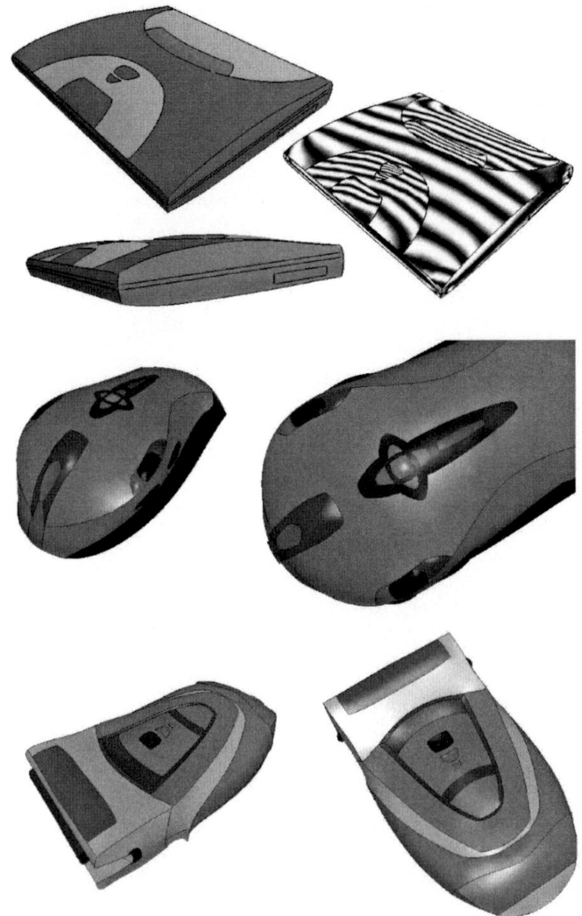

Figure 9: *Example models created by our system.*

at interactive speeds on a consumer level PC (2.0GHz with 1MB of RAM), except for the optimization-based surface modification process. In this case, our experiments have shown that it takes anywhere between 5 to 30 seconds to determine the optimal surface deformation.

7. Conclusions and Future Work

We have described a new approach to computer aided design of 3D geometry using a sketch-based interface. Our techniques are particularly useful for *styling design*, where a fully sketch-based interaction is an appealing natural alternative to traditional menu-and-mouse-based interaction. Our system supports a wide range of sketch-based 3D modeling operations including wireframe construction through curve creation, wireframe modification, surface creation, surface deformation, and boundary condition specification. Besides these main modeling operations, a trainable gesture-based command interface allows many of the frequently used commands to be invoked via a set of stroke gestures. With the

proposed techniques, users of our system can design a wide variety of 3D models exclusively through the use of a digital pen. We believe the proposed techniques demonstrate that a sketch-based interaction is a viable alternative to the traditional interaction mechanisms found in existing software. Moreover, it is particularly advantageous for styling design purposes where typical tasks would be tedious, if not complicated, using conventional interaction techniques.

While our current system is an effective tool, there are several directions for future improvements. Currently our curve modification algorithm requires curves to be modified individually, and each curve must be modified in its entirety. This means local modifications to a curve are currently not permitted. We plan to extend our curve modification techniques to allow local curve modifications. Also, our current surface deformation tool uses a uniform pressure field to deform a surface. We are currently exploring other means, such as non-unform pressure fields, for a more flexible control of the deformed surfaces. Also, while our techniques are tailored toward the creation of *curvy* edges and surfaces, we plan to incorporate options for creating more standard geometry such as straight lines, arcs, fillets etc. Finally, we are planning to conduct field studies with real industrial designers to better assess our system, and to see how it can be improved.

References

[BCCD04]　Bourguignon D., Chaine R., Cani M.-P., Drettakis G.: Relief: A modeling by drawing tool. In *EUROGRAPHICS Workshop on Sketch-Based Interfaces and Modeling* (2004).

[CCP*04]　Cheutet V., Catalano C., Pernot J., Falcidieno B., Giannini F.: 3d sketching with fully free form deformation features (d-f4) for aesthetic design. In *EUROGRAPHICS Workshop on Sketch-Based Interfaces and Modeling* (2004).

[CSSJ05]　Cherlin J. J., Samavati F., Sousa M. C., Jorge J. A.: Sketch-based modeling with few strokes. In *SCCG '05: Proceedings of the 21st spring conference on Computer graphics* (2005), ACM Press, pp. 137–145.

[DDGG05]　Das K., Diaz-Gutierrez P., Gopi M.: Sketching free-form surfaces using network of curves. In *EUROGRAPHICS Workshop on Sketch-Based Interfaces and Modeling* (2005).

[DE03]　Draper G., Egbert P.: A gestural interface to free-form deformation. In *Graphics Interface 2003* (2003), pp. 113–120.

[EBE95]　Eggli L., Bruderlin B. D., Elber G.: Sketching as a solid modeling tool. In *SMA '95: Proceedings of the third ACM symposium on Solid modeling and applications* (1995), ACM Press, pp. 313–322.

[HQ03]　Hua J., Qin H.: Free-form deformations via

sketching and manipulating scalar fields. In *SM '03: Proceedings of the eighth ACM symposium on Solid modeling and applications* (2003), ACM Press, pp. 328–333.

[IMT99] IGARASHI T., MATSUOKA S., TANAKA H.: Teddy: a sketching interface for 3d freeform design. In *SIGGRAPH '99: Proceedings of the 26th annual conference on Computer graphics and interactive techniques* (1999), pp. 409–416.

[KDS06] KARA L. B., D'ERAMO C., SHIMADA K.: Pen-based styling design of 3d geometry using concept sketches and template models. In *ACM Solid and Physical Modeling Conference* (2006).

[KG05] KHO Y., GARLAND M.: Sketching mesh deformations. In *SI3D '05: Proceedings of the 2005 symposium on Interactive 3D graphics and games* (2005), ACM Press, pp. 147–154.

[KHR02] KARPENKO O., HUGHES J. F., RASKAR R.: Free-form sketching with variational implicit surfaces. In *Eurographics* (2002).

[KWT88] KAAS M., WITKINS A., TERZOPOLUS D.: Snakes: active contour models. *International Journal of Computer Vision 1*, 4 (1988), 312–330.

[MKL05] MASRY M., KANG D. J., LIPSON H.: A freehand sketching interface for progressive construction of 3d objects. *Computers and Graphics 29*, 4 (2005), 563–575.

[MSK00] MITANI J., SUZUKI H., KIMURA F.: 3d sketch: Sketch-based model reconstruction and rendering. In *Workshop on Geometric Modeling 2000* (2000), pp. 85–98.

[NSACO05] NEALEN A., SORKINE O., ALEXA M., COHEN-OR D.: A sketch-based interface for detail-preserving mesh editing. *ACM Transactions on Graphics 24*, 3 (2005), 1142–1147.

[PT97] PIEGL L., TILLER W.: *The NURBS Book*. 1997.

[PYJH04] P.A.C.VARLEY, Y.TAKAHASHI, J.MITANI, H.SUZUKI: A two-stage approach for interpreting line drawings of curved objects. In *EUROGRAPHICS Workshop on Sketch-Based Interfaces and Modeling* (2004).

[Ruc96] RUCKLIDGE W. J.: *Efficient Visual Recognition Using the Hausdorff Distance*. Number 1173 Lecture Notes in computer Science,. Springer-Verlag, Berlin, 1996.

[SL03] SAUND E., LANK E.: Stylus input and editing without prior selection of mode. In *UIST '03: Proceedings of the 16th annual ACM symposium on User interface software* (2003), ACM Press, pp. 213–216.

[SWSJ05] SCHMIDT R., WYVILL B., SOUSA M. C., JORGE J. A.: Shapeshop: Sketch-based solid modeling with blobtrees. In *EUROGRAPHICS Workshop on Sketch-Based Interfaces and Modeling* (2005).

[TBSR04] TSANG S., BALAKRISHNAN R., SINGH K., RANJAN A.: A suggestive interface for image guided 3d sketching. In *CHI '04: Proceedings of the SIGCHI conference on Human factors in computing systems* (2004), pp. 591–598.

[ZHH96] ZELEZNIK R. C., HERNDON K. P., HUGHES J. F.: Sketch: an interface for sketching 3d scenes. In *SIGGRAPH '96: Proceedings of the 23rd annual conference on Computer graphics and interactive techniques* (1996), pp. 163–170.

EUROGRAPHICS Workshop on Sketch-Based Interfaces and Modeling (2006)
Thomas Stahovich and Mario Costa Sousa (Editors)

Parts, Image, and Sketch based 3D Modeling Method

Jun Murakawa, Ilmi Yoon, Tracie Hong[1] and Edward Lank[2]

[1]Computer Science Department, San Francisco State University, 1600 Holloway Ave., San Francisco, CA, 94132
[2]David R. Cheriton School of Computer Science, University of Waterloo, Waterloo, ON, Canada, N2L 3G1
junmura@gmail.com, yoon@cs.sfsu.edu, traciely@sfsu.edu, lank@cs.uwaterloo.ca

---

Abstract

Despite their many benefits, challenges exist in the creation of 3D models, particularly for individual not currently skilled with 3D modeling software. To address this, we explore the creation of 3D modeling software for non-domain experts that uses a hierarchical parts database of generic 3D models, and deforms models into specific related target objects using image guided 3D model morphing. A human-in-the-loop sketching interface supports image registration and constrains our geometrical transformation to support real time morphing of generic models into accurate representations of new objects for which users wish a 3D model. Applying the application to the study of insects in biology, we find that the application supports the creation of realistic 3D models, and that the application is of value to educators and researchers in entomology.

Categories and Subject Descriptors (according to ACM CCS): I.3.3 [Computer Graphics]: Line and Curve Generation, H5.m [Information interfaces and presentation] (e.g., HCI): Miscellaneous.

---

1. Introduction

3D models allow an enhanced representation of the structure of an object in various fields, including engineering (CAD), design (architecture), and art (sculpture). One factor inhibiting more extensive use of 3D models is the relatively complex and time-consuming process associated with generating these models. Typical 3D modeling software requires significant expertise. As well, the time-consuming, pedantic nature of 3D model construction makes these software applications ill-suited to exploratory processes by end users. The time investment required to create 3D models argues, instead, for their use at later, rather than earlier stages of object construction or analysis.

In our work, we explore the design of 3D modeling tools to support researchers and students in the biological sciences. In particular, our goal was to design 3D model creation tools that would be useful for biological researchers or biological students during the early stage of structure object examination. Our first target domain in biology is entomologists, and we explore the creation of 3D models of various insects for education and early analysis of physical characteristics. Current 3D modeling applications require a significant time investment to create 3D models, and users with a new insect specimen have few simple options for creating a 3D model of an insect they are studying.

Recent research in 3D modeling software seeks to address the shortcomings the modeling software in two ways. The first is the design of systems that allow simplified creation of 3D objects, based on techniques such as suggestive geometries and other informal drawing methods that are augmented with computational intelligence. Two challenges exist with this method of 3D model creation. First, systems that support the creation of 3D models of objects do allow users to create simple 3D models, but complex objects are more difficult to model, requiring extensive, painstaking drawing of physical structure. Consider using pen-based sketches and suggestive geometries to create a 3D model of an ant. A user would need to extensively sketch all parts of the ant, adjusting geometries as needed. While this is possible for simple mechanical systems, the complex surface deformations of living organisms make this process prohibitively time consuming, even with enhancements such as image-guided sketching [TBS04].

The second method for end-user 3D model specification allows users to construct new 3D objects by combining or altering pre-existing 3D models of real world objects. Altering existing 3D models shows more promise for the creation of 3D models in domains such as biology. Current techniques in the research literature do this by pasting together parts to create 3D models of chairs, for example [FKP04], or by editing existing meshes into new shapes using techniques like sketching to intelligently manipulate control vertices [NSA05].

This paper describes a 3D modeling tool based on semi-automated, image-guided 3D model deformation. Taking a complex 3D model that is similar to a target object a user wishes to model, we describe a process where images, superimposed on the model, serve as a guide for model deformation. Users use a pen to select parts of the 3D model based from a parts database of 3D models of objects in the target domain, select a portion of an image of an object of which they wish a 3D model using lasso based selection, and our geometrical transformation algorithms alter the meshes on the 3D model to correspond to the shape of the target image. Using our model deformation strategy, we give biologists the ability to easily create near perfect 3D models of target organisms. Biologists have identified this tool as useful for education and in early stages of biological research.

This paper is organized as follows. In Section 2, we describe related work. Section 3 presents our modeling method. Section 4 displays modeling results. Finally, we conclude by describing current contributions and future work.

2. Related Work

The creation of 3D models of objects is a time-consuming process, particularly for individuals unfamiliar with 3D modeling tools, or users attempting to re-create 3D models from complex perspective images. Authors have noted this shortcoming, and the opportunity that exists to make 3D modeling accessible to end users [IMT1999, TBS04, NSA05, ZHH96].

To design 3D modeling tools for end-users unskilled with complex 3D modeling software, researchers have explored two alternative approaches. The first uses a 2D sketch of 3D objects coupled with some form of computational intelligence to infer 3D geometries. The second is the manipulation of pre-existing 3D models, for example the combination of parts of models into a new composite model or the guided deformation of pre-existing models.

2.1. Sketch-Based 3D Modeling

Sketch-based 3D modeling can be further decomposed into three distinct approaches to the recognition of 3D structure from the sparse information conveyed by a 2D sketch. These approaches are sketch-based geometry generation, gesture-based 3D modeling, and predictive and suggestive interfaces.

The best-known sketch-based geometry generation system is Teddy [IMT99], which examines the contours created by 2D lines and constructs plausible 3D polygonal surfaces from the 2D line drawing. Users begin by drawing the simple contour of the object on the screen and the system constructs a candidate 3D shape for the 2D contour. The shape can be rotated and modified through the addition of additional strokes which define new 3D shapes, or by drawing a series of gestures to transform existing shapes, for example cut gestures, smoothing gestures, extrusion gestures, or painting and erasing gestures. Other researchers have extended this work [IH03, CSS05], but the basic nature of 3D model creation remains unchanged. Using knowledge of likely candidate shapes, a sketch defines a new 3D model. While this system does allow users to create simple 3D models, creating complex models is a much more time-consuming process, and may be impossible using these approximate 3D model generation systems.

Gesture-based 3D modeling, such as Zeleznik's *Sketch* system [ZHH96] are geared more toward near-expert users who want more intuitive 3D modeling tools. A pen-based system is used to sketch contours, and gestures augment the input by allowing users to manipulate and more fully refine 3D models. The basic gesture-based system allows users to create, scale, and orient objects in 3D environments using gestalt commands, and enhanced systems exist to support various domain experts such as engineers. While the system does allow effective 3D model creation, it places a significant burden on users to master a series of multistroke gestures to create precise 3D models.

Finally, predictive and suggestive systems suggest relevant geometries to the user using either a database of prior geometries. Tang et al. [TBS04] describe a 3D modeling that supports drawing directly in 3D perspective by displaying a 3D rectangle defining "faces" of a 3D model. The rectangle on which users draw can be rotated, and images for tracing can be placed on each face. Users can then trace images or draw freehand on a face, and the lines drawn are rendered in three dimensions. Geometrical information "suggests" good line placement, and switching views permits a user to adjust the three-dimensional position of the lines.

While the 3D sketching interface does permit line-drawn 3D objects to be created, two points merit note. First, for all but the simplest of outlines, the drawing and repositioning process is very time consuming. 3D sketching is inappropriate for complex 3D models, such as of biological specimens where many smooth contours shaded with appropriate texture maps must be generated. Second, the system requires a good awareness, on the part of the user, of the 3D model being constructed. As such, sketch-based 3D modeling is inappropriate for non-3D modeling experts.

2.2. 3D Model Transformation

The second approach to end-user creation of 3D models transforms pre-existing 3D models or combines pre-existing 3D models into new 3D models of objects. Two recent approaches to this are Nealen et al.'s detail-preserving mesh editing [NSA05] and Funkhouser et al.'s technique of creating 3D models by combining parts of pre-existing 3D models.

Mesh editing allows users to sketch on meshes to suggest edits to the mesh [NSA05]. Using discrete models of 3D meshes, contours can be moved while preserving much of the existing geometric surface detail. The user first selects a silhouette segment to be transformed, and draws a new candidate shape for the silhouette. Vertex normals on the silhouette segment are linearly interpolated based on the new candidate shape's position. The silhouette vertices are then mapped to new locations based on a transformation calculated from the overall movement defined by the new candidate shapes location.

In the modeling by example approach, a parts database is mined for 3D models of interest. Portions of these meshes can be segmented from the models and selectively added to other models. For example, using rough shapes drawn using a mouse to indicate position, arms from one 3D model can be glued onto a 3D model of an armless statue or different styles of chair arms can be combined into a new chair design.

2.3. Shortcomings of Existing Work

While many of the components to support non-expert creation of 3D models have been proposed, no one solution fully addresses the needs of the non-expert in the rapid creation of complex 3D models of real world objects. Sketching systems require the depiction of every line, and 3D Model transformation either requires painstaking alteration of 3D models or the need for an extensive parts database that contains all possible pre-existing 3D models that you might want to use.

In domains such as biology, researchers and students may examine new, un-modeled species containing structures that, while similar to pre-existing models of other species within a broader family of organisms, have unique characteristics not currently represented. Our goal is to provide domain experts with access to informal 3D modeling tools that allow the creation of near-perfect complex 3D representations rapidly.

3. Proposed Modeling Method

To provide interfaces for domain experts with little 3D modeling experience, we propose a modeling tool that supports interactions on 2D images to guide 3D model deformation. Users start with image(s) of their subject and choose a generic 3D model from the list of available ones for their particular domain of study.

The proposed modeling process is as below (Figure 1). A user first provides images of the subject that is going to be modeled and selects a generic 3D model from the list of models available. Ideally, the selected model is "similar" to the subject; for example, a 3D model of one ant species would be used to model a target ant species. Second, given the generic 3D model and images of the subject to be modeled by the user, the system displays the selected 3D model overlaid on the target images. The user then selects a part to be morphed. The hierarchical structure of the generic 3D model aids with this selection, as shown in figure 2, by providing a natural segmentation of the 3D meshes in the generic 3D model. Next, the user draws a stylus lasso that selects the corresponding part of the target subject on top of the image of the target subject. Finally, the system morphs the generic 3D model based on the silhouette of the part extracted from the selected component of the image. The user can repeat this process for each part until significant parts of the 3D model are deformed to the desired shapes in the subject of interest to the domain expert.

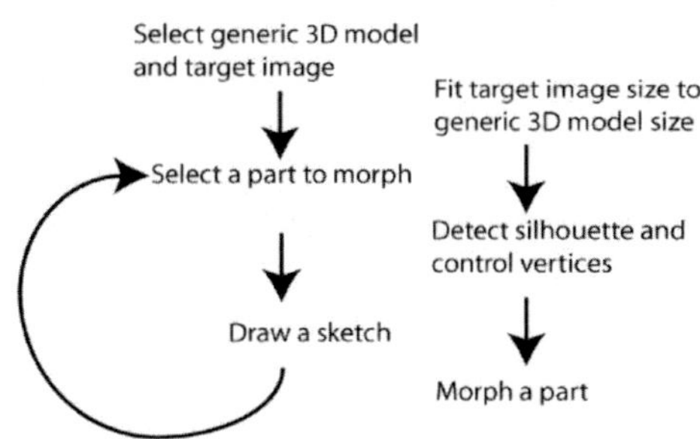

Figure 1: Overall Modeling Process

When the user selects the part from the 3D model, the system detects the silhouette of the 3D model component and identifies control vertices from the silhouette as source points for morphing. When the user later defines the silhouette of the corresponding part from the image using a pen-based selection gesture, the system computes sequences of points as a destination of the morphing. The details of each step in our modeling process are described in the following subsections.

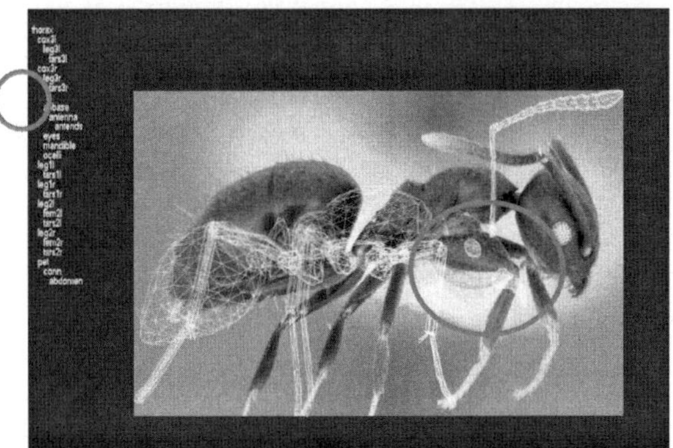

Figure 2: Tree Display of Hierarchical Structure of Parts on the left side (and the top) and the selected part (circled) is highlighted as red.

3.1. Parts Database

The idea of parts database is inspired by research in modeling by example [FKP04]. In our research, the generic parts database which categorizes 3D geometry by model structure was designed. Using this database, the system allows a user to search, browse and select body parts of interest. This parts database was inspired by biology education, where species taxonomy is based on the structure of physical parts of the body of a target species to be classified. Users with knowledge of how physical structure defines species classification can search and assemble body parts to create a generic model that can be easily morphed to the desired shape depicted by photos of a subject of interest.

3.2 Generic 3D Model and Target Image

Generic 3D models are used as the starting point for the modeling process. A hierarchy structure is defined for a category of insects. As one example, in ants the thorax is the root of a hierarchy, and a head, legs, and abdomen as the children of the Thorax part. The hierarchy structure is not mandatory for the modeling process but aids the process by allowing the user to select body parts efficiently.

In this first step, the user also provides target image(s). The target image can be a single view of a subject or multiple views of the same subject, preferably from various perspectives if such images are available. For example, the antweb [ANTWEB] provides a large number of images of different species of ants. If multiple images are available, the user can select images for the top, front, side or another random non-orthogonal view of the ant subject to be modeled. Then, the system displays the generic 3D model on top of the target images. Internally, this 3D rendering is done by the OpenGL 3D library. Images are also rendered as texture applied on large quads.

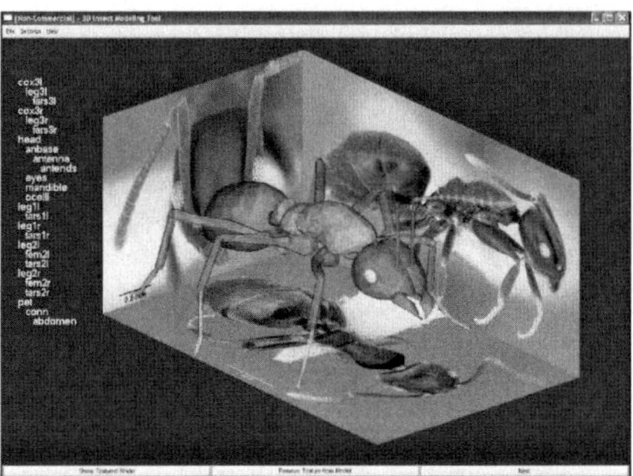

(a) Image and model alignment in 3D view

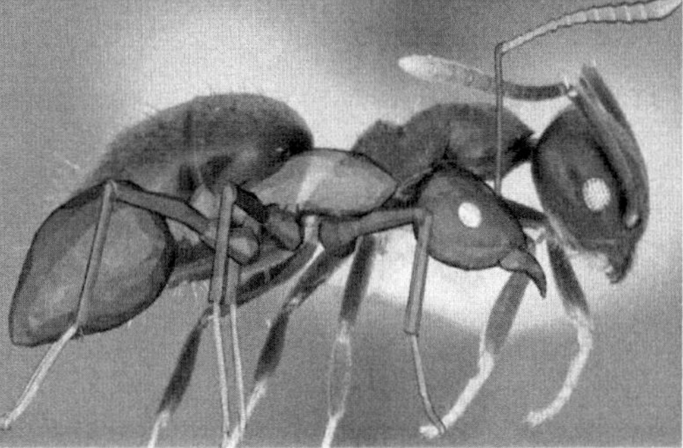

(b) Modeling view in 2D

Figure 3: Modeling View: Generic Ant Model rendered on Top of Target Image – User selects thorax part (red – half transparent part) to be morphed.

The simplest images to use for a user are orthogonal views, specifically the front, top, rear, and side views at perpendicular angles to the dominant axes of a species being modeled. Using a random, non-orthogonal photo does require some additional user-directed adjustment to accurately align the image with the generic 3D model.

The application interface that supports this step allows the user to browse target images and 3D models in multiple views. Basic navigation tools (zoom in/out, rotation, and 3D centering) are implemented for convenience. The application interface for model and image selection and alignment is shown in Figure 3a and 3b.

3.3 Part Selection

Live organisms consist of several body parts and parts are interconnected in varying orientations. The variation in orientation creates poses. Automatic recognition of every body part based on diverse poses from photos is challenging. Instead, our system asks the user to choose a body part from the 3D model and use a pen sketch to outline the corresponding part in images of the subject being modeled. This human-in-the-loop image registration task simplifies the morphing algorithm, specifically to support real time morphing of our 3D models. Due to the use of generic parts, the user need only morph significant body parts, leaving insignificant parts unaltered from the generic model. To help the user select a part of the 3D model to be modified, the list of part names is displayed on the left side of the modeling screen in a tree view that depicts the hierarchical structure of the parts, shown at figure 2.

The use of 3D model deformation is not unique to our work, but has been recognized as an effective way to draw, select, and manipulate objects in a sketch guided two-dimensional interface. Pen-based input devices such as Tablet PCs or data tablets support sketching operations by leveraging familiarity with pen and paper to create precise outlines of relevant structure. Initially, the user sketch is a set of points on the screen. To use the sketch to deform the 3D geometry, the screen coordinates are converted into 3D world coordinates using un-projection.

3.4. Silhouette and Control Vertices

The silhouette is the boundary of the 3D object projected onto the 2D screen. For the morph algorithm to deform the 3D geometry using the user drawn 2D outline of a target shape, vertices on the silhouette are used as control vertices for the 3D geometry deformation. We don't use a popular silhouette edge detection algorithm that requires connectivity information [BS03]. Instead of building the connectivity information, we detect silhouette vertices directly from the dot product of a normal vector and a camera vector. As visualized in figure 4, the red color shows small values of the dot product (near 0.0), and the green color shows large values of the dot product (close to 1.0). Those (red) vertices with smaller dot products are orthogonal to the camera view and are selected as control vertices for morphing.

3.5. Correlation between Control Vertices and Sketch Points

After the user sketch and control vertices are obtained, the center point of the shape defined by the control vertices and the center of the shape defined by the sketch points are aligned using global translation. The system then finds a corresponding sketch point for each control vertex, and this correspondence is used to compute movement vectors.

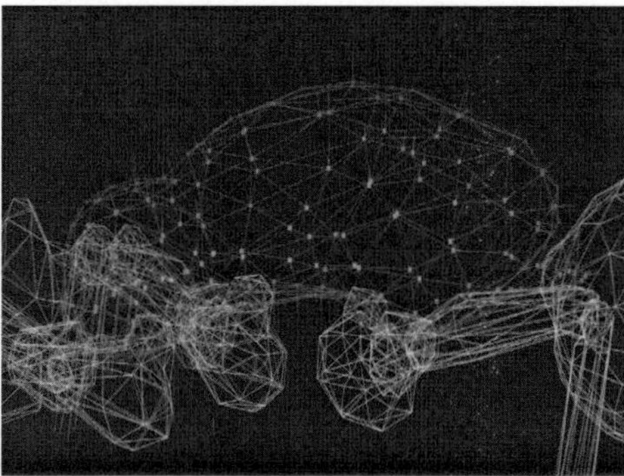

Figure 4: Dot Products of Normal Vectors and Camera Vector

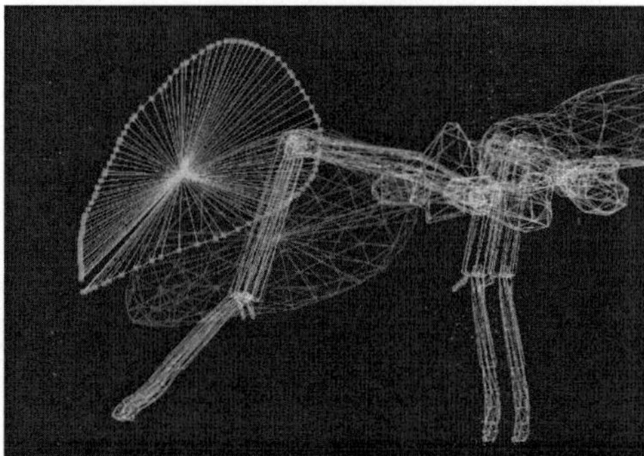

Figure 5: Control Vectors and Sketch Vectors

For each control vertex, the algorithm identifies the point in the user gesture on the image which has the closest angle to the control vertex. This is done by computing the dot product of two vectors: the control vector (a vector from the centre of the 3D shape to the control vertex) and the sketch vector (a vector from the centre of the sketched outline to the point on the gesture). The sketch vertex which has maximum dot product value with the specific control vertex is selected as the corresponding sketch point. Figure 5 visualizes control vectors and sketch vectors before global translation.

3.6. Movement Vectors

Once a corresponding sketch point for the control vertex is found, movement vectors are computed. A movement vector is a vector originating at the control vertex and directed to the corresponding sketch point. However, control vertices are not necessarily contained in the plane of the sketch points. Therefore, movement vectors have to be computed as if movements are parallel with the sketch plane. We compute the movement vector as the sum of local movement and global translation. The local movement is computed by multiplying the sketch vector by the ratio between the length of the sketch vector and control vector, and the global translation is a vector from the center of the 3D geometry to the center of the sketch.

$$\text{Movement Vector}: MV = \frac{|SV| - |CV|}{|SV|} SV + T$$

CV is a control vector
SV is the corresponding sketch vector
T is the global translation vector

Figure 6 shows an example of movement vectors. Figure 6a shows the movement vectors in side view, and figure 6b shows the same movement vectors in perspective view. The movement vectors are in 3D space, but point to the user drawn 2D sketch points. The movement direction is restricted to the sketch plane.

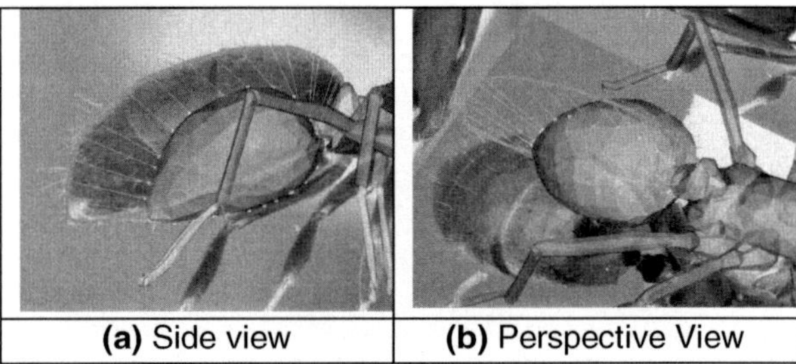

| (a) Side view | (b) Perspective View |

Figure 6: User Drawn Sketch, Control Vertices, and Movement Vectors.

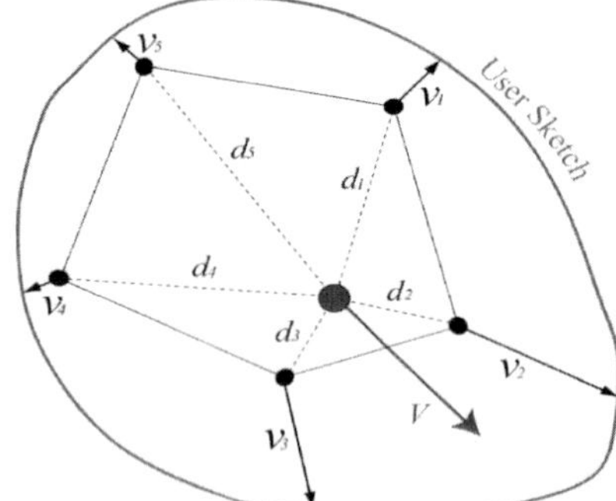

Figure 7: Vertex, Movement Vectors and Displacement Vector

After the movement vectors of all control vertices are computed, the movement is distributed throughout all vertices in the 3D mesh. The displacement vector of each vertex in the 3D mesh is computed as a weighted sum of

movement vectors. Figure 7 shows geometrical relationships between movement vectors and the displacement vector. To morph an example geometry with five vertices to the user drawn sketch shown as the green curve, the displacement vector V for the red colored vertex in the 3D mesh is computed as the weighted sum of the movement vectors $v_{1,2,...,5}$, according to their distances $d_{1,2,...,5}$.

To examine the effects of weight functions on the morphing algorithm, both parabolic and linear weight functions were tested. The parabolic weight function uses the reciprocal of relative distance from a vertex to the control vertex as the weight, and the linear weight function uses the relative distance from the vertex to the control vertex as the weight. Mathematically, the displacement vector of a vertex in the mesh is defined by the following equations. Here v_i is a movement vector for each control vertex i, V is displacement vector for each vertex and computed as a weighted sum of movement vectors:

$$V = \sum_{i=0}^{n} \frac{w_i}{W} v_i.$$

where the weight w_i for a control vertex i is defined using attenuation factor p:

$$w_i = \left(\frac{D - d_i}{d_i} \right)^p \quad \text{- Parabolic weight function}$$

and the total weight W is sum of weights across all vertices:

$$W = \sum_{i=0}^{n} w_i,$$

where D is the longest distance in all control vertices:

$$D = Max(d_i)$$
$$i=0,1,...n$$

When applied on a 3D mesh, parabolic and linear weight functions result in different shapes. Figure 8 shows the different morphed shapes of an insect abdomen using parabolic and linear weight functions. The part is morphed in the side view and observed in the top view.

The parabolic weight function places higher weight on control vertices close to the vertex, and lower weight on more distant control vertices. In this way, it preserves the shape of the original mesh, especially in the area close to control vertices. On the other hand, the linear weight

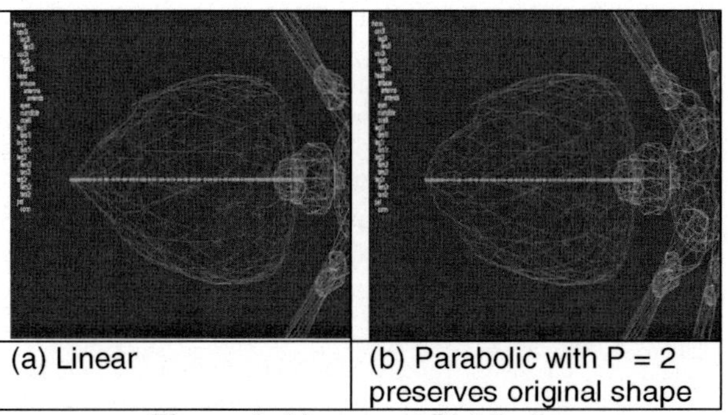

| (a) Linear | (b) Parabolic with P = 2 preserves original shape |

Figure 8: Movement Distribution

function takes a larger number of control vertices into account because of its gentle fall off, thus resulting in lower geometrical noise.

Since both functions have advantages in certain types of geometry, both are left as options. The parabolic function is used as the default weight function because it shows better morphing results in the general case. For either the parabolic or linear weight function, the attenuation factor, p, also affects the result of the morph. The weight function shows a sharper attenuation curve for higher attenuation factors, p, and the differences in restuls are shown at figure 8. Various attenuation factor values were tested and p=2 appears to balance speedy convergence with low noise in our deformation of generic models of biological organisms.

Figure 9: **Morphed Ant Model**

In figure 9, the silhouette of the 3D part is precisely matched to the bounds drawn by the user's sketch, while the topology and shape of the original geometry is preserved. The morph algorithm also supports multiple views. Figure 10 shows the user sketch and morph results applied in the side view first and then in the top view. Note the head part has already been morphed in the side view prior to the top view morph; the user can apply morphing in multiple views in any order they prefer, and continue working on significant parts until the desired shape is

obtained. As well, as shown in these figures the topology of the 3D geometry is well preserved after multiple morphings.

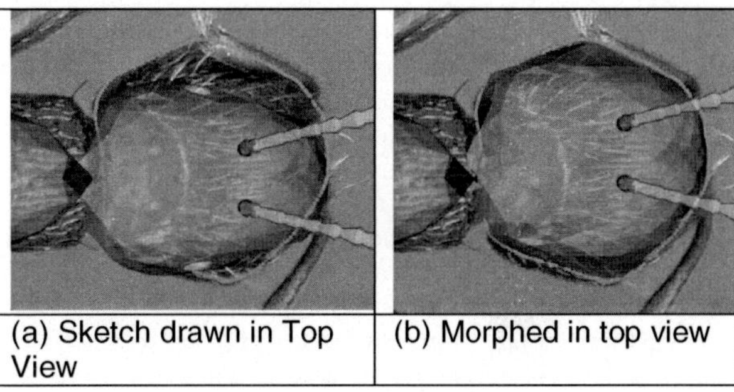

| (a) Sketch drawn in Top View | (b) Morphed in top view |

Figure 10: Adding top view image for refining the shape

3.7. Texture Extraction

Texture is an important attribute of the 3D model for realistic appearance. We utilize the symmetry of the insect model and also utilize view-dependent texture blending to use textures from multiple view images. These textures are applied to the new 3D model to provide a more realistic depiction of the subject organism.

4. Results

4.1. Modeling Algorithms

To model insects, we used 13 insect models from the virtual insect web site [VRI]. The original VRML format was converted to 3DS format using 3D Studio Max [3DS], and loaded into the system. For the ant example model which is used throughout this research, a hierarchy structure is also configured by 3D Studio Max as follows.

In only a few morphing steps by a user, the shape of each body part in a 3D insect model is matched to the target images. Textures are extracted from multiple views and blended smoothly. A new ant model is created from the generic ant model as shown in figure 11.

4.2. Supporting Biological Research

The 3D modeling application has been well-received by entomologists. There are two particular ways that entomologists feel the modeling tool will aid them in their work.

First, entomologists view the application as a high valued aid to teaching. When teaching organism classification, an appreciation of physical structures, and how the physical structures of an organism feed into its taxonomy must be communicated to students. The 3D modeling tool allows students to perceive the structural similarities and differences clearly, and provides a simple morphing algorithm to convert a generic 3D model into a model of a specific insect under examination. While 2D photos can convey similar information, the realism of a 3D perspective view will, in the view of biological educators, more clearly depict for students the structural similarities and differences of various categories (phyla, classes, order, families, and genera) of species.

In research, too, it is often less interesting to examine 2D representations of structure, whereas 3D can more compellingly allow communication and discussion during early biological research into new species identification. While more information is not present, the depiction of the information spurs more interest and is more easily described by highlighting areas and structures on a 3D model.

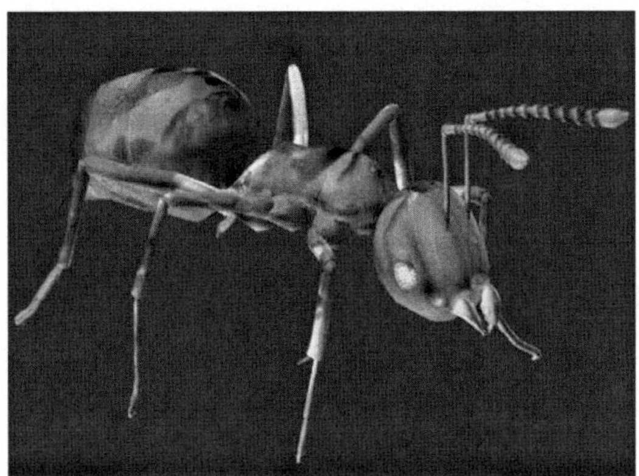

Figure 11: Final Ant Model

5.　Conclusion

In this paper, we propose a new parts, image, and model morphing application to support 3D model generation by non-3D modeling experts. The goal is to make accessible 3D models to those individuals who can make use of models without requiring them to master the intricacies of 3D modeling software. Our application has proven effective for the generation of 3D models of biological organisms, specifically focused on insect modeling.

Biology is only one area of 3D modeling, but is undoubtedly the most suited to our 3D modeling application. While engineers and artists need access to 3D models, it is true that our system has disadvantages when applied to these fields. First, engineers are currently comfortable with CAD software, multiple images, and generated, accurate 3D representations of objects. Generating near approximate, one-off models of pre-existing objects is of less interest in this domain. Similarly sculptural artists, another demographic interested in 3D models, generally seek new, novel objects to visualize, depict and create, where our tool seeks to generalize from similar structures.

Despite its focus on biological research, our application has been successful in providing biological researchers and educators with an alternative 3D modeling platform for the rapid generation of accurate 3D models of organisms. We continue to examine modifications to our algorithms, and additional application domains for these techniques.

Acknowledgements

This research was funded by the National Science Foundation, grants DBI-0234980 and IIS-0448540, and by the Natural Science and Engineering Research Council of Canada.

References

[ANTWEB] Antweb: Ants of the world. http://antweb.org.

[BV99] Blanz V., Vetter T.: A Morphable Model for the Synthesis of 3D Faces. SIGGRAPH 99 Conference Proceedings.

[BS03] Stefan Brabec and Hans-Peter Seidel: Shadow Volumes on Programmable Graphics Hardware, Eurographics 2003 (Computer Graphics Forum)

[CSS05] Cherlin J. J., Samavati F., Sousa M. C., Jorge J. A.: Sketch-based modeling with few strokes. Spring Conference on Computer Graphics 05.

[FKP04] Funkhouser T., Kazhdan M., Shilane P., Min P., Kiefer W., Tal A., Rusinkiewicz S., Dobkin D.: Modeling by Example. SIGGRAPH 04, p 652-663.

[IH03] Igarashi T., Hughes J. F.: Smooth meshes for sketch-based freeform modeling. SIGGRAPH 03.

[IMT99] Igarashi T., Matsuoka S., Tanaka H.: Teddy: A Sketching Interface for 3D Freeform Design. SIGGRAPH 99.

[NSA05] Nealen A., Sorkine O., Alexa M., Cohen-Or D.: A sketch-based interface for detail-preserving mesh editing. SIGGRAPH 05.

[SYN05] Sebe I. O., You S., Neumann U.: Rapid Part-Based 3D Modeling. ACM Symposium on Virtual Reality Software and Technology (VRST) 05.

[VRI99] Sharov A.: Virtual Insect. http://www.ento.vt.edu/~sharov/3d/virtual.html.

[TBS04] Tsang S., Balakrishnan R., Singh K., Ranjan A.: A suggestive interface for image guided 3D sketching. SIGCHI 04.

[YSP05] Yang C., Sharon D., Panne M.: Sketch-based Modeling of Parameterized Objects. SIGGRAPH 05, Sketch Session.

[ZHH96] Zeleznik R. C., Herndon K. P., Hughes J. F.: SKETCH: An Interface for Sketching 3D Scenes. SIGGRAPH 96. p. 163-170.

EUROGRAPHICS Workshop on Sketch-Based Interfaces and Modeling (2006)
Thomas Stahovich and Mario Costa Sousa (Editors)

Transformation Strokes

Aaron Severn[1], Faramarz Samavati[1] and Mario Costa Sousa[1]

[1]University of Calgary, Calgary, Canada

Abstract

In this paper, we present a sketch-based technique for specifying transformations for general models by means of a single stroke, offering a more streamlined form of user interaction. The shape of the stroke is interpreted to allow composition of translation, rotation and scaling. We extract two main directions from the input stroke using Principle Component Analysis and use them to obtain an appropriate transformation for the model. Our method helps to have a more natural and faster way of assembling 3D structures. It is general and does not depend on specific knowledge about the type of models. As such, it can fit in the majority of graphics systems or modelling techniques.

Categories and Subject Descriptors (according to ACM CCS): I.3.5 [Computer Graphics]: Computational Geometry and Object Modeling: Modeling packages

1. Introduction

Today, 3D modelling systems are used in a wide variety of applications such as designing mechanical parts, architecture, and creating scenes in animated films. Computer models have replaced traditional drawings and physical models in many areas. The demands of precision modelling have led to complex interfaces, where parameters must be carefully supplied by the users, which often require significant skill and expertise to use effectively. These systems, while effective at producing precise three dimensional models, are not well suited to applications where exact precision is not essential.

One of the key components of any 3D modelling or viewing system is user controlled transformations. Transforming models is a fundamental operation in computer graphics. Traditional systems usually support transformations through a click and drag interface, where translation, rotation, and scaling are divided into three distinct operations, or by defining complicated relationships between models. Simply a mouse click in 3D is not enough to provide a reasonable three dimensional transformation. This presents difficulties, making even simple manipulations surprisingly hard to perform([TDM01], [CSSJ05]). Positioning two models for a Boolean operation, for instance, can involve a sophisticated

set of transformations until the alignment of the models is as desired.

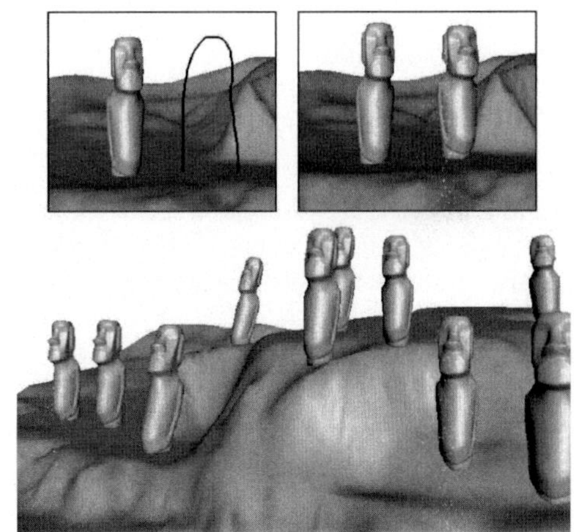

Figure 1: *A scene created in a few minutes with transformation strokes.*

We present a novel approach to performing transformations in a modelling system using a single stroke. This is a justifiable effort because a stroke provides more information than a mouse click. In addition, it not only gives a better visual impact but also approximates our regular drawing metaphor([ZHH96], [IMT99]). Our transformation stroke is designed to interpret the likely intensions of the user so that a previously difficult transformation can be performed easier. From a single stroke, we interpret the translation, rotation, and non-uniform scaling intended by the user and apply these to a model. When used in conjunction with traditional transformation interfaces our method may allow users to position models with less difficulty and effort (Figure 1).

It is possible to specify the transformation more accurately when we take into consideration more information from the models. However, our goal is to find a general method that can specify the transformation without any (or with a minimized amount of) specific knowledge about the type of models. This assumption helps to have a method general enough to be fit in any graphics system or modelling technique. On the other hand, it makes the problem harder with several ambiguities.

1.1. Related work

Few works have explored the use of simple sketch-based stroke indicators or commands for specifying linear transformations for modeling 3D objects. Pereira et al. [PJBF03] present a calligraphic sketching metaphor for a CAD/drawing system (GIDeS) providing a paper-like interaction for various modeling operations including translation. Gomis et al. [GACN04] use strokes for indicating 2D symmetry operators in a calligraphic editor for tile and textile design. Igarashi and Hughes [IH02] present a sketch-based indicator approach for putting clothes on a 3D character and manipulating them. The user paints freeform marks on the clothes that are then placed around the body so that corresponding marks match. Ijiri et al. [IOOI05] present a SBIM system used together with floral diagrams and inflorescences to provide the positional information for assembling individual flower components.

Our approach is based on a single stroke-based technique allowing translation, rotation and scaling into a single operation. We use our transformation strokes as a tool for transforming models, rather than modelling by transformation. As such, they are general and can be used in any kind of modelling.

1.2. System overview

Our transformation stroke supports manipulation of arbitrary models, freely and with respect to other models, in a three dimensional environment. We have employed it in a system that supports loading multiple mesh models, which can be manipulated and have operations performed on them such as Boolean operations and subdivision. Strokes are performed by tracing with the mouse along the intended stroke path. The mouse position is sampled at discrete intervals in order to create a polyline representation of the stroke.

Our system supports an *active model*, which can be selected by the user if desired. If an active model is selected, transformation strokes will use it as a reference for aspects of the transformation that are difficult to interpret using two dimensional input, such as the desired depth of a model.

2. Method

2.1. Stroke interpretation

A 2D stroke is not enough to determine all parameters and freedoms of a 3D transformation. We need to come up with natural and simple interpretations for ambiguities. While our system accepts and interprets any generic stroke, for clarity of understanding we can perceive the strokes to be U-shaped, with the height of the U being greater than its width (Figure 2). We need to determine three sets of information from our stroke: the target position of the model; the target orientation; and the target scale. To obtain these transformations we extract four measurements from the stroke. We find a vector from the base to the top of the U, which we call the *major axis*, and determine its magnitude, which will be used to determine the target scale. We find a vector perpendicular to the major axis in the plane of the stroke, the *minor axis*, and determine its magnitude, also for use in scaling. We use the centre of the stroke to determine the target position, and the orientation of the major axis for the target orientation.

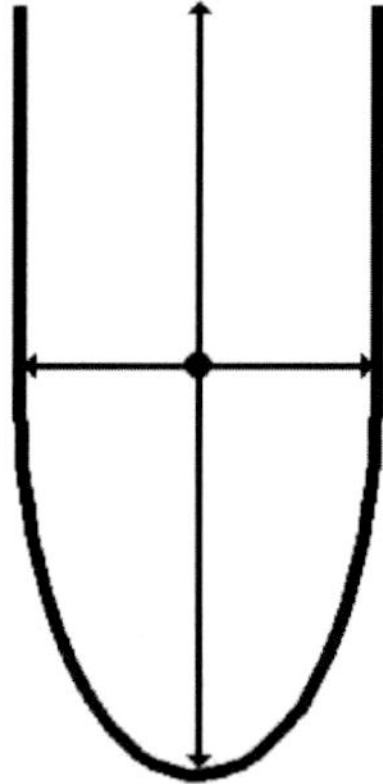

Figure 2: *Interpretation of the transformation stroke.*

The major and minor axes of the stroke are computed using principle component analysis [DH73]. We compute the covariance matrix

$$M = \frac{1}{n} \sum_{i=0}^{n-1} (P_i - C)(P_i - C)^T$$

where P_i denotes the points of the stroke, and C denotes the mean of those points. Since the stroke lies in the xy-plane, this results in a 2x2 matrix. The principle components, which will form the axes of the stroke, are the eigenvectors of M

and can be computed by solving a quadratic equation in the 2x2 case. These two orthogonal vectors are the axes of maximum and minimum variance, thus indicating the orientation of the stroke. We determine the magnitude of the axes by projecting each of the points of the stroke on to each of the axes to determine how far the stroke extends in each direction. By taking the midpoint of the extents along each axis we can determine the centre of the stroke (Figure 3).

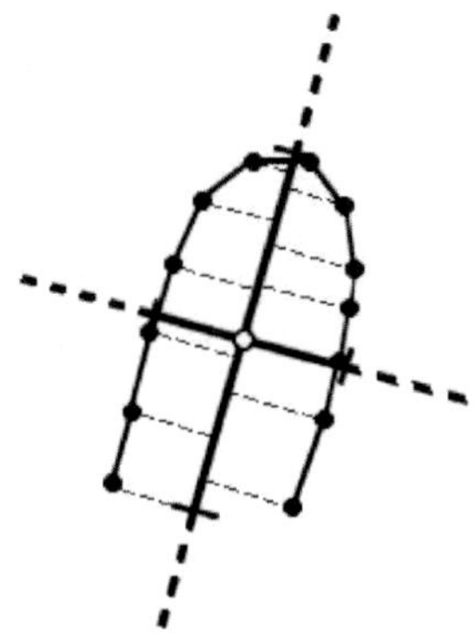

Figure 3: *Stroke extents are determined by projecting each stroke point on to the computed axes, the stroke centre is at the midpoint along each axis.*

2.2. Translation

Our translation works by moving the centre of a model to the centre of the stroke. We compute the centre of the model as the centre of an axis-aligned bounding box around the model since this is the fastest and easiest approach, and typically gives good results. Alternately, it could also be computed as the centre of an oriented bounding box, the centre of mass, or any other means that is appropriate.

Since the stroke is defined only in the xy-plane, this simple translation does not deal with the depth of the model. We make use of two heuristics for resolving this issue. The first is to simply maintain the current depth of the model. The second involves selecting another model for reference, which we call the *active model*, and using its depth.

2.2.1. Active model

When using an active model to determine the intended depth, the depth of the active model will vary across its surface. Thus we interpret the desired behaviour in three different ways.

- If the start and end points of the stroke lie over the active model (Figure 4) then we determine the stroke as follows. We cast two rays from the view point, through the start and end points of stroke, to determine where the rays enter and exit the active model. We then take the average of these four points and use its depth as the new depth of the

model that is being transformed. This method allows the user to define a region of interest in the active model, to which the transformed model should be moved.

- If the start and end points do not lie over the active model then we approximate the desired depth using the centre of a bounding box around the active model (Figure 5). Here, the active model is used as a kind of reference for the depth.
- The user is allowed to select a point on the surface of the active model, which we call the *active point*, and if this point is selected it will define the depth (Figure 6).

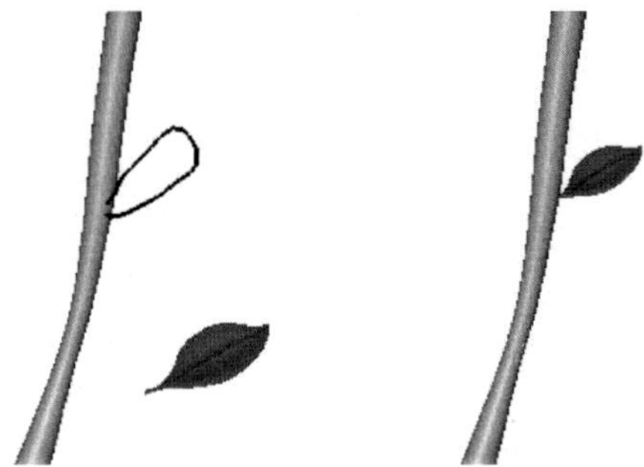

Figure 4: *When the stroke is drawn with its end points above the active model, this defines a region of interest on the active model. Here, the leaf is placed on the stem.*

Figure 5: *The active model (the sphere) is used to bring the cylinder to the front.*

Figure 6: *An active point can be used when the centre of the model doesn't provide an accurate enough depth. Here, the active point is on the left ear.*

After a depth reference is determined we project the stroke centre to the desired depth, using an appropriate projection to match up with the viewing transformation, and then compute the translation from the model centre to the stroke centre at that depth. It is important to note that simply translating the stroke centre to the desired depth often will not produce the desired result, such as when a perspective transformation is being used.

2.3. Rotation

When determining the rotation we have more degrees of freedom than what can be expressed in the stroke, thus we must choose an appropriate interpretation. The intention of our rotation is to align the longest axis of the model to the stroke's major axis. This approach gives a logical and predictable result that is useful in practice. In our default interpretation, we assume that the model will be axis-aligned in some sense, so that the longest axis of an axis-aligned bounding box will yield a meaningful orientation. This is often true of manufactured objects such as pipes or nails, but can also be true for natural objects. We determine the longest axis out of the x-, y-, and z-axes using an axis-aligned bounding box which, in the case of our system, has already been computed around each model. We have used two different methods for finding the axis of rotation. In the first, the axis of rotation is the cross product of the longest axis of the model and the major axis of the stroke, and the angle of rotation is the inverse cosine of the dot product of those same two vectors, normalized (Figure 7). In the second method we can simply use the normal to the screen as the direction of the axis. In the first method the proportion of the source and the target axes is important, while in the second method the orientation of the model towards the viewer is kept unchanged.

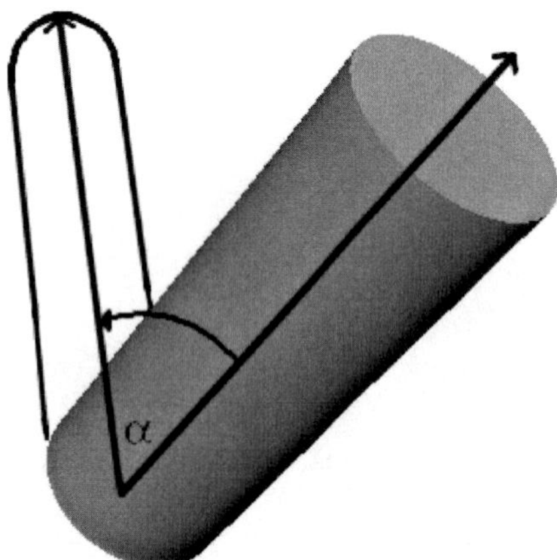

Figure 7: *Rotation from the longest axis of the model to the stroke major axis.*

We would like to be able to predict which direction the model will be oriented based on the direction of its main axis

and some property of the stroke. Here, we choose the curved portion of the U-stroke to indicate which way the major axis is pointing. Principle component analysis produces a vector in the first or fourth quadrant (having a positive x coordinate) for the axis of maximum variance, so there is a danger that our stroke's major axis will be oriented in the opposite direction of what we want. To determine whether or not this is the case, we project the start point of the stroke and a middle point of the stroke on to the major axis. If the dot product between the first point of the stroke and the major axis is greater than the dot product between a middle point and the major axis then our axis must be reversed, so we correct the orientation by multiplying the major axis by -1.

In some cases using a main axis aligned to either the x-, y-, or z-axis will perform poorly, since many freeform models are not axis-aligned. To handle these situations we also allow the user to define the main axis directly. It may seem appropriate to use the longest axis of an oriented bounding box around a model when computing a rotation, however the axis-aligned approach performs well in many common cases. It is also quicker and works better with our scaling method, in which scaling is applied only along the x-, y-, or z-axes, thus we prefer to use an axis from the standard basis to define the rotation.

2.4. Scaling

Scaling is also a difficult transformation to fit into our framework for transformation strokes. When combined with rotation it creates an ambiguity: the model could either be scaled to the dimensions suggested by the stroke without rotation, or it could be rotated first and then scaled. Also, since our two dimensional strokes are intended to represent the non-uniform scaling of a three dimensional model we are missing information along one axis.

We have resolved the first problem by choosing to always rotate first and then scale. This choice is appropriate since it results in a close aspect ratio between the original model and the transformed version, which is typically what the user would expect. The second problem is resolved by assuming that the model should only be stretched or compressed along the longest axis, while the aspect ratio between the other two-axes should be maintained. We only need two scaling factors to define such a scale, which is what we have from the stroke.

Initially, we use the magnitude of the stroke major axis to scale along the longest axis of the model. This is the same axis that we used to rotate the model. The scale factor will be the magnitude of the stroke major axis divided by the magnitude of the longest model axis. This scale stretches or compresses the model to the same length as the stroke.

Next, we determine the aspect ratio of the two remaining axes, v_0 and w_0, which is calculated as $a = |v_0|/|w_0|$. We intend to scale the diagonal of the rectangle defined by v_0

and w_0 to the magnitude of the stroke minor axis (Figure 8), we will call this magnitude d. Thus, we can solve for the scaled magnitude of v_0 and w_0

$$|w| = \sqrt{d^2/(a^2 + 1)}$$

$$|v| = a * |w|$$

where v and w represent the scaled vectors. We then compute the scaling factors as $|v|/|v_0|$ and $|w|/|w_0|$ respectively.

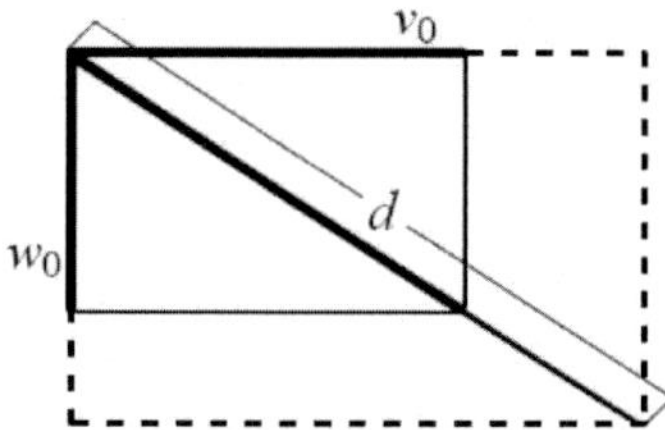

Figure 8: *We scale the diagonal of the shorter two sides to the magnitude of the stroke minor axis.*

3. Results and discussion

We have used our transformation stroke to position and re-size models in a wide variety of modelling applications. Figure 1 depicts a scene where ten statues were positioned on a landscape using only ten strokes. It makes use of the active model feature to position the models so that their bases are located on the part of the terrain lying under the stroke end points. Since precise positioning of the statues is unnecessary to create the desired scene (and may even be detrimental to the realistic appearance) a sketch-based approach works well.

Transformation strokes can be used to quickly place models. We have used them to assemble larger models from their parts, for both natural objects such as the dead tree in Figure 9, which was created from a single simple primitive, and the vine in Figure 10, and mechanical objects such as the various gears shown assembled in Figure 11. Note that the gears were placed without using scaling since the parts were already precisely sized.

Our method is best suited to models that have a well defined main axis, which is true of many real world objects. This property can be seen in man-made objects, such as nails and cars, and also in natural objects like leaves and trees (Figure 12). The ability to specify a user-defined main axis extends the usefulness of our transformation stroke to additional objects, however those where no reasonable main axis exists, such as spherical objects, present difficulties.

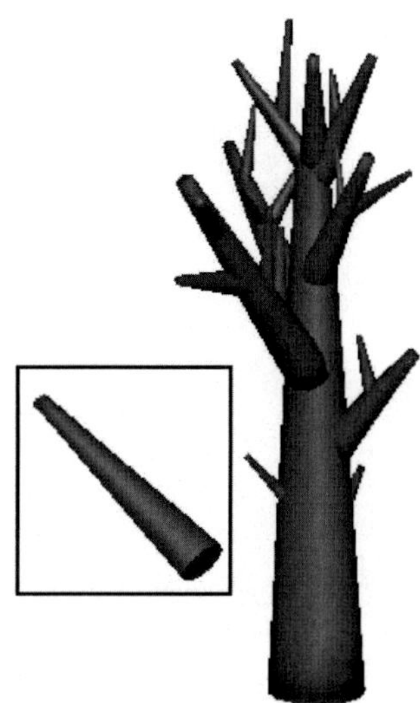

Figure 9: *A dead tree is constructed by positioning copies of a primitive using strokes.*

Figure 10: *Many leaves can be quickly added to a stem to produce a vine.*

4. Conclusion and future work

We have presented a stroke based method for performing transformations in a modelling system. Our transformation stroke is capable of interpreting the desired translation, rotation, and non-uniform scaling in many common situations. By building a complex transformation from a single stroke, we allow for quicker and easier manipulation of models than

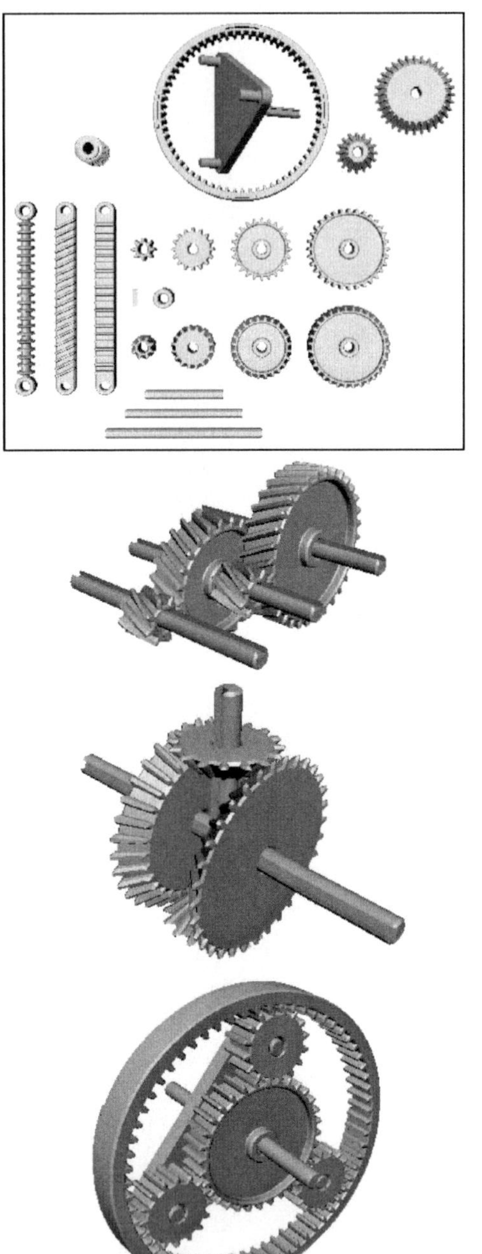

Figure 11: *The gears were assembled using transformation strokes in conjunction with standard transformation techniques.*

was previously possible with a mouse. This transformation stroke is relatively easy to implement and does not involve a high computational cost.

While our transformation stroke interprets many of the desired manipulations of a user, it is not yet comprehensive.

Figure 12: *Many real world objects have a well defined main axis, such as the ones shown here.*

Our stroke is best suited for models with a well defined main axis, and while this encompasses a wide variety of models, further work is required to produce a transformation stroke that will interpret the user's intentions under more circumstances. Although using a bounding box's axes and the major axis of the stroke can provide a useful default interpretation of the user's intension, it is not always correct and requires additional information that might be directly supplied by the user. However, it would be better if all necessary properties could be determined automatically by the system.

Many aspects of our system involve choosing an appropriate interpretation among a variety of possibilities. These choices have a profound impact on the behaviour of our transformation strokes, in particular for rotation and scaling. While we have attempted to choose the best interpretation for all ambiguous situations, some other interpretation may prove to be more appropriate. These alternate interpretations require further study to determine the best choice. User studies need to be conducted to determine the best interpretations and to assess the overall effectiveness of the method.

References

[CSSJ05] CHERLIN J. J., SAMAVATI F., SOUSA M. C., JORGE J. A.: Sketch-based modeling with few strokes. In *21st Spring Conference on Computer Graphics* (2005).

[DH73] DUDA R. O., HART P. E.: *Pattern Classification and Scene Analysis.* John Wiley and Sons, 1973.

[GACN04] GOMIS J. M., ALBERT F., CONTERO M., NAYA F.: Calligraphic editor for textile and tile pattern design system. In *Proceedings of SmartGraphics '04. Lecture Notes in Computer Science vol. 3031* (2004), pp. 114–120.

[IH02] IGARASHI T., HUGHES J. F.: Clothing manipulation. In *15th Annual Symposium on User Interface Software and Technology, ACM UIST* (2002), pp. 91–100.

[IMT99] IGARASHI T., MATSUOKA S., TANAKA. H.: Teddy: A sketching interface for 3d freeform design. In *SIGGRAPH 99 Conference Proceedings* (1999).

[IOOI05] IJIRI T., OKABE M., OWADA S., IGARASHI T.: Floral diagrams and inflorescences: Interactive flower modeling using botanical structural constraints. *ACM Transactions on Graphics (Proc. of SIGGRAPH '05) 24*, 3 (2005), 720–726.

[PJBF03] PEREIRA J. P., JORGE J. A., BRANCO V. A., FERREIRA F. N.: Calligraphic interfaces: Mixed metaphors for design. In *Interactive Systems: Design, Specification and Verification, DSV-IS 2003 Proceedings* (2003), pp. 154–170.

[TDM01] TOLBA O., DORSEY J., MCMILLAN L.: A projective drawing system. In *ACM Symposium on Interactive 3D Graphics* (2001).

[ZHH96] ZELEZNIK R., HERNDON K., HUGHES J.: Sketch: An interface for sketching 3d scenes. In *SIGGRAPH 96 Conference Proceedings* (1996).

EUROGRAPHICS Workshop on Sketch-Based Interfaces and Modeling (2006)
Thomas Stahovich and Mario Costa Sousa (Editors)

A Sketching Interface for 3D Modeling of Polyhedrons

D. C. Ku, S. F. Qin and D. K. Wright

School of Engineering and Design, Brunel University, Middlesex, UB8 3PH, UK

Abstract

We present an intuitive and interactive freehand sketching interface for 3D polyhedrons reconstruction. The interface mimics sketching with pencil on paper and takes freehand sketches as input directly. The sketching environment is natural by allowing sketching with discontinuous, overlapping and multiple strokes. The input sketch is a natural line drawing with hidden lines removed that depicts a 3D object in an isometric view. The line drawing is interpreted by a series of 2D tidy-up processes to produce a vertex-edge graph for 3D reconstruction. A novel reconstruction approach based on three-line-junction analysis and planarity constraint is then used to approximate the 3D geometry and topology of the graph. The reconstructed object can be transformed so that it can be viewed from different viewpoints for interactive design or as immediate feedback to the designers. A new sketch can then be added to the existing 3D object, and reconstructed into 3D by referring to the existing 3D object from the current viewpoint. The incremental modeling enables a 3D object to be reconstructed from multiple sketching sessions from different viewpoints. However, the interface is limited to reconstructing trihedrons from sketches without T-junctions to avoid ambiguity in the hidden topology determination.

Categories and Subject Descriptors (according to ACM CCS): I.3.6 [Methodology and Techniques]: Interaction techniques I.3.5 [Computational Geometry and Object Modeling]: Geometric algorithms, languages, and systems

1. Introduction

Freehand sketching is a fast and efficient way to visualise an idea in conceptual design. A sketch assists designers by allowing their mental images to be expressed externally for further mental synthesis. With the introduction of faster computers, there is a stronger interest in using a CAD system for conceptual design that allows designers to sketch a series of drawings and transfer them to 3D models automatically. There are many advantages to such a computerized system. Some of these relate to how the sketch data is stored (i.e., digital). For example, recent advancements in data storage make it relatively inexpensive to store many sketches in a single data drive (e.g., hard disk). Furthermore, with digital data, sharing and communication of ideas through sketches can be performed easily without loss of information (e.g., strokes sketching sequence, sketching speed and pressure).

However, currently available commercial CAD systems, such as SolidEdge and Pro/ENGINEER, cannot create 3D objects directly from freehand sketches. In particular, extensive menu selections are needed to create a 3D object. Such a

process is not as intuitive as sketching with pencil on paper, and hence is not suitable for conceptual design.

In this paper, we present an interactive freehand sketching interface to assist the designers in the early design stage. The interface is intuitive, allowing the designers to sketch out their desired shapes without enforcing gesture sketching, while avoiding excessive menu selection that adds overhead to the design process. In addition, it provides a more natural sketching environment by enabling discontinuous strokes and overtracing, and interpreting natural line drawing (hidden line removed). A novel 3D reconstruction approach is developed to interpret inaccurate online freehand sketches and reconstruct into 3D objects. The 3D object can be transformed by designers to evaluate their design from different viewpoints. The interface is interactive so that designers can work on the sketches progressively. Finally, the reconstructed objects are rendered in sketchy style that have the appearance similar to the original sketches. Figure 1 shows an example of progressive 3D object reconstruction from incremental freehand sketching along the processing pipeline of the prototype system. Figure 1(a) shows an initial input freehand sketch. Figure 1(b) shows the line drawing drawing from the vertex-edge graph after 2D tidy-up. Figure 1(c) is the 3D object after the 3D geometry approximation and hidden topology determination. Figure 1(d) shows the transformed object from a different viewpoint rendered in sketchy style. Figure 1(e) shows the object from another viewpoint with new sketches added into the scene. Figure 1(f) shows the updated object with the new sketches reconstructed into 3D. Figure 1(g-h) show the object after several sketching and reconstruction sessions.

There are always ambiguities in hidden topology determination from a natural line drawing because there are infinite possible hidden topology interpretations. However, we have chosen the simplest interpretation, although it might not always be the most plausible. The prototype system is limited to line drawing with T-junction to minimise the ambiguities in hidden topology determination. To date, there is no general solution to determine hidden topology from such line drawing [VMS05]. However, the objects with T-junction can be modelled from incremental reconstruction with multiple sketching sessions.

2. Related Works

There is extensive research in 3D modelling systems based on freehand sketching. It can be grouped into three approaches, based on the sketch interface and 3D reconstruction algorithms utilised by the systems.

1. *Gesture-sketching*: Gestural sketching interprets freehand sketches in a specific way so that some sketching gestures actually mean the 3D reconstruction commands, besides being the objects profile lines. This approach has the advantage of being able to reconstruct 3D objects almost instantly without sophisticated 3D reconstruction algorithms. Zeleznik et al. [ZHH96] was the first to introduce sketching gestures for 3D object reconstruction. [EHBE97] uses a combination of gesture and graph-based geometric constraints to reconstruct 3D objects. In [QWJ00], a system based on fuzzy knowledge is developed to infer user's sketching intentions. SMART-PAPER [SC04] uses a combination of gesture and modified optimization proposed by [LS96] to reconstruct 3D objects. [IMT99] extended the method to model objects with free-form surfaces.

   Although the systems enable direct 3D object reconstruction in real-time from freehand sketches, they are limited in providing a natural sketching interface. Users cannot sketch freely in the gesture-based systems as some of the sketch gestures are interpreted as operation commands rather than sketch contents. Meanwhile, users need to learn and memorise the gestures in advance, and adopt to the associated sketching sequence. Furthermore, new gestures are needed for new objects and must be designed carefully to avoid repetition. Eventually, users will be loaded with too many gestures and get confused.

2. *Geometric correlations approach (analytic heuristic)*: Lipson and Shiptalni [LS02] introduced an optimisation-based 3D reconstruction approach based on geometric correlations between a 3D object and its projection on a 2D plane. Company et al. [CCCP04] improved the approach by introducing tentative model and regularities categorization in the optimisation algorithm. Oh and Kim [OK03] modified the approach by acquiring correct sequence of line sketching.

   Although the systems avoid setting threshold values in decision-making (e.g., parallel and perpendicular lines), the optimisation process is computationally expensive. Furthermore, finding the global minima during the optimisation process still remains a challenge in the implementation of the approach. It fails to generate the most plausible 3D objects when the process fails to reach its global minima. The overall response speed is slowed down by the optimisation process, which makes it inappropriate for interactive sketch-based applications. In [MKL05], an angular distribution graph (ADG) of strokes is used to obtain a preliminary estimation of the shape of the objects. This reduces the complexity of the optimisation method and improves the reconstruction speed. However, it only works well with drawings of objects whose edges predominantly conform to some overall orthogonal axis system.

3. *Perceptual approach*: Lamb and Bandopadhay [LB90] proposed an approach that reconstructs 3D objects from line drawings along the identified principal axis in the axonometric view. A junction is chosen as the 3D reference. The 3D vertices for other junctions are then propagated along the associated axis, referring to the reference junction. Digital Clay [SG00] implemented the algorithm to reconstruct 3D objects from freehand sketches. [CNJC03, NJC*02] extended the approach by using an axonometric inflation method to reconstruct quasi-normalon objects.

   The systems are insusceptible to inaccuracies in the freehand sketches and always return meaningful 3D objects. However, ambiguities can exist in some cases when applying the heuristic perceptive rules. Another limitation is that the approach is only applicable to objects with edges parallel to the principal 3D axes, with vertices lying on an oblique plane that can be identified, or where a symmetry rule can be used to obtain the unknown vertex.

In general, the development of an intuitive sketching interface for conceptual design remains a challenge that has yet to be fully addressed.

3. 3D Modelling Approach

The proposed sketch-based 3D modelling method interprets sketches in an isometric view, which is the preferred viewpoint of most designers. The input is a freehand sketch that is

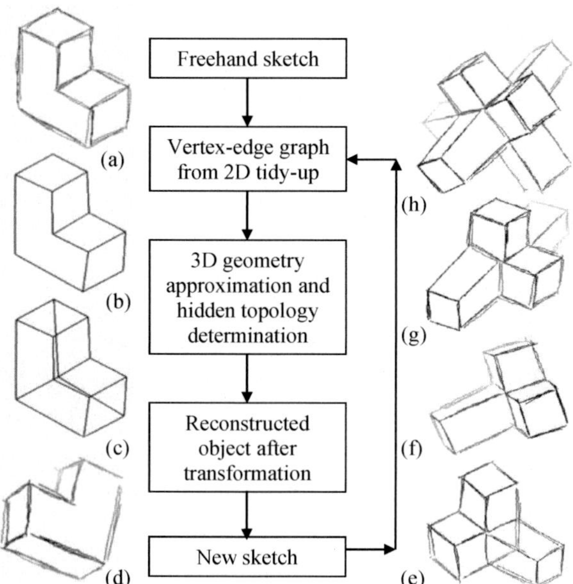

Figure 1: *The processing pipeline of the prototype sketching system.*

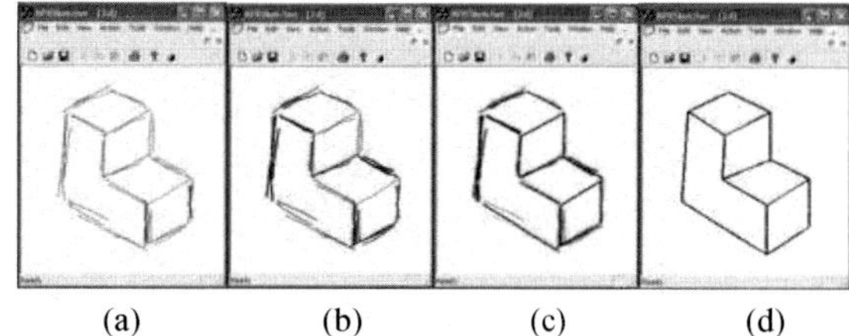

Figure 2: *An example of the 2D tidy-up: (a)Initial sketch; (b)strokes are grouped into segments, which are indicated by different colour; (c)strokes are fitted into parametric lines; (d)the line drawing generated from the vertex-edge graph after 2D tidy-up processing.*

captured through a calligraphic interface (Figure 2(a)). The sketch with overtracing is interpreted by a series of tidy-up processes to produce a vertex-edge graph. The graph consists of 2D coordinates and their connectivity of tidied-up line segments from the sketched strokes. The tidy-up process consists of four stages: stroke classification, strokes grouping and fitting, 2D tidy-up with endpoint clustering, and in-context interpretation. Figure 2(d) shows the output after the 2D tidy-up process. The overtracing strokes are grouped into the appropriate segments by grouping process (Figure 2(b)). The grouped strokes are least-square fitted to obtain parametric equations (Figure 2(c)). The endpoint clustering ensures the corresponding edge endpoints meet together and loops are closed formed in the vertex-edge graph (Figure 2(d)). The in-context interpretation ensures that the graph has no 'open' endpoints, i.e., a line drawing depicting a 3D geometry has no unconnected endpoints (more details are discussed in [KQW06]).

After that, a 3D object is reconstructed from the graph. The reconstruction process involves reference junction determination, three-line-junction analysis, vertices approximation, hidden topology determination and planarity enforcement. The approach is not computationally expensive, thus it is simple, easy to implement and able to generate output almost instantaneously. Similar to the perceptual approach that uses the chain propagation process, the proposed approach always returns meaningful 3D objects as output. It is able to reconstruct non-symmetrical, non-perpendicular and non-axis-aligned objects. The characteristics of the reconstruction approach allow 3D objects to be modelled in-

crementally from multiple sketching sessions. The 3D objects can then be transformed so that it can be viewed from different viewpoints with an appearance similar to the original sketches.

3.1. Reference Junction Determination

The proposed 3D reconstruction approach begins with the identification of edge circuits from the vertex-edge graph that corresponds to actual faces in 3D object. For a natural line drawing with the hidden lines removed, a 3D face corresponds to a non-self-intersecting closed contour without internal circuit [LF92]. It is followed by selection of a reference junction in the sketch plane to be set as the 3D reference. The junction is selected based on the following criteria:

1. The junction consists of only three lines. The reference junction needs to be a junction with three lines so that the three-line-junction analysis can be applied to the line drawing.
2. The junction consists of only three lines. The reference junction needs to be a junction with three lines so that the three-line-junction analysis can be applied.
3. The junction with the longest lines. Longer lines are taken to be more important than shorter lines in the sketch. Effects due to the dimensions represented by the longer lines are more prominent compared to that of the shorter lines. As such, we start the reconstruction process from the longer lines to minimise the deviation while approximating the vertices for the line drawing. Let the lines in a junction be represented by vectors, $\vec{L}_i \mid i = 1, 2, 3$. The line with the shortest length is $L_{short} = min(|\vec{L}_i|)$. The junction that satisfies this criterion is the junction with the longest L_{short}. The longer shortest-line in the junction minimises the deviation. Such selection ensures the junction with the three individual longer lines to be selected as the reference.
4. The junction with lines most aligned to the projection

axes (x, y and z in Figure 3). That is, the junction with

$$max\left(\sum_{i=1}^{3} max\left|\left(\vec{L}_i \;\middle|\; \begin{matrix} \vec{L}_i.\vec{x} \\ \vec{L}_i.\vec{y} \\ \vec{L}_i.\vec{z} \end{matrix}\right)\right|\right)$$

The selected reference junction is set as (0, 0, 0). The three-line-junction analysis will be applied to the junction to approximate the vertices at the opposite end of the lines.

3.2. Relationship between 2D sketch plane and 3D space

In this section, we identify the relationship of a vertex in 3D world coordinate system and its isometric projection. The relationship allows a line segment in the 2D plane to be interpreted as a corresponding 3D components that give a 3D vertex. Let the 2D sketch plane defined in (u, v) unit. In the isometric projection, the principal axes of the 3D world coordinate system X, Y, Z are projected as x, y, z (Figure 3). The y-axis is parallel with the v-axis, the x and the z-axis are $30°$ below the u-axis from the origin.

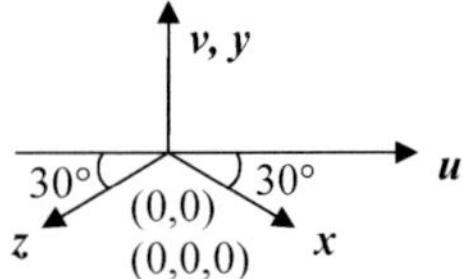

Figure 3: *The axes of the 2D sketching plane and the 3D world coordinate system in the isometric projection.*

A three-line-junction in the sketch represents a three-edge-corner on a 3D object. A three-line-junction with the isometric lines, i.e. lines that are parallel to the projection axes, represents a perpendicular corner. An edge in 3D can be represented by a vector, $\vec{E} = w\vec{X} + h\vec{Y} + d\vec{Z}$, with w, h and d representing width, height and depth in the world coordinate system, respectively. The length of the edges shown in the isometric projection is approximately 0.8165 times shorter than the actual length of the edges on the object itself. In the isometric projection, the vector $\vec{E}$ becomes

$$\vec{L} = a\vec{x} + b\vec{y} + c\vec{z}, \tag{1}$$

with $a = 0.8165w$, $b = 0.8165h$ and $c = 0.8165d$ (Figure 4).

In the 2D sketch plane, a line represented by a vector $\vec{L}$ (Figure 4) can be derived as follows:

$$\vec{L} = i\vec{u} + j\vec{v}, \tag{2}$$

where i and j are the values of the associated 2D vectors, $\vec{u}$

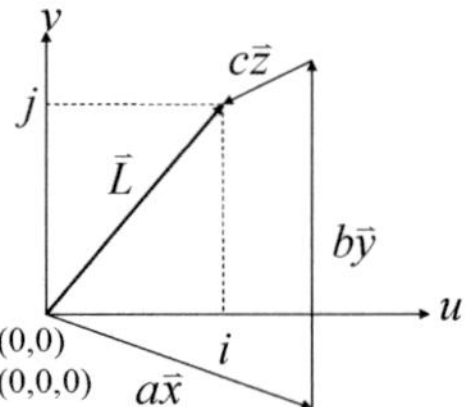

Figure 4: *A vector $\vec{L}$ in 2D and 3D vectors.*

and $\vec{v}$. From equation (1) and (2), decomposition of the vector $\vec{L}$ to its vertical and horizontal components results with the following:

$$i = a\cos 30° - c\cos 30°, \tag{3}$$

$$j = -a\sin 30° + b - c\sin 30°. \tag{4}$$

For the isometric lines, two of the unknown a, b or c are zeros and the 3D vertices of the lines can be calculated from the equation (3) and (4). However, for non-isometric lines, all unknowns are non-zeros. With only two equations available, there is no direct solution to the values. We introduce a novel approach to approximate the values in the following section.

3.3. Three-line-junction Analysis and Assumptions

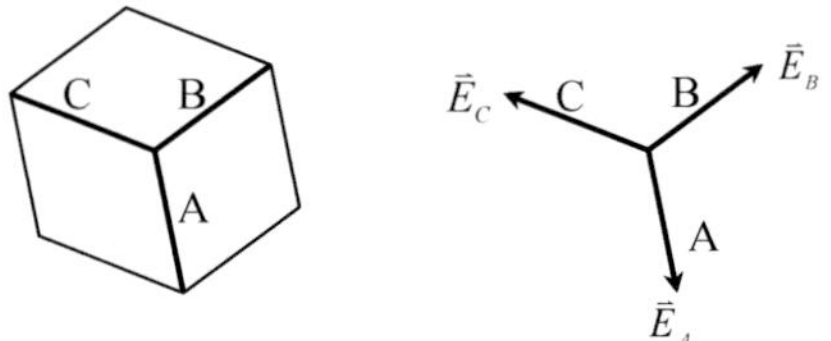

Figure 5: *A three-lines-junctions in a 2D sketch.*

Vertical edges in 3D are more likely to be drawn as vertical lines in 2D sketches based on observation by [LS96]. In a three-line-junction (Figure 5), the line with the greatest slope, line A, is assumed to have $|b_A| \gg |a_A|$ and $|b_A| \gg |c_A|$. Therefore, eliminating either c_A or a_A has little effect on the vertex approximation. That is, the line A is simplified as lying on the XY-plane or the YZ-plane:

$$\vec{L}_{A1} = a_A\vec{x} + b_{A1}\vec{y}$$

or

$$\vec{L}_{A2} = b_{A2}\vec{y} + c_A\vec{z}.$$

With the above assumption, the solution that generates the

greater b_A value is selected. Line B and C in the junction (Figure 5) are assumed to have least change in the height compare to the line A, which means $|b_A| \gg |b_{B,C}|$. We simplify the solution for the line B and C as lying on the *XZ*-plane,

$$\vec{L}_{B,C} = a_{B,C}\vec{x} + c_{B,C}\vec{z}.$$

Substituting the equation (3) and (4) into the above equations, the value a, b and c can be calculated. The vetices for the lines in the junction can be determined by using the appropriate equations from the above, based on their orientation in the junction.

Note that there is no assumption of the junction being perpendicular, i.e., the line A is not set perpendicular to the line B and C, and the line B is not set perpendicular to the line C.

3.4. Vertices Approximation

Having selected the reference junction and approximated the vertices for the associated lines, the 3D face equations for the faces touching the junction can be calculated. From the face equations, we can approximate the vertices for the rest of the junctions in the faces. Let a 3D face equation be $px + qy + rz = s$. The 3D vertex for a point in the face with coordinates (i, j) is

$$\begin{bmatrix} x \\ y \\ z \end{bmatrix} = \begin{bmatrix} p & q & r \\ 0.7071 & 0 & 0.7071 \\ 0.4082 & 0.8165 & -0.4082 \end{bmatrix}^{-1} \begin{bmatrix} s \\ i \\ j \end{bmatrix}.$$

After the vertices in the faces touching the reference junction are obtained, the 3D geometric approximation can be propagated to adjacent faces. The vertices for the adjacent faces can be obtained by repeating the above process as long as there are at least three vertices known for the faces. The process is repeated until the vertices for all junctions in the line drawing are obtained. There could be more than one vertex for a junction calculated from the touching faces, the junction will be assigned to the average of the vertices.

3.5. Hidden Topology Determination

Mathematically, there are infinite hidden topology interpretations for a natural line drawing. We assume the simplest possible objects from the sketches by assuming that every front face and hidden face in the objects meets at an occluding edge.

Determination of the hidden topology generally involves interpretation of junctions. The junctions give information about the existence of hidden edges. To simplify the analysis, the system is limited to interpret trihedrons. There are exactly three lines (front and hidden edges included) connecting to a complete junction in the line drawings.

The analysis starts by searching through junctions in the line drawing. The junctions formed with only two lines are identified. The two-line-junction is the junction with a hidden edge blocked by other parts of the object in the current viewpoint. Two two-line-junction indicating a hidden edge, three two-line-junction indicating a hidden vertex of the object. The hidden edge is the edge connecting the two two-line-junction. For the object with a hidden vertex, the hidden face equations can be calculated from the visible vertices of the faces in the sketch. The hidden vertex is the intersection point of the three hidden faces. Geometry symmetry and mirror are used for the hidden topology determination when there are more than one hidden vertex (also see [VMS04]).

3.6. Planarity Enforcement

A closed contour without internal circuit in a line drawing represents a face in a 3D object, and the contour formed by straight-lines represents a 3D planar face. The vertices approximated in the sections 3.4 might not lie on the associated planar faces. The errors can be caused by the imperfections in the freehand sketches, e.g., the parallel edges are not sketched parallel, the edges that are supposed to be the same length are not sketched to have the equivalent length, and others. We apply the unambiguous planarity constraint to correct the errors on the reconstructed objects. The best-fit face equations are computed from the data points as in [LS96]. The inaccurate vertices are adjusted to form planar faces. Figure 6 shows an example of the reconstructed object before and after the planarity enforcement.

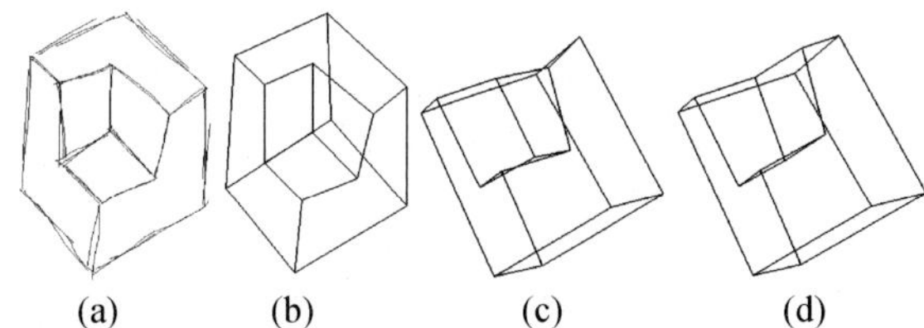

Figure 6: *An example of a reconstructed object before and after planarity enforcement; (a) initial sketch; (b) reconstructed 3D object; (c) the object before the planarity enforcement; (d) the object after the planarity enforcement.*

The new vertex is obtained by solving the three face equations of the faces connecting to the associated junction. Let the faces connecting to the junction represented by $F_i | i = 1, 2, 3$ with face equation $p_i x + q_i y + r_i z = s_i$. The intersection vertex of the faces is

$$\begin{bmatrix} x' \\ y' \\ z' \end{bmatrix} = \begin{bmatrix} p_1 & q_1 & r_1 \\ p_2 & q_2 & r_2 \\ p_3 & q_3 & r_3 \end{bmatrix}^{-1} \begin{bmatrix} s_1 \\ s_2 \\ s_3 \end{bmatrix}.$$

Although the best geometry might not be approximated through the process, the approach ensures a consistent (though not always accurate) approximation. We repeat the reconstruction process from different reference junction to obtain different sets of the 3D vertices, and then have the plane equation calculated from the sets of vertices to minimize the inaccuracies.

3.7. Progressive 3D Reconstruction from Incremental Sketching

Referring to Figure 1, the new input sketch received after the first 3D object reconstruction will be tidied-up to generate a new vertex-edge graph. A new 3D object will be generated from the graph with the same reconstruction procedures as discussed in the previous sections. However, the new 3D object is reconstructed with a new 3D reference, which is on a local reference system (the 3D reference for the first object is taken to be the global reference). The new object needs to be incorporated with the first object in the global reference system to be interpreted in a scene. With the objects in the same viewpoint, changing from the local to the global reference system is simply by translating the new object by the difference between the reference systems. The new object needs to be attached to the first object at the appropriate face. We assume the new object is always added to the visible part of the first object, thus limiting the possible attaching face to visible faces for the first object and hidden faces for the new object. We further apply the condition that only a face from the new object is attaching to a face on the first object. The two faces will be touching each other only when they are overlapping in the sketch and parallel in 3D. However, the perfectly parallel faces seldom present in practical, especially the objects are reconstructed from inaccurate freehand sketches. Let the normal vectors for the visible faces on the first object, $N_i = (l_i, m_i, n_i) \mid i = 1, 2, 3 \ldots$; and the normal vector for hidden faces on the new object, $N_j = (l_j, m_j, n_j) \mid j = 1, 2, 3 \ldots$. The attaching faces are the faces with

$$max \left(\frac{l_i l_j + m_i m_j + n_i n_j}{\sqrt{l_i^2 + m_i^2 + n_i^2} \sqrt{l_j^2 + m_j^2 + n_j^2}} \right).$$

After the parallel faces pair is identified, the overlapping point of the faces in the sketch is identified. The point might be a junction for the new object in the first object face's boundary and vice versa, or an intersection point of the new and first object edges. The global vertex for the overlapping point can be calculated by referring to the first object; meanwhile the local vertex for the point is obtained by referring to the new object. The difference between the global and the local vertex is the translation needed to incoporate the new object with the old object.

Finally, the attaching face on the new object is adjusted so that it is lying on the attaching face of the first object. After this, the two objects are using the global reference system

and can be treated as a uniform scene during transformation. The sketching and reconstruction process is repetitive.

3.8. Personalised Non-photorealistic Rendering (PNPR)

The reconstructed objects are rendered in non-photorealistic rendering (NPR). The silhouettes of the objects are rendered with the sketched strokes, which give the objects an appearance similar to the input sketches (PNPR). The strokes are also rendered in various grey tones to provide depth cues for the 3D objects, with darker tones indicating the closer end and lighter tones indicating the further end.

4. Results

Figure 7 shows examples of the objects reconstructed with the prototype system. The results show that the system is able to reconstruct non-symmetrical, non-perpendicular and non-axis-aligned objects from freehand sketches. It is also able to reconstruct 3D objects incrementally from multiple sketching sessions, as shown in Figure 1(a-h). Figure 8 shows more objects reconstructed by incremental modelling.

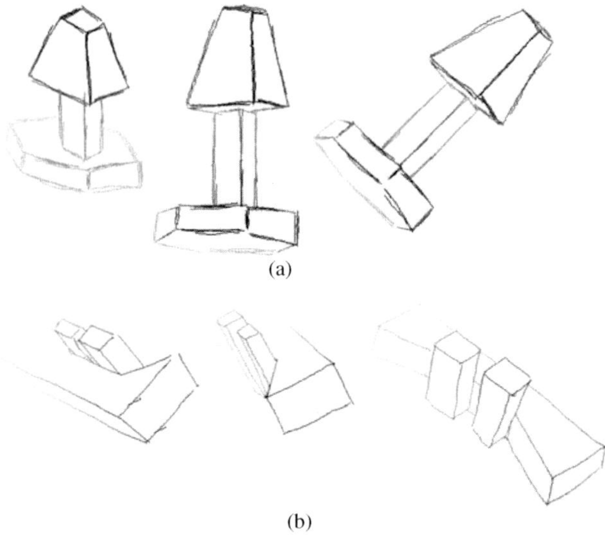

(a)

(b)

Figure 8: *Examples of 3D objects reconstructed from incremental sketching with our prototype sketching system.*

5. Discussion

The sketching interface presented in this paper aids designers in the early design stage by reconstructing 3D objects from freehand sketches. It helps designers to compare the spatial relations and relative sizes of objects. The interface provides a natural sketching input environment by handling the freehand sketches with overtracing. Designers can sketch over existing sketches to enhance, complete or correct a line.

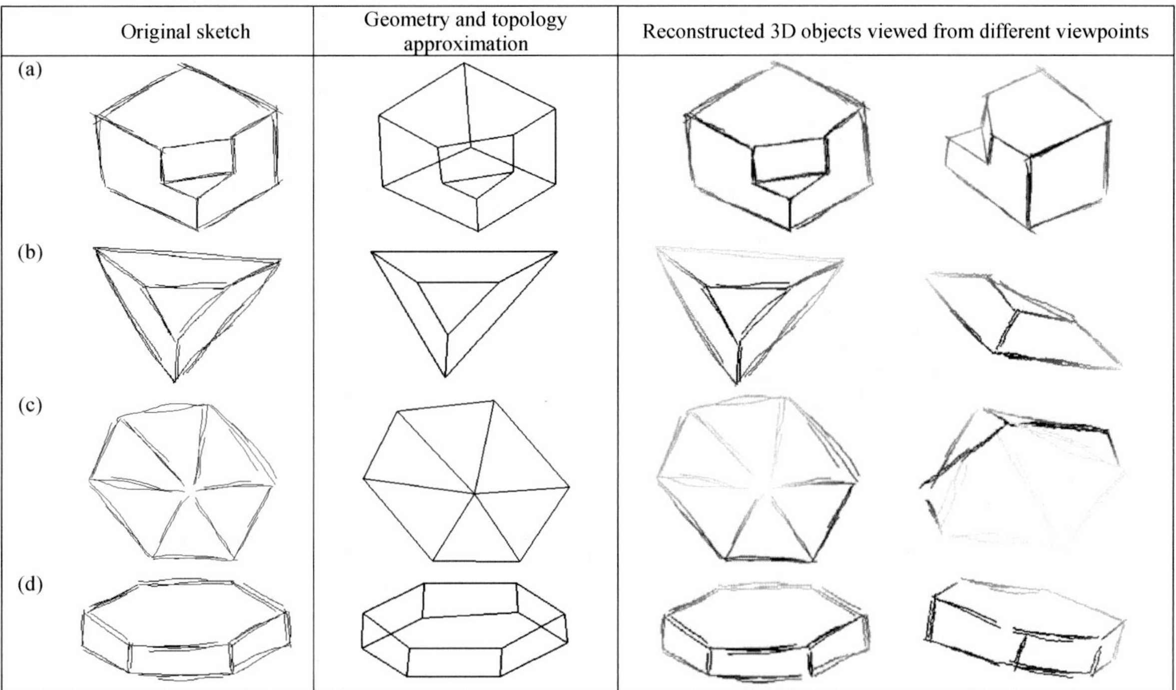

Figure 7: *Examples of 3D objects reconstructed from freehand sketches with our prototype sketching system: (a) non-symmetrical object; (b) non-perpendicular object; (c-d) non-axis-aligned objects.*

Sketches are tidied-up to extract the vertex-edge graph that represents the connectivity of the sketched strokes.

The sketch is then reconstructed into a 3D object by a novel 3D reconstruction algorithm. The reconstruction algorithm utilised by the system is computationally inexpensive, simple and robust compared to algorithms involving many computational parameters and extensive searches, e.g. compliance function and optimization processing [LS96, CCCP04, OK03, MKL05]. In addition, it can be applied to more objects compared to the perceptual-based systems [LB90, SG00, CNJC03, NJC*02], i.e. it interprets not only normalons and quasi-normalons, but also the non-axis-aligned, non-symmetrical and non-perpendicular objects. Extended trihedrons can be reconstructed incrementally from multiple sketching sessions (Figure 1(a-h)). It also avoids the ambiguous heuristic rules. Furthermore, it does not use gestural sketching input that enforces constraints about how objects can be sketched out as in [ZHH96, EHBE97, QWJ00, SC04].

The proposed 3D reconstruction approach is novel and suitable for online sketching applications. The approach approximates the 3D geometry from inaccurate sketches with three-line-junction analysis and unambiguous planarity constraint. In the three-line-junction analysis, the 3D vertices for the lines in the junction are approximated by limiting the changes of up to two 3D components (x, y and z).

The approach automatically corrects the inaccuracies in the sketches by enforcing the planarity constraint to the associated faces.

The process of sketching and 3D object reconstruction is repetitive. Designers can sketch directly on any part of the reconstructed object from different viewpoints. The new sketches are reconstructed into 3D and incorporated with the existing 3D objects. The incremental sketching allows the progress of the design to be recorded. The design process can be reused completely or partly to modify or explore other possibilities of the design. The record can be interpreted in a specific manner for evaluation, e.g., a video generated from sketches across a fixed time interval to show the flow of the design process. The output is rendered in a sketchy style with a similar appearance to the original sketched strokes. This helps designers to focus on the design instead of being distracted by the output appearance.

In addition, the 3D reconstruction approach can be extended to reconstruct 3D non-solid objects. Figure 9 shows an example of the non-solid object reconstructed from a freehand sketch with a modified version of the prototype system.

6. Conclusion and Future Work

Several contributions have been made with this prototype sketching system. First, it supports a natural freehand sketching environment with overtracing, which allows designers to

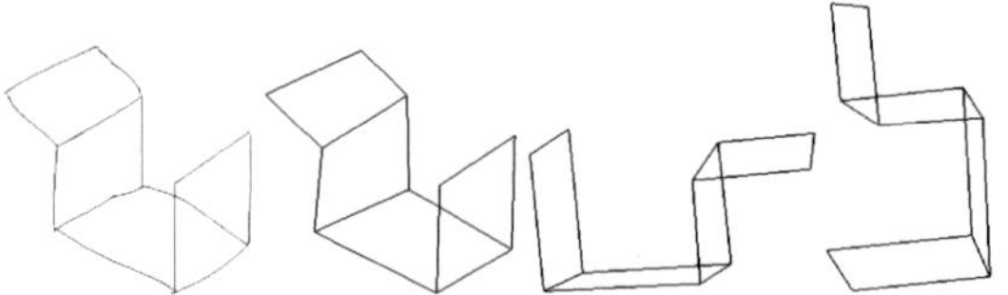

Figure 9: *An example of the non-solid object reconstruction.*

sketch more freely as with pencil and paper. Second, it uses a novel 3D reconstruction algorithm to reconstruct sketches into 3D objects. The nature of the approach, e.g., computationally inexpensive, heuristic-free, insusceptible to input inaccuracies and fully automatic, allows it to support an intuitive and interactive calligraphic interface for conceptual design sketching. In addition to removing the need for gestural sketching, the approach is able to reconstruct the non-axis-aligned, non-symmetrical and non-perpendicular objects. Third, it allows incremental modeling by sketching directly on any part of the reconstructed 3D objects from various viewpoints. Fourth, the objects are rendered in an appearance similar to the original sketches to discourage distraction from the designers to the presentation on the computer.

The system presented here is part of our personalised-sketched-based 3D modelling and rendering system for conceptual design. Further study is required for more polyhedrons and simple curve object reconstruction. The rendering effect of the reconstructed scenes could be improved with more detailed sketches e.g. shadows and textures.

References

[CCCP04]   COMPANY P., CONTERO M., CONESA J., PIQUER A.: An optimisation-based reconstruction engine for 3d modelling by sketching. *Computers & Graphics (Pergamon) 28*, 6 (2004), 955–979.

[CNJC03]   CONTERO M., NAYA F., JORGE J. A., CONESA J.: Cigro: A minimal instruction set calligraphic interface for sketch-based modeling. In *ICCSA (3)* (2003), Springer-Verlag GmbH, pp. 549–558.

[EHBE97]   EGGLI L., HSU C., BRUDERLIN B. D., ELBER G.: Inferring 3d models from freehand sketches and constraints. *CAD Computer Aided Design 29*, 2 (1997), 101–112.

[IMT99]   IGARASHI T., MATSUOKA S., TANAKA H.: Teddy: A sketching interface for 3d freeform design. In *Proceedings of the 26th annual conference on Computer graphics and interactive techniques* (1999), ACM Press/Addison-Wesley Publishing Co, pp. 409–416.

[KQW06]   KU D. C., QIN S. F., WRIGHT D.: Interpretation of overtracing freehand sketching for geometric shapes. In *Proceedings of the 14th International Conference in Central Europe on Computer Graphics, Visualization and Computer Vision'2006* (2006), UNION Agency - Science Press, pp. 263–270.

[LB90]   LAMB D., BANDOPADHAY A.: Interpreting a 3d object from a rough 2d line drawing. In *VIS '90: Proceedings of the 1st conference on Visualization '90* (1990), IEEE Computer Society Press, pp. 59–66.

[LF92]   LECLERC Y. G., FISCHLER M. A.: An optimization-based approach to the interpretation of single line drawings as 3d wire frames. *Int. J. Comput. Vision 9*, 2 (1992), 113–136.

[LS96]   LIPSON H., SHPITALNI M.: Optimization-based reconstruction of a 3d object from a single freehand line drawing. *CAD Computer Aided Design 28*, 8 (1996), 651–663.

[LS02]   LIPSON H., SHPITALNI M.: Correlation-based reconstruction of a 3d object from a single freehand sketch. In *AAAI Spring Symposium on Sketch Understanding* (2002), AAAI Press, pp. 99–104.

[MKL05]   MASRY M., KANG D., LIPSON H.: A freehand sketching interface for progressive construction of 3d objects. *Computers & Graphics 29*, 4 (2005), 563–575.

[NJC*02]   NAYA F., JORGE J. A., CONESA J., CONTERO M., GOMIS J. M.: Direct modeling: from sketches to 3d models. In *1st Ibero-American Symposium on Computer Graphics - SIACG02* (2002).

[OK03]   OH B., KIM C.: Progressive reconstruction of 3d objects from a single free-hand line drawing. *Computers & Graphics 27*, 4 (2003), 581–592.

[QWJ00]   QIN S. F., WRIGHT D. K., JORDANOV I. N.: From on-line sketching to 2d and 3d geometry: A system based on fuzzy knowledge. *CAD Computer Aided Design 32*, 14 (2000), 851–866.

[SC04]   SHESH A., CHEN B.: Smartpaper: An interactive and user friendly sketching system. *Computer Graphics Forum 23*, 3 (2004), 301–301.

[SG00]   SCHWEIKARDT E., GROSS M.: Digital clay: Deriving digital models from freehand sketches. *Automation in Construction 9* (2000), 107–115.

[VMS04]   VARLEY P. A. C., MARTIN R. R., SUZUKI H.: Can machines interpret line drawings? In *Sketch-Based Interfaces and Modelling, EUROGRAPHICS* (2004), pp. 107–116.

[VMS05]   VARLEY P. A. C., MARTIN R. R., SUZUKI H.: Frontal geometry from sketches of engineering objects: Is line labelling necessary? *Computer-Aided Design 37*, 12 (2005), 1285–1307.

[ZHH96]   ZELEZNIK R. C., HERNDON K. P., HUGHES J. F.: Sketch: An interface for sketching 3d scenes. In *SIGGRAPH '96: Proceedings of the 23rd annual conference on Computer graphics and interactive techniques* (1996), ACM Press, pp. 163–170.

EUROGRAPHICS Workshop on Sketch-Based Interfaces and Modeling (2006)
Thomas Stahovich and Mario Costa Sousa (Editors)

A New Sketch Based Interface using the Gray-level Co-occurrence Matrix for Perceptual Simplification of Paper Based Scribbles

A. Bartolo[1], K. P. Camilleri[1], P. J. Farrugia[2], J. C. Borg[2]

[1]Department of Electronic Systems Engineering, University of Malta, Malta
[2]Department of Manufacturing Engineering, University of Malta, Malta

Abstract

The sketching activity has an important role in conceptual design and a variety of tools exist which help designers to facilitate the generation of 3D models form sketched drawings. This paper describes a new sketch-to-3D tool, which uses annotations to aid the interpretation of the drawing. Over-traced lines present in the designer's scribbles provide an interpretation challenge, which must be resolved in order to obtain 3D models from these sketches. Perceptual grouping techniques used to interpret such images require that the drawing is represented as vectors. These are generally obtained through thinning or edge detection. However, we show that processing scribbles using these techniques result in a large number of vectors which do not provide a faithful representation of the drawing. This paper investigates the use of the co-occurrence matrix to perceptually simplify these drawings, thus obtaining a smaller number of vectors which describe the drawing more faithfully.

Categories and Subject Descriptors (according to ACM CCS): I4.6 [Image Processing and Computer Vision]: Edge and feature detection I.5.4 [Pattern Recognition]: Computer Vision

1. Introduction

A designer is sitting at a cafeteria table, pondering upon the design of a perfume bottle that complements the marketing program of a new perfume. Suddenly, the designer manages to come up with an idea, which is quickly externalised on a readily available piece of paper. A 'dialogue' between the sketch and the designer is created leading to a candidate form solution of the perfume bottle. The designer would now like to obtain a three dimensional (3D) virtual model of this sketch, which will aid the designer in visualising better the form intent. This will help the designer verify whether the bottle will look as appealing in 3D. Situations such as this are not uncommon and studies show that very often, ideas come to mind when we least expect them [SH99]. Studies also show that despite the increasing number of portable computer systems, people still prefer to use paper and pen as a sketching medium, especially in the conceptual design stages [FBCS05].

What makes sketches so important in design? Before addressing this question, it is necessary to distinguish between different drawing categories. This may be done by classifying the drawings into a hierarchy according to their accuracy and detail. Accurate technical drawings are found at the highest level, giving a detailed description of an object, including its dimensions. The freehand sketch is less accurate, yet it is drawn after certain shape features have been clearly established. Thus, it is placed at a lower level than the technical drawing. At the lowest level one finds scribbles, which are drawn when the shape of the object is still being explored, since scribbles are the type of paper drawings often used during the conceptual design stage.

In the scenario above, the designer captured an idea on paper. In this sense, the paper based scribble acts as a storage device. This ensures that when the designer returns to the office, the idea can be remembered. Once the mental model has been externalised on a visualising medium, the designer may need to adjust some aspects of the preliminary form. This is one of the roles of scribbles in the designer's visual thinking process. Moreover, scribbles can be a source of knowledge and insight for an alternative or even completely different idea [Mul01]. The scribble can also be considered as a thought process, where the evolution of the designer's ideas are captured on paper. Finally, to obtain a better visualisation of the design idea, the designer would like to generate a 3D model of the scribble. To do this, the designer would have to either manually transfer the sketch into a CAD system, or use a sketch-based interface which acts as an intermediary step between the drawing and the CAD system.

This paper describes a method which can be used to perceptually simplify the scribble strokes for subsequent processing as well as an intuitive method for annotating the scribble to enable the correct interpretation of the intended form. The main problems involved in the interpretation of scribbles and the perceptual grouping techniques which may be applied to the interpretation of scribbled drawings are described in Section 2. A different image preparation method is suggested in Section 3 whilst a novel interface which facilitates the interpretation of these scribbles is given in Section 5. Section 6 compares the results obtained by the proposed perceptual simplification methods and the standard methods image preparation methods.

2. Scribbles: The interpretation challenges

Scribbles are challenging for a number of reasons. A scribble reflects the drawing habits of an individual and one cannot determine a single correct method of representing an object. A typical example of this is demonstrated by the different possibilities with which one can represent a 3D object on a 2D plane. The interpretation of the scribble must be in accordance to the projection with which it is drawn and humans can do this intuitively, because they know what views are normally used. Paper based scribbles provide an additional challenge as they are by their nature made up of several overlapping line strokes rather than single crisp strokes, thus 'fuzzifying' the shape drawn. This fuzziness arises from the fact that in the conceptual design stage, the designer does not yet have a definite object shape. Human interpretation of multiple line strokes follows the Gestalt laws [Sau03], which form the basis of perceptual grouping techniques. Since scribbling is part of a thought and object exploration process, the designer might find it necessary to adjust some of the features in the scribble, without necessarily rubbing off the old features. It is therefore necessary to select as more salient those line strokes that form the object's features over others which were discarded by the designer when scribbling.

Sha'ashua and Ullman [SU88] do this by describing the image as a network of orientation vectors. A vector ρ_i may have one of two states; it is active if it has an underlying line segment and virtual otherwise. The state and orientation of each vector ρ_i contributes to the saliency of the curve of which it is part. This algorithm will thus classify each line stroke in the image according to its saliency, favoring long, smooth, continuous curves. Gui and Medioni [GM93] argue that the physical evidence extracted locally from images is

ambiguous and does not correspond to the expected perception of the image. For this reason, they impose global perceptual constraints by introducing the concept of an *extension field* which is a maximum likelihood directional vector field describing the contribution of a single unit-length edge element to its neighbours. Each pixel site in the image accumulates votes from the vector field of its neighbours, such that the most salient sites will obtain the highest vote count. A global saliency measure is also used by Guichard and Tarel [GT99], who define saliency as the gain in 'energy' obtained after introducing a new edgel to an existing set of edgels describing a curve. Guichard and Tarel assume that the salient curves in the image may be modelled as parametric curves of the form $x = f(y)$ where x and y are the coordinates of points on the curve. The Kalman filter framework is used to recursively update the curve parameters and hence determine the edgel groups forming a salient curve. Whilst recognizing the need for a global saliency measure, Saund [Sau03] proposes a saliency measure based on figural closure, arguing that this is considered as a salient feature in sketches and drawings. The algorithm proposed traces through a number of segments in attempt to obtain closed contours. Segment tracing may be done according to two preferred directions, namely maximally turning or smooth continuation. The smooth continuation preference is similar to the saliency criterion proposed by Sha'ashua and Ullman, and highlights paths drawn with the same pen stroke. In contrast, maximally turning preferences seeks the most compact and tightly closed paths. Junction preference scores are used to weight decisions taken at each junction and are required to resolve ambiguities when multiple tracing options are available. Whilst the junction preference scores provide a local saliency measure, Saund defines a global figural goodness, which is based on the compactness of the figure, and the distance between the endpoints of the traced curve. The algorithms discussed so far required either an iterative computation of the saliency measure, or an iterative path tracing. Kelley and Hancock [KH00] propose a single pass grouping algorithm, based on a measure of geometric affinity between segments. This affinity is obtained using a probabilistic linking field based on the length and orientation of a virtual linking segment formed by the endpoints of two segments. Thresholding this linking field using an adaptive entropy based threshold, will result in an affinity matrix. Eigen decomposition can then be applied to this matrix to separate the image segments into clusters according to the objects in the image.

The techniques described above require some image preprocessing before the saliency measures may be obtained. Sha'ashua and Ullman [SU88], assume that the image is binarised, whilst the algorithms proposed in [GT99, Sau03, KH00] require that the image data is represented as line segments. These segments may be obtained by either performing image binarisation, line thinning and then segmentation or, as proposed in [GT99] by performing edge detection followed by segmentation. In either case, this may result in a large number of segments, and one of the problems encountered by these algorithms is the need to avoid an exhaustive search amongst all the segments. Figure 1 shows the performance of a simple iterative global thresholding technique and Sobel's edge detection on a noisy binary test image. In Figure 1(c) the binarised image shows misclassification of several foreground pixels, which will be in interpreted as short line segments. This results in a number of vector data for which there is no supporting image foreground. In Figure 1(d) the foreground noise breaks the smooth edges, hence splitting a single vector into a number of smaller vectors. Although better thresholding or edge detection techniques will reduce the effect of noise, these do not necessarily reduce the number of redundant segments. Scribbles consist of multiple line strokes, most of which are supporting line strokes which the human vision system can immediately group as one single stroke. However, pre-processing scribbles with binarisation or edge detection techniques will result in separate segments for each of these strokes. These line strokes must be grouped by a perceptual grouping algorithm. Ideally, the image pre-processing would be able to provide the perceptual grouping algorithm with a single segment for these supporting line strokes. This would allow the perceptual grouping algorithm to identify curve saliency from a smaller number of segments, thus reducing the search required by the algorithm. The following section investigates the use of the co-occurrence matrix, a technique traditionally applied to texture analysis, to group these supporting line strokes into a smaller number of appropriate line strokes.

3. The co-occurrence matrix

The co-occurrence matrix [HS01] records the number of times a pixel with gray level g_1 occurs in the vicinity of a pixel with gray level g_2. The location defining the pixel's vicinity may be determined by a vector of length d and orientation θ. Thus the co-occurrence matrix will compare the gray levels of pixel pairs having co-ordinates (r,c) and $(r+d\sin(\theta), c+d\cos(\theta))$ where c and r represent the horizontal and vertical axis of the image respectively. Thus for each gray-level pair combination in an image f, the matrix $T_{g_1,g_2,d,\theta}$ given by Equation 1 may be evaluated,

$$T_{g_1,g_2,d,\theta}(r,c) = \begin{cases} 1 & , \quad (f(r,c) = g_1) \ and \ (f(r',c') = g_2) \\ 0 & , \quad otherwise \end{cases}$$

(1)

where $r' = r + d\sin(\theta)$ and $c' = c + d\cos(\theta)$. The co-occurrence matrix $C_{d,\theta}$, can thus be defined as the accumulation of the values in $T_{g_1,g_2,d,\theta}$ for each gray level in the image, as given in (2)

$$C_{d,\theta}(g_1,g_2) = \sum_{c=1}^{C} \sum_{r=1}^{R} T_{g_1,g_2,d,\theta}(r,c)$$

(2)

As shown in Figure 2 the co-occurrence matrix for line drawing images has a maximum point located in the background-background region. Since scribbled images contain a small number of foreground pixels in comparison to the number of background pixels this maximum point will be present for all combinations of d and θ since, given any vector length and orientation, the number of background-background matches will always be greater than any other match combination. Figure 2 also shows a local maximum in the foreground-foreground region. Unlike the global maximum, a local maximum in this region of the co-occurrence matrix will occur only when the vector (d,θ) is aligned with the image foreground. Thus if the co-occurrence matrix were to be evaluated for a range of θ values, as shown in (3) the

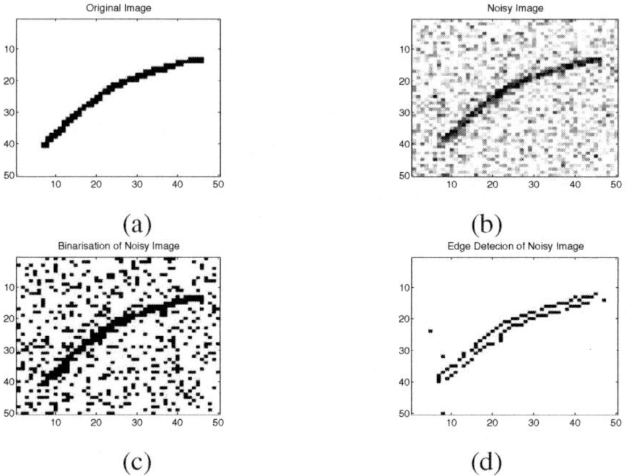

(a)

(b)

(c)

(d)

Figure 1: *Performance of simple image pre-processing techniques under noise conditions. (a)A binary test image. (b) image corrupted with additive zero mean Gaussian distributed noise, having a variance of 0.12. (c) result of global thresholding (d) result of Sobel's edge detection.*

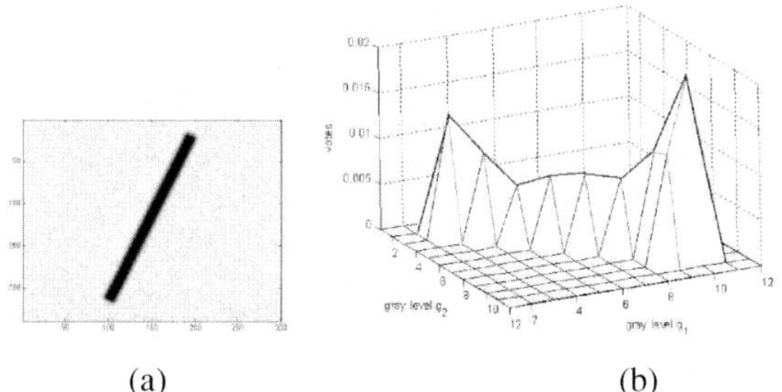

(a)

(b)

Figure 2: *A 3D plot of the co-occurrence matrix for the test line with orientation of 110° shown in (a). The matrix parameters were chosen as $d = 8$ and $\theta = 110°$*

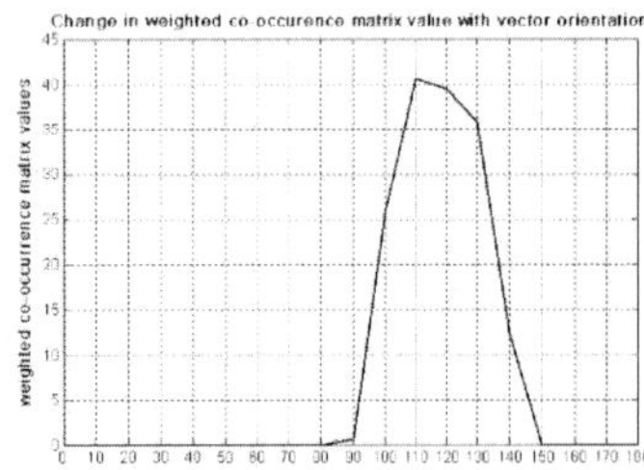

Figure 3: *The weighted co-occurrence vector*

presence of a local maximum in the foreground-foreground region of the matrix will indicate the orientation θ of the image line.

$$M_d(g_1, g_2, \theta) = \sum_{c=1}^{C} \sum_{r=1}^{R} T_{g_1, g_2, d, \theta}(r, c) \qquad (3)$$

It is therefore beneficial to identify and separate the local maxima as these will indicate the line orientations in the image. This may be done by multiplying the co-occurrence matrix obtained for each value of θ with a weight matrix such as that given by Equation 4, which attenuates the background-background transitions.

$$W(g_1, g_2) = e^{\frac{(1 - g_1 g_2)}{(2^l - g_1)(2^l - g_2)}} \qquad (4)$$

This matrix returns a value of 1 when both g_1 and g_2 are 1 (black) and a value of 0 when either one of g_1 or g_2 is equal to 2^l (white), where l defines the bit-depth of the image. We can now represent the co-occurrence matrix as a function of the orientation θ (5), indicating the significance, or otherwise, of foreground-foreground transitions in relation with orientation.

$$D_d(\theta) = \sum_{g_1=1}^{2^l} \sum_{g_2=1}^{2^l} W(g_1, g_2) M_d(g_1, g_2, \theta) \qquad (5)$$

Figure 3 gives a plot of the weighted co-occurrence vector obtained for the image shown in Figure 2. As given in (6) the orientation $\hat{\theta}$ of lines in the image may be deduced from the maxima of this vector.

$$\hat{\theta} = \arg\max_{\theta} D_d(\theta) \qquad (6)$$

Since images consist of many lines, it will be necessary to localise the orientation information derived from the co-occurrence matrix. In order to localise the orientation information, the image is split equally into sub-regions, us-ing a quad-tree split for each subsequent region. This allows the co-occurrence matrix to focus on regions containing the line strokes, disregarding others which consist only of background pixels. The quad-split is carried out up to a certain resolution depth, which depends on the length d, since reasonable data may be obtained only for sub-regions whose size is greater than the value of d. Choosing d such that it is slightly larger than the stroke width, will ensure that the smallest subregion spans the width of a line stroke. The orientation deduced from each subregion may be applied to all the pixels within the region, thus representing the line strokes falling within that region with a single orientation vector.

Although the co-occurrence matrix can be used as described here to represent the scribble with less clutter, the 3D form represented by the scribble is generally ambiguous. Thus, in order to resolve the intended form, additional information about the 3D form has to be provided by the designer. Online systems provide the designer a set of tools via an interactive user interface, which the designer may use while drawing. Paper-based offline systems cannot provide an interactive interface, however, the designer may make use of specific pre-defined sketching languages which will aid the interpretation process.

4. The sketch based interface: what should it be like?

Several sketch-based interfaces have been developed, each catering for a particular drawing method. Interfaces such as Celesstin [VT92] and MDUS [DW99] may be used to convert 2D paper-based machine drawings to CAD systems. If the designer wishes to sketch directly in 3D, interfaces such as CIRGO [NCC*03] may be used. This interface distinguishes between different types of strokes according to the pressure with which they are drawn. Thus, the interface must be used in conjunction with tablet PCs, requiring the designer to reproduce the final sketch on an active medium. From a computational point of view, including symbols and using pre-defined drawing languages to incorporate the designer's intent will facilitate the interpretation process [FBC*05]. However, the designer would like an interpretation system that functions on sketches and scribbles that are as close as possible to the designer's natural drawing habits. The sketch based interface should therefore provide a suitable compromise between ease of use and ease of interpretation.

Ideally a sketch based interface should be capable of making a distinction between different view points and interpret the sketch accordingly. The interface should also support all kinds of geometries, including objects having 'form features' such as through or blind holes, and 3D primitives such as spherical or conical sections. Since the interpretation of the paper-based scribble requires the aid of symbols, these should be chosen such that they resemble standard drawing

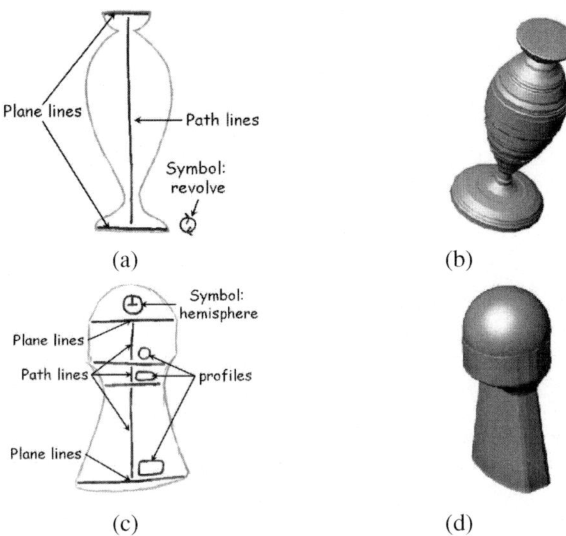

Figure 4: *An example of the sketching procedure*

symbols. This ensures that the symbols are easily remembered, making the language easier to use and develop.

5. The Annotator

The sketch based interface being proposed is a paper-based interface which uses the raw scribble drawn by the designer as the core mechanism for interpretation. This interface is a continuation of the interface described in [FBY*06], however, rather than requiring that the designer redraws the sketch according to some prescribed language, the designer is asked to annotate the scribble *after* this has been drawn. In this way, the sketch based interface is closer to the designer's natural drawing habits, hence achieving an easy-to-use interface. The annotations serve to facilitate the automated interpretation of the designer's scribble by the sketch-based interface and are made in such a way that they complement the designer's perception of the scribble.

In order to evaluate the concept proposed in this paper and develop a prototype tool which may be tested with designers, the extent of forms that can presently be represented by the implementation of the proposed sketch-based interface is limited to objects that may be represented using a single planar view and which contain a single axis. These include objects whose geometry may be described by rotation, extrusion or lofting operations. Furthermore, the sketch based interface is designed to extract the object's geometry; this work does not attempt to investigate the extraction or representation of form features, such as pockets or blind holes.

5.1. The annotation procedure

Figure 4 gives an example of two annotated scribbles and their corresponding 3D models. As can be seen in Fig-

ure 4(a) and (c), the designer is presented with four different annotation tools, namely cross-sectional profiles, plane lines, path lines and symbols. In order to facilitate the separation of the annotations from the scribble, the annotation is drawn in a colour that contrasts with the colour of the scribble.

Profiles are used to specify the cross-sectional shape of the object at particular planes orthogonal to the drawing plane. These are necessary to indicate the geometric shape of the object, which cannot be deduced from the scribble since this is assumed to be a front-elevational view of the object. The relation between the cross-sectional profiles and the scribble is shown by *plane lines*. These give the position and inclination of the plane at which the profiles are taken. It is not necessary to draw the cross-sectional profiles to scale, since their aspect ratio may be scaled according to the length of the plane lines. In some instances, the cross-sectional profiles may be replaced by *symbols*. The 'revolve' symbol in Figure 4(a) indicates that the intended form has a rotational symmetry along the nearest path line. In this case, profiles are unnecessary since rotational objects must have a circular cross-section. On the other hand, in Figure 4(c), the symbol indicates that the object terminates with a 3D primitive, namely a hemisphere. *Path lines* are drawn in the center of the scribble and perpendicular to the plane lines. The meaning associated with the path lines differs according to the context in which they are used. In Figure 4(a), which represents a rotational object, only one path line was necessary and this reflects the axis of rotation of the object. Figure 4(c), which has four plane lines, three path lines - one between each pair of plane lines was necessary. In this case, the object is to be represented by a loft operation, and so the path line indicates the path along which the operation is to be carried out.

5.2. Interpreting the annotated scribble

The first step in the interpretation process would be to distinguish between the scribbles and the annotations. Since the designer makes the annotations in a different colour, the two may be separated on this basis. However, since the designer is free to use any two contrasting colours, it is also necessary to identify which of the coloured line strokes form the scribble and which form the annotations. This distinction is carried out after perceptual simplification of the two coloured components, since after simplification of the scribble, the number of disconected line strokes forming the annotations will be greater than the number of line strokes forming the scribble.

Once the annotations have been identified, they are further classified into path lines, plane lines, profiles or symbols. The scribbled drawing is used to help identify between the plane lines and path lines. This is done by taking two directed run-lengths perpendicular to the line in consideration at specific intervals along the line. Since the path line is drawn towards the center of the scribble, the directed run-

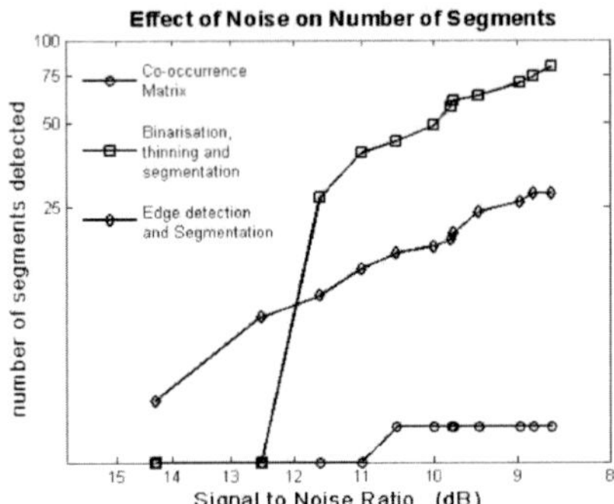

Figure 5: *Effect of noise on number of segments.*

lengths at each specific interval should be approximately equal. Thus if the average difference between the directed run-lengths along the line is less than a predefined threshold, the line is classified as a path line.

If a 'revolve' symbol is identified in the annotations, the interpretation process is only required to specify the shape profile to rotate and the axis of rotation about which the shape profile will be rotated. The axis of rotation is defined by the end points of the path line, whilst the shape profile is obtained from the scribble. If no rotational symbol is identified, it will be assumed that the 3D object can be generated by using a combination of extrude or loft operations. To achieve the 3D model, the annotations must first be grouped into sets. This is done by ordering the path lines such that the first path line is the bottom-most path line, and then locating the plane line and profile closest to each of the path line's endpoints. Thus, each annotation set will consist of a path line, two plane lines and two profiles. The minimum bounding box of each profile is used to determine the profile's size. The width of the minimum bounding box is compared to the length of the corresponding plane line and the profile is scaled accordingly. The position of the profile is then shifted such that the center of the minimum bounding box lies on the center of the plane line, thus aligning all the profiles in the drawing.

It is now necessary to identify the CAD operation required to propagate the profile from one plane to the next. This is carried out by taking the width of the scribble at intervals along the path line. An extrude operation will be assumed when the width of the scribble remains constant and the profiles at the start and end of the operation have the same geometric shape. If any one of these conditions fails, then a loft operation is assumed.

6. Results and Discussion

Perceptual simplification using the co-occurrence matrix is expected to have a good noise immunity since it is unlikely that random noise pixels give a high response to a particu-

lar vector (d, θ). This is verified in Figure 5 which compares the number of segments returned by binarisation, edge detection and the co-occurrence matrix for the image shown in Figure 1 which was corrupted with varying degrees of noise.

The co-occurrence matrix can also group together multiple line strokes falling within the same subregion. This is illustrated in Figure 6 which compares the line segments generated after processing part of a scribble with the co-occurrence matrix, binarisation and thinning and edge detection. Fewer and 'cleaner' line segments are generated by the co-occurrence matrix, making these segments more suitable for further processing by perceptual grouping algorithms.

Figure 8 shows the results obtained after applying the co-occurrence matrix on three test scribbles and a comparison of the performance of the co-occurrence matrix with simple binarisation and edge detection pre-processing techniques is given in Figure 7 (refer to `http:www.eng.um.edu.mt/~inpro/activities/` for further results). Comaparison of the computinal times yields average time of 80s for the co-occurrence matrix 5s for binarisation and 4s for edge detection, thus the co-occurrence matrix causes a 94% and 95% increase in computational times respectively. However, this additional computational time is compensated for by the decrease in the number of line segments generated, which reflects the computations required in subsequent perceptual grouping algorithms. The co-occurrence matrix results in an average of 9 segments whereas binarisation and edge-detection give an average of 200 and 485 segments respectively. Assuming a computational complexity of $O(n^2)$ defined in [GT99, GM93], where n is the number of line segments, pre-processing the images using the co-occurrence matrix reduces the computations required by 98% and 99% for the low noise images in comparison with the pre-processing by binarisation and edge detection tech-

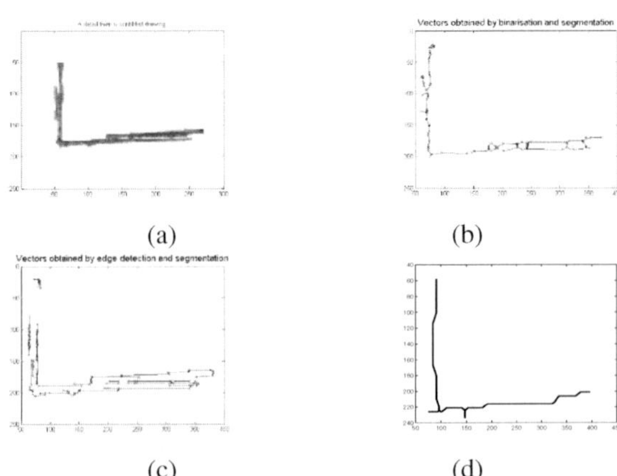

Figure 6: *A scribbled L-junction and its vector data after pre-processing with (b) Global binarisation (c) Sobel's edge detection (d) Co-occurrence Matrix.*

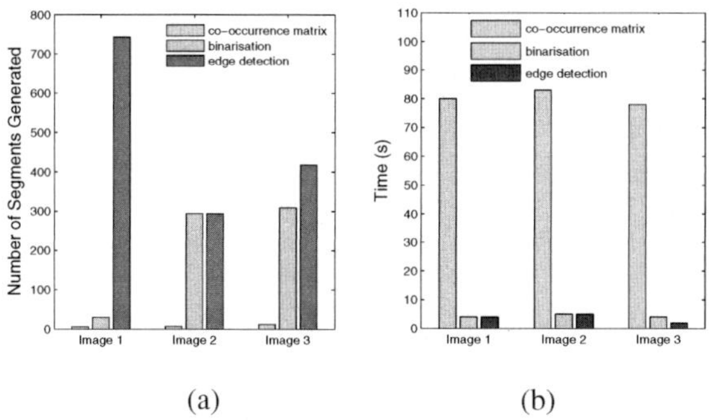

(a)   (b)

Figure 7: *Comparison of (a) number of line segments and (b) computational times of the proposed algorithm and simple global thresholding and edge detection techniques.*

niques respectively. Simple binarisation and edge detection do not perform well under noise conditions, in fact, for the image shown in Figure 1 binarisation and edge detection would increase the computations of the perceptual grouping algorithm by a factor of 99.86% and 97% respectively. The co-occurrence matrix would only increase the computations by a factor of 44%, thus 55.86% and 53% less than the increase brought about by binarisation and edge detection.

7. Conclusion

The co-occurrence matrix determines the orientation of a pattern in a sub-region of the image. This effectively groups together multiple line strokes falling within that region, whilst giving a good noise immunity. Thus the co-occurrence matrix performs perceptual simplification of the image, making it easier for perceptual grouping algorithms to identify the most salient parts of the scribble. This is important in sketch-based interfaces, since the ability to interpret a designer's scribble brings the interface closer to the designer's natural drawing habits, and hence more user friendly.

8. Acknowledgements

This research is part of the research project 'Innovative Early Stage Design Product Prototyping' (InPro), (http:www.eng.um.edu.mt/~inpro) which is supported by the University of Malta under research grant IED 73-529-2005 .

References

[DW99] DORI D., WENYIN L.: Automated CAD Conversion with the Machine Drawing Understanding System: Concepts, Algorithms, and Performance. *IEEE Transactions On Systems, Man, and Cybernetics Part A: Systems and Humans 29*, 4 (July 1999), 411 – 416.

[FBC*05] FARRUGIA P. J., BORG J. C., CAMILLERI K. P., GIANNINI F., YAN X.: Extracting 3D shape models and related life knowledge from paper-based sketches. *International Journal on Computer Application in Technology (IJCAT), special issue on "Models and methods for representing and processing shape semantics. 23 (2/3/4)* (2005), 120 – 137.

[FBCS05] FARRUGIA P. J., BORG J., CAMILLERI K. P., SPITERI C.: Experiments with a Cameraphone-Aided Design (cpad) System. In *15th International Conference on Engineering Design (ICED05)* (2005), pp. 130 – 131.

[FBY*06] FARRUGIA P., BORG J. C., YAN X. T., CAMILLERI K. P., GRAHAM G.: A Sketching Alphabet for Paper-based Collaborative Design. *Journal of Design Research (JDR), special issue on Fostering Innovation During Early Informal Design Phases (to appear)* (2006).

[GM93] GUY G., MEDIONI G.: Iferring Global Perceptual Contours from Local Features. *Image Understanding Workshop* (1993), 881 – 892.

[GT99] GUICHARD F., TAREL J.: Curve Finder Combinng Perceptual Grouping and a Kalman-like Fitting. In *IEEE Conference on Computer Vision* (1999), pp. 1003 – 1008.

[HS01] HARALICK R. M., SHAPIRO L. G.: *Computer and Robot Vision*. Addison-Wesley, 2001.

[KH00] KELLEY A. R., HANCOCK E. R.: Grouping Line-segments using Eigendecomposition. In *Proceedings of the 11th British Machine Vision Conference* (2000), pp. 586 – 595.

[Mul01] MULLER W.: *Order and Meaning in Design*. Lemma Publishers, 2001.

[NCC*03] NAYA F., CONESA J., CONTERO M., COMPANY P., JORGE J.: Smart Sketch System for 3D Reconstruction Based Modelling. In *Third International Symposium on Smart Graphics* (2003), pp. 58 – 68.

[Sau03] SAUND E.: Finding Perceptually Closed Paths in Sketches and Drawings. *IEEE Transactions on Pattern Analysis and Machine Intelligence 25*, 4 (Apr. 2003), 475 – 491.

[SH99] STAPPERS P. J., HENNESSEY J. M.: Towards Electronic Napkins and Beermants: Computer Support for Visual Ideation Skills. In *VRI'99* (1999), pp. 220 – 225.

[SU88] SHA'ASHUA A., ULLMAN S.: Structural Saliency: The Detection of Globally Salient Structures using a Locally Connected Network. In *Second International Conference on Computer Vision* (Dec. 1988), pp. 321–327.

[VT92] VAXIVIERE P., TOMBRE K.: Celesstin: CAD Conversion of Mechanical Drawings. *IEEE Computer Magazine 25* (1992), 46 – 54.

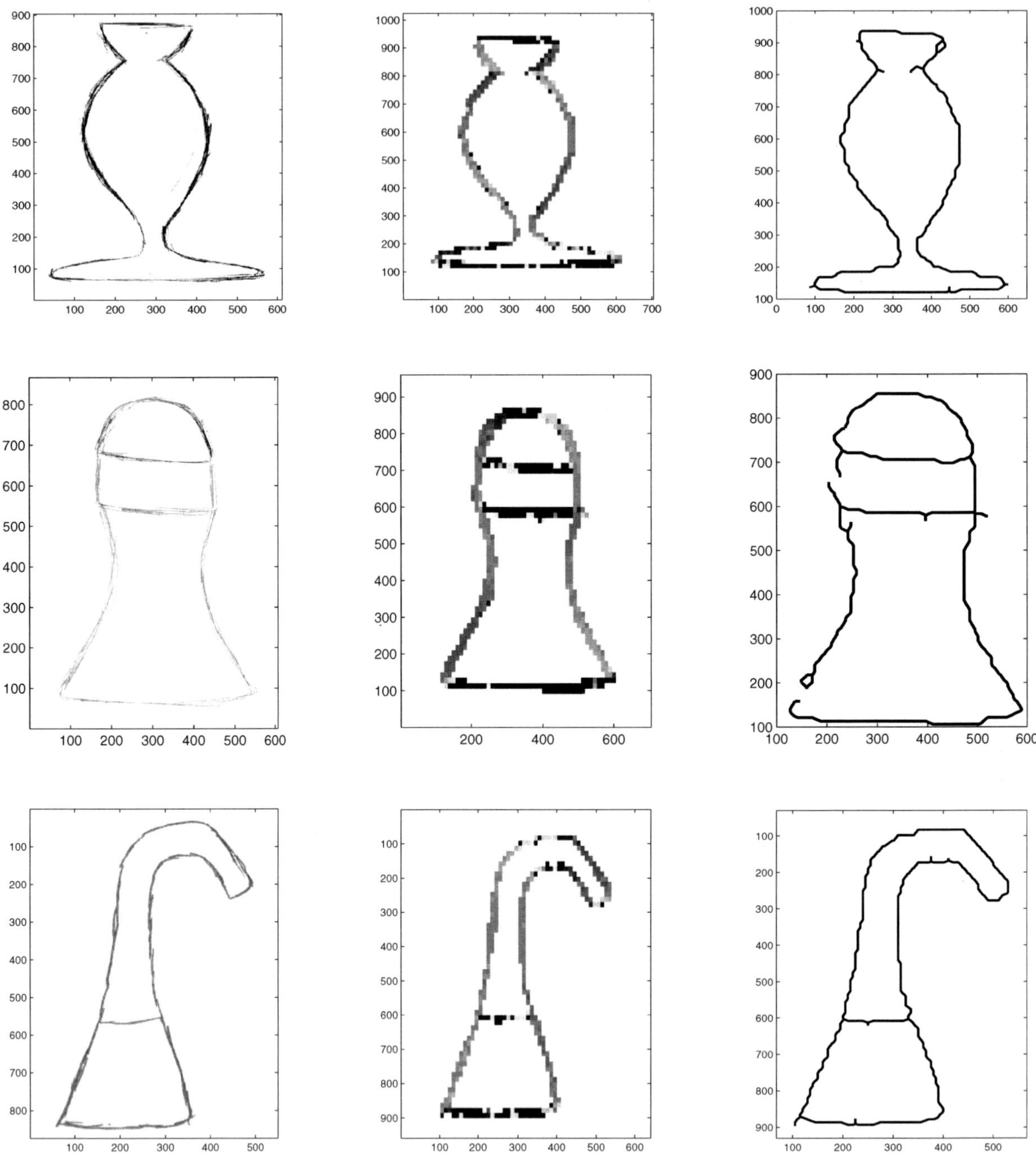

Figure 8: *The results obtained for three test scribbles which have been drawn with a black pencil on plane white paper and scanned at 96dpi. The first column shows the original scribble. The second column shows the orientations $\hat{\theta}$ obtained from the co-occurrence matrix, where black regions indicate an orientation of $0°$ and white represents an orientation of $180°$. The last column shows the number of line segments that are extracted from the orientation response matrix. In these examples, the length of the vector d, used to evaluate the co-occurrence matrix, was set to 8*

EUROGRAPHICS Workshop on Sketch-Based Interfaces and Modeling (2006)
Thomas Stahovich and Mario Costa Sousa (Editors)

Modeling Plant Variations through 3D Interactive Sketches

L. Streit[1]   P. Lapides[2]   M. C. Sousa[1]   E. Sharlin[1]

Departments of [1]Computer Science, [2]Electrical and Computer Engineering, University of Calgary, Canada

Abstract

Modeling realistic looking plants is still a complex problem requiring specification of plant structure, geometry and surface characteristics. Modeling a collection of plants is more problematic especially since each plant is slightly different. Altering the shape of branches and stems is one of the most dramatic and natural methods of creating differing instances of the same plant type. We present a sketch-based interface for modeling plant variations through specification of branch and stem shape. Our system is based on interaction with the 3D Tractus: a new physical interface we developed to support direct 3D sketching. The 3D strokes from the 3D Tractus are used as input to a biologically-based modeling method that mimics natural growth variation factors of real plants.

Categories and Subject Descriptors (according to ACM CCS): I.3.5 [Computer Graphics]: Computational Geometry and Object Modeling: Modeling packages

1. Introduction

In nature no two instances of a single plant type are exactly the same. This fact must be preserved when trying to model a large collection of the same type of plant. As computer generated scenes become more complex, the desire to include many plants in a scene increases. The most profound difference between plant instances is often the shape of the branches and stems of the plant.

To model a collection of differing plant instances it is desirable to interactively specify and control branch and stem shape. Other modeling systems allow the user to control a variety of parameters, which often reflect features of the geometry [OHKK03] rather than structure. Some previous work has interactively specified structural components such as branch and stem shape, but are restricted to specifying these shapes in a 2D domain [LD99, OOI05] and often assume certain constraints (i.e. clamping to the surface, constant curvature) in order to create a 3D curve.

Interactively specifying plant shape parallels 3D curve design [CMZ*99, CHZ00]. The most direct method of defining 3D curves is to draw them; however drawing 3D curves and strokes is problematic when working in a 2D domain. Sketch-based modeling has recently been used for creating plant models [IITS04, IOOI05, OI03, OOI05]. All these methods rely on certain assumptions or techniques to infer the 3D shape or model from the 2D strokes.

We present a system for creating a variety of plant instances from a single plant model using direct 3D strokes (Figure 1). We use a physical 3D drawing-board interface for sketching stem and branch shapes in 3D. The sketched stems and branches are directly employed as realistic variations to the original plant model [SFS05]. Our main contribution is the unique system which combines the 3D drawing-board with creating plant model variation for creating plant collections. Our technique includes a unique method of creating and editing strokes as well as associating them with a base model. The result is an intuitive, direct, and quick method for creating a variety of plants from a single model, to facilitate creating large plant model collections.

2. Related Work

Modeling of plants has been addressed by the computer graphics community for decades [AK84, PL90]. Since our focus is to create variations in plant model instances, we overview previous work that permits interactive editing of models to create different plant model instances rather than creation of models. Also, since we use a 3D interface in a sketch-based paradigm, we overview work in this context.

2.1. Interactive Plant Design

With increases in computational power, interactive modeling of complex models such as plants has recently become possible. As Lintermann and Deussen [LD99] describe, many plant modeling approaches can be classified as either biologically motivated to simulate natural plant development, or to generate visually correct shape. Interactive modeling applications belong to the latter and is likewise our focus.

Interactive plant modeling techniques target three aspects: data, means and method of interaction. The data is typically surface geometry [OHKK03], a structural representation [PBPS99, BPF*03], or some combination of these two [LD99]. The interaction means is traditionally manipulation of the 3D model in a 2D view plane while selecting various joints or plant aspects using a 2D pointer (e.g. mouse) or a 3D magnetic tracker [OHKK03]. The interaction method has involved applying editing operations to various amounts or levels of plant structure simultaneously to reduce tedium with highly complex models. Some techniques use the spatial arrangement to select components or aspects of the plant within a particular region [OHKK03], some use silhouettes for bounding regions [BPF*03], some craft the model's parameters to allow for multi-resolution editing through parameter alteration [LD99] and others use the model's structural representation [LD99, BPF*03].

The goal is often the control of shape. To improve realism some techniques assist the user by imposing physical constraints given the user's input such as the inverse-kinematic approach of Power et al. [PBPS99], or the use of transformation or developmental rules such as growth of buds or leaves of Onishi et al. [OHKK03]. Lintermann and Duessen [LD99] provide a few options to control overall shape including functional modeling, tropisms or freeform deformation, but their method seems more difficult when specifying individual branch and stem shape. Boudon et al. [BPF*03] allow specification of shape through editing of 2D curves by manipulating control points in 3D space to represent axes of structures.

While these editing methods as well as various commercial procedural methods for creating plants [IDV05, OC05] provide a means of creating variation by specifically interacting with the parameters or geometry of the model, individually editing the many components of the model numerous times to create a large collection of these varied models is too tedious. A common method to quickly introduce variations involves randomly [OC05] or systematically varying parameters [LD99, Xfr05], however these methods are not controllable and are often too sensitive.

Our objective is to make use of the skeletal representation for multi-resolution editing while providing a means of intuitive direct 3D manipulation. Similar to Power et al. [PBPS99] and Onishi et al. [OHKK03] we use a L-system to represent the plant structure. However, we do not constrain the user by physical parameters [PBPS99] and do not force the user to manipulate individual controls [BPF*03, LD99] or joints to communicate transforma-

tions [OHKK03], but rather the user simply draws the intended branch and stem manipulations directly in 3D.

Furthermore, since our goal is create variation for a collection of plants the sketch-base interaction provides a natural means of creating variation in the same way artists create a 'likeness' of a plant. A painting or drawing of a plant can be easily recognized as a particular plant, but is rarely if ever an exact representation of the real plant.

In addition to using sketch input for variation we use the sketched information as input to the procedural method of Streit et al. [SFS05] to add biological variation that occurs naturally through development. With the combined technique we can create user controlled differences in the plant model, particularly in the shape of branches and stems with an underlying biology-based variation.

2.2. Three-Dimensional Interfaces

Sach's et al. [SRS91] 3-Draw system and other free space devices using six degrees of freedom (DOF) [BBMP97, HRPGK94, PTW98] are early examples of pioneering 3D interfaces for sketching, manipulation and drawing. These systems require the use of a virtual reality environment, typically including head mounted displays (HMD), stereo shutter glasses, and tethered 6 DOF trackers. All of this complex and usually expensive equipment can be seen as a disadvantage, and designers who are used to working on physical surfaces often find these systems difficult to use.

Both the CAT and Interaction Table [HGRT03, HG02] use a physical touch sensitive surface to provide the user 6 DOF. However, both interfaces rely on physical pressure instead of movement to navigate a virtual world. ArtNova and in-Touch [FOL02, GEL00] use SensAble's PHANTOM Haptic device [ST05] to allow the user to directly interact with virtual 3D objects. The PHANTOM provides force-feedback directly to the user's arm or hand.

The Boom Chameleon [TFK*02] lets the user interact with a touch sensitive display mounted on a position sensitive arm. The display acts as a window into the virtual space, and the user can annotate and interact with the 3D scene. To our knowledge this apparatus is neither simple, nor inexpensive and has not been used for 3D drawing.

2.3. Sketch-based Plant Modeling Interfaces

Recently, systems have been developed to create and manipulate plant models through a sketch-based interface. Ijiri et al. [IITS04, IOOI05] introduce a methodology for modeling flowers using floral diagrams and inflorescence. Their geometry editor uses two sketched cross-sectional strokes to shape a flat leaf into a curved one. An additional sketched stroke defines the central axis of a selected inflorescence. From the 2D free-form strokes they create 3D geometry by adding depth to the strokes using the assumption of constant

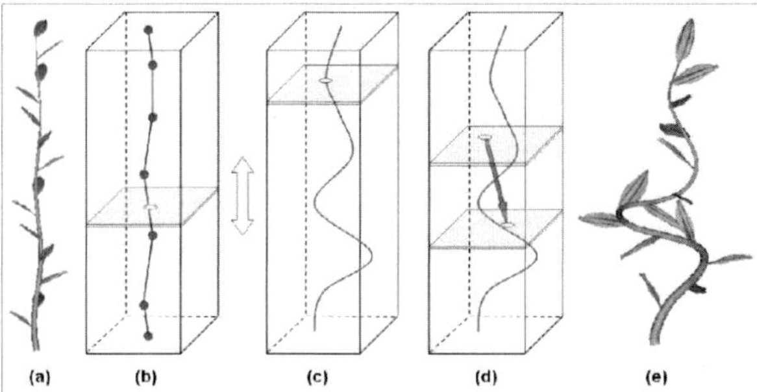

Figure 1: *Given a 3D plant model (a) and its extracted skeleton (b) the user selects segments (blue) from the skeleton (b) and sketches corresponding strokes (c) using the* 3D Tractus. *These strokes together with macro sketch-based motion indicators for overall growth direction (d) are used to control growth variation (e).*

Figure 2: *A user interacting with the* 3D Tractus.

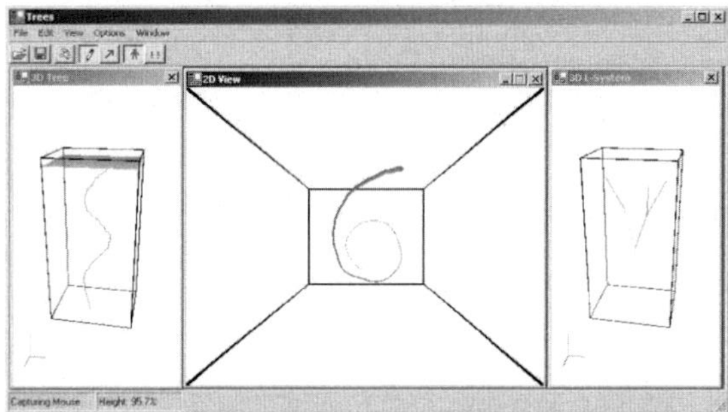

Figure 3: *A screenshot showing a spiralling stroke (left and center) and the plant skeleton (right).*

curvature. Other parameters and a flower diagram help define various model characteristics.

Okabe et al. [OI03, OOI05] present a method for modeling trees from sketches. Their technique generates 3D geometry from a 2D sketch by assuming that botanical trees tend to maximize the distance between branches and that most users tend to draw branches that extend sideways rather than into or out of the drawing plane. They introduce three editing modes to assist the user in creating repetitive arrangements, rather than specifying rules or parameters to create the model. As the authors state, currently their system is limited to single trees. Creation of other types of plants and similar trees for forming collections of plants is not possible. Our focus is the creation of varied models for the purposes of generating collections of a wide range of plant models.

3. System Overview and Interface

Our system is based on a 3D interface which permits users to draw strokes directly in 3D space. As shown in Figure 1, the user selects a base plant model, to which they would like to add variations. Following the system extracts the skeleton of this model. We currently use an L-system description of the plant model and a wire-frame interpretation of the L-system string for the skeleton. The user then sketches strokes directly in 3D using the 3D Tractus [LSSS06], as shown in Figure 2. These strokes indicate how the branches of the base model's skeleton should be varied. These strokes are used as input to a procedural method which adds variation to the model through a growth-based simulation.

The 3D Tractus is a simple physical interface that allows the user to draw on a flat surface (such as a tablet PC) while moving the surface up and down, as shown in Figure 2. The 3D Tractus uses a simple and inexpensive string-potentiometer to measure the interaction surface height. Following, all the user's surface interactions are mapped in 3D, and the system can display related 3D feedback to the user

in real time according to the surface height [LSSS06]. The result is that the user can generate 3D curves directly, without having to resort to GUI widgets as in other 2D interfaces such as commercially available Maya^{TM} or 3DS Max^{TM}.

The software presented to the user is controlled exclusively by a pointer, facilitating sketching without interruptions or need to resort to the keyboard. There are three main areas of the application that the user sees. The first is the tree skeleton, which shows the L-system in a 3D view that can be rotated, as shown on the right in Figure 3. The user selects branches that they want to add variations to from this view. In another window, the user employs the 3D Tractus to draw the 3D curve that describes the branches that they selected, as shown in the center. Finally, the user sees the curves that they have drawn in a 3D view shown on the left.

4. Creating Variation

Variation is added to the base model through alteration of branch and stem shape. This can have a profound affect on the look of the plant without changing any other attributes of the model. Variation can be added to the branches and stems in three forms: intentional artistic, unintentional artistic and growth-based [SFS05]. Direct inputting of variations using 3D Tractus sketches employs the artistic variation form. By drawing the shape of the branches, variation can be deliberately introduced through definitive alterations in the branch orientation and direction as well as unintentional imprecision due to hand gestures in the drawing of the stroke. Using sketched strokes in free-form drawing as a source of variations, results in better approximations of the process of traditional illustration production.

Mapping the user-drawn strokes to the original model is not an easy problem and parallels graph-matching problems. Without imposing some ordering on the drawing the complexity of the matching problem grows exponentially with each stroke drawn. To avoid imposing restrictions on drawing order and to improve interaction even with complex models, we chose to have the user first indicate to which branch or branch component they are associating a stroke through selection. Of course selecting each and every branch and associating a stroke with it can be tedious with overly complex models, thus a means of propagating the stroke to utilize the natural repetition in botanical models is used. The stroke propagation facilitates hierarchical editing of the model to assist in both control over fine details and quick, efficient definition of models. As the user associates strokes a view of the model is updated and the user can choose to render the complete geometry of the model at any stage.

4.1. Plant Skeleton and Selection

To generate variation, the user starts with a base plant skeleton which is generated from geometric transformations of an L-system [PL90] string. Hierarchical information is computed from the set of line segments representing the skeleton by forming joints at common endpoints. This information is constructed from root to tip such that any segments (herein branches) that stem from a common branch are its' children resulting in an n-ary tree (Figure 4). The user then selects branches from the n-ary tree and adds variation by associating drawn strokes with the selected branches.

A painter's algorithm [FvDFH96] is used for skeletal segment selection. The user draws a 2D stroke on top of the tree skeleton, displayed in 3D, and any branches that lie under the stroke are selected. This lets the user directly select the desired branches. However, most interesting tree skeletons have a large number of branches, many of them small, meaning that simply selecting branches that lie under the stroke may erroneously select many unwanted branches.

Smart decisions about the user's intended selection are made using the hierarchical information. We restrict selection of branches to one direction, descending down the n-tree, for example, you cannot select a child branch and then select its parent. Although restrictive, it is common practice to draw trees from the main trunk outward to more minor branches [Mal99].

Each branch segment can transition between three states: unselected, selected or undetermined as shown in Figure 5. The undetermined state is similar in appearance to the unselected state. As the user draws the selection stroke, selected

Figure 4: *Left: Conceptual n-ary tree where child and parent associations occur at joint locations **Right:** 3D n-ary tree from skeleton of base model.*

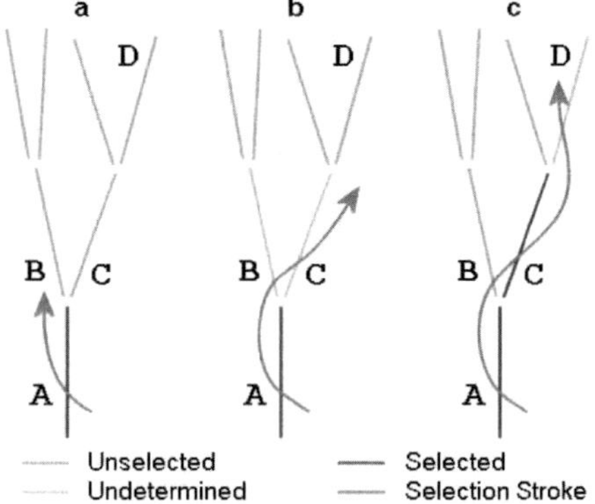

Figure 5: *Selection of branches A-D; Coloured segments show selected, unselected, and undetermined branches with progress of curved selection stroke (a–c).*

branches are drawn in a different color to indicate that they are selected. Branches can be in an undetermined state when the system cannot decisively determine if the segment was intended for selection. Like in a linked list, only a sequential path of branches may be selected.

Assume the user starts selection; all branches are unselected (Figure 5). The user initially draws a stroke over top of some branch A. No branches have previous been selected or marked undetermined, so branch A is immediately selected. The user continues the stroke upward and accidentally draws on top of one of A's children; the child branch B is temporarily marked as undetermined. Continuing the stroke upward, the user intentionally draws over another one of A's children and branch C is also temporarily marked as undetermined. Continuing the stroke upward, the user intentionally draws over another one of A's children and the branch, C, is also temporarily marked as undetermined. The two branches B and C are marked undetermined because the system is unsure which branch the user really wanted to select.

As the stroke is drawn further upward, it is drawn over top of a branch, D, that is one of C's children (A's grand-

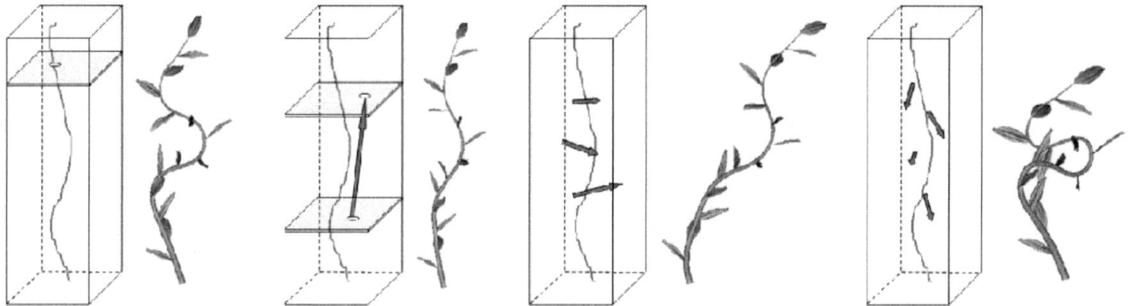

Figure 6: *Motion indicators representing dominant environmental factors which affect overall stem shape.*

child). This additional information helps to resolve our previous undetermined state. Since the user is now selecting C's child, the system determines that the user did not intend to select branch B but intended to select branch C. At this point, branch C is marked selected, branch B is marked as unselected, and branch D is marked as undetermined. The selection process continues as before until the user finishes the selection action (finishing the stroke and raising the stylus). At this point any remaining undetermined branches will become selected. Conversely, had the user drawn over top of B's children, the system would have unselected C.

4.2. Sketching Strokes

After selecting which branches will have variations added, users draw the 3D curves that defines the path of branch growth. These 3D curves are generated by sketching on top of the interaction surface while moving the 3D Tractus up or down. The tablet PC placed on top of the 3D Tractus behaves as a 'window' that allows the user to view the volume that they may draw in. Because we are viewing 3D curves on a 2D display, users must be given additional information that intuitively conveys the depth of these lines, or distance from the viewing window. Several approaches were designed, but we found that the most intuitive and clear communication of depth information is the use of line thickness when viewed with a perspective projection, as shown in Figure 3 (versus orthographic projection) [LSSS06].

4.3. Stroke Propagation for Multi-resolution Editing

As mentioned, the most interesting tree skeletons consist of a large number of branches, some of which may be very short. It would not make sense for the user to give the same amount of attention to the small leaf branches as they do to the main trunk or other large branches. At the same time, having variation in the small branches is still essential to generate realistic looking plants. We propose a feature where the user may control the resolution of the branches that the curve is applied to with two modes.

The first mode applies the curve only to the selected branches. However, this is insufficient for editing many branches quickly, especially small ones. The other mode handles the problem of defining variation for many small branches by applying the same curve to every single branch that is a descendant of the selected branches, all the way down to the leaf branches. The user may wish to combine both modes, so that all the descendants and the selected branches themselves are associated with a drawn stroke. This propagated editing can be over-ridden by simply selecting the desired branches and drawing the stroke to be associated with these branches. This flexibility allows the user to add variation to small branches without spending a lot of time drawing, but still allows details to be added if required. Multi-resolution editing can be applied to many branches whose shape is intended to be similar. However if the collection of associated branches includes branches of varying scales, due to re-sampling of the stroke the shape of very small branches may not always appear visually similar making the tree look more realistic.

4.4. Sketching Motion Indicators

In traditional sketching, artists use light line strokes to indicate aspects such as wind, sun, or rain. For example, an image with many long vertical lines, would indicate it was raining, and particularly hard. If the lines were shorter, it would convey a feeling of lighter rain. We use the same principle in our system. Influences such as wind, water, or sunlight may all be added through the creation of motion indicators. Motion indicators are sketch-based vectors which are added together to skew the overall growth of the plant. They are created by drawing and moving the 3D Tractus up and down, just like curves, except that only the start and end points are used. If the user wishes to add wind, so that the plant will be skewed to one side, he/she would draw a series of motion indicators in a horizontal direction. Sunlight may be added by drawing long upward motion indicators. Rain may push the plant down slightly, so downward motion indicators would be drawn. See Figure 6 for motion indicator examples.

4.5. Further Variation with a Biological Basis

Once the drawn strokes and motion indicators are associated with the base model, this determines the predefined growth

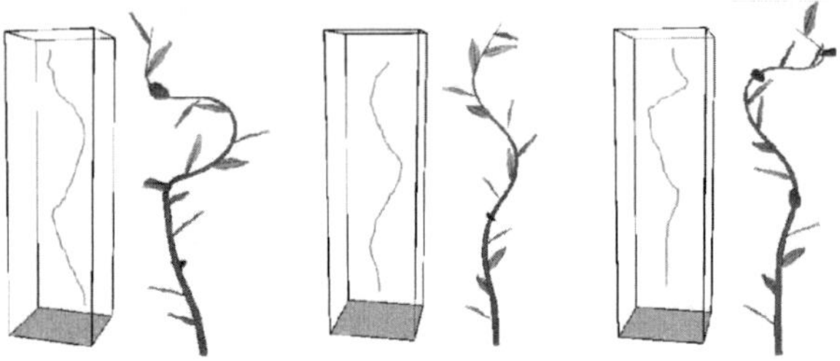

Figure 7: *Examples showing variations of original plant model (leftmost image) from user drawn 3D strokes.*

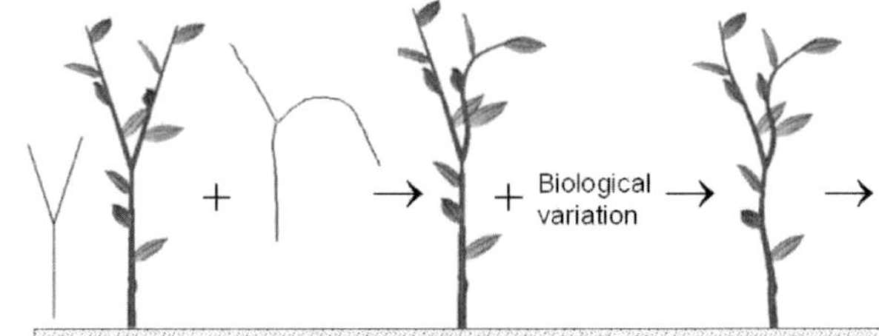

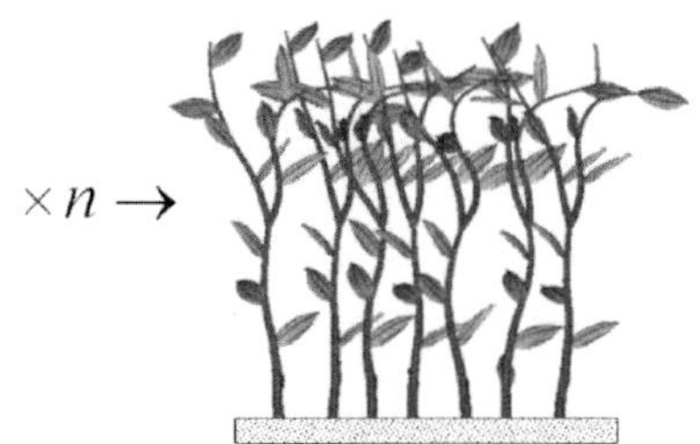

Figure 8: *Sketch-based variation of branching structures.* ***Top Row:****Original model and skeleton with stroke and biological variation* ***Bottom row:*** *collection of seven instances.*

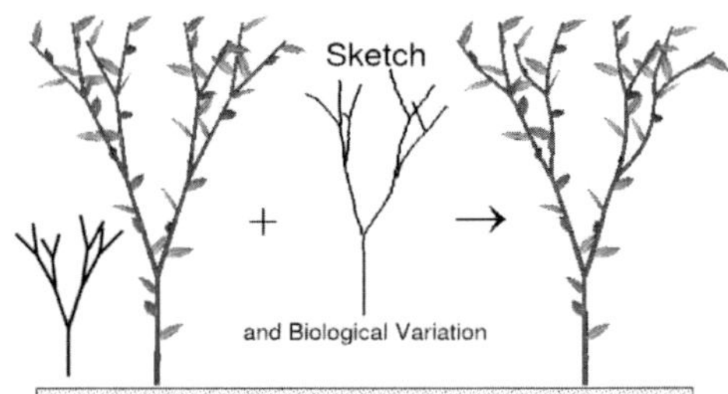

Figure 9: *Figure 8's model with more branching levels.*

direction and dominant influence respectively, in the growth simulation [SFS05]. The simulation incorporates numerous environmental factors affecting plant growth as random influences. These influences with the user data indirectly determine growth direction throughout the growth simulation. As the plant grows, a difference between the current and predefined (user's strokes) growth directions is determined. This difference is used to add further subtle, biological variation in branch and stem shape beyond what is specified by the user's strokes. Since the strokes are aligned with the branches, the branch topology and orientation remain consistent with the base model. This approach facilitates generating a large number of plants which have identical overall controlled branch and stem shape as defined by the user's stroke association with the base model, but with subtle variation. Section 5 shows example results.

5. Results and Discussion

Figure 7 shows examples of strokes in 3D space with corresponding resulting plants. Examples of plant collections generated by our method are shown in Figures 8 and 10. Our method facilitates quick creation of a collection of similar plants though direct sketch-based variation of branch and stem shape. Our approach maintains the branch location and orientation defined by the base-model, so that the resulting branch arrangement does not differ from the desired model. Due to variations in stroke path (Figure 7) and growth simulation (Figures 8 to 10) the resulting shape of the branch and direction of the tip can differ. Also, the overall direction of branch growth can be altered by adding indicators representing environmental factors as outlined in Section 4.4. Our selection method (Section 4.1) allows users to quickly and efficiently associate strokes with branches to create variation even with more complex models. Figure 9 shows an example with four branching levels. Furthermore, with our system, users have true 3D interaction for drawing the strokes.

We performed a preliminary small-scale user study to gather feedback about our system's usability. We recruited three computer science graduate students, two with strong art backgrounds. The participants were first informed about the purpose of our system and shown a brief demo. Each participant went through a training session using a simple L-system model and then got to use the application freely with two different and more elaborate L-system models. Each experiment took about 40 minutes. The experiment was evaluated by a simple qualitative, direct observation method using a video camera for documenting the sessions and the participants' interaction and feedback, and a structured interview for collecting comments at the end of each experiment.

All the participants enjoyed using the 3D Tractus-based application and commented that since every curve they drew generated a different looking plant it was easy and intuitive to generate random plants. All participants were able to effectively use the motion indicators and simulate wind and sun effects quickly and accurately. Selection was found to be very effective and assisted the participants when attempting to refer to branches in a large plant. Participants commented that the system was able to correctly resolve which branch they wanted to select, allowing them to choose branches quickly and with accuracy.

While our system was generally well received, participants indicated the desire for more control of the plant's

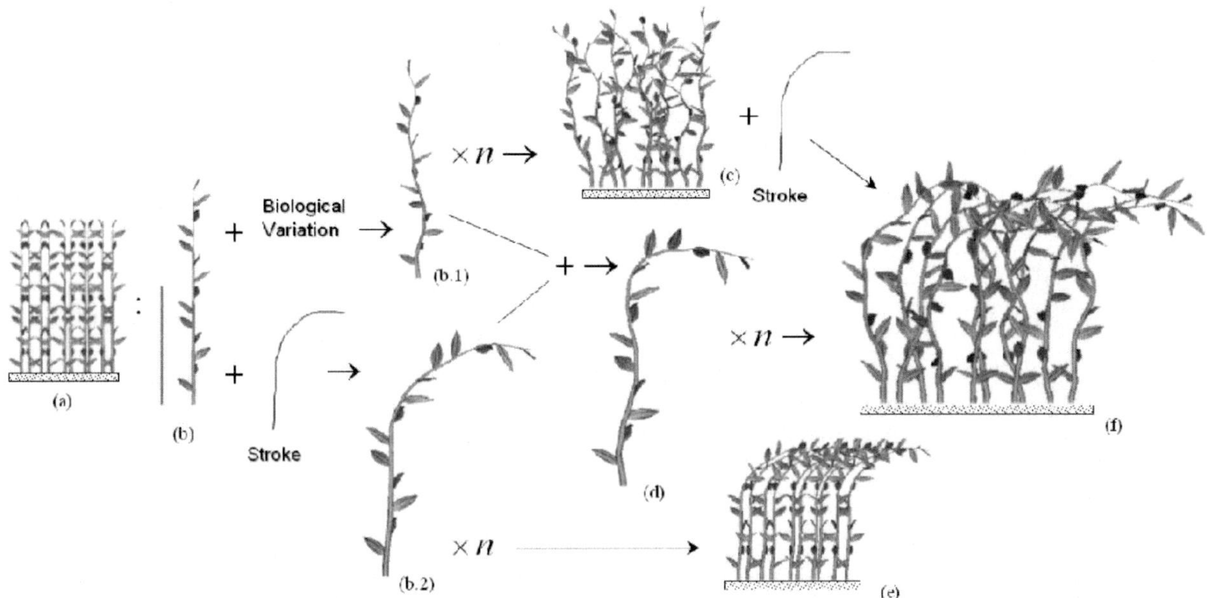

Figure 10: *A pipeline from original plant model on the far left to a collection of plants on the far right created by combining stroke and biological growth variation in each instance.*

growth. More precise control of motion indicators was requested: one participant asked to be able to map specific motion indicators to influence only specific parts of the plant. Although participants commented very positively about the smart selection technique, two suggested adding an intermediate selection visualization feedback indicating undetermined branches through color. Finally, one participant suggested we support selecting long paths by specifying only start and end branches of a selection and automatically selecting intermediate branches. We are planning to address and implement these suggestions in the future.

6. Conclusions and Future Work

We described a method for directly controlling branch stem and shape in plants for the purposes of creating variation among instances of the same plant model. The proposed method uses the 3D Tractus, a physical 3D interface, to allow the user to interact with the plant model intuitively in 3D and communicate shape information by drawing the intended shape in a 3D environment. To facilitate ease of specifying shape for numerous branches a method for propagating stroke shape through multi-resolution editing was used and a smart selection algorithm was used to associate strokes with branches. Further indicators of shape such as direction of light, wind or other environmental factors could be added by drawing sets of lines which indicate the direction and strength of these factors directly to the 3D environment.

The associated branch shape strokes were then used as input to a growth simulation framework. The simulation results in variation (aside from stroke variation) by adding

variation through growth. Overall, the simulation models the randomness in growth while trying to maintain the intended curvature of the branches and stems as indicated by the user-defined strokes. In this manner, the overall shape of stems and branches is as intended, with subtle variations in the shape introduced through free-handedness of sketch and simulation. The preliminary user evaluation we performed demonstrates the potential effectiveness of our approach in creating varied plant models.

Extending this framework of control and 3D creation beyond stems and branches to plant organs could be a useful direction of future work. This may include not only creating and controlling the shape of plant organs, but also their spatial 3D distribution and orientation on the plant.

Acknowledgments

This research was funded by several grants provided by the National Sciences and Engineering Research Council (NSERC), Canada.

References

[AK84]　AONO M., KUNII T. L.: Botanical tree image generation. *IEEE Computer Graphics and Applications* 4, 5 (May 1984), 10–29, 32–34.

[BBMP97]　BILLINGHURST M., BALDIS S., MATHESON L., PHILIPS M.: 3D palette: a virtual reality content creation tool. In *Proc. of Virtual Reality Software and Technology* (1997), pp. 155–156.

[BPF*03] BOUDON F., PRUSINKIEWICZ P., FEDERL P., GODIN C., KARWOWSKI R.: Interactive design of bonsai tree models. *Computer Graphics Forum (Proc. of Eurographics '03) 22*, 3 (2003), 591 – 599.

[CHZ00] COHEN J. M., HUGHES J. F., ZELEZNIK R. C.: Harold: A world made of drawings. In *Proc. of the First International Symposium on Non Photorealistic Animation and Rendering (NPAR '00)* (2000), p. 83 Ű 90.

[CMZ*99] COHEN J. M., MARKOSIAN L., ZELEZNIK R. C., HUGHES J. F., BARZEL R.: An interface for sketching 3d curves. In *Proc. of the 1999 symposium on Interactive 3D graphics (SI3D '99)* (1999), pp. 17–21.

[FOL02] FOSKEY M., OTADUY M., LIN M.: ArtNova: Touch-enabled 3D model design. In *Proc. of IEEE Virtual Reality Conference* (2002), pp. 119–126.

[FvDFH96] FOLEY J., VAN DAM A., FEINER S. K., HUGHES J. F.: *Computer Graphics. Principles and Practice. 2nd Edition in C.* Addison-Wesley, 1996. FOL j 96:1 1.Ex.

[GEL00] GREGORY A., EHMANN S., LIN M.: inTouch: Interactive multiresolution modeling and 3d painting with a haptic interface. In *Proc. of IEEE Virtual Reality Conference* (2000), pp. 45–54.

[HG02] HACHET M., GUITTON P.: The interaction table - a new input device designed for interaction in immersive large display environments. In *Proc. of 8th Eurographics Workshop on Virtual Environments* (2002), pp. 189–196.

[HGRT03] HACHET M., GUITTON P., REUTER P., TYNDIUK F.: The CAT for efficient 2d and 3d interaction as an alternative to mouse adaptations. In *Proc. of Virtual Reality Software and Technology* (2003), pp. 205–212.

[HRPGK94] HINCKLEY K., R. PAUSCH J., GOBLE, KASSELL N.: Passive real-world interface props for neurosurgical visualization. In *Proc. of CHI '94* (1994), pp. 452–458.

[IDV05] INTERACTIVE DATA VISUALIZATION I. I.: Speedtree. *http://www.speedtree.com/* (2005).

[IITS04] IJIRI T., IGARASHI T., TAKAHASHI S., SHIBAYAMA E.: Sketch interface for 3d modeling of flowers. In *Technical Sketch SIGGRAPH '04* (2004).

[IOOI05] IJIRI T., OKABE M., OWADA S., IGARASHI T.: Floral diagrams and inflorescences: Interactive flower modeling using botanical structural constraints. *ACM Transactions on Graphics (Proc. of SIGGRAPH '05) 24*, 3 (2005), 720–726.

[LD99] LINTERMANN B., DEUSSEN O.: Interactive modeling of plants. *IEEE Computer Graphics and Applications 19*, 1 (1999), 56 – 65.

[LSSS06] LAPIDES P., SHARLIN E., SOUSA M. C., STREIT L.: The 3D Tractus: A three-dimensional drawing board. In *The First IEEE International Workshop on Horizontal Interactive Human-Computer Systems (TableTop2006)* (2006).

[Mal99] MALTZMAN S.: *Drawing Trees Step by Step.* North Light Books, 1999.

[OC05] ONYX COMPUTING: Onyxtree. *http://www.onyxtree.com/* (2005).

[OHKK03] ONISHI K., HASUIKE S., KITAMURA Y., KISHINO F.: Interactive modeling of trees by using growth simulation. In *Proc. of the ACM symposium on Virtual reality software and technology (VRST '03)* (2003), pp. 66–72.

[OI03] OKABE M., IGARASHI T.: 3d modeling of trees from freehand sketches. In *Technical Sketch SIGGRAPH '03* (2003).

[OOI05] OKABE M., OWADA S., IGARASHI T.: Interactive design of botanical trees using freehand sketches and example-based editing. *Computer Graphics Forum (Proc. of Eurographics '05) 24*, 3 (2005), 487–496.

[PBPS99] POWER J. L., BRUSH A. J. B., PRUSINKIEWICZ P., SALESIN D. H.: Interactive arrangement of botanical L-system models. In *Proc. of the 1999 symposium on Interactive 3D graphics (SI3D '99)* (1999), pp. 175–182.

[PL90] PRUSINKIEWICZ P., LINDENMAYER A.: *The algorithmic beauty of plants.* Springer-Verlag New York, Inc., New York, 1990.

[PTW98] POUPYREV L., TOMOKAZU N., WEGHORST S.: Virtual notepad: Handwriting in immersive vr. In *Proc. of Virtual Reality Annual International Symposium '98* (1998), pp. 126–132.

[SFS05] STREIT L., FEDERL P., SOUSA M. C.: Modelling plant variation through growth. *Computer Graphics Forum (Proc. of Eurographics '05) 24*, 3 (2005), 497 – 506.

[SRS91] SACHS E., ROBERTS A., STOOPS D.: 3-draw:a tool for designing 3d shapes. In *IEEE Computer Graphics and Applications* (1991), pp. 18–26.

[ST05] SENSABLE TECHNOLOGIES I.: PHANTOM®arm. In *www.sensable.com* (2005).

[TFK*02] TSANG M., FITZMAURICE G., KURTENBACH G., KHAN A., BUXTON B.: Boom chameleon: Simultaneous capture of 3d viewpoint, voice and gesture annotations on a spatially-aware display. In *Proc. of Symposium on User Interface Software and Technology* (2002), pp. 111–120.

[Xfr05] XFROG: Greenworks Organic-Software. *http://www.xfrog.com/* (2005).

EUROGRAPHICS Workshop on Sketch-Based Interfaces and Modeling (2006)
Thomas Stahovich and Mario Costa Sousa (Editors)

Sketching Reaction-Diffusion Texture

Ly Phan[1] and Cindy Grimm[2]

[1]Southern Arkansas University, Arkansas, United States
[2]Washington University in St. Louis, Missouri, United States

Abstract

In this work, we present an interactive interface for sketching synthesized textures. Reaction-Diffusion (RD) is used as the basis for texture synthesis. RD allows an unlimited amount of non-repeating texture and offers great flexibility for mapping textures to arbitrary surfaces. However, it can be difficult to find starting values of parameters that will produce interesting patterns. We use machine learning to resolve the difficulty of determining appropriate initial values of the RD system. The system described here allows a user to sketch a pattern of spots or stripes with arbitrary orientations, and then automatically generates a pattern with the same attributes as the sketch. It also allows the user to interactively create more complex textures by adding another layer of pattern, as well as manipulate the color of the resulting texture. We also show that this procedure can be applied to realistic 3D surfaces.

Categories and Subject Descriptors (according to ACM CCS): I.3.7 [Computer Graphics]: Color, shading, shadowing, and texture; I.3.8 [Computer Graphics]: Applications

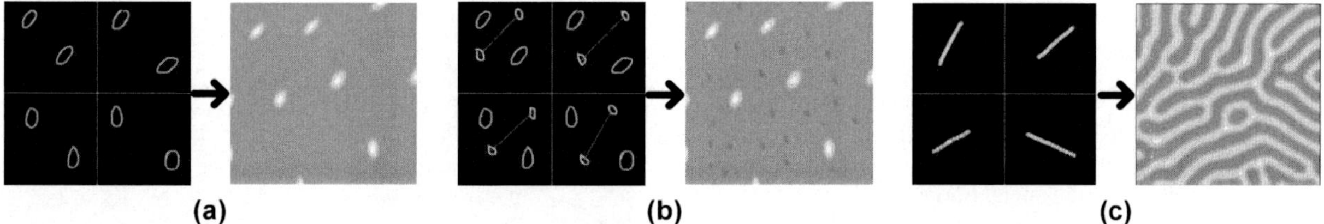

(a)   (b)   (c)

Figure 1. *(a) User sketches ellipses with different orientation. Our system generates dots with similar size, shape, and orientation. (b) User adds smaller ellipses to the sketch. The system generates smaller dots in between larger dots. (c) User sketches lines with different slopes. The system generates random stripes with similar orientation.*

1. Introduction

Textures are two-dimensional images or three-dimensional volumes that can be mapped onto an object's surface. Very often, the object's surface is larger than the texture sample available, hence the need for texture synthesis – generating more of a texture from a given sample. There are two main types of textures: raster textures, and procedural textures. Raster textures can be scanned pictures or painted images. They are ready-to-map, but the cost of memory storage is very high and resampling and mapping them to an arbitrary surface can be very difficult. Procedural textures, on the other hand, are defined mathematically, and therefore take little memory to store. They are also easier to resample and map to a surface. In this paper, we focus on textures generated from a method called Reaction-Diffusion. In addition to allowing an unlimited amount of non-repeating texture, this approach also offers greater flexibility for both controlling the attributes of patterns and mapping textures to arbitrary surfaces.

Reaction-Diffusion (RD) was first introduced as a model of morphogenesis, a biological pattern-formation process in which two or more chemicals – called morphogens – diffuse over a surface and react with each other. The differences in concentration of morphogens form certain animal coat patterns, such as spots and stripes [Tur52]. This process is defined by differential equations, which control the change in concentration of one morphogen relative to other morphogens over time.

A RD system consists of numerous parameters, a few of these being the reaction rates k/s, the diffusion rates D, and the random factor β (Section 3). At present there is no intuitive way to determine the values of these parameters that will produce interesting patterns, much less a pattern that has certain attributes. Thus, although RD can produce interesting and varied textures, it is difficult for a user to use a RD system without having a deep knowledge of its internal workings. We solve this problem by developing an interactive interface that allows users to sketch a rough version of their desired pattern. Our system then automatically generates a texture sample that contains similar features (Figure 1). This is done by analyzing the sketch's attributes and using machine-learning technique to map these attributes to the appropriate starting parameters. Our approach allows for more control over the attributes of the patterns produced by the RD system (in case of Figure 1, the size and orientation of spots and stripes). The system also includes a coloring interface that gives the user freedom to vary the color of the generated textures. Finally, we show that our approach can be applied to generate patterns, as defined by a user, on a 3D surface.

The rest of this paper is organized as follows. In Section 2, we present our interface for sketching RD textures. In Section 3, we provide a brief background of RD systems. In Section 4, we summarize the previous work that has been done on generating textures with RD. Section 5 contains a detailed description of the implementation of this system, including our extension to existing techniques and our application of machine learning to solve the problem of finding the appropriate parameter values. In Section 6, we illustrate how our method extends to 3D surfaces. We conclude with a discussion of the future work in Section 7.

2. Sketching RD textures using the interface

Initially, the user sketches ellipses and lines in the sketch window, which act as inputs to the system. The system then generates a texture consisting of spots or stripes that has similar attributes as the initial sketch. These attributes are shape, size, spacing, and orientation of the spots and stripes that form the textures.

The sketch window is divided into smaller regions to allow for a pattern with varied attributes across the entire image. For the purpose of experimenting, the sketch was divided into four regions (Figure 2), but this could be *n by n* regions for a larger texture. Average values of attributes in each region are used in determining the final attributes of the output texture. Since patterns in different regions can vary in size, shape, or orientation, linear interpolation of the attribute values between neighboring regions gives the output texture a smooth transition from one region to the next.

2.1. Sketching spots

2.1.1. Controlling size of spots. Spots are described by their size, shape and orientation. The user can generate spots by sketching ellipses in the sketch window. The system calculates the average size of ellipses in each region. A mapping function then maps these values to a set of starting parameters such that the spots generated by this system will have the same size as those sketched. This mapping function is described later in Section 5.4.1. As shown in Figure 2, the spots are varied in size across the image with a smooth transition in size from the top left to the bottom right corner.

2.1.2. Controlling orientation of spots. Using the same technique as that for varying the size of spots as explained above, their orientation can also be varied across the image (Figure 3). Implementation details for generating textures with arbitrarily oriented spots can be found in Section 5.3.

2.1.3. Controlling spacing among spots. In general, a RD system of spots would have the spacing between spots determined by the size of spots. Implementing cascaded RD system as described in [Tur92], our system allows the user to generate patterns from a sketch where arbitrary sized spots can have arbitrary spacing between them (Figure 4). This technique will be described in detail in Section 4.

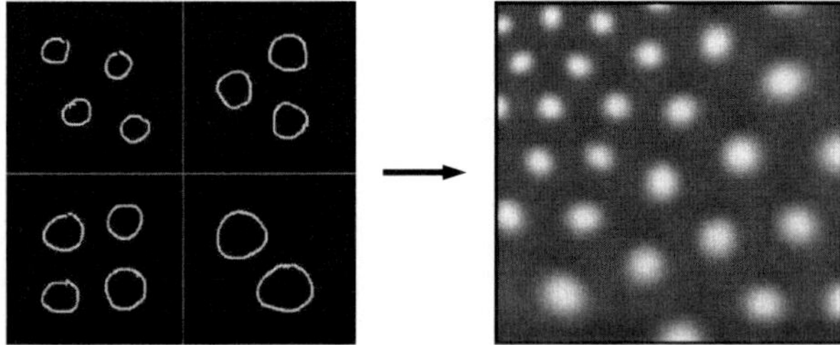

Figure 2. *Size of the spots produced varies over the grid (right), as depicted in user's sketch (left).*

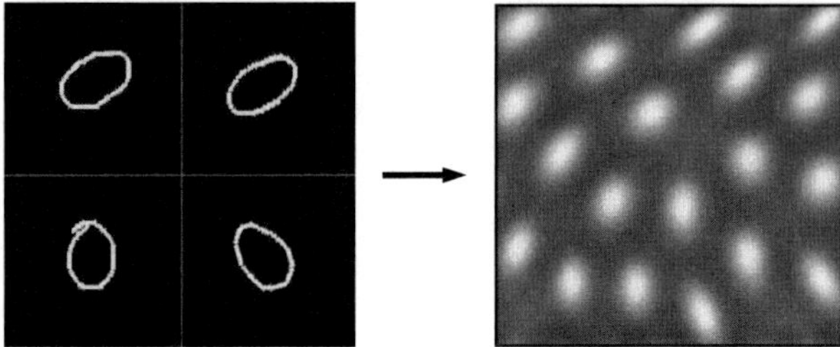

Figure 3. *Orientation of spots produced (right) varies over the grid as sketched (left).*

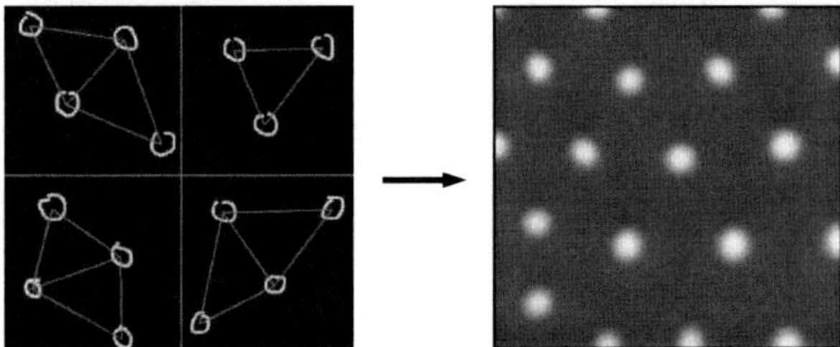

Figure 4. *Small spots with large spacing (right) as sketched in the sketch window (left). The red lines are produced when the sketch is analyzed. These lines correspond to the distances among the spots.*

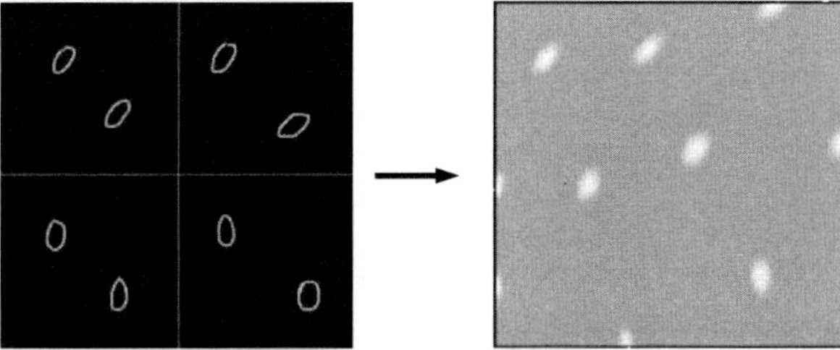

Figure 5a. *The first simulation produces yellow spots (right) based on the sketch of the larger ellipses (left).*

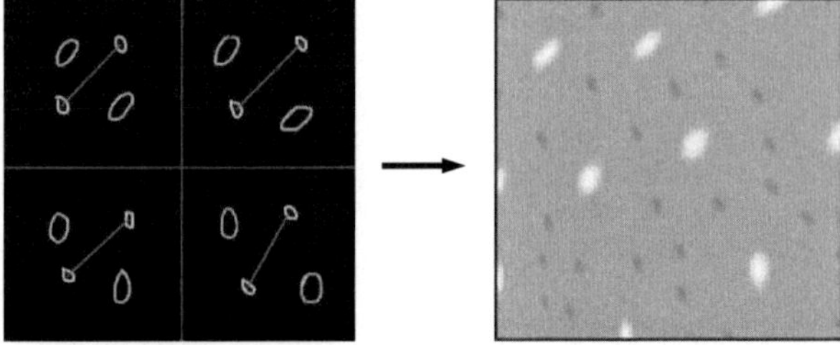

Figure 5b. *The second simulation produces red spots (right). Red lines between smaller ellipses in the sketch are produced when the sketch is analyzed (left).*

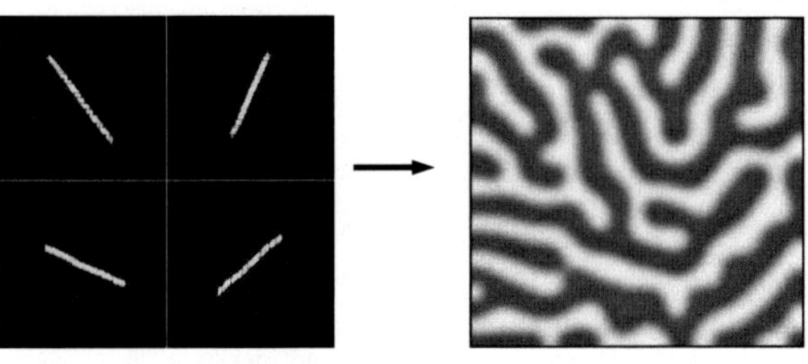

Figure 6. *The system generates pattern of stripes (right) that have the same orientation as in user's sketch (left).*

2.1.4. Complex patterns. The previous subsections described how spots with desired size, orientation and spacing can be obtained. However, the spots generated in this way have only one size in each region. In order to have small spots interspersed with larger spots through out the image (Figure 5b), we implement cascaded RD system as described in [Tur92].

Using our interface, the user first sketches only the large ellipses in the sketch window (Figure 5a). The system generates spots with spacing and orientation as sketched. These spots form the first layer of patterns, with a coloring scheme as described in Section 2.3. To add more spots into this texture, the user first freezes these larger spots (set the morphogens concentration in these cells constant). A second set of ellipses can now be drawn in the sketch window (Figure 5b). The system produces a second set of spots (the second layer of patterns), with orientation as sketched, in between the first set. The outcome of this second set of spots depends on the spacing among the first set and the size of the second set. The size of the second set of spots should be small enough for them to form in between the larger spots.

2.2. Sketching stripes

Stripe pattern can be generated by sketching straight lines in the sketch window (Figure 6). Stripes are described by their width and orientation. The user needs to draw at least one line representing stripes in each region of the sketch window. The system calculates average slopes of lines in each region. Based on these values, the system then generates stripes with orientations similar to those in the sketch. The detailed description of this implementation can be found in Section 5.1. The user can choose one of four different sizes to draw the line, resulting in four different thicknesses of the stripes.

2.3. Color control

Our system generates textures by imitating the RD process between morphogens. The concentration of each morphogen is mapped to a color. The patterns of spots and stripes are formed through the variations in concentration of the morphogens as a result of the RD process. After the texture is produced, the user can use the color control interface provided by the system to vary the color of the texture by changing the mapping of the morphogen concentrations to colors.

The color control interface is based on the work presented in [KTBG03]. The interface provides two sets of colors illustrated by the two long spacing bars in Figures 7 and 8. The upper bar displays the set of colors used for the first layer of patterns while the lower bar displays the set of colors used for the second layer (this second color set is used only in the case of complex patterns, as in Figure 8). A user can use the Red/Green/Blue slide bars to define the colors to be used for either of the two sets. Colors can be added, modified, removed or the order of colors can be changed for each of the two sets. A user can also adjust the spacing between colors in one set by moving the buttons (one for each color) on the spacing bar. Apart from the spacing bar, the user can use a Bezier curve to blend between colors. The blending of colors in each set is based on the distance between two adjacent colors on the spacing bar, and by the shape of the corresponding Bezier curve.

The concentration of a given morphogen is mapped to the continuous set of colors; the lowest concentration (valley) corresponds to the first color in the set, and the highest concentration (peak) corresponds to the last color (Figure 7).

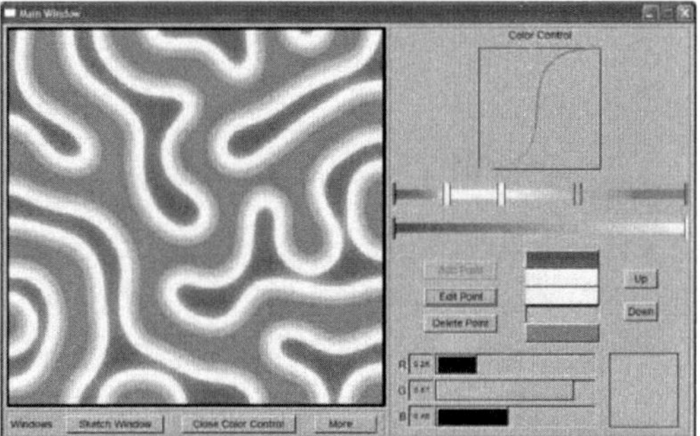

Figure 7. *Concentration of morphogen A is mapped to the upper set of colors, with the lowest concentration mapped to violet and the highest concentration mapped to pink. Transition between the valley to the peak of the morphogen's concentrations is visualized by a change in color, from violet to yellow, to green, and then to pink.*

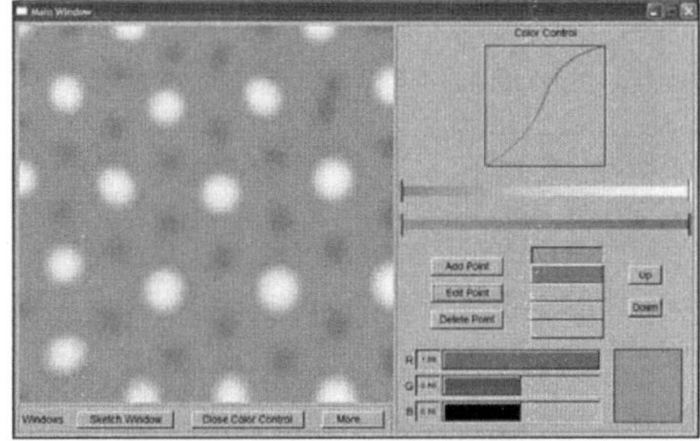

Figure 8. *Spots belonging to the first layer are mapped to the first color set (pink to yellow), while spots belonging to the second layer are mapped to the second color set (pink to red).*

3. Background of Reaction-Diffusion

A Reaction-Diffusion (RD) system consists of two (or more) morphogens *diffusing* over a surface and *reacting* with one another to form a stable pattern. This pattern is visualized by mapping each morphogen's concentration to a color. In general, this process can be modeled by the following differential equations [Tur91]:

$$\frac{\partial a}{\partial t} = F(a,b) + D_a \nabla^2 a \qquad \text{(Eq. 1)}$$

$$\frac{\partial b}{\partial t} = G(a,b) + D_b \nabla^2 b$$

where a and b represent the concentrations of morphogens A and B, and D_a and D_b are diffusion rates of A and B, respectively. At any point in time, the concentrations a and b are determined by the above functions. $F(a,b)$ and $G(a,b)$ describe the change in the concentration of A and of B, respectively, as a result of the reaction processes between A and B. These functions will decide if one morphogen inhibits the other, or sustains the other at the same position. Laplacians $\nabla^2 a$ and $\nabla^2 b$ are the measures of how high the concentrations of A and B are relative to the concentrations of the same morphogens, respectively, in the surrounding cells. In the case of a grid (Figure 9a), the formula for $\nabla^2 a$ is as follows:

$$\nabla^2 a = a_{i-1,j} + a_{i+1,j} + a_{i,j-1} + a_{i,j+1} - 4a_{i,j} \qquad \text{(Eq. 2)}$$

In general, for an arbitrary surface, e.g. a mesh (Figure 9b), the formula will be:

$$\nabla^2 a = \sum_{k=1}^{n} a_{ik} - na_i \qquad \text{(Eq. 3)}$$

For a given morphogen A, if the concentration of A in the current cell is higher than that of A in the surrounding cells, Laplacian $\nabla^2 a$ is negative. In the next time step, A diffuses away from this cell, thus the concentration of A reduces. The reverse occurs if the concentration of A is lower in the current cell relative to the surrounding cells. D_a and D_b specify how fast A and B diffuse across the surface. At any time t, the concentration of A is the sum of a reaction process between A and B – denoted by $F(a,b)$ – and a diffusion process of A – denoted by $D_a \nabla^2 a$ (see Appendix).

4. Previous work

The work by Turing in [Tur52] describes a RD system of two morphogens that forms spots (Turing spot system). Other researchers have since shown that simple patterns, from spots to stripes, can also be generated with reaction-diffusion mechanisms using different systems of morphogens and equations [Bar81, Mur82, Mei82]. In [Mei82], Meinhardt described a RD system of two morphogens that produces spots (Meinhardt spot system), and another RD system of five morphogens that produces stripes (Meinhardt stripe system). In 1991, Witkin and Kass adapted RD for texture synthesis and added anisotropy by varying diffusion across the surface [WK91]. It was also shown that complex patterns could be generated using double simulations of cascaded RD systems [Tur91].

Using the three RD systems (Turing spot, Meinhardt spot, and Meinhardt stripe), we can generate random spots or stripes by applying random variations to the concentrations of morphogens in the system. We can also generate regular stripes by raising the initial concentration of one morphogen at certain cells, called "initiator cells." During RD simulation, stripes radiate from these cells (Figure 10).

Cascaded systems built upon these three basic forms can generate more complex patterns, such as leopard spots or mixed spots of different sizes [Tur92]. Mixed spots of different sizes are obtained by first generating large spots. These large spots are then frozen – the concentrations of morphogens in those cells that form the spots are kept constant. The second simulation then creates small spots in between the large spots (Figure 11a). Leopard spots, or rosettes (Figure 11b), are generated using the Turing spot system in a similar way, but with one extra step. After freezing the large spots, the concentrations of morphogens in cells that form these spots are reset to the initial level [Tur92]. During the second simulation, the small spots tend to form a circle around the large spots instead of in between them.

Iterations

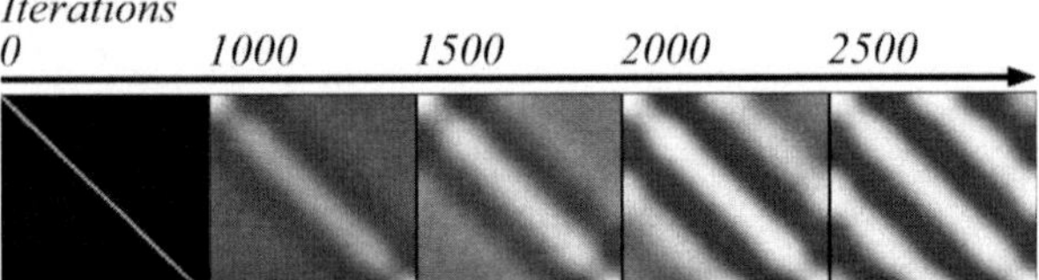

Figure 10. *Regular stripes radiate from initiator cells during RD process.*

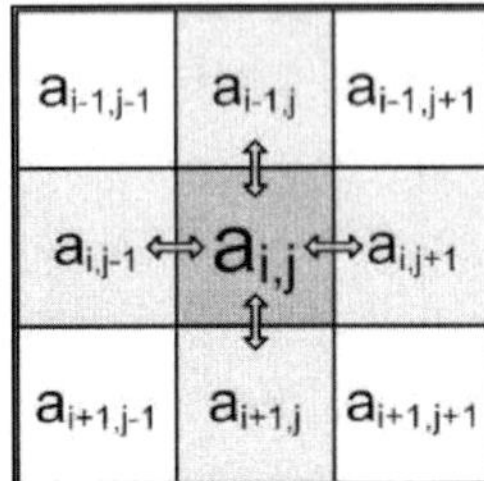

Figure 9a. *Morphogen A diffuses to and from four adjacent cells.*

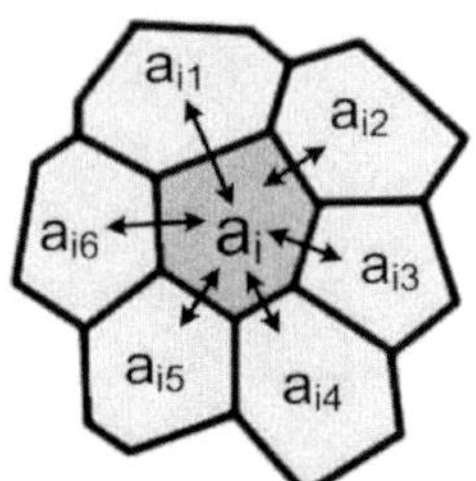

Figure 9b. *Morphogen A diffuses to and from all adjacent cells.*

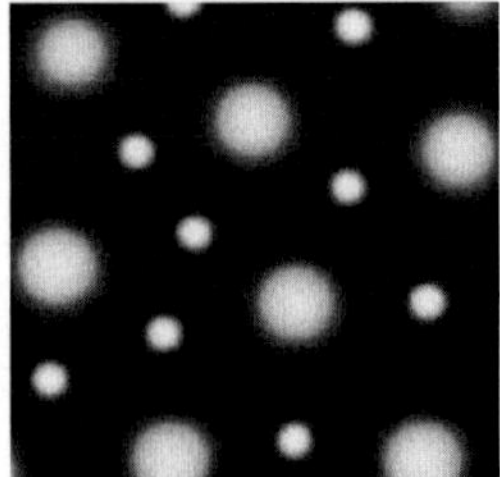

Figure 11a. *Mixed spots generated by the Meinhardt spot system.*

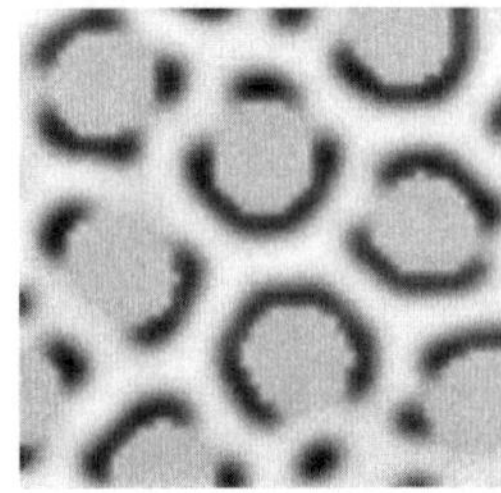

Figure 11b. *Leopard spots produced by Turing spot system.*

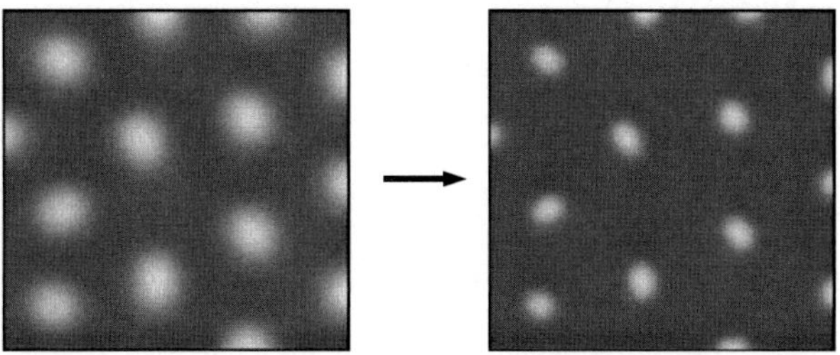

Figure 12. *Two-step generation of small spots with large spacing using cascaded Turing spot system. First, large spots with large spacing are produced (left). Next, small spots are produced at the same sites where large spots had been (right).*

When single RD simulation is employed to generate spots, the distance between spots, or spacing, is proportional to the size of the spots. However, using cascaded Turing spot systems as described in [Tur92], small spots with large spacing can be generated (Figure 12). The first simulation yields large spots with large spacing. The concentration of morphogens from the first simulation is then used to set up the second simulation such that smaller spots are produced at the same positions where the large spots had been, thus maintaining large spacing.

The existing systems of spots and stripes described above have limited flexibility. For example, the spots and stripes described before cannot be oriented in any arbitrary direction that the user may desire. More importantly, the user needs to directly tweak parameters of the RD system in order to get a desired pattern. It can be difficult to find initial values of morphogens that produce interesting patterns, much less a pattern that has certain desired attributes. In the following section we describe our interface with which a user can sketch RD texture. This is an intuitive method for a user to generate patterns automatically, without the need for knowledgeable tweaking of RD parameters. In order to allow more flexibility to the textures that can be generated, we also provide extensions that support arbitrarily oriented spots and stripes. In the following section, we will show how we give additional control to the attributes of the patterns, and how we apply machine learning to map from our high-level spot description to RD parameters.

5. Implementation

5.1. High-level description for spots

The main objective of this work is to develop an intuitive and easy way for a user to automatically generate a desired texture. The first step is the intuitive sketch interface described in Section 2. However, the RD systems which are used to generate the textures require values of various parameters as inputs. In order to extract the parameter values from the sketch, we devised a high-level description for the spots in terms of the three parameters: size, orientation and spacing.

When the user draws spots in the sketch window, the system fits ellipses to the spots, and extracts their centers, orientations and radii. The area of a spot is used to describe its size; the ratio of minor radius to major radius to describe its shape, and the major axis to describe its orientation. We then use Delaunay triangulation method to determine the closest neighbors of a spot, and then calculate the distance from this spot to its neighbors. The average distance between adjacent spots in the user's sketch is then used as the spacing between all the spots for the purpose of generating the texture.

5.2. Application of Machine learning for mapping user's sketch to RD parameters

In the previous section, we describe how physical attributes of the sketch are calculated. Once these values have been extracted, we use machine learning to map between the physical attributes and RD parameters. This step is described in the following paragraphs.

5.2.1. Preparing training data for machine learning.

The purpose of our machine learning function is to map the spot attributes to parameter values. The first step is to learn how a set of initial parameter values map to spot attributes. Since the parameters used to determine orientation and size with spacing are independent, learning the mapping for the orientation and for the size with spacing can be done separately. To reduce the total number of data points, we generated four different sets of training data, two for Turing and Meinhardt spots' orientation and two for Turing and Meinhardt spots' size and spacing. The RD system was run 15,600 times with different parameter settings to generate textures with various patterns that serve as training data for this learning process. For each RD spot system, we use a different threshold value for morphogen A or B to trace the boundary of the spot. We then fit ellipses to these spots. Bad textures (e.g. when the patterns are not well formed, or if the size of the spots is too small to perform ellipse fitting) are excluded. Using the same method as for extracting spot attributes from user's sketch, we calculate the physical attributes of spots generated by the RD system (Figure 13). During the texture generation process, the training data were fed to a machine learning function to map the spot attributes from the user's sketch to corresponding RD parameters.

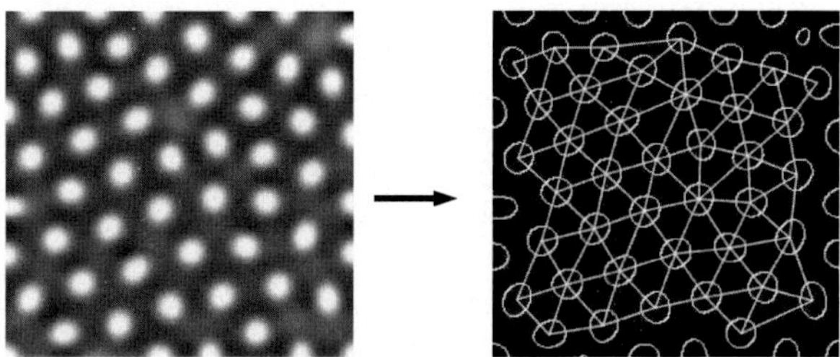

Figure 13. *Ellipses (left) are fitted to RD spots (right). Yellow lines connect each ellipse to their closest neighbors as determined by Delaunay triangulation.*

5.2.2. Locally Weighted Regression. To implement machine learning, we choose Locally Weighted Regression (LWR) because it does not require an extremely large collection of training data, and yet it is highly efficient for learning complex mappings from real-valued input vectors to real-valued output vectors using noisy data.

Locally Weighted Regression is a memory-based algorithm for learning continuous curves that uses only training data close to the particular point X. Points nearby are weighted by their distance to point X. A nonlinear regression – an estimation technique using interpolation to predict one variable from one or more other variables – is then calculated using these weighted points. We use the LWR Matlab function presented in [SA94].

5.2.3. Mapping functions. The results we get from mapping size and spacing of spots to RD parameters are not always reliable because of the random nature of the Reaction-Diffusion technique. Therefore, we build a mapping function for size and spacing of spots using linear interpolation. The function takes spacing or area as input and returns reaction rate as output (one to one relationship). For orientation of spots, the mapping function is a LWR function that takes as inputs the ratio of minor radius to major radius as well as the two (x & y) components of the major axis vector of the sketched ellipses, and returns direction coefficients as outputs.

Inputs	Outputs	Mapping functions
Spacing	Reaction rate (k or s)	Linear Interpolation
Area	Reaction rate (k or s)	Linear Interpolation
Ratio of minor radius to major radius, x component of major axis vector, y component of major axis vector	Direction coefficients (E-W, S-N, SE-NW, SW-NE)	Locally Weighted Regression

Table 1. *Input sketch parameters with their related output RD parameters and mapping functions.*

5.3. Extensions to existing RD spots

5.3.1. Arbitrarily oriented spots. The existing RD systems described in the Section 4 can generate only anisotropic spots, which are elliptical spots in vertical or horizontal directions. This is because these systems allow the morphogens to diffuse to four neighbors only, along the directions North, South, East, and West (Figure 9a). In this work, apart from using anisotropic diffusion rates, we also allow the morphogens to diffuse from and to each of the eight neighbors (Figure 14a). In addition to diffusion rates D_a and D_b shown in Equation 1, we also expand the formula calculating Laplacians (Equation 2) and add direction coefficients to the flow of morphogens to and from neighbor cells (Figure 14a). These coefficients specify preferential directions in which morphogens diffuse faster,

thus the spots are elongated in these directions. As a result, spots can have arbitrary orientation.

Even though morphogens can flow from and to all eight directions, they always flow equally in symmetrically opposite directions. Therefore, four direction coefficients (E-W, S-N, SE-NW and SW-NE) are enough to define the diffusion of chemicals to all eight neighboring cells.

5.3.2. Non-homogeneous patterns. In a RD system, there are several parameters such as the reaction rates, diffusion rates, and direction coefficients that determine the size, shape, spacing, and orientation of the spots. In order to allow non-homogeneous patterns, instead of using the same parameter values everywhere, we blend the parameter values across the grid. The result is patterns of spots that have size, orientation, and spacing changing across the image (Figure 15).

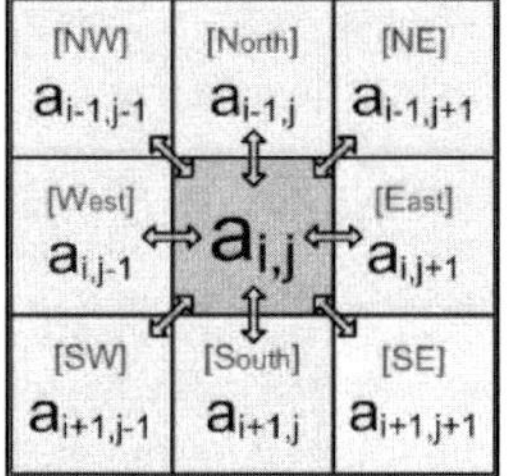

Figure 14a. *Morphogens from one cell can diffuse from and to all eight of its neighbors. Direction coefficients give the spots shape and orientation.*

Figure 14b. *Anisotropic Turing spots with the user-supplied direction indicated by arrow*

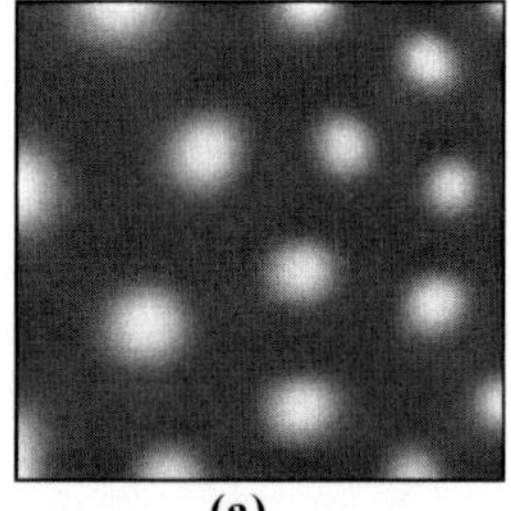

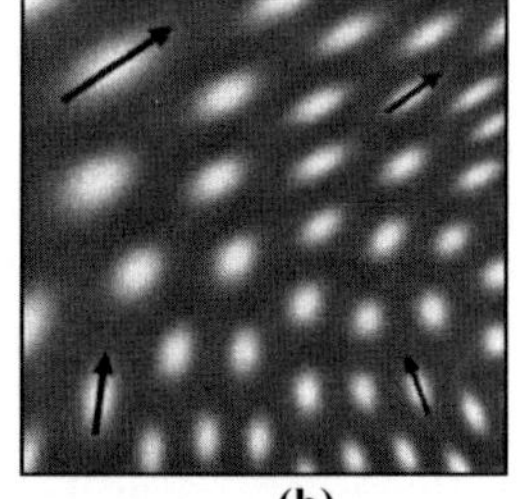

(a)   **(b)**

Figure 15. *Examples of non-homogeneous textures of spots with size (a) and orientation (b) changing across the image.*

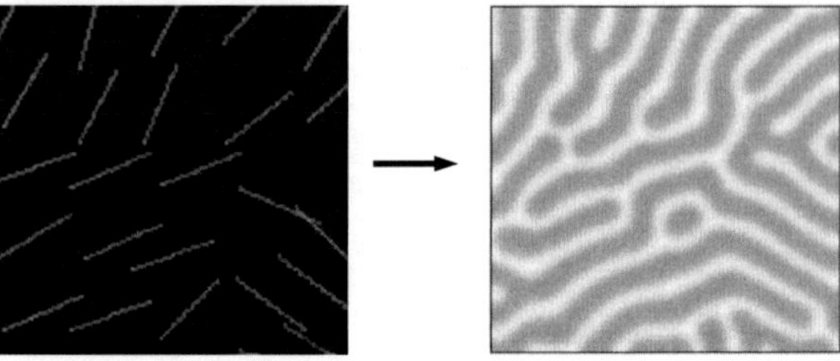

Figure 16. *Seeding the stripe system with line segments (left) results in a texture with similar orientation (right). Note that slopes of the stripes vary across the image.*

5.4. Oriented random stripes

Direction coefficients can be used to generate oriented spots (as explained in Section 5.3.1), but they do not help in generating oriented stripes. Initiator cells that form oriented random line segments, however, can create oriented random stripes. The system calculates the average slopes of the lines sketched by the user in each of the regions of the sketch window. These values are used to seed random lines with slight variations of these average slopes. The Meinhardt stripes system then generates random stripes that have similar orientations (Figure 16).

6. Sketching RD texture on a 3D mesh

We demonstrate our interface for creating RD textures on 3D surfaces. Instead of drawing on a separate sketching window, the user can draw spots directly on a mesh. The system then fits ellipses to the spots, computes their attributes, maps these to appropriate parameters, which are then associated with vertices of the mesh that lie within these ellipses. The remaining vertices are assigned parameter values that are a linear combination of the values at vertices lying within the closest ellipses.

To generate spots of different sizes on the bunny in Figure 19, the diffusion rates of morphogens A and B are propagated and blended over the mesh based on the size and position of spots sketched by the user. The relative proportions of morphogen flowing to each of the neighboring vertices are calculated as explained below.

For each vertex i in the mesh and its neighboring vertex ik (among its n neighboring vertices numbered $i1$ through in), the term d_{ik} denotes the distance between centroids of the two triangles on either side of the edge connecting vertex i to vertex ik (Figure 17). The percentage coefficient P_{ik} for the flow of morphogens between these two vertices is calculated as the ratio:

$$P_{ik} = \frac{d_{ik}}{\sum_{k=1}^{n} d_{ik}} \quad \text{(Eq. 4)}$$

And the Laplacian $\nabla^2 a$ for vertex i is given by Equation 5, where a_i is the morphogen concentration in vertex i.

$$\nabla^2 a = 4 \times \left(\sum_{k=1}^{n} P_{ik} a_{ik} - a_i \right) \quad \text{(Eq. 5)}$$

To generate oriented spots, the vector showing the orientation of the ellipse is projected onto the tangent plane at each vertex (Figure 18). During RD simulation, the faces surrounding each vertex are rotated so that this projected vector becomes parallel to the x axis. These faces are then scaled down along the x axis according to the ratio of the minor radius to the major radius of the ellipse sketched by the user. Finally, the relative proportions of morphogen flowing to each of the neighboring vertices are determined based on these transformed faces surrounding the vertex in the same manner as described above. Once the differential flow of morphogens has been calculated, it is applied to the

original mesh to generate the desired pattern. As shown in Figure 20, the method produces spots with desired orientation on a cube. However, due to irregular distribution of vertices, the orientation of spots is not as clear when generated on the bunny.

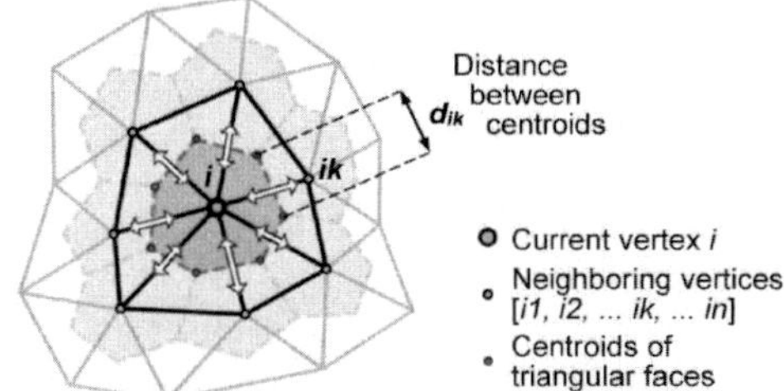

Figure 17. *Proportional flow of morphogens along each edge between the current vertex and its neighboring vertices is determined by the normalized distances between the centroids of the two faces on either side of that edge.*

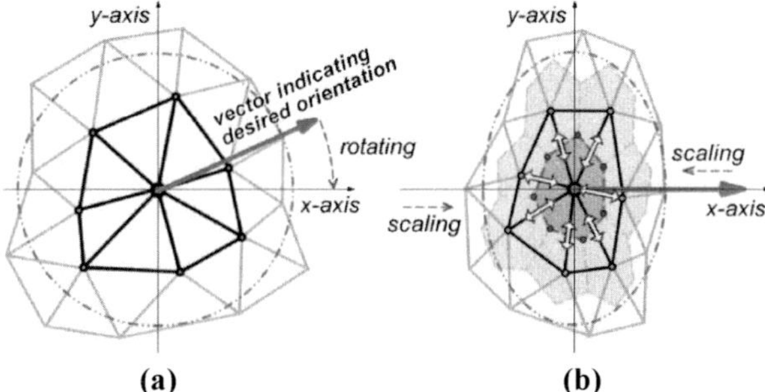

Figure 18. *(a) The original mesh showing the current vertex and its surrounding vertices. The arrow shows the projection of the sketched ellipse's major axis vector onto the tangent plane at the current vertex. (b) Illustration of the vertices after a rotation followed by scaling down the faces along the x-axis.*

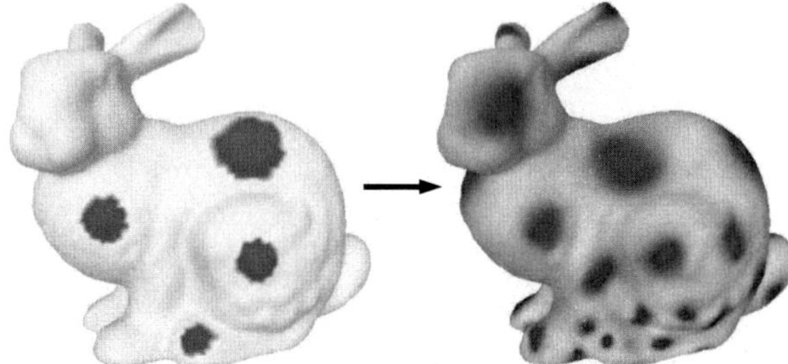

Figure 19. *Spots of different sizes generated on a 3D mesh.*

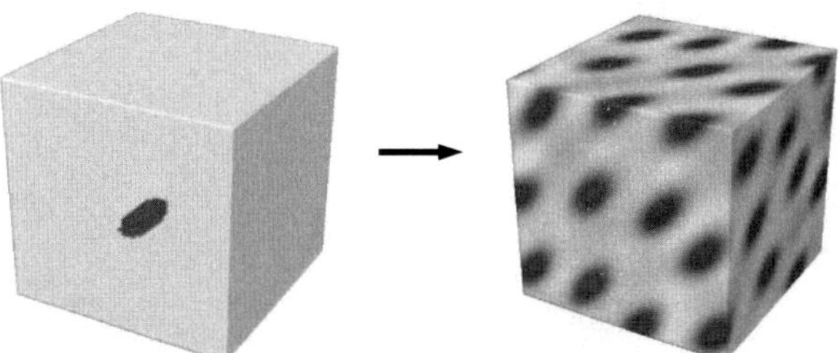

Figure 20. *Oriented spots generated on a cube.*

7. Summary and future work

The system described here allows a user to make a simple sketch of a desired pattern and then automatically generates a large amount of texture that has a similar pattern. This interface allows the user to produce a desired texture with ease and without the need for any internal knowledge of the Reaction-Diffusion process. Instead of having to run the system several times to find the right set of parameters that will produce desired texture, the user can sketch the patterns they want and have the system automatically generate a texture with similar attributes. This is a much more natural and intuitive method.

As part of future work, the dimension and resolution of the grid can be dynamically determined based on user's sketch, such as number and size of ellipses or stripes, in order to make the texture synthesis more flexible. As demonstrated here, this system can be extended to support automatic texture synthesis on canonical 3D surfaces. The next step will be the development of a stable and robust system for automatic texture synthesis on a 3D model.

8. Appendix:

8.1. Formulae for Turing spot system

$$\frac{\partial a}{\partial t} = speed\left[k_a\left(16 - ab\right) + D_a\nabla^2 a\right]$$

$$\frac{\partial b}{\partial t} = speed\left[k_a\left(ab - b - \beta\right) + D_b\nabla^2 b\right]$$

8.2. Formulae for Meinhardt spot system

$$\frac{\partial a}{\partial t} = speed\left[s\left(\frac{0.01\,a^2\beta}{b} - ap_1 + p_3\right) + D_a\nabla^2 a\right]$$

$$\frac{\partial b}{\partial t} = speed\left[s\left(0.01\,a^2\beta - bp_2 + p_3\right) + D_b\nabla^2 b\right]$$

8.3. Formulae for Meinhardt stripe system

$$\frac{\partial a}{\partial t} = speed\left[\frac{0.01\,a^2 e\beta}{c} - ak_{ab} + D_a\nabla^2 a\right]$$

$$\frac{\partial b}{\partial t} = speed\left[\frac{0.01\,b^2 d}{c} - bk_{ab} + D_b\nabla^2 b\right]$$

$$\frac{\partial c}{\partial t} = speed\left[0.01\,a^2 e\beta + 0.01\,b^2 d - ck_c\right]$$

$$\frac{\partial d}{\partial t} = speed\left[\left(a - d\right)k_{de} + D_d\nabla^2 d\right]$$

$$\frac{\partial e}{\partial t} = speed\left[\left(b - e\right)k_{de} + D_e\nabla^2 e\right]$$

9. References:

[Bar81] BARD J. B. L.: A Model for Generating Aspects of Zebra and Other Mammalian Coat Patterns. *Journal of Theoretical Biology*, Vol. 93, No. 2, pp. 363–385 (November 1981).

[EMP*02] EBERT D. S., MUSGRAVE F. K., PEACHEY D., PERLIN K., WORLEY S.: *Texturing & Modeling: A Procedural Approach*, Morgan Kaufmann, 3rd edition, (December 2002).

[KTBG03] KULLA C. D., TUCEK D. J.., BAILEY R., GRIMM C. M.: Using Texture Synthesis for Non-Photorealistic Shading from Paint Samples. *11th Pacific Graphics Conference on Computer Graphics and Applications*, pp. 477 (October 2003).

[Mal82] MALDELBROT B. B.: *The Fractal Geometry of Nature*, W. H. Freeman and Company, New York, 1982.

[Mei82] MEINHARDT H.: *Models of Biological Pattern Formation*, Academic Press, London, 1982.

[Mur81] MURRAY J. D.: On Pattern Formation Mechanisms for Lepidopteran Wing Patterns and Mammalian Coat Markings. *Philosophical Transactions of the Royal Society B*, Vol. 295, pp. 473–496 (October 1981).

[Per85] PERLIN K.: An Image Synthesizer. *Computer Graphics*, Vol. 19, No. 3 (SIGGRAPH '85), pp. 287–296 (July 1985).

[PH89] PERLIN K., HOFFERT E. M.: "Hypertexture," *Computer Graphics*, Vol. 23, No. 3 (SIGGRAPH '89), pp. 253–262 (July 1989).

[SA94] SCHAAL S., ATKESON C. G.: Assessing the quality of learned local models. *Advances in Neural Information Processing Systems 6* Morgan Kaufmann, San Mateo, CA, pp. 160-167, 1994.

[Tur52] TURING A.: The Chemical Basis of Morphogenesis. *Philosophical Transactions of the Royal Society B*, Vol. 237, pp. 37–72 (August 14, 1952).

[Tur91] TURK G.: Generating Textures on Arbitrary Surfaces Using Reaction-Diffusion. *Computer Graphics*, Vol. 25, No. 4 (SIGGRAPH '91), pp. 289–298 (July 1991).

[Tur92] TURK G.: Texturing Surfaces Using Reaction-Diffusion. PhD Dissertation, The University of North Carolina at Chapel Hill, 1992.

[WK91] WITKIN A., KASS M.: Reaction-Diffusion Textures. *Computer Graphics*, Vol. 25, No. 4 (SIGGRAPH '91), pp. 299–308 (July 1991).

EUROGRAPHICS Workshop on Sketch-Based Interfaces and Modeling (2006)
Thomas Stahovich and Mario Costa Sousa (Editors)

Living Ink:
Implementation of a Prototype Sketching Language
for Real Time Authoring of Animated Line Drawings

Bill Rogers

The University of Waikato, Hamilton, New Zealand

Abstract

Sketching with pen on paper is often used as a way of augmenting spoken descriptions: to help explain how some mechanical device works; to show the flow of information in an organisation, to show the action in a story, and so on. Sketches serve as a focus for the attention of viewers and help make abstract concepts more concrete. But images on paper don't move. Where the time and resources are available, as in preparing a lecture in advance, or producing a television program, authors recognize that moving images are often superior at conveying concepts and holding people's attention. An electronic display is capable of generating moving images in real time. We argue that such a display need not be used just to mimic pen and paper. After all paper is cheap, plentiful, has a wide viewing angle, and doesn't have batteries to run flat. Our 'Living Ink' system is a prototype implementation of a user interface for generating animated line drawings (animated sketches). Our goal was to provide a user interface which can be used in real-time, making interesting animations while an audience watches. This paper describes progress to date towards that objective and discusses proposals for further development.

I.3.4. [Computer Graphics: Graphics Utilities]: Graphics Editors; Picture Description Languages

1. Introduction

There are many circumstances in which people use informal sketches. When explaining how a mechanical gadget works, how we would like a user interface to function, or when telling stories, we often quickly draw pictures, to support our descriptions. This might happen in a teaching situation, where a teacher draws on a overhead projector screen or board. It might happen in a formal meeting or brainstorming session where participants draw on boards or pieces of paper. It might happen in a restaurant where ideas are jotted onto table napkins. The quality of the pictures does not have to be high, because the accompanying explanation compensates for their limitations. Indeed, in many situations the audience can ask for further clarification, and the sketch author can immediately make extensions to a picture, or invite their questioner to indicate or even draw themselves on the image to explain what aspects they do and do not understand. The crucial aspect is the immediacy. In a very short space of time it is possible to get onto paper some information that will significantly improve the level of communication being achieved between participants. Of course, given more time, sketches can be improved, and there is a continuum of circumstances between those in which a quick sketch is the most useful, and those in which a well planned and carefully constructed diagram is the most useful. In this paper we are interested in the use of rapid sketching for communicating ideas, or telling stories.

Sketch interfaces of one kind or another are available in many kinds of computer technology. PDA's and Smart Phones support pen input, and we can write sketch applications for them. Notebooks and desktop computers can have graphics tablets or 'write-on' screens for pencil and paper like sketching. It is also possible, albeit awkward, to draw with a mouse. The current technology most like the pen and paper though is the tablet computer, where software not only supports drawing strokes 'directly' on to a surface, but also simulates other aspects of real pens, like smooth anti-aliased lines, line weight that depends on pen pressure and the pen top eraser. This kind of technology is clearly well designed for use in the informal sketching domain. Our approach to animation sketching is designed for technology like a tablet computer, although our prototype implementation functions perfectly well with a mouse and a desktop PC.

Computer based sketching is significantly different to using pencil or pen and paper. The disadvantages of computer systems lie in limited resolution, imperfect pen devices, restricted drawing space, and in many cases restricted viewing angles. The advantages usually offered by the computer are the ability to store sketches, restore previous work, transmit information to other locations, and the capability of erasing, editing and transforming sketch data. In either case some kind of projection equipment can be used to make sketches visible to a large audience. Overall it is not clear that the advantages of computer sketching outweigh the disadvantages in most circumstances. Paper is cheap, plentiful and doesn't have batteries that run flat. In order to make computer equipment more attractive in this role we need to offer compelling capabilities that paper cannot. The most obvious capability of the electronic display is that of rapid update. Sketching software already makes use of this by allowing lines to be erased or changed, which is a largely unsatisfactory process on paper. However we still have software that is oriented mostly to generating static finished sketches. In the kinds of scenario in which we see informal sketching being used, we argue that animated sketches would be of value, especially when telling stories or explaining how gadgets work.

Imagine telling a story to a child about the sea. On paper you might show a wavy line to represent the water surface, and draw a boat above it and a fish below. On a computer display such a line could really move. Figure 1 is a screen shot from our system of such a 'water surface' line. (For the purposes of presentation in print, the software has been modified to fade the lines from previous frames rather than erase them – giving an onion skin (ghost) effect. The real system just shows one moving line. In Figure 1, because of the small movement, the onion skin lines show as shaded grey patterns.)

Figure 1: Animated wave in Living Ink

Of course this only works if it is possible to generate animations quickly – in real time – while observers are watching. If this could be achieved then electronic sketches would offer capabilities that really were not possible with paper, and we really might expect to see tablet computers replacing table napkins as the information exchange medium of choice in restaurants.

We take as inspiration for our work the sketch style animations produced by Big Time Pictures [BTP05], included in the British Television Channel 4 series 'Scrapheap Challenge'. In that series, contestants build mechanical devices. A programme host explains, with the aid of the animations, just how planned devices are expected to work or might fail. The animations are in a sketch style (see Figure 2) with enough detail to support the explanations. Some of the content shows devices operating. In Figure 2, the truck moves and the axe rotates. Some is background only – the clouds drift across the sky, and the truck driver has a worried expression. The animations provide a beautifully appropriate basis for explanation, showing moving parts, but including humorous elements that support a commentary that is entertaining as well as informative. Of course, these animations were not produced as the commentator spoke. They were probably the result of hours or days of effort. However, even if we cannot match them fully, we are interested in seeing how close we can get with real time authoring.

Figure 2: 'Scrapheap Challenge' animation still

The remainder of this paper is organized as follows. Section two reviews related work. Section three outlines our interface design, and shows examples of the interface in action. Section four gives some extended examples, showing how our primitive commands combine to produce complex effects. Section five reports some qualitative results from a limited informal user evaluation, and section six presents our conclusions and plans for further work.

2. Related Work

There is a compelling body of literature, eg: [LM01, PA03] that emphasizes the importance of using and retaining the imprecise sketch style in design documents. Any attempt to tidy documents can lead to authors being sidetracked into spending time on perfecting position and appearance at the expense of content. In the design context this spending of time can lead to premature commitment to early design ideas. In our authoring context sketching must be done quickly. We interpret the evidence in favour of design sketching as implying that adding precision controls to our interface would pressure authors towards time wasting adjustments of their work. Largely then, we need an interface that is as completely sketch based as possible.

The term 'sketch animation' is used in a number of ways in the literature. First there is the kind of animation shown in Figure 2. The overall appearance of the animation is of a sketched line drawing. The animation process itself seems to vary in these animations. Sometimes objects move with no internal change, suggesting that a single sketch is being moved and imaged in different positions. At other times it looks as though frames have been sketched independently, and irregularities between frames in the drawn strokes give the animation a slight 'squirminess'. So, even within this one set of examples we can distinguish sketch as a source of objects that are smoothly animated, and actual sketching constituting the animation itself.

The term 'sketch animation' has also been used to describe line animation in which the lines are found by searching for edges in the output of 3D scene rendering software. The goal there being to generate a sketch style of animation from scenes modeled fully in 3D. Examples are "Loose and Sketchy Animation" [CUR98] and the sketch animation feature of Lightwave 3D [NT05]. Although the result is sketch like, these systems are not built by sketch input.

A third use of the term is in progressive sketch animation [DIC05]. In these systems the strokes drawn by an artist are recorded and replayed. Usually the goal is a single, often quite detailed, sketch; for example, a portrait. The result is interesting to watch, and gives insight into the way the artist develops their work. It is usual to play back the drawing at a much higher rate than drawing speed. However this kind of animation is quite similar to the form we are trying to design. If the drawing is simple enough, it can be played at drawing speed. For example in describing a user interface it makes sense to describe each element as it is sketched – the animated drawing focusing audience attention on items, one at a time, as they are described. This is a common style of sketching used by teachers at a whiteboard.

Sketching has also been used in 3D animation systems, to specify the animation. In 'Motion Doodles' [THO03] sketch lines are used to quickly specify motion of articulated characters. The characters and their basic animations are modeled in a standard 3D graphics package manner: characters with skeletons and 3D meshes; basic animations elements, such as walk cycles, done using skeleton poses in keyframe sequences. Sketching is then used to define longer animation sequences. This is a gesture recognition system in which gestures are translated into motion sequences. A sketched loop, for example, specifies that the character perform a summersault; a sequence of arcs commands a sequence of steps. The system is interesting from a sketch viewpoint because it makes more use of the sketched information than just extracting gestures as abstract symbols. The position of the lines specifies location and direction of motion; the size of gestures dictates the scale of movements (large steps), and the timing of drawing controls the speed of motion. The system thus leverages the richness of detail in a sketch line to allow quick delivery of instructions that would otherwise require extensive parameter setting.

The same idea is also developed in "Animation Sketching", Moskovich et al [MH04]. They address the problem of animating 2D sketched shapes using "motion by example". In their system sketched items can be grabbed and moved. The track and timing of that motion is recorded. Elaborate motion, in which movements must be coordinated is handled by layering motion tracks. For example to have a bird's two wings flap, the user first moves one wing, then rewinds and records the movement of the second wing. Where two objects must move in a coordinated way Moskovich's system supports time warping. For example, to make a door open just before a

character passes through, the user records the movements of door and character with approximate timing, then marks a coordination point on the time line of each movement, and lets the system warp the timing of each motion to make coordination points occur simultaneously.

Poliakov's MorphInk [POL01] uses automatic morphing from shape to shape. In this system the primary motivation is achieving good compression of animation information for transmission over networks. However, its automatic morphing is a valuable approach to specifying animation. Computer animation easily provides tween frames for animation actions that are simple transformations. MorphInk extends the range of tweens that can be produced automatically, reducing authoring effort (and data size).

In [KST04] Kato et al, describe a system using sketched 'Effect Lines'. In their system, line gestures, styled to be similar to the motion lines used in comic book cartoons, are interpreted as motion commands (Figure 3). A variety of gestures are used to specify rotation, translation and oscillatory motions. A particular advantage of this system in our context would be the appropriate and familiar style of the lines. They are commands that would communicate well to a real time observer, as well as to the animation system. In contrast to our planned system however, Kato's system uses sketching only to specify animation. More conventional modeling techniques are used to generate the scenes being animated. This modal use of sketching avoids any difficulty that might arise in distinguishing motion commands from sketch content.

Figure 3: Effect lines from [KST04]

The K-Sketch project [DAV05] has as its goal, drastic reduction of the time taken to produce simple animations. Their project report includes a useful survey of the effects used in a collection of animations by a number of artists. Their prototype system animates sketched (line drawn) content. Animation is controlled partly by gesture and partly by pen operated controls. Gestures are used for selection and to specify motion tracks. Controls include a time slider and a multi-transformation widget (Figure 4). The transformation widget is popped up whenever content is selected. The user places their pen in the appropriate part of the widget for the kind of transformation they require (translate, rotate, etc), and drags to initiate and specify movement (Figure 4). The widget then disappears. The user sees the content move and also a low intensity motion line that grows with the motion and remains on screen to allow edit access to the motion later (Figure 5). As in Moskovich's system, position and speed of motion are recorded for exact reproduction in replay. The system also appears to run a clock continuously, so that successive animation actions each occur at the time at which they were entered (modulo explicit rewinding).

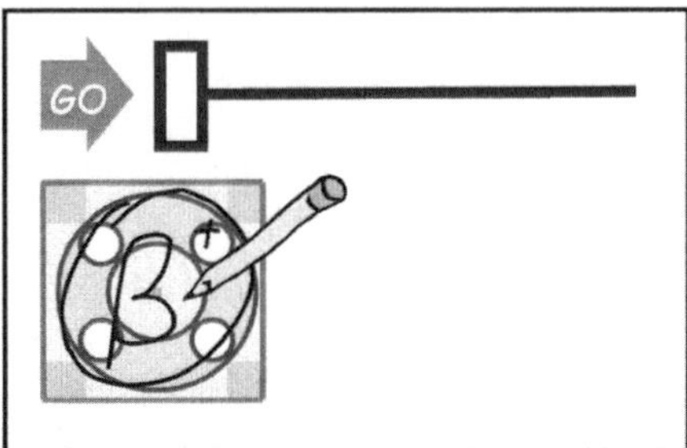

Figure 4: K-Sketch's multi-transformation widget, over sketch content (circled beta plus).

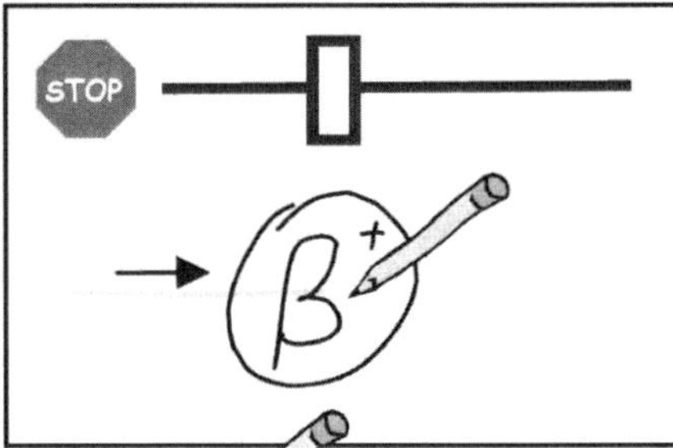

Figure 5: K-Sketch content moving with low intensity motion line showing track.

Perlin, eloquently puts the case for "The Animated Napkin Sketch" [PER02]. His goal is *allowing people to capture the immediacy and power of rapid creation of "drawings over time".* His prototype system is called DrawPad. The concept is of a sequence of drawings or 'shots'. The timing and sequence of stroke drawing is retained so that a shot can be replayed as an animation. A simple gesture allows linking of 'sub-drawings'. The program can 'zoom' in and out of sub-drawings, thus providing a means of structuring the presentation/recording of ideas. An application of zooming occurs, for example, when the primary document is a mind map. Associated with each concept can be a (hierarchy of) sub-documents. The system is not really an animation system in the normal sense. Rather it is a way of retaining and structuring a sequence of sketch items, so that they can be presented or explored later. Its strength is the simple user interface which can be used to capture in real time a complex presentation of ideas.

In summary, a great deal of work has been done on using sketching interfaces to generate animations of different kinds. Considerable success has been achieved in reducing authoring time and ease of interaction, sometimes at the expense of reduction in precision. From these successes, we formed an optimistic view of the prospects for doing real time animation. In the following section, as part of the description of our prototype design, we comment on the relationship to the systems surveyed.

3. Living Ink Interface Design

In most graphic design software there is a strong element of selection and markup with tools. Usually there is a currently selected shape, highlighted in some way and decorated with tool handles: like corners to be used for scaling, or handles for curve adjustment. The usage process is to: add a primitive, complete with control scaffolding; and adjust until it looks right. Sketch interfaces can avoid much of this with stroke primitives. The artist draws lines and it can be assumed that they are correct immediately they are drawn, thus avoiding any adjustment process (except sometimes removing a stroke altogether and trying again). This allows us to avoid scaffolding associated with item construction. The design issues that remained are to do with specifying animation actions.

Our goal was to produce an animation program which could be used in front of an audience. This imposed strong constrains on the nature of the interface. Initially we took the view that we should avoid having any 'construction marks' or 'scaffolding' on the display. Ideally all that would ever appear would be the sketch, appropriately animated. As design proceeded we relaxed that constraint in favour of having the artist sketch 'track' lines for animation actions.

It would have been possible to achieve a 'no visible scaffolding' effect by using two displays – one of which was visible to the artist and one to the viewer. This would be viable in a teaching situation in which the artist could use a computer with local display attached to a projector, providing the viewer's image. Then it would be possible to decorate the artists view in any way desired. Of course, the dual display solution is not viable for using a shared tablet computer at a restaurant table, but more significantly, we felt that having the artist work on invisible controls would not support the 'draw and explain' task very well. It would be very easy for there to be periods of time during which the viewer would experience visual inactivity while the artist was busy with invisible adjustments and therefore probably not commenting either. For both reasons we decided that a common view for artist and viewer was necessary.

Specifying animation actions involves: selecting objects to be transformed, choosing the transformation, and specifying the track and timing that will be applied.

In K-Sketch, users select objects by drawing around them. Other systems allow the user to click on an object to select it, and then highlight the object to show that it has been successfully selected. Highlighting seemed undesirable, particularly if it persisted for an indefinite time (as is usually the case). Drawing around an object was less objectionable, as it would fit naturally with explanation – "and the fish (draw around it) swam to the …" After some initial experimentation we observed that objects were often manipulated immediately after being drawn, and adopted the idea of implicit selection. Actions apply to the last object(s) created. Our system does have a selection operator (drag an outline with side button on pen held down), but it is rarely used. Explicit selection is acknowledged by briefly flashing the selected object red (for approx $1/3^{rd}$ of a second). If several objects are selected in one operation, they are flashed in sequence.

Selecting a transformation, its track and timing were addressed together. Of other systems we have considered, the one that seems best suited to working in front of an audience is Kato's Effect Lines. At the time we were designing our system we were unaware of that work. In retrospect, though, using the idea would have been problematic for us in two ways. Firstly it would have been difficult to distinguish effect markup from object sketch lines. Secondly, whilst the idea of setting an object (like the car in Figure 3) moving by drawing effect lines is appealing, it would have put our artists under pressure to catch and stop the object in a timely manner. Instead we opted for a more conservative solution. We decided that movements could be specified with visible sketched strokes, and that there would be a toolbar holding buttons for each kind of animation action (operator buttons).

The basic interaction paradigm is stack based. The artist draws lines (strokes) which are put into a first-in last-out stack. Strokes can be either sketch data, or operator 'track' specifications. Each operator pops its operand(s) from the top of the stroke stack, and pushes its result(s) back. Most operators have two operands – data and track. For example, to draw an object and specify that it move over some track, the artist sketches the object, sketches the track and then clicks the 'path' (translation) operator. This is illustrated in Figure 6.

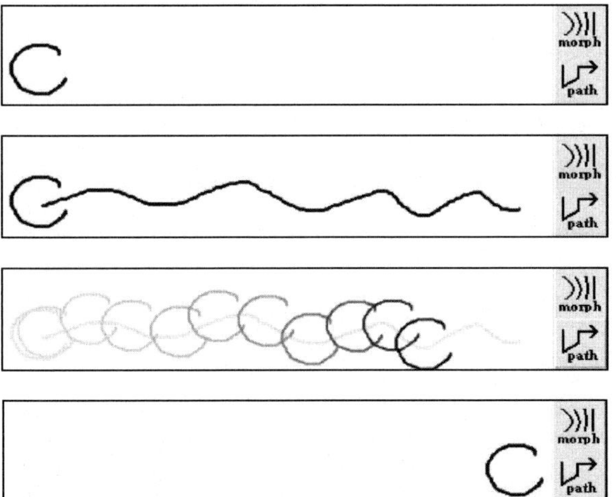

Figure 6: Using the path operator. (Part of a screen shot positioned to make the relevant part of the toolbar visible.)

The stack principle allows operations to be combined in a way that is not possible in a system in which tracks are specified directly by dragging. Almost any object can be used as a track. In particular it is possible to use an animated line as a track.

In terms of our design goals we think that this works reasonably well. The track lines have some contextual meaning. It is acceptable for the artist to say "and now the fish moves along this way (drawing the track)", then click the operator button and let it happen. In this way it is acceptable that track lines are visible to the audience. In fact, the system seems to result in more 'positive' animation. If the artist grabs and moves an object it tends to look as though it is floating about purposelessly. Showing where it is going and then letting it go there quickly and smoothly looks better. The toolbar doesn't occupy very much screen space, and the artist doesn't spend much time working with it.

That just leaves the problem of specifying timing. We were suspicious of the idea of recording detailed timing of pen movement – of animation by example – even though it was the main metaphor used in all the sketch controlled systems reviewed, other than Kato's Effect Lines. In our early experiments we found that it was difficult to adjust objects with any kind of timing accuracy. When people draw lines they are thinking more about shape than time, and speed of drawing tends to be dictated mostly by the complexity of the shape. It therefore seemed unnatural to reproduce drawing timing exactly. We also observed that having a running clock determine the timing at which actions began was 'oppressive' and that pauses which seemed appropriate while creating the animation were often annoying on playback.

Our timing is largely implicit. Initially, animation actions all take one second to perform. There is a system clock, but it doesn't move except when an action is entered, in which case it moves forward by one second. There are two timing buttons: 'Meanwhile' and 'Then'. 'Meanwhile' moves the system clock back in time to the start of the last action. 'Then' takes it forward. There is still, however, an element of timing retained from tracks. Actions do not follow tracks at a fixed speed (in the pixels per frame sense). When the pen is moved slowly, the system samples its position more often than when it is moving rapidly. Each animation action runs by using a uniform number of samples per frame, chosen to finish the given track in one second. This wasn't really a design decision. It was just what the first implementation was coded to do. Because it retains some of the 'sketchy' feel of imprecise pen movement we decided to leave it that way. As explained later, it was also helpful in matching strokes appropriately during morph operations. The one second time for actions can be adjusted after the animation is complete. Each action has start and end handles on a timeline. These can be moved to speed or slow the animation. A number of other controls are also provided in the timeline area, to permit adjustment of other aspects of actions.

The operators provided in the current version of the program design are: hide, show, bits, delete, morph, path, break, turn, size, group, one and split. They are invoked by buttons down the right hand edge of the screen, as shown in the full screen dump of Figure 14.

'Hide' and 'Show' make objects invisible and invisible. The transition occurs at the current time, but can be moved on the timeline if needed. 'Delete' completely removes an object from the system. 'Path' has been described already and illustrated in Figure 6.

'Turn' and 'Size' provide rotation and scaling respectively. Size is not implemented in the current prototype. 'Turn' works in a similar manner to 'Path', except that the track except that the track is used differently. Its starting point is the centre of rotation, and rotation 'follows' the tangent of the track (see Figure 7). A spiral track allows rotations of more than 360°.

Figure 7: Rotation with the 'Turn' operator

'Morph' takes two operands. It animates the transformation of one into the other. The normal mode of operation for Morph is to 'cycle' – the object transforms backward and forward. It can be set (radio buttons on the timeline) to 'one-shot' or 'repeat'. The 'repeat' option is like 'cycle' except that the shape changes from first to second form, then reverts instantly to first form and morphs again. The 'one-shot', 'cycle', 'repeat' options are actually available for other operators, but 'one-shot' is the default in those cases. Morph is illustrated in Figure 8.

In contrast to the MorphInk system we have not implemented any special algorithm for matching points in morphing. Our system can morph between composite (grouped) objects. In that case the component strokes of each composite object are matched pair-wise in sequence between the first and last morph positions, giving the artist some control of the process. With single objects, the way that pen motion happens usually leads to quite good morph point matching. Because pen movement usually slows in drawing cusps, there are many sample points on cusps and few on long straight line segments. For this reason morphing tends to map cusp to cusp in reasonably similar shapes. This happens in Figure 8. In addition the system forms a new cusp in the middle of the bottom line of the triangle to complete the square.

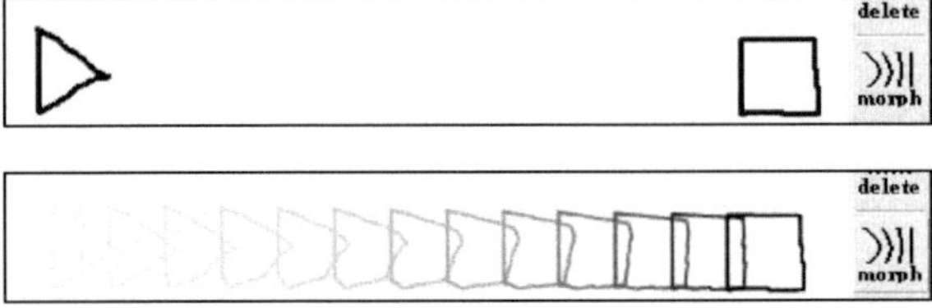

Figure 8: Morph operation.

'Group' combines two items to form a composite item. It can be applied repeatedly for form larger composites.

The grouped object is flashed briefly to confirm the grouping. 'Split' separates a composite object into its components, flashing them in sequence to confirm. 'One' is a variant of 'Group'. It also makes two items into a composite. However, only one of the pair is displayed – ie: the composite is a set of items from which one is chosen for display every time the 'group' is instantiated. This is of value when the composite is used as a particle emitter.

The 'Break' operator allows an item to be cut in two. The track is used as a 'knife'. In Figure 9, an egg shape is 'cut' with a zig-zag line. In the third image of Figure 9 the two halves have been move apart by a small distance to better show the sections.

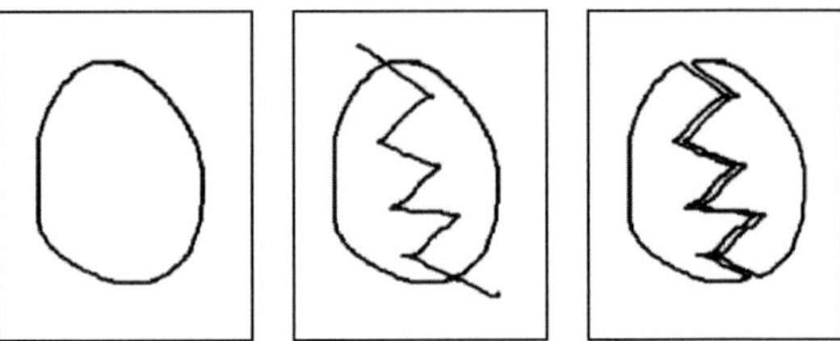

Figure 9: 'Break' cutting an egg

Finally the 'Bits' operator makes an item into a particle emitter. Controls are provided to set the set of directions and speeds, particle lifetime and emission frequency. Figure 10 starts with a sketch of a ship. The second image shows a single smoke puff above the funnel. The 'Bits' operator is applied to make it into a particle emitter, and in the last image a line of smoke puffs can be seen rising from the funnel.

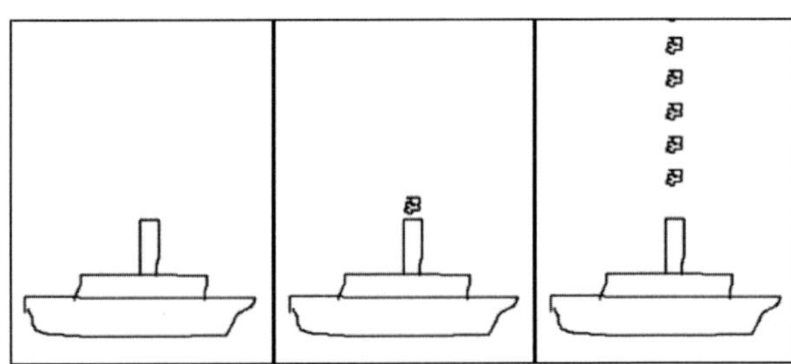

Figure 10: 'Bits' operator makes a particle emitter

4. Composite Operations

The stack style of command makes it possible to apply almost any kind of object as a control track to any other object (the main exception is that it is not possible to use a particle emitter as a track). In this section we will give three examples to provide an indication of the possibilities.

The first example is a small extension to Figure 10. The smoke emitter is grouped to the ship (which is itself a group of three lines), and a path is applied to move the ship across the screen to the right. The result is in Figure 11. The second example shows the 'One' operator in action. The letters 'a' to 'e' were drawn and grouped together using the 'One' operator. The resulting group was made into a particle emitter. The direction of emission was set to all upward angles. The result is a screen full of letters, some of which is shown in Figure 12.

The final example is a very crude bee fluttering from flower to flower. The bee is just a circle with loops for wings. The wings are drawn in the top position, grouped to form a pair; then drawn again in the bottom position and grouped again. Clicking the 'morph' button makes the wings flap. An adjustment to the timeline speeds the flapping. Once the wings are grouped to the body, the whole bee can follow a 'Path' from flower to flower.

Figure 11. Ship moving with 'smoke' particle emitter

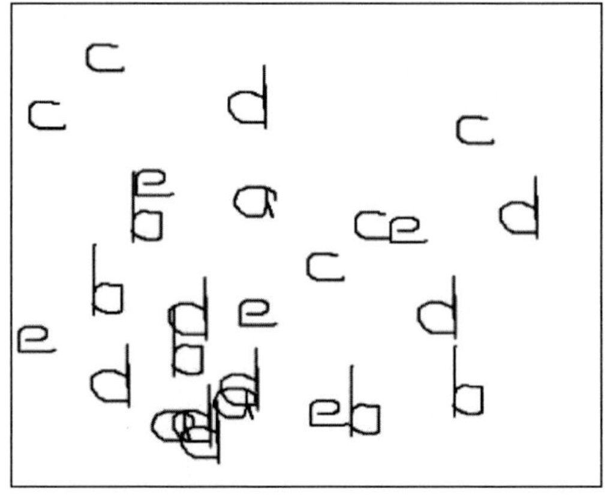

Figure 12. Particle emitter from 'One' grouped letters

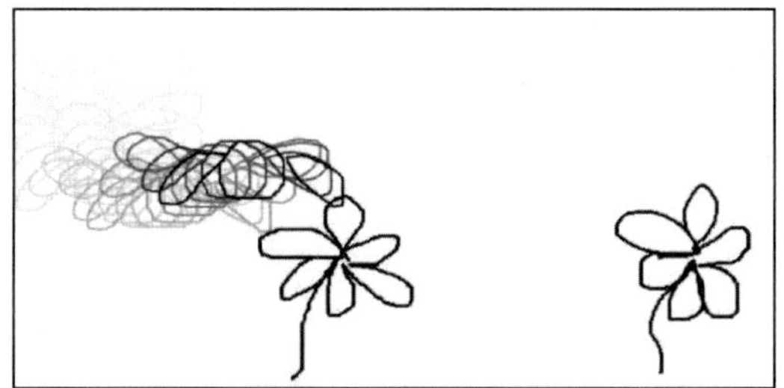

Figure 13. Bee flying

Clicking 'Bits' converts the flying bee into a swarm, in this case all following the same path (Figure 14.). If a number of different paths were needed, then those paths could be drawn, grouped with 'One' and applied with 'Path' to the bee. Each bee particle instantiated would itself instantiate a randomly chosen path. Note also that Figure 14 shows the whole application window with operator toolbar at the right, and timeline at the bottom including controls for adjusting particle emitter settings.

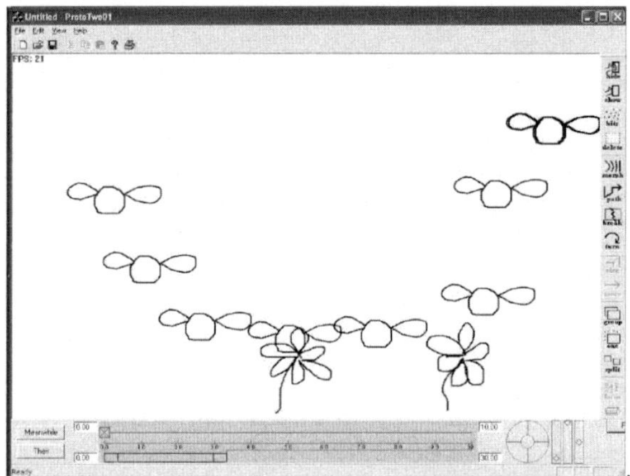

Figure 14: Line of bees following a path

5. Evaluation

We can report on the current state of the project in two ways. Firstly, the goal of producing a reasonably powerful animation system that can be used rapidly. Davis [DAV05] undertook a survey of features used in a number of animations. From their list of features Living Ink is currently capable of generating animations including: Translation, Appearing/Disappearing objects, Rotation, Repeating Sequences, Translation combined with rotation, Motion Hierarchies, and Morphing. It is not currently capable of Sequence reuse, Animation cells, Keyframing, Physical modeling or Sound. Scaling is included in the program design, but not yet implemented. The number of features included is the same as that included in K-Sketch, but the features sets are different.

Secondly, we undertook a small informal user evaluation. Five people took part: 3 children ranging in age from 11 to 16, and 2 adults. All were able to operate the program quite quickly. However, the kinds of results achieved varied considerably. Each person was allowed to experiment for as long as they wanted. All, especially the children, found the program engaging and spent an hour or more working with it. The bee visiting flowers was an invention of the 16 year old. Her experience was typical. She did not find the exact sequence of operations to make the animation obvious. She devised the idea, and set about experimenting to see how the effects could be achieved. It took 10 attempts to get a result she was satisfied with. Early attempts mostly failed because of operations applied in the wrong order, for example applying a path to the bee before grouping it to its wings (which led to the wings flying off without the body). This experience partly indicates that the command set is complex, and that users have to work quite hard to translate their objectives into the command set provided. It can also be interpreted partly as a limitation of the current implementation. At present there is no 'undo' command, and once a control track has been bound to an object, there is no way to reverse the operation and change the track or the underlying object.

Finally, we were surprised by the number of lines that the participants put into drawings. In our own testing we had mostly used very simple drawings, usually no more than 10 lines. Participants put more items into each picture, and often used lines to shade areas. Because the rendering of digital ink is not very fast, animations with a large number (100's) of lines slow down significantly. Presumably this occurs because digital ink is rendered by the CPU rather than the graphics card. On a 2.16GHz Athlon processor with GEForce 2 graphics card, rendering 130 ink strokes (averaging approximately 100 pixels in length) with the Tablet PC ink library, occupied 100% of CPU time at 20 frames per second. In contrast, rendering the same 130 strokes as sequences of straight line segments ten times per frame at 30 frames per second involved only 50% of CPU time. We have done some preliminary experiments with alternative rendering methods.

6. Conclusions and Continuing Work

We have designed a notation/command set that allows production of a wide range of simple sketch animations. Operations include standard geometric transformations as well as breaking an object into pieces and using objects as exemplars for particle generation. Our goal was to support the production of animations in real time during teaching, design and story-telling sessions. Early user testing supports the assertion that our system allows very rapid authoring; however the evidence suggests that it is essentially an expert tool. It is simple enough for users to discover ways of achieving effects by themselves. It is fast enough for users to generate in real time effects that they have previously practiced, but it seems unlikely that people could create new effects in real time. This is not an unsatisfactory result, and is perhaps as much as we should have expected.

The current prototype has limitations that make it difficult to modify an animation. When trying to work in real time, this may not matter, because it would not be appropriate to tinker with an incorrect animation in front of an audience. However, it may be possible to improve the ease with which people learn to achieve effects with the system, by making it easier to correct faults. The next prototyping iteration will therefore include an undo facility. We are also working towards providing a way of 'looking inside' groups and operator bindings to change strokes without undoing the structures they belong to. The current proposal is a 'focus' command which would focus the editor on a single composite object, perhaps fading out other parts of the animation. Applying 'unfocus' would then return to the outside view.

References

[BTP05] BIG TIME PICTURES, `http://www.bigtimepicturescom/examples/scrapheap.aspx`

[CUR98] CURTIS, C.: Loose and Sketchy Animation `http://www.otherthings.com/uw/loose/sketch.html`

[DAV05] DAVIS, R: Informal Animation Sketching with K-Sketch, *Doctoral Consortium UIST 2005*, Seattle, WA, October, 2005

[DIC05] DECLERICO, D, Sketch Animation, `http://www.chrisdiclerico.com/2005/11/12/sketch-animation`

[KST04] KATO, Y., SHIBAVAMA, E., & TAKAHASHI, S. Effect lines for specifying animation effects. In *Proc IEEE Symposium on Visual Languages and Human-Centric Computing*. Rome, Sept 2004, pp. 27-34.

[LM01] LANDAY, J. A. and MYERS, B. A.: Sketching Interfaces: Toward More Human Interface Design. *IEEE Computer*. 34, 3 (2001), pp. 56-64.

[MH04] MOSCOVICH, T. & HUGHES, J.F.: Animation Sketching: An Approach to Accessible Animation. *Technical Report, CS-04-03*, Computer Science Department, Brown Univ. 2004

[NT05] VAUGHAN, W.: Sketch animation with Lightwave 3D, `http://www.newtek.com/products/lightwave/tutorials/rendering/sketch/index.html`

[PA03] PLIMMER, B.E., APPERLEY, M.: Software for Students to Sketch Interface Designs, Interact, Zurich, 2003.

[PER02] PERLIN, K: The Animated Napkin Sketch, `http://www.mrl.nyu.edu/~perlin/draw/` (2002)

[POL01] POLIAKOV, V: MorphInk: Morphing Technology for Web and Wireless Animation, `http://www.morphink.com/e/tools/WhitePaper1.pdf`

[THO03] THORNE, C.; Motion Doodles: A Sketch Based Interface for Character Animation; *Masters Thesis*, University of British Columbia, 2003.

EUROGRAPHICS Workshop on Sketch-Based Interfaces and Modeling (2006)
Thomas Stahovich and Mario Costa Sousa (Editors)

Sketch-based Volumetric Seeded Region Growing

H. L. J. Chen[1]   F. F. Samavati[1]   M. C. Sousa[1]   J. R. Mitchell[1,2] †

[1]Department of Computer Science, University of Calgary, Canada
[2]Seaman Family MR Research Centre, Foothills Medical Centre, Calgary, Canada ‡

Abstract

Interactive volume segmentation is an essential and important step in medical image processing. Conventional interactive methods typically demand significant amounts of time and do not lend to a natural interaction scheme with the 3D volume. In this paper we present a sketch-based interface for seeded region growing volume segmentation. In our approach, the user freely sketches regions of interest (ROI) directly over the 3D volume. Parts of the volume outside the ROIs are then automatically cut out in real-time. The user repeats this process as many times as necessary until he/she decides to specify the seed point 3D location directly at the ROI. To prevent unexpected segmentations, the region growing is restricted to the specified ROI. Our sketch-based system utilizes GPU programming to achieve real-time processing for both rendering and volumetric cutting independent from the size and shape of the sketched strokes.

Categories and Subject Descriptors (according to ACM CCS): I.4.6 [Image Processing and Computer Vision]: Segmentation, partitioning

1. Introduction

Medical imaging systems, such as computerized tomography (CT), magnetic resonance imaging (MRI) and ultrasound, are becoming increasingly ubiquitous. Clinicians and surgeons often use computer-based segmentation to identify and analyze anatomical structures of interest in medical image datasets. For example, neuroradiologists often segment and examine the internal carotid artery to determine its degree of stenosis in patients suffering from transient ischemic attacks (TIAs - "mini" strokes). The degree of carotid stenosis is a critical factor to determine if TIA patients should have surgery to open up this vital vessel. Other measurements (such as the shape, topology, and cubic volume) could also be obtained during the segmentation process [ONI05]. Therefore, volume segmentation is an essential and important step in medical image processing.

Segmentation is often broken down into "edge based" or "region based" methods. Each of these in turn may be

"manual" or "computer assisted" (including completely automatic). Along the edge-based category, a typical manual segmentation process requires a trained specialist to draw contours around the region of interest (ROI) on cross-sectional images. These contour lines are then linked and reconstructed into a 3D representation for further analysis (Figure 1, top). This procedure can become a challenging task if the target is, for example, blood vessels in the brain, which by nature involves complex shape and unpredicted turning directions. Automatic methods currently focus on low-level features such as edge detection and texture analysis. An example of an edge detection algorithm exists in the use of histograms by considering the relationship between three quantities: the data value and its first and second directional derivatives along the gradient direction [KD98]. A number of contributions and efforts were made in the research direction for obtaining automatic segmentation results. However, the difficulty for a complete automatic approach is limited in one sense or another. Kirbas and Quek [KQ03] pointed out that all such attempts for developing automatic segmentation algorithms are limited to some global parameters or can fail with certain data.

The region growing [RK82] algorithm is one of the well-

† http://www.ImagingInformatics.ca

‡ http://www.mrcentre.ca

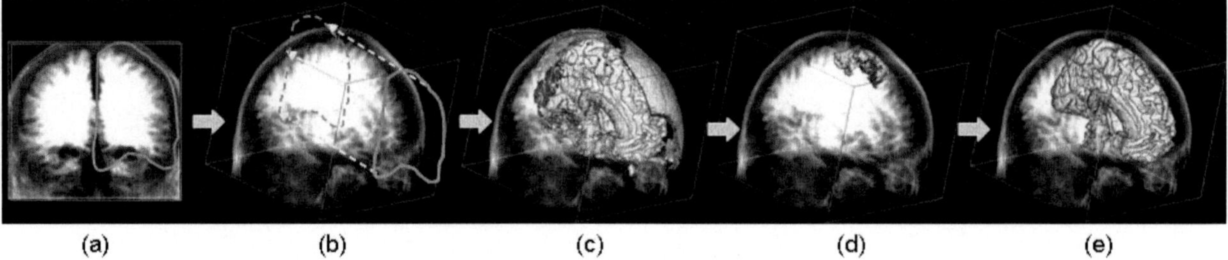

Figure 2: *Our sketch-based volume segmentation method: user sketches a ROI directly over the data (a), the ROI is extruded (b), volume outside is cut out and user plants the seed point (c), region grows (d) and segments volume portions within the extruded ROI (e).*

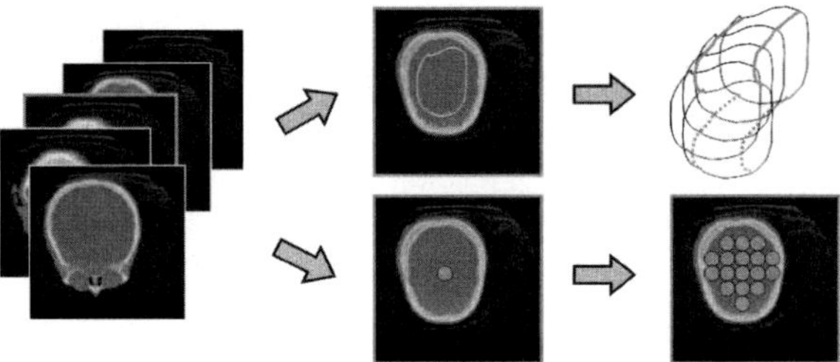

Figure 1: *Conventional segmentation methods. Top row: edge-based method. Bottom row: region-based method.*

known region-based segmentation methods that is simple to compute and applicable to a wide range of data types. Seeded region growing was first introduced by Rolf Adams and Leanne Bischof [AB94]. Their algorithm requires the planting of an initial seed point in the 3D volume dataset. However, the challenge of specifying a 3D coordinate from a 2D device, such as the mouse, is associated with providing an intuitive interface in assisting with the mapping process. Existing methods for specifying the seed point [SHN03] can be outlined as follows: the user navigates from a stack of 2D image slices; a desired slice is selected (i.e. equivalent to selecting one of the axis as a first step); and then the user places the seed point from the cross-sectional view of the data (Figure 1, bottom). As a result the seed point is propagated to the entire volume based on certain criteria the user defines.

The key limitations with the conventional seeded growing region process are the large amount of cross-sectional images a user has to go through. The user is also required to have a priori knowledge of the data in order to quickly identity the correct slice number and the appropriate seed location on the 2D grey-scaled image. This procedure demands a significant amount of time and does not lend to a natural interaction scheme with the 3D volume (i.e. direct manipulation of the 3D data).

In this paper, we propose a sketch-based interface for volumetric seeded region segmentation. Figure 2 illustrates the

key stages of our method applied over a raw MRI super-brain dataset (152x154x181). At first, the user loads the volumetric data and defines an intensity range from the histogram. And then the user directly sketches a ROI over the displayed volume (Fig. 2, a). The system extrudes the ROI along the viewing direction within the entire volume (Fig. 2, b - dotted lines). The volume outside the extruded ROI is cut out and the user places the seed at the red cross (Fig. 2, c). The region starts to grow (Fig. 2, d) and finally the complete segmentation inside the extruded ROI is obtained (Fig. 2, e). In addition, the user could place multiple sketches from different views to form arbitrary-shaped ROI. Our system uses GPU programming for real-time rendering and interactive sketching. Furthermore, we utilize the stencil buffer to achieve a processing rate that is independent of the sketch complexity.

The rest of the paper is organized as follows. In Section 2, we review related work and current sketch-based interfaces for volume segmentation. In Section 3, we outline our system framework. In Sections 4, 5, and 6, we provide details of our sketch-based system for volume segmentation. Results are discussed in Section 7, and conclusions are presented in Section 8.

2. Related Work

Interactive seeded region growing. Many segmentation approaches have been proposed for the 2D image segmentation task. The set of well-known techniques include thresholding, k-means clustering, watershed segmentation, and level-set methods (see the survey conducted by Pham et. al. [PXP99]). For segmenting 3D medical datasets, these techniques could also be applied and adapted easily by re-using the 2D image techniques. Sherbondy et. al. [SHN03] developed a fast volume segmentation system using GPU. Their work was based on seeded region growing. The seed selection step allows the user to paint seeds by drawing on the sectional views of the volume. Their segmentation merging criteria are based on non-linear diffusion metric. They also incorporated image smoothing algorithms for noise conditions. More recently, Schenke et. al. [SWD05] analyzed the GPGPU paradigm and implemented the seeded region growing method with fragment shaders and VTK. In order to fully take advantage of the GPU parallelism, the user was encouraged to specify as many seed points as possible.

Sketch-based interfaces for volume segmentation. For general sketch-based modeling of volumetric data, Owada et. al. [ONNI03] presented a system that captures hand-drawn sketches and creates volumetric objects with internal structures. Owada et. al. [ONOI04] further extended the interface for users to define internal volumetric textures of a model. The system allowed interactive design and browsing for volumetric illustrations. Recent work for segmenting volumetric data have also focused on incorporating user intervention and developing interactive segmentation systems. Tzeng et. al. [TLM03] developed a novel interface for volume data classification. They allowed the user to draw strokes on the cross-section of volume data that roughly indicate foreground and background regions. The stroke information was used to train a classifier that is designed for segmenting voxels. Yuan et. al. [YZNC05] presented a novel method to cut out volumetric structures by drawing simple strokes directly on volume rendered images. Owada et. al. [ONI05] proposed an intuitive user interface for volume segmentation. The user traces the contour of the target region using a 2D free-form stroke on the screen. The volume catcher system then returns a plausible 3D region inside the stroke.

Similar to Owada's approach [ONI05], the concept of our system extends the stroke and sweeps through the volume. We use histograms as a first classification step whereas they applied opacity transfer functions. In contrast, we adapt closed strokes that include free-form and other variations. Most importantly, our approach allows the user to interact with a simple sketch-based interface for navigating to the ROI instead of browsing through hundreds of cross-sectional slices ([SHN03]; [SWD05]). For seed planting, our technique is fundamentally 3D and the user no longer needs to look at texture-mapped 2D planes. In addition, we enable the user to define a sub-volume of arbitrary shape with few sketches to constrain the region grow and provide rapid segmentation feedback.

3. Particle System Framework

In our sketch-based system, we utilize a particle system framework. Because of the generality and the fundamental design of the framework, the system can be easily extended to work with irregular datasets. Other potential applications include general point-based systems and polygonal meshes (which were converted to a point-cloud).

At the first stage of our system, a desirable range of intensities is selected by using the intensity histogram to define target voxels from the volumetric dataset. Since only a subset of the entire volume is rendered to the scene, we represent the target voxels by a particle system. We use lists of particles for rendering and processing. This avoids the need to traverse the 3D array containing the original dataset every time we access these target voxels.

In order to maintain the lists of particles, we organize them with a central particle system scheme. The particle system contains a list of particle objects. Each particle object can be organized and displayed by using the display list or vertex buffer objects (VBOs). When the display list option is used, each particle object contains an object color if particles do not possess color information. The particle object also maintains a list of particles and each particle contains information such as: position (x, y, z), color (r, g, b, a), and reference to voxel (which contains intensity and gradient). Position is used during the sketch-based volume cutting (Section 4). Reference to voxel is required to locate neighboring voxels during segmentation (Section 5). For rendering (Section 6), position, color, and voxel gradient (normal) are needed.

Alternatively, particle objects can utilize the various VBOs stored in a collection of *particle buffersets*. Each *particle bufferset* contains a vertex buffer (i.e. voxel position), normal buffer (i.e. voxel gradient), and color buffer (i.e. voxel intensity). Each of these buffers is stored on the GPU texture memory using VBO. The required voxels only travel across the system bus once whenever the histogram is defined. Each particle object then maintains only index information into the corresponding *particle bufferset*. Particles are rendered in either X-ray mode or surface mode (Section 6). Each particle object contains an attribute for its assigned rendering mode.

4. Sketch-based Volume Cutting

To place the seed for the region growing, we use a novel sketch-based interface. In the first stage, the user specifies a ROI by a closed free-form sketch on the screen. The extrusion of this sketch forms the ROI and likely contains the target area (organ). This approach has several benefits: it increases the performance of seed-growing after extrusion and cutting, the user is able to navigate and place the seed more easily, and finally it is very intuitive.

The main challenge here is to cut the extrusion from the volume at an interactive rate. With the defined histogram intensity range, a collection of particles is composed from the 3D volume array. The set of particle attributes is packaged into vertex buffer, normal buffer, and color buffer using VBO. These buffers are sent only once and stored on the GPU texture memory for successive rendering and processing. The sketched area is extruded along the view direction and pierces into the entire volume (Figure 3). The computed sub-volume is rendered in the surface mode and the background volume is rendered in the X-ray mode (Figure 9, right). Subsequent sketches affect only the 'visible' sub-volume currently rendered in the surface mode. Then the remaining task is to distinguish the particles that fall 'inside' the extrusion from the ones that are 'outside'.

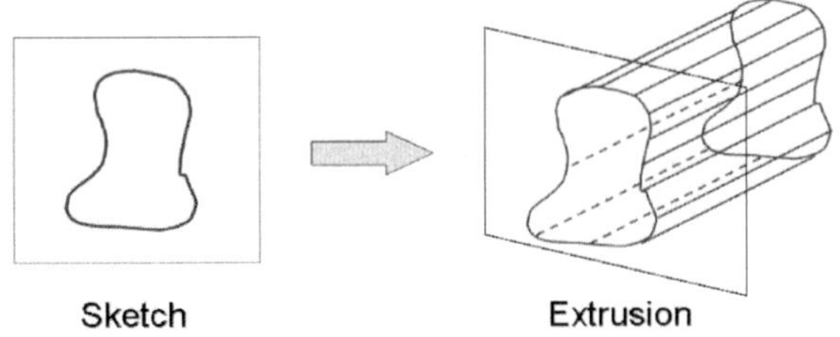

Figure 3: *Sketch extrusion.*

In order to find the list of selected particles that fall inside the sketched extrusion, one possible strategy is to use the standard polygon fill or crossing test algorithms [Hai94] [Fra]. For this, we can project the particle to the screen and check whether it is inside of the sketched stroke. The speed of this method depends on the number of points on the stroke (as a polygon). Unfortunately, this method suffers from a slow speed when the stroke (polygon) has a good quality. Although we could implement the crossing test in GPU, the speed is still dependent on the complexity of strokes and the level of interactivity can vary depending on the user input. Instead, we adapt a novel GPU-based technique that is independent of the sketch complexity.

4.1. Computational Mask

The fundamental concept of our sketch-based system is a real-time filtering process employing a computational mask (Figure 4). We move the mask to traverse the entire volume in a front-to-back order and pick up the particles (or voxels) that are inside the sketched area. The particles which are not visited by this process are labeled as being 'outside'. As depicted in figure 4, the volumetric dataset can be in any orientation with respect to the computational mask.

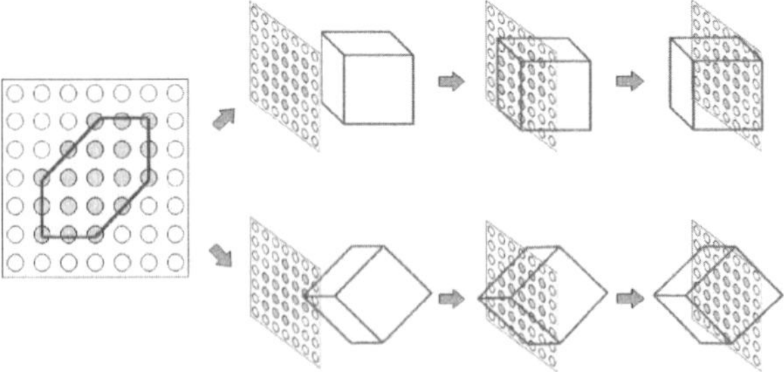

Figure 4: *Computational mask.*

The computational mask is composed of 1s and 0s, where 1 indicates that the pixel is covered by the sketched area and 0 means that the pixel is outside the area. Figure 5 illustrates the process for generating the mask. At first, the user places strokes on the screen and a closed curve is obtained. Next, we fill the enclosing area using the stencil buffer with a 1-bit

color [WNDS99]. Then we save the content of the stencil buffer as a texture as demonstrated in Figure 5.

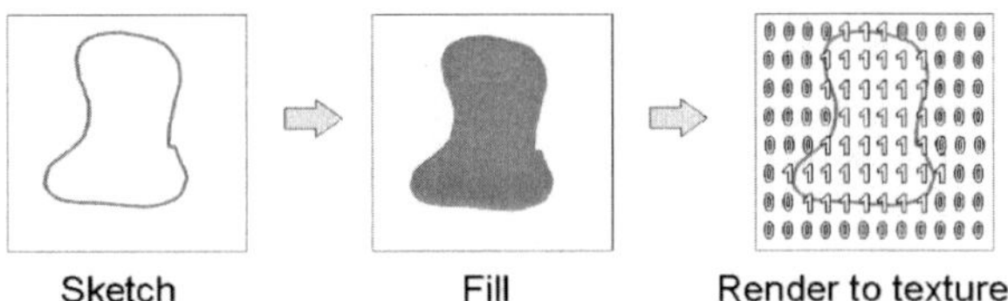

Figure 5: *Generating the computational mask using the stencil buffer.*

4.2. GPU-based Sketch System

In order to quickly filter the entire volume with the generated computational mask, we perform all of our computation in GPU and send back the result as a single texture to the CPU. We leverage the workload to both vertex and fragment shaders and optimize the speed by minimizing the program complexity. Notice that we use the fragments (pixels) and the framebuffer somehow different from their regular functions. Instead of sequential processing of the particles, we map many particles to the fragments at a time. This helps us to use parallel architecture of GPU for processing of the particles. Therefore, the fragments' "position" in our method is an index to the particles instead of being a position of visible pixels. We also use a binary "value" for the fragments to show whether the particle is inside of the extrusion. To map the index of particles, which has a linear order, to the position of fragments, that has two components, we use a 2D texture coordinate buffer. In addition, not all particles can be uniquely mapped to the screen. Consequently, to process all of the particles, we need to do the process in several passes of saving the current screen and mapping a new set of particles. For saving the current screen, which contains binary values, we use a one-bit plane of the framebuffer (off-screen). For example, with a given 100x100 sized screen, we are able to process 10,000 particles for each pass through the graphics pipeline. Figure 6 gives an overview of the processing pipeline.

4.2.1. Preparing Data Buffers for Pipeline Processing

The vertex buffer (1) contains all particles collected from the histogram pre-classification phase. It is not deleted unless the intensity range has been redefined. This enables the system to quickly fetch the target particles whenever a sketched region shall be resolved. This mechanism prevents unnecessary traffic of particles traveling across the system bus for every processing cycle. The texture coordinate buffer (2) stores a 2D array of screen coordinates (0, 0), (0, 1), ..., (s, t), ..., (height - 1, width - 1). Each particle is mapped to a screen coordinate using the associated seeded texture coordinate. During the execution of the processing pipeline, we redirect every particle to its designated screen location.

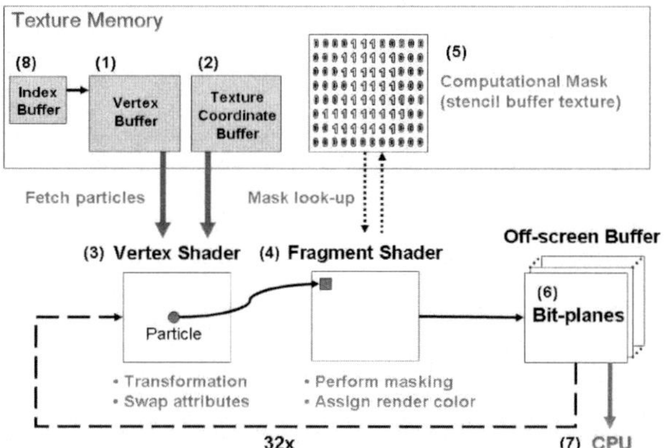

Figure 6: *Sketch system implemented in GPU.*

4.2.2. The Vertex and Fragment Programs

The vertex shader (3) is used to perform the particle coordinate transformation. In order to rasterize the current vertex (e.g. rendered as a 3D point) to the designated fragment location, we swap the incoming attributes as follows. The vertex (input) is multiplied by the model-view matrix, and the result is assigned to the texture coordinate (output). The accompanied texture coordinate (input) is multiplied by the projection matrix, and the result is assigned to the position (output). After the vertex shader has finished processing, both the resulting texture coordinate and position are rasterized and passed onto the fragment shader.

The fragment shader (4) performs the masking operation and assigns a pre-defined render color if the mask value is valid. The input texture coordinate (i.e. the particle's position assigned by the vertex shader) is adjusted with respect to the projection parameters and the value is looked up from the computational mask stored as a stencil buffer texture (5). If the texture look-up results a value of 1, then the particle processed by the current fragment program is inside the sketched region; otherwise, it is outside.

4.2.3. Parameter Calculations

Note that we only need one bit in the off-screen buffer (6) to store the selection information (i.e. one being selected, and zero being not selected). For a typical off-screen color buffer with RGBA components, and each component having 8-bit resolution, it is possible to encode 320,000 particle selections information by adding all render colors. Thus, the required off-screen buffer dimension is $\lceil \sqrt{N/32} \rceil$, where N is the total number of particles to be processed from the vertex buffer. The calculated buffer dimension becomes the width and height of the off-screen buffer.

4.2.4. Composing the Result

Finally, the CPU (7) receives the texture and decodes the selected particles to construct two index buffers, one con-

taining indices of the selected particles and the other one for the non-selected particles. These index buffers are then sent and stored in the GPU texture memory for the next processing cycle as well as for rendering purposes. In subsequent sketch operations, the index buffer (8) (storing the indices of the previously selected particles) is used to index into the vertex buffer when the 'fetch particles' command has been issued.

5. Seeded Region Growing

After describing a rough estimate of the target area using the sketch-based volume cutting, the user can navigate the volume and place a seed point directly on the visible surface to obtain an accurate segment. To find out the seed location in the 3D object-space from a 2D input device (e.g. the mouse), we use an intuitive interface that is consistent with our sketch-based system. In this interface, the user inputs a visible voxel (particle) by clicking the mouse on the screen. The entered pixel can be associated with several particles in various depths and we need to find the best candidate. To do this, we extend the pixel area to a larger rectangle whose extrusion in the volume contains all the involved particles (see Figure 7). To extrude the rectangle in the volume, we use the same technique as described in section 4. After determining all the involved particles, we select the one that has the shortest distance to the entered seed point (Figure 7). The selected particle is then used as the actual 3D seed point. For the region growing algorithm, we start from the seed point as the current voxel and move to adjacent voxels with intensity values close to the current intensity. We use the breath-first search algorithm as appears in the context of graph traversing techniques [CLRS01]. This approach helps to maintain a balanced and coherent growth. We use a threshold for the closeness of the intensities. It is obvious that the growing process can be sensitive to thresholds and the resulting region can be dramatically enlarged when the threshold is increased by one or two scales. However, as a benefit of our volume cutting tool, we can constrain the growing region to be inside of the cut sub-volume as a rough estimate of the desired region.

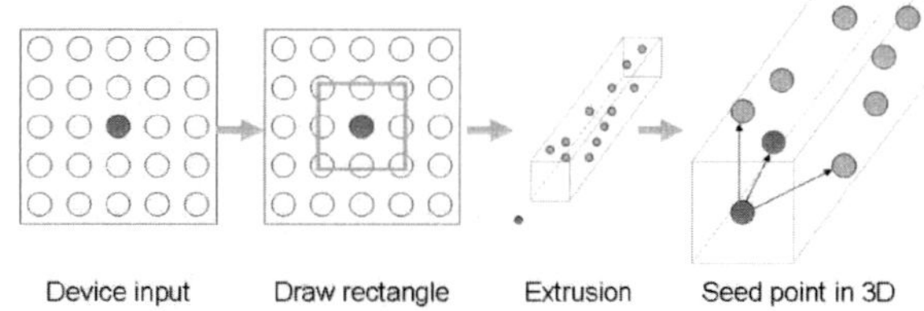

Figure 7: *Searching the seed point.*

6. Rendering

In our approach, we adapt the splatting technique [Wes91] for direct volume rendering using GPU programming. For rendering the volumetric data, each particle associated with a voxel is rendered as a square texture using the OpenGL hardware accelerated point sprite. Point sprite enables us to send only a single vertex information for each particle (voxel) through the rendering pipeline. We adapt the Gaussian kernel as our texture generation function (Figure 8, left).

In the fragment shader, we simply check the incoming opacity value and discard the current fragment if alpha is less than 0.2. We adapt two rendering modes for point-based splatting: X-ray and surface modes (Figure 8, middle and right, respectively).

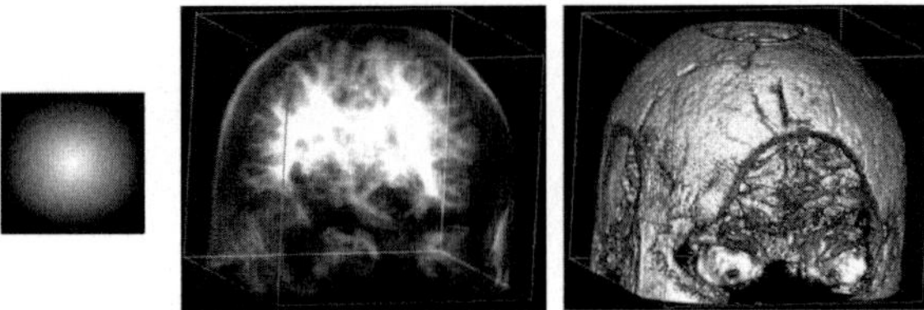

Figure 8: *(left to right) Disk texture with Gaussian distributed transparency values. Different rendering of the brain: X-ray and surface modes.*

The X-ray mode accumulates all fragments to compute the final pixel value with the following OpenGL formulation: $I_f(x) = \alpha_{new}(x)I_{new}(x) + I_f(x)$ [XC04]; where $I_f(x)$ is the frame-buffer intensity value at pixel location x, $I_{new}(x)$ is the incoming fragment value, and $\alpha_{new}(x)$ is the opacity of the new fragment. We use glBlendFunc(GL_SRC_ALPHA, GL_ONE) to perform the accumulation [XC04].

In order to render particles and obtain a surface representation, we apply a two-pass rendering technique that consists of the visibility pass followed by the shading pass [BHZK05]. During the visibility pass, we perform the so-called ε-test operation. For implementing the ε-test, we perform the following steps. First, we scale all the particles with the value of ε in the negative z-direction. Then we render to the depth buffer and turn off the color buffer. During the shading pass, we perform lighting computation for each particle processed by the vertex shader. Note that in both passes, we discard fragments whose opacities are less than 0.2. We also combine the X-ray mode and the surface mode to form the hybrid mode as follows: (1) render the particles (X-ray mode) to the frame buffer using alpha-blending with no lighting and (2) render the particles (surface mode) and perform the visibility pass and the shading pass respectively. However, during the visibility pass while rendering the surface mode particles, we enable writing to both the depth buffer and the color buffer. In the fragment shader, we output black pixels for all fragments processed (i.e. to overwrite the X-ray mode particles).

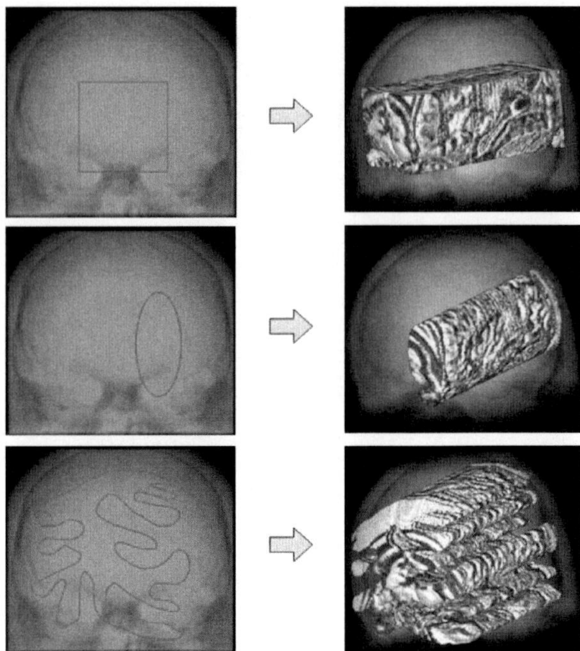

Figure 9: *Sketch types: (a) rectangular strokes, (b) elliptical strokes, and (c) free-form strokes.*

7. Results and Discussions

All the results were generated on an AMD Anthlon 64 X2 3800 with a GeForce 7800 GT, 256 MB card. We selected raw volumetric datasets of the brain (MRI, 152x154x181), skull (MRI, 256^3), and angiography (3T MRT, 256x320x128).

For all datasets, the sketch response time (SRT) was below 1 second. From loading a full-range histogram, Figure 2 shows the segmentation of grey and white matter of the left hemisphere of the brain (SRT = 0.384 sec). Figure 9 illustrates the before/after effects on the brain dataset after sketching rectangular, elliptical and free-form ROIs (SRT = 0.515, 0.392 and 0.384 sec, respectively). Figure 10 (top row) shows a successful segmentation of the right ventricle with SRT = 0.267 sec. Figure 10 (bottom row) illustrates a series of volume cutting after free-form sketched ROIs (SRT = 0.261 sec) and the resulting segmented portions of the teeth. With the 3T MRT time-of-flight angiography dataset of a human head (Figure 11), we were able to quickly segment the carotid and cerebral arteries with SRT = 0.224 sec.

Our system also allowed a real-time preview of seed locations as the user moves the mouse. The interactive rate of seed searching was achieved by utilizing the core system implementation and from the aid of GPU. Note that in order to obtain smooth sketching lines, we froze the background rendering (i.e. the volume splatting) by saving the entire scene to a texture. Thus when the user placed strokes on the screen, we rendered the screen-sized texture first followed by the ROI strokes.

8. Conclusion and Future Work

We presented a novel interface for volume segmentation based on seeded region growing. Instead of the traditional way of browsing from hundreds of cross-sectional slices, we proposed a sketch-based interface for interactive volume exploration and navigation for the ROI. We provided real-time rendering when the user interacts and places the seed point from a truly 3D environment. More importantly, our sketch-based system constrained the region grow from the cut subvolume to enforce focus-of-attention. In designing from a particle system perspective, our approach can be easily extended to a number of applications including other point-based systems, polygonal meshes, and irregular volume with changing topology.

Future improvements include extending our system with other algorithms for sketch-based volume manipulation. It would also be useful to have the capability of multiple sketched ROIs assigned in different regions of the volume to allow, for instance, better control of the level of detail in selected regions of the dataset. The criteria that we used to judge the quality of the results were solely based on our observations on the speed and flexibility of volume data cutting, exploration, and seed planting/growing control. It is important to conduct more formal evaluations and user/clinical studies to provide quality sketch-based volume segmentation tools for professionals in medical science.

References

[AB94]   ADAMS R., BISCHOF L.: Seeded region growing. *IEEE Trans. on PAMI 16*, 6 (June 1994), 641 – 647.

[BHZK05]   BOTSCH M., HORNUNG A., ZWICKER M., KOBBELT L.: High-quality surface splatting on today's gpus. In *Proc. of the Eurographics Symposium on Point-Based Graphics '05* (2005).

[CLRS01]   CORMEN T. H., LEISERSON C. E., RIVEST R. L., STEIN C.: *Introduction to Algorithms.* MIT Press and McGraw-Hill, 2001.

[Fra]   FRANKLIN W. R.: Pnpoly - point inclusion in polygon test. http://http://www.ecse.rpi.edu/Homepages/wrf/Research/Short_Notes/pnpoly.html.

[Hai94]   HAINES E.: Point in polygon strategies. *Graphics Gems IV* (1994), 24–46.

[KD98]   KINDLMANN G., DURKIN J.: Semi-automatic generation of transfer functions for direct volume rendering: Methods and applications. In *Proc. of Visualization '98* (1998), pp. 79 – 86.

[KQ03]   KIRBAS C., QUEK F.: Vessel extraction techniques and algorithms: a survey. In *Proc. of Bioinformatics and Bioengineering '03* (2003), pp. 238 – 245.

[ONI05]   OWADA S., NIELSEN F., IGARASHI T.: Volume catcher. In *Proc. of the Symposium on Interactive 3D graphics and games '05* (2005), pp. 111 – 116.

[ONNI03]   OWADA S., NIELSEN F., NAKAZAWA K., IGARASHI T.: A sketching interface for modeling the internal structures of 3d shapes. In *Proc. of 3rd International Symposium on Smart Graphics* (2003), pp. 49 – 57.

[ONOI04]   OWADA S., NIELSEN F., OKABE M., IGARASHI T.: Volumetric illustration: Designing 3d models with internal textures. *Proceedings of ACM SIGGRAPH(SIGGRAPH2004)* (2004), 322–328.

[PXP99]   PHAM D. L., XU C., PRINCE J. L.: A survey of current methods in medical image segmentation. *In Technical Report JHU/ECE 99-01, The Johns Hopkins University* (1999).

[RK82]   ROSENFELD A., KAK A.: Digital picture processing. *New York Academic Press 2* (1982), 138 – 145.

[SHN03]   SHERBONDY A., HOUSTON M., NAPEL S.: Fast volume segmentation with simultaneous visualization using programmable graphics hardware. In *Proc. of IEEE Visualization '03* (2003), pp. 171 – 176.

[SWD05]   SCHENKE S., WUENSCHE B., DENZLER J.: Gpu-based volume segmentation. In *Proc. of IVCNZ '05* (2005), pp. 171 – 176.

[TLM03]   TZENG F.-Y., LUM E. B., MA K.-L.: A novel interface for higher-dimensional classification of volume data. In *Proc. of IEEE Visualization '03* (2003), pp. 505 – 512.

[Wes91]   WESTOVER L.: *Splatting: A Parallel, Feed-Forward Volume Rendering Algorithm.* PhD thesis, Department of Computer Science, University of North Carolina at Chapel Hill, 1991.

[WNDS99]   WOO M., NEIDER J., DAVIS T., SHREINER D.: *OpenGL Programming Guide Third Edition.* Addison-Wesley Publishing Ltd, 1999.

[XC04]   XUE D., CRAWFIS R.: Efficient splatting using modern graphics hardware. *Graphics Tools 3*, 8 (2004), 1ąV21.

[YZNC05]   YUAN X., ZHANG N., NGUYEN M. X., CHEN B.: Volume cutout. *The Visual Computer (Special Issue of Pacific Graphics 2005) 21*, 8-10 (2005), 745–754.

EUROGRAPHICS Workshop on Sketch-Based Interfaces and Modeling (2006)
Thomas Stahovich and Mario Costa Sousa (Editors)

Sketch-based 3D Engineering Part Class Browsing and Retrieval

Suyu Hou and Karthik Ramani

Purdue University, West Lafayette, IN, USA

Abstract

We present a two-tier sketch-based engineering part retrieval system enhanced with classifier combination. Given a free-hand user sketch, we propose to use an ensemble of classifiers to estimate the likelihood of the sketch belonging to each category by exploring the strengths of individual classifiers. This supports high quality part retrieval by motivating user feedback with a ranked list of top choices. Three shape descriptors have been used to generate the probability-based classifiers independently. Experiments are conducted using the Engineering Shape Benchmark database in order to evaluate the selected combination rules before we integrate the best rule for sketch classification. User studies with the system show that users can easily identify the desired groups and then the parts. In addition, the precision attained using the synthesis is better than results from independent classifiers when applied to both user sketches and 3D models.

Categories and Subject Descriptors (according to ACM CCS): I.3.6 Interaction techniques, I.5.4 Application

1. Introduction

It is well-recognized that engineering design starts with a sketch. Sketch-based part retrieval is a more natural form for searching during the stage of earlier concept design than example-based part retrieval. When a 3D query example is not available, sketch will be especially useful. Therefore, it is necessary to have a fast and effective system for sketch-based engineering part retrieval.

Most of the sketch-based retrieval systems focus on searching of 2D sketches/images. Recently, several studies have been conducted to retrieve 3D models based on 2D sketches [FMK*03, PR05]. A common method to retrieve 3D models using sketches is to represent the sketch and views of the database model by a set of shape descriptors. The system then computes the similarity metric between the query and the database model based on a predefined cost function. However, the system often retrieves mixed classes of models without fully considering the user intent embedded in the query, thus causing a gap between user expectations and system retrievals. For engineering reuse, it is important not only to retrieve parts with similar shape, but also to match retrievals with similar functions to the query. Therefore, it is important for the user to obtain functional class consistency besides shape matching.

In this paper, we introduce an approach to support sketch-based engineering part class browsing and retrieval driven by classification. We mainly focus on applying sketch-based classification for the goal of high quality retrieval. The key idea is to elicit the user to provide a relevance feedback to a list of part categories obtained by sketch classification. In addition, the strategy of classifier combination is employed to boost the performance of sketch classification.

The main advantage of the proposed approach is its use of a probability-based classification to orienteer the user in a two-tier search framework. The probability-based classification can narrow down the choices for user

Figure 1: *Similar engineering model from different classes*

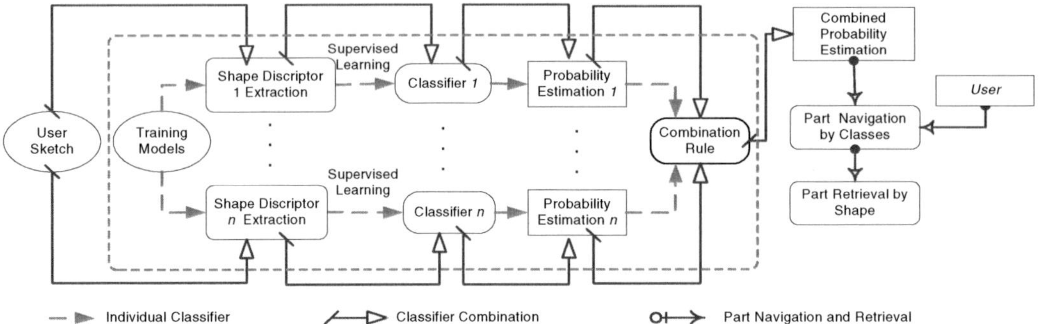

Figure 2: *System architecture*

selection without the risk of binary decisions obtained from regular classifiers. This is especially beneficial for sketch-based engineering part retrieval. First, sketches are always ambiguous. By motivating the user to disambiguate the intermediate result, the system actively gets the consent from the user. Secondly, engineering parts have a more complex scenario than regular multimedia models for categorization. There is no unique criterion for classifying engineering models. Even one engineering model sometimes can be classified into different classes by various standards [IR05, JKI*06]. Figure 1 shows an example of some similar engineering models from different classes. Therefore, another objective of this paper is to provide applicable classification mechanisms for engineering parts. Lastly, the probability estimation can facilitate post processing. The interpretation of the probability output is independent of the types of classifiers; only its quality depends on classifiers. We take advantage of this fact to attain a combined estimation so as to improve the confidence for the decision making.

To the best of our knowledge, we do not know of any existing work that supports sketch-based 3D part class browsing and retrieval using classification. The rest of this paper is organized as follows. In Section 2, we briefly describe the system architecture of the proposed framework. We then present the major modules of the framework in Section 3. Section 4 shows the user studies and includes a discussion. The paper concludes in Section 5.

2. System Architecture

We use a 3D part retrieval system, ShapeLab [PR05], and the Engineering Shape Benchmark database (ESB) [JKI*06] as the test bed for this study. Given a query in the form of sketches from three orthogonal views of a 3D object, we allow the user to browse the most possible classes based on the query sketch. This is obtained by a probability-based classification engine. The classifier differentiates the likelihood of the query belonging to each 3D part category from ESB. A ranked list of top categories is provided to the user based on the degree of agreement between the query sketch and the classifier for each class. The system will then perform the shape matching within the categories that the user prefers. The idea of classifying a query sketch into 3D part category comes from the notions that i) engineers usually express their concept of a 3D shape with three 2D orthogonal views without losing much

information [PR05]; ii) consistency exists between the user sketch of orthogonal views of 3D objects and the views automatically generated from the 3D model by the pose estimation method based on Virtual Contact Area (VCA) used by the ShapeLab system [PR05]. In this paper, instead of using a conventional single classifier, we propose to synthesize independent classifiers to improve classification performance and avoid a biased decision.

Figure 2 presents the system work flow. First, training data from ESB is used to finalize the individual classifiers as shown inside the left dotted window of Figure 2. Each shape descriptor corresponds to a specific classifier. Different classifiers which output the probability estimation of data being classified to a particular class are developed separately using supervised learning. Meanwhile, we exploit the classification output from the training data to estimate the optimal weight for the linear combination model used later for the real searching. The main idea is that given a classifier, its contribution to the combined prediction of the testing data is dependent on its performance with the training data. A classifier with better classification accuracy is considered to have better predication capability and will be given more weight for the combination model. Several candidate combination rules are proposed for this work which will be presented in Section 3. Testing data from ESB is employed to assess these combination rules before the rule is applied to the sketch input. The testing data and the sketch pass through the same processes of shape descriptor extraction and the classification estimations before reaching the combination stage, except that the sketch input utilizes the combination rule selected by the testing data. The combination rule designated in Figure 2 is the one finalized by the testing data. At the end, the system enables the user to browse the parts organized in classified groups and then to pinpoint the desired parts while avoiding browsing irrelevant parts. In some form our system performs the function of relevancy feedback using part classes.

3. Approach

3.1. Sketch Acquisition and Representation

The sketch acquisition module records users' search intent using sketch. Users can employ a pen or a mouse to sketch. In our system design, the sketches are drawn

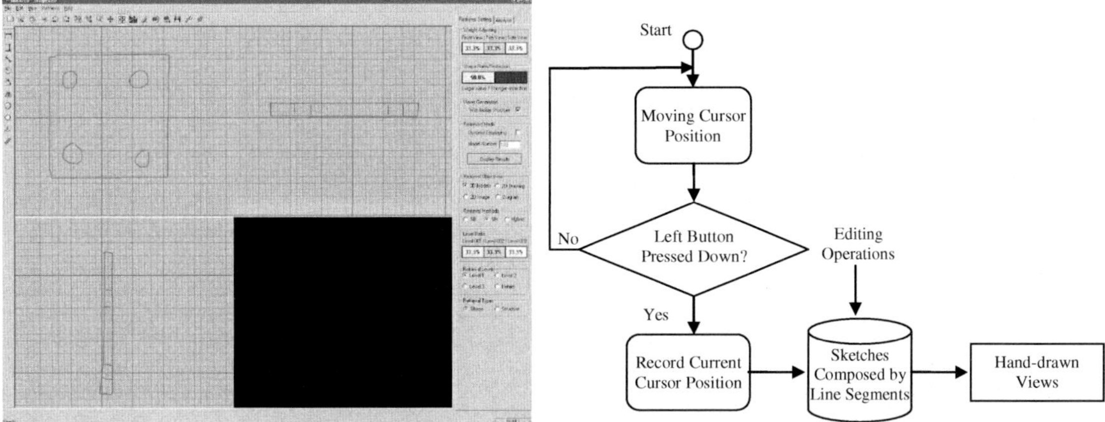

Figure 3: *Sketch acquisition module: (left) sketch editor, (right) information work flow*

through a sequence of strokes. Figure 3 shows the visual appearance and the architecture of the sketch editor. During the sketching process, the system monitors the action of the mouse or the pen. Once the mouse cursor is moving and the left button is pressed down, it can be concluded that users have begun to draw sketches. Now the moving path of the cursor is recorded in real time with the end of the stroke indicated by the release of left button.

Each track of a stroke S is composed of a sequence of small line segments rather than image bitmaps: $S = \{((x_i, y_i), (x_{i+1}, y_{i+1}), t_i) \mid 0 \leq i \leq n\}$ where n is the total number of line segments included in a single stroke S, (x_i, y_i) and (x_{i+1}, y_{i+1}) are the two ending points of a small line segment at time t_i. Consequently, sketching activity A is usually formed by a sequence of stroke $A = \{S_i \mid 0 \leq i < m\}$ where m is the number of strokes. In the end, the desired shape descriptor will be extracted from these strokes [PR06].

In the sketch process, it is inevitable that the user will make some mistakes. Therefore, besides the sketch operations, some editing operations are also provided to users. Some basic operations, such as erase, trim, move, rotate, zoom, and view copy are included. More operations can be added into this system, although only a few basic operations are provided in this system. In the future, sketch beautification from [PHR06] will be integrated with the current system to regulate the freehand sketch, which is expected to boost the performance of sketch-based shape analysis.

3.2. View-based 3D Shape Description and Its Benefits for Sketch Recognition

In our system, three 2D orthogonal views by pose determination and projection are automatically generated from each 3D triangulated model [PR05]. Therefore, given a shape description from views of a query, the system can find similar 3D models. Compared to most other existing 3D shape descriptors which capture the form from 3D models directly, shape signatures generated from views perform well and can be applied to view-based 3D model

retrieval directly [COT*03]. Similarly, it is intuitive to accept the idea of sketch-based 3D model classification given the fact that sketches are the most natural form for shape expression. Sketch-based 2D symbol classification/recognition has progressed extensively in the past decades. Most classifiers/recognizers either use a coded template for matching [CDP*04, FPJ02, FJ00, VCC01, AD04] or require sets of training data to reliably learn new symbols [LQX01, SD05, HN04, KS04, KS05, RUB91]. Among them, methods using statistical learning for symbol classification share a similar background with this paper even though we mainly focus on sketch-based 3D part classification. In [KS05], classifier combination is applied to sketch symbol recognition using user-defined training examples. This method can reach higher classification accuracy because the sketch query is consistent with the training data. However, the idea is not applicable for 3D engineering parts because the engineering part classification scheme and training data are hard to define on the fly. Besides, engineering parts are difficult to sketch formally for training purposes. Therefore, we motivate the user to help the system obtain the best retrieval with the classification engine defined by real engineering models.

For our work, we rely on shape descriptors as feature vectors for the classification problem. Our experience with sketching has shown that users prefer to draw a model at a higher level, thus closer to the contour level of the view generated from the 3D model , which captures an outer boundary and internal boundaries from a specific view of a 3D model [PJH*06]. In this paper, two criteria are needed to meet the shape descriptor selection. First, it has to be applicable to both 2D views and the sketch. Second, it is rotation invariant so that optimal alignment identification can be saved. Three shape descriptors are chosen to represent the shape content from the sketches/views in this context: 2.5D Spherical Harmonics (SH) from the contours [PR06], Fourier Transform (FT) from the outer boundary [ZL01], and the Zernike moments (ZM) from the region inside the outer boundary [KH90]. These three shape descriptors have been shown empirically to perform well in the task of shape matching. Although our framework is independent of the shape descriptor selected, we choose

Table 1: *Classification accuracy for testing data from ESB*

	Individual Classifiers			Combination Rules				
	SH Contour	Fourier	Zernike	Majority Vote	Product Rule	SA	WA MSE	WA MCE
Case I	68.69%	66.38%	63.35%	71.80%	74.50%	75.00%	73.31%	75.00%

2.5D SH, FT and ZM because they complement the shape description from different perspectives using dissimilar techniques. For example, 2.5D SH includes the internal boundaries in addition to the outer boundary considered by FT, while ZM reflects more of the internal details by describing the distribution inside the region. Therefore, it is expected that classifier combination can achieve a better performance. For the current work, we concatenate shape signatures generated from three views to form a single feature vector $x \in \Re^n$. Data produced at this stage will then be employed for classifier recognition.

3.3. Probability-based Classification

Many algorithms have been presented to classify 3D objects using machine learning techniques [BD06, HLR05, IR05, and ZC02]. Given a classification scheme of C classes $\Omega = \{\omega_1, \omega_2, ... \omega_C\}$, and a set of labeled training examples $X = \{(x_i, y_i), i = 1, ... N\}$ with $x_i \in \Re^n$ and $y_i \in \Omega$ from database, a common goal is to classify a unique example x into a particular class ω_i. A simple method is to recognize the classifiers using the training data and to assign the query to the class that has the largest confidence from the prediction. Usually, the system outputs binary decision $P = \{p_1 = 0, ... p_k = 1, ... p_C = 0\}$ when $x \in \omega_k$, indicating that only the class that has the largest confidence wins the verdict. This approach, however, may lead to an inappropriate consequence for sketch-based engineering part classification. Unlike the binary classifier which hardens confidence measurement into a binary decision, the proposed probability-based classifier normalizes the confidence measurement into a probability output $P = \{p_1, ... p_k, ... p_C\}$ with $\sum_{k=1}^{C} p_k = 1$. Besides, there is no need to normalize the classification output for synthesis because the probability can be universally interpreted. Several algorithms have been presented to produce the probability output from pattern classifiers [WLW04]. In this paper, we chose Support Vector Machines (SVM) [CL01] as the classifier because of its quality although there are other applicable classifiers such as KNN [KUN04], Gaussian linear classifier [TBD*00]. Steps following the conventional procedures are taken to produce a classifier for each shape descriptor. A set of probability estimations $\{P_{2.5DSH}, P_{FF}, P_{ZM}\}$ for the query will then be generated in a parallel way using the resulting independent classifiers.

3.4. Classifier Combination Rules and Evaluations

Recent applications in combining multiple classifiers for the classification problem have shown strong evidence that strategies of taking advantage of various resources outperform traditional monolithic classifiers [RKW04]. The combined estimation theoretically always avoids the worst case and it even outperformed individual classifiers in our experiment as we demonstrate later. Inspired by this observation, we employ the strategy of classifier combination for sketch-based classification. The competency of classifier combination also implies that the system does not require as much training data as a monolithic classifier in order to reach the same performance. Therefore, the tradeoff between classification accuracy and amount of training data can be coordinated with the tactic of classifier combination in case the database does not have enough training data, as is often seen in reality. Several existing popular classifier combination rules are presented here for selection: Majority Vote, Product Rule [KHD*98], Simple Average (SA) [KHD*98, FR05], Weighted Average (WA) using Minimum Square Error (MSE) for weight estimation [BSE*97] and WA using Minimum misclassification Error (MCE) for weight estimation [UED00].

We examined the combination rule proposed above using real data from ESB. There are a total of 856 models in ESB with 55 out of 856 models which are miscellaneous and do not belong to each of the 42 classes. Therefore, there are a total of 801 models grouped in 42 classes in ESB. The size of each group varies. The maximum size of a group in ESB is 58, while the minimum size of a group is only 4. Half of the data from each group is randomly selected as the training data. The average training size from the 42 groups of training data with different sizes is 19.6 with a standard deviation of 14.6, which indicates the complexity of our classification problem. Training data from half of the ESB is first used to recognize the classifier and then to estimate the weight for a linear combination using MSE or MCE. Testing data from the remainder of the database will then be employed to evaluate the quality of the combination rules using the classification estimation from independent classifiers.

The results from Table 1 show that each combination rule outperformed the classification performance from individual classifiers. Even the worst combination (Majority Vote) had over 3% accuracy increase over the best individual classifier. SA and WA using MCE had the most competitive performance than other combination rules over our testing data. However, WA by MCE needs training data for weight estimation but without guarantee of better synthesizing results. The product rule also shows good performance in this experiment. However, the risk associated with this method when one classifier has a large

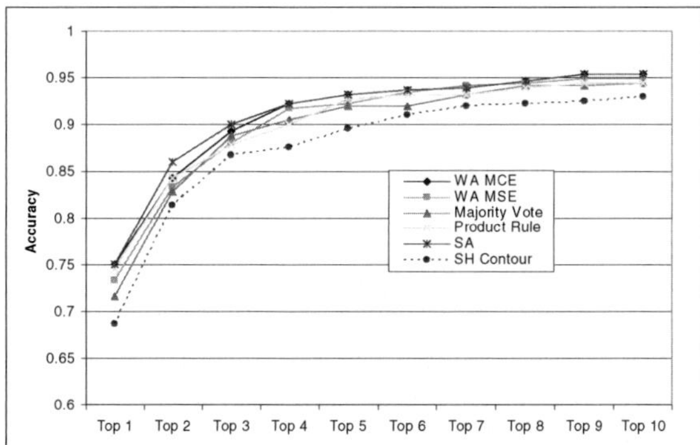

Figure 4: *Relaxed classification accuracy*

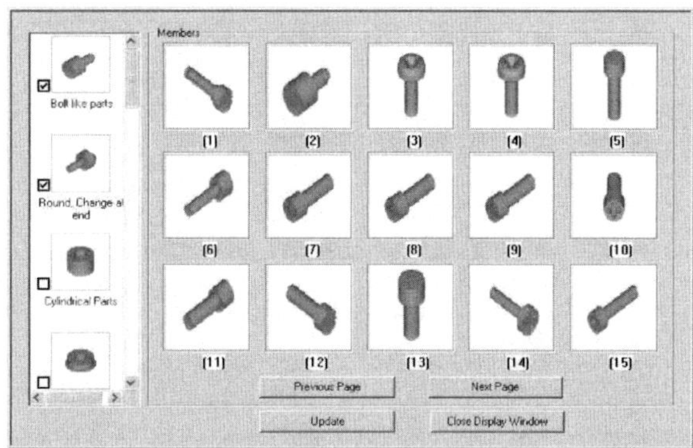

Figure 5: *GUI of part class browsing and retrieval*

estimation discrepancy from others [KHD*98] rules it out from our selection. The results are consistent with the experiment studies in [FR05] which conclude that SA is as good as WA sometimes in reality although the author also claims that WA is better than SA theoretically. We therefore choose SA as our sketch-based classifier combination rule. Besides, high quality and dissimilar classifiers can be further inserted into the combination without making modifications to the current system.

Figure 4 shows the relaxed classification accuracy for selected classifiers up to the top 10 using the testing data from ESB. The relaxed classification accuracy for top K is defined as $RCA(K) = \dfrac{\sum_{i=1}^{K} n(i)}{N}$ where $n(i)$ is the number of correct classifications at i^{th} rank, and N is the total number of the testing data. Solid lines represent the relaxed classification accuracy under different combination rules, while the dotted line comes from the best individual classifier, the one developed from 2.5D SH. The combination rule can reach about 92% within the top five for the testing data. After the top 8 results, the relaxed classification accuracies become stable and approximate to 96% at top 10. At this stage there is not much difference among different combination rules. The output shows some promising results given the classification complexity in this problem: 42 classes with non-uniform training size. Difficulties may arise when the classification engine is applied to the sketch input. However, the overall performance boosts our confidence in using the proposed framework for sketch-based 3D part retrieval.

3.5.   GUI Design

We have implemented the proposed sketch-based part retrieval for ShapeLab. After the user submits the sketches using the sketch editor described in Section 3.1, the system will provide a list of 20 classes sorted by the probabilities from the classification output. We let the user browse the top 20 out of the total of 42 classes to show the advantages of the proposed work while at the same time avoiding missing identifications. Figure 5 shows the GUI of the implementation. On the left-hand side of the GUI are the class images of the ranked list that prompt the user to choose. Models of the selected class will be shown in the order of shape similarity to the query on the right-hand side. The default images of the models will be the ones belonging to the class that has the highest possibility. The user is then able to browse groups of models based on the selection that he/she thinks as the right classes. The proposed framework can not only improve the search effectiveness and efficiency, but also enhance user interaction by involving only a limited number of highly possible choices. This design will be especially useful for a large database with a large number of classes.

4.   User Studies

The overall purpose of the experiments is to appraise the proposed idea with respect to the system performance for query by sketch. Besides, we formally quantify how well the combination rule can improve the performance over single classifiers. The results assist us to understand the difference between sketches and views from a 3D model. To obtain an objective evaluation, we conduct a user study consisting of two independent experiments. In the first experiment, users are given examples of models from our ESB to sketch. In the second experiment, engineering CAD models outside ESB are provided for the user to sketch.

In this experiment, people with no background of ShapeLab system are chosen to participate in the study. Users are allowed to take some time to acquaint themselves with the hardware and the system. During the practice, users did not encounter any problem. Typically they spend several minutes before the real tests begin. There is no instruction on how to sketch the 3D object in particular, for example, the view definition for the orthogonal views (e.g., front, side, or the top view), or the amount of detail to sketch (e.g. whether to sketch the external contour alone or the complete drawing with hidden lines).

Five different users are asked to generate a freehand sketch for each example. For each sketch input, two kinds of classification engines are used for the tests. The first one is the best individual classifier which employs 2.5D SH feature vector. The other is the combined classifier using Simple Average rule selected through the ESB testing data.

Table 2: *Results for sketches of examples from ESB*

	Average Best Rank by Sketch	Overall Average Rank by Example	Average Best Classification Accuracy		
			Top 1	Top 5	Top 10
Classifier by 2.5 SH	3.33	1.67	33.33%	75.00%	100.00%
Classifier by SA Combination	3.00	1.50	33.33%	75.00%	100.00%

Table 3: *Results of sketches of examples from outside ESB*

	Average Best Rank by Sketch	Average Best Classification Accuracy			
		Top 1	Top 5	Top 10	Top 15
Classifier by 2.5 SH	7.29	28.57%	28.57%	71.43%	100.00%
Classifier by SA Combination	6.29	28.57%	42.86%	85.71%	100.00%

Each sketch goes through the two classification engines separately. The user is then asked to give his/her evaluation of the rank of the right class as shown by the class images on the left hand side of the window. We then record the ranks for this example from the results of the five sketches. The overall performance of the selected classification engine can then be evaluated based on the results from sketches of all the examples.

4.1.   Sketch Examples from ESB

There were a total of 12 examples, 60 user sketches tested in this experiment. The examples containing a wide variety of engineering shapes are randomly picked from the testing dataset of ESB. These examples are not involved in the training process. Besides, the sketch inputs are different from the views generated from the training examples. Therefore, it is fair to say that this experiment can objectively reflect the performance of the system. However, it is expected that the result will be different from the result of the second experiment since these examples come from the same database and belong to one of the 42 classes in the training data. Table 2 shows the average best performance of each classification engine for the sketched input. We pick the best rank for each example. This is because the sketches created by the users are sometimes different from the view permutation generated from the 3D models as we find out during the experiments. Figure 6 gives an example shown to the user and the five sketches involved in this experiment. It is obvious that the user sketches have some dissimilar characteristics from each other and are not guaranteed to have the consistent view correspondence compared to the views generated by the system as shown in Figure 6 (a).   The views generated by the ShapeLab system have certain patterns driven by the VCA algorithm. Therefore, it decides the classifier produced by the training models. If the sketch does not follow the convention of view generation, it is impossible to get the best matching. The overall performance expressed by relaxed classification accuracy is obtained by putting the best rank of each example into a histogram. We also provide the average rank of these examples in Table 2, with the views automatically generated by the system instead of user sketch. The purpose is to compare how much influence the user sketch can have on the classification performance. From the results, it can be seen that there is certain difference between classification for views generated from examples and classification for sketches of the examples. The difference is mainly because of the sketch ambiguities between the training views and the sketches. This is because we have already excluded the reason for different view correspondence in calculating the overall rank. The combination rule marginally improves the classification performance from the best individual classifier. A smaller value of the average rank indicates a better performance of the classifier. Although it is not the determining factor for the classification output, the strategy of classifier combination can certainly help the system to obtain the best performance when no prior knowledge of the individual classifier is available.

4.2.   Sketch Examples from outside ESB

The aim of this experiment is to find out how flexible and robust our system is when the data is outside the range of our database. Half of these examples do not conceptually belong to any of our ESB classes. Some of them are even hard to sketch based on user experiences. There are a total of 7 examples and therefore 35 user sketches to evaluate the performance of the classifiers. Since there is no information as to which classes these examples belong to, we let the user decide the rank based on the similarities between the query and the class images shown on the left-hand side of the window. It is possible that the same query may belong to multiple classes. Therefore, the rank evaluated by the user is the highest rank from possible classes given by the system. We calculate the overall performance for each example following the same procedure as the first experiment. Table 3 lists the results obtained from this experiment. The results are not as good as those of the first experiment as expected. We further investigated the results and found out that those examples not belonging to any of the classes have lower rank evaluations. However, the user can still find promising categories as he/she browses the classes. Similarity, the combination rule improves the classification performance.

Both experiments demonstrate that the sketch has more uncertainties compared to real examples. In fact, query by sketch commonly does not have as good retrievals as query-by-example. The goal for our work is to improve the end retrieval by orienteering user feedback at the first tier. Therefore if we successfully obtain the user feedback for the second tier search, we can still achieve the goal. The experimental results support our proposition of providing the user with the desired choices within a certain range.

5.   Conclusions and Future Work

This paper presented and explored a framework to support fast and effective sketch-based 3D engineering part retrieval driven by classification. We described the idea of

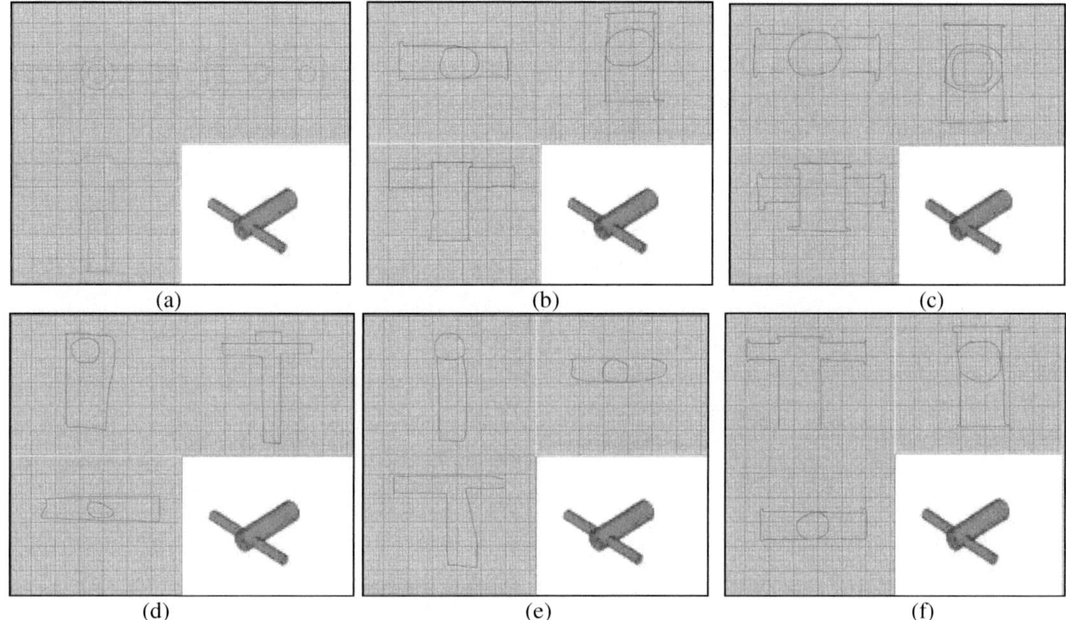

Figure 6: *(a) views generated by system for the example, (b-f) sketches created by different users for the same example*

using classifier combination to improve the sketch classification performance for the good of downstream part class browsing and retrieval. The use of a probability-based classifier and its merits in classifier combination can be applied to any type of two-tier content-based search system. We then conducted two user studies to evaluate the robustness of the proposed work. Different datasets were used to examine the classification accuracy of two classification engines: the best individual classifier and the Simple Average combination rule. The experimental results showed that the system can output the right class within a tolerance range, thus guiding the user to choose the preferred class for shape matching. The use of an ensemble of classifiers improved the classification accuracy both for sketches and 3D models. In addition, our system showed distinction in classification output to examples that did not come from any of the classes of ESB. Important factor to decide the classification performance for sketches included the ambiguities and inconsistencies of the sketches with regards to the training views. In the future, the sketch beautification will be integrated into the current system in order to regulate the sketch input. It is possible that sketching three views of a complex object will be hard for most people. We will use sketch beautification to partially help the user to draw complex views, and we may add more sketch utilities to address this issue in the future. Also the user may be able to use a photograph of an object and use a model with detected edges as input. In addition, for better classification performance, we will permute the sketches in order to find the best correspondence with the training views.

Acknowledgements

We would like to acknowledge partial support of the National Science Foundation Grant (IIS 0535156).

Reference

[AD04] ALVARADO, C., DAVID, R.: SketchREAD: a multi-domain sketch recognition engine. *In Proceedings of the 17th Annual ACM Symposium on User Interface Software and Technology*, (2004), 23-32.

[BD06] BARUTCUOGLU,Z., DECORO, C.; Hierarchical shape classification using Bayesian aggregation. *Shape Modeling International.* (June 2006)

[BSE*97] BENEDIKTSSON, J.A., SVEINSSON, J.R., ERSOY, O.K., SWAIN, P.H.: Parallel consensual neural networks, *IEEE Trans. Neural Networks*, 8, 1, (1997),54-64.

[CDP*04] COSTAGLIOLA, G., DEUFEMIA, V., POLESE, G., RISI, M.: A parsing technique for sketch recognition systems. *In Proceedings of 2004 IEEE Symposium on Visual Languages-Human Centric Computing* (VLHCC'04), (2004), 19-26.

[CL01] CHANG, C-C., LIN, C-J.: LIBSVM : a library for support vector machines. Software available at http://www.csie.ntu.edu.tw/~cjlin/libsvm. (2001).

[COT*03] CHEN, D-Y., OUHYOUNG, M., TIAN, X-P., SHEN, Y-T.: On visual similarity based 3D model retrieval. *Computer Graphics Forum*, (2003) 223–232.

[FJ00] FONSECA, M.J., JORGE, J.A.: Using fuzzy logic to recognize geometric shapes interactively. *In Proceedings of the 9th IEEE Conf. on Fuzzy Systems*, 1, (2000), 291-296.

[FMK*03] FUNKHOUSER,T., KAZHDAN, M., CHEN,J.,HALDERMAN,A.,DOBKIN,D.,

JOCOBS,D.: A search engine for 3D models. *Transactions on Graphics*, 22, 1 (2003), 83-105.

[FPJ02] FONSECA, M.J., PIMENTEL, J., JORGE, J.A.: Cali-an online scribble recognizer for calligraphic interfaces. *In Proceedings of the 2002, AAAI Spring Symposium on Sketch Understanding*, (2002), 51–58.

[FR05] FUMERA, G., ROLI, F.: A theoretical and experimental analysis of linear combiners for multiple classifier systems. *IEEE Trans. Pattern Analysis and Machine Intelligence*, 27, 6, (2005) 942-956.

[HLR05] HOU S., LOU K., RAMANI K. SVM-based semantic clustering and retrieval of a 3D model database, *Computer Aided Design and Application*, 2, 2, 2005, 155-164.

[HN04] HSE, H., NEWTON, A.R.: Sketched symbol recognition using Zernike moments. *In Proceedings of 17th International Conference on Pattern Recognition* (ICPR'04,, (2004),367-370.

[IR05] IP, Y., REGLI, W. C.: Manufacturing processes recognition of machined mechanical parts using SVMs, *AAAI2005*, (2005), 1608-1609.

[JKI*06] JAYANTI, S., KALYANARAMAN, Y., IYER, N., RAMANI, K.: Developing an engineering shape benchmark for CAD models, the Special Issue on Shape Similarity Detection and Search for CAD/CAE Applications, *Journal of Computer Aided Design*, in print, (2006).

[KUN04] KUNCHEVA, L.I., *Combining pattern classifiers: methods and algorithms*. Wiley, 2004.

[KH90] KHOTANZAD, A., HONG, Y.: Invariant image recognition by Zernike moments. *IEEE Trans. Pattern Analysis and Machine Intelligence*, 12, 5, (1990), 489-497

[KHD*98] KITTLER, J., HATEF, M., DUIN, R. MATAS, J.: On combining classifiers. *IEEE Trans. Pattern Analysis and Machine Intelligence*, 20, 3,(1998),226–239.

[KS04] KARA, L.B.., STAHOVICH, T.F.: An image-based trainable symbol recognizer for sketch-based interfaces. *In Proceedings of AAAI Fall Symposium Series 2004*: Making Pen-Based Interaction Intelligent and Natural, (2004), 99-105.

[KS05] KARA, L.B.., STAHOVICH, T.F.: An image-based, trainable symbol recognizer for hand-drawn sketches. *Computers & Graphics* 29, 4, (2005) 501-517.

[LQX01] LIU, W.Y., QIAN, W.J., XIAO, R. Smart sketchpad - an on-line graphics recognition system, *In Proceedings of Sixth International Conference on Document Analysis and Recognition*, (2001), 1050-1054.

[PHR06] PU, J.T., HOU,S., RAMANI K.: Toward freehand sketch beautification driven by geometric constraint. Submitted to *ACM Transactions on Graphics*.

[PJH*06] PU J.T., JAYANTI S., HOU S., RAMANI K.: Similar 3D model retrieval based on multiple level of detail. Accepted by *the 14th Pacific Conference on Computer Graphics and Applications*, (2006).

[PR05] PU, J.T., RAMANI K.: A 3D model retrieval method using 2D freehand sketches. *Lecture Notes in Computer Science,* vol. 3515 (2005) 343-347.

[PR06] PU, J.T., RAMANI K.: On visual similarity based 2D drawing retrieval. *Journal of Computer Aided Design*, 38, 3 (2006) 249-259.

[RUB91] RUBINE, B.: Specifying gestures by example. *ACM Transaction on Computer Graphics*, 25, 4, (1991), 329-337.

[RKW04] ROLI, F., KITTLER, J., WINDEATT, T., eds.: Multiple classifier systems, *Lecture Notes in Computer Science*, 3077, (2004).

[SD05] SEZGIN, T.M., DAVIS, R.: HMM-based efficient sketch recognition. *In Proceedings of the 10th International Conference on Intelligent User Interfaces,* (2005) 281-283.

[TBD*00] TAX, D., BREUKELEN, M. VAN., DUIN, R. KITTLER, J.: Combining multiple classifiers by averaging or by multiplying? *Pattern Recognition*, 33, 1, (2000), 475-1485.

[UED00] UEDA, N.: Optimal linear combination of neural networks for improving classification performance. *IEEE Transactions on Pattern Analysis and Machine Intelligence*, 22 (2000), 207-215.

[VCC01] VALOIS, J.P., CÔTÉ, M., CHERIET, M.: Online recognition of sketched electrical diagrams. *In Proceedings of Sixth International Conference on Document Analysis and Recognition*, (2001), 460-464.

[WLW04] WU, T.-F., LIN, C.-J., WENG, R. C.: Probability estimates for multi-class classification by pairwise coupling. *Journal of Machine Learning Research*, (2004)

[ZC02] ZHANG, C., CHEN, T.: A new active leaning approach for content-based information retrieval, *IEEE Trans. On Multimedia Special Issue on Multimedia Database*, 4, 2, (2002), 260-268.

[ZL01] ZHANG D. S., LU. G. J.,: Shape retrieval using Fourier descriptors. *IEEE International Conference on Multimedia and Expo (ICME)*, (2001)1139- 114.

EUROGRAPHICS Workshop on Sketch-Based Interfaces and Modeling (2006)
Thomas Stahovich and Mario Costa Sousa (Editors)

A Study of Usability of Sketching Tools
Aimed at Supporting Prescriptive Sketches

P. Company[1], M. Contero[2], F. Naya[2], and N. Aleixos[1]

[1]Department of Mechanical Engineering and Construction, Universitat Jaume I, Spain
[2]DEGI-ETSII, Polytechnic University of Valencia, Spain

Abstract

Prescriptive sketches are usually drawn, after conceptual design is over, to prepare the creation of digital 3D models. Designers and draftsmen use them as "screenplays" that guide the creation of the final 3D model. Prescriptive sketches are still paper-and-pencil, in spite of the existence of some academic or even commercial, computer tools.

In this paper, we defend the hypothesis that this is because current computer tools are less usable than paper-and-pencil sketches and do not posses significantly improved functionality. A pilot study was conducted to validate this hypothesis. Both the study and its main conclusions are described in detail.

Categories and Subject Descriptors (according to ACM CCS): J.6.1 [Computer-Aided Engineering]: Computer-Aided Design. H.5.2 [User Interface]: *Interaction styles, Input devices and strategies,* Evaluation/methodology.

1. Introduction

According to the classification by Ferguson [Fer92], we distinguish among *thinking sketches* used to focus and guide non-verbal thinking, *talking sketches* employed to support discussion on the design with colleagues and *prescriptive sketches* applied to give instructions to the draftsman who is in charge of making the final drawing. From the point of view of machine interpretation of sketches, prescriptive sketches clearly differ from both thinking and talking sketches, as prescriptive sketches contain many standardized conventions (like symmetry lines, dimensions, hatched cut views, etc.) that greatly affect to both the input and the reconstruction process of a final model.

The machine interpretation and reconstruction of thinking sketches has attracted a lot of attention. A number of different authors and groups using different techniques have contributed to this field (see the recent survey in [CPC*05]). Besides, the judgment of designers about computer support for thinking sketches in the conceptual design of industrial products has been a field of interest for some time and is still very active at present (see, for instance, [BD03] and [LQP*04]). Talking sketches, which are aimed at enhancing communication among design teams, have not received so much attention. Some recent developments from the computer support collaborative work (CSCW) scientific community are aimed at both collaborative creation and the sharing of 2D sketches.

However, relating to the objectives of this paper, few differences separate them from thinking sketches in terms of its automatic interpretation and conversion into 3D digital models. Finally, although it obviously benefits from the general advances in pen-based interfaces and the like (e.g. Computers & Graphics 29(4), special issue on pen-based computing), few works were found in the literature aimed at studying the singularities of the input and the transfer from prescriptive sketches into 3D computer models. Although concerned with architecture rather than product design, the work by the Lucid group (e.g. [JLA05]) is a pioneering effort in this field. Prescriptive sketches were ignored at the time when a lot of effort was concentrated in automatic digitalization of engineering drawings, since, at that time, they were considered to be more "noisy" than line-drawings, and just temporary documents (instead of valid documents containing long-term information). In our opinion, this point of view obviates the fact that prescriptive sketches are typically done by head designers, and are later converted into final line-drawings by draftsmen. Certainly, some draftsmen are very expert in solving geometrical incoherencies and not well defined details of the sketches. But many of them simply tidy up (or, in the worst cases corrupt!) the original prescriptive sketch, which already contains all the relevant information. Hence, creating prescriptive sketches, then converting them into line-drawings and finally creating a 3D model is a clearly inefficient flow. Yet, the need of prescriptive sketches is clear, as they are still drawn (after conceptual design is over), in order to prepare the creation of digital 3D models: designers and draftsmen use them as "screenplays" that guide the creation of the final 3D model. Hence, the first question is whether or not creating a paper-and-pencil prescriptive sketch is more or less efficient than creating a "digital" prescriptive sketch. This question is relevant since digital sketches are the output of computer-aided sketching (CAS) tools, which should become the new design paradigm.

In this paper, we defend the hypothesis that paper-and-pencil is still preferred because current CAS tools are less *usable* and do not posses significantly improved *functionality*. A pilot study was conducted to validate this hypothesis. Both the study and its main conclusions are described in detail.

Apparently, creating a prescriptive sketch and then creating its 3D model from scratch is also inefficient: prescriptive sketches should be the input for the automatic creation of 3D models. This should constitute the functionality improvement that greatly compensates the reduced usability of digital prescriptive sketches. Hence, this shift would convert digital prescriptive sketches into a valid alternative. Sometimes, it is assumed that current "pseudo-sketchers" embedded into CAD applications solve this problem, i.e. they can substitute hand made prescriptive sketches without loss of usability and they can also increase functionality by semi-automatically aiding the user in creating the final model from the different views of the sketch. In our pilot study we have tried to measure the validity of this belief.

2. Discussion

The absence of digital prescriptive sketching tools in the design process is not due to prescriptive sketching not being necessary any more. It is just that appropriate hardware was not available until the recent advent of tablet PCs, and currently available SBIM tools are still too academic, and no commercial tools have yet arrived to the end users.

However, it is to be noticed the difference with the origin of other CAD tools. Indeed, even the most primitive and simple advances in "digital" curves, from the field of CAGD, were anxiously adopted by designers' community as soon as they became available. Furthermore, they were considered to be such a technological advantage that they were kept under trade secret for as long as their owners could do so [Far02].

In our opinion, this was because "digital" curves solved a critical problem in aeronautical and automotive industries that traditional tools could not solve. Designers and manufactures needed a mathematical description of curves (ready to CAM), which had to be, at the same time, meaningful and simple for design purposes. Traditional approaches to curves from descriptive geometry were limited to conics. Analytical curves depended on abstract parameters and its behaviour was not intuitive for designers.

On the other hand, sketching is certainly a powerful way to communicate design ideas and to enhance the designer

creativity! Many studies ([Tve02], [PA02], [BD03]...) guarantee sketching to be an important conceptual design tool. A recent survey conducted by the Engineering Design Graphics Division of the American Society for Engineering Education (ASEE) includes the ability to sketch engineering objects in the freehand mode as the second main engineering students' outcome [Bar04], [BKA04]. The same happens in the American Society of Mechanical Engineers ASME [Ros05].

However, apart from the advantages of paperless office, "plain" digital prescriptive sketches do not solve any *real* problem, since paper-and-pencil sketching is simpler, polyvalent and well suited for giving instructions to the draftsman in charge of making the final drawing or 3D model. We have not found direct evidence of the previous asseveration, but Lim et al [LQP*04] conducted a study aimed at identifying the requirements for developing a computer-based sketching system. They focused on thinking sketches, as they tried to validate sketches as input interface for 3D free-form surface modelling. Nevertheless, they designed a questionnaire whose results aroused our interest. The first one was that the main reason to use paper-and-pencil is because it allows fast expression and it is easy to capture impulsive ideas. The second was that there are no appropriate tools that fully support free-hand sketching and recognition. And the third was the list of weaknesses of existing CAD tools: too time consuming with slow feedback, different feeling to paper and pencil, difficult interface, too expensive and poor results. In sum, the respondents wanted a simple sketching environment with qualities as good as real paper. In addition, the drawing tool in a system should be able to be used as a multiple purpose (in terms of the stroke thickness and possibly colour support) just like a real pencil does. All these conclusions appeared to be plausible for prescriptive sketches too, as far as commercially available CAD tools with some "pseudo-sketching" capabilities have been considered to be clearly oriented towards detailed design [Ott98]. Hence, they may represent the nucleus of the future paradigm in prescriptive CAS tools.

As a consequence, it can be concluded that achieving or even enhancing the usability of paper-and-pencil appears to be a key issue for the success of digital prescriptive sketching. Following this assumption, we did not investigate existing research tools for sketch input because our pursuit was digital sketches obtained in a simple virtual paper and pencil scenario, i.e., sketch space should be deliberately minimalist [PA02]. On the contrary, adding some extra functionality, without suffering any reduction in usability, should increase the acceptance of those tools.

Some additional considerations must be taken into account, as we can agree with Plimmer and Apperley [PA02] that giving the user feedback of whether a glyph, and edge or an entire model has been recognized distracts him or her from the creative activity. Hence, future CAS tools should simulate a *minimalist* virtual paper-and-pencil scenario. To emulate this minimalism, the three modes suggested by Plimmer and Apperley (draw, handwrite and edit) can even be simplified to two, as text processing belongs to a relatively separate research field. An *edit* mode can be maintained apart from *draw* mode, since we assume that cut, copy, paste, resize, and similar transformations are explicit actions that the designer uses in a higher conscious plane, and, hence the explicit invocation of such action from a menu does not broke the thinking process.

Other evidence exists. Some relevant works compare traditional versus digital media, although they are mainly oriented towards ideation sketches. Some of them are not directly related to this study, because they are particularly oriented to conceptual sketching and, besides, they do compare 2D sketching versus 3D gesture based modelling [OSD05]. However, other studies are related in some way. For instance, in their interesting work, Bilda and Demirkan [BD03] decompose the entire problem into segments, where prescriptive sketches may be classified in the particular segment: "F reproduction of design", i.e. copy the design/tracing on a new sheet/redraw the layout. They consider four action categories, and again, prescriptive sketches also fit into the three sub-categories of "physical" action category (draw, modify and copy). Hence, their conclusions can be considered valid for prescriptive sketches. It is particularly relevant that their main conclusion about physical actions was that the mean frequency of "draw" actions was lower in CAD than in HAND, while "modify" actions are more frequently used in CAD when compared to HAND. They concluded that this is because current commercial CAD software usually works on "draw and then modify" principle.

In sum, maintaining usability while increasing functionality of future digital prescriptive sketches seems to be the goal. Current levels of sketching usability can be derived from a comparison among a) paper-and-pencil, b) "pseudo-sketching" capabilities commercially available CAD tools, and c) a minimalist virtual paper-and-pencil scenario.

3. Hypothesis

Our current goal is making easier the input of geometrical information into CAD applications. Our hypothesis is that the less intrusive the interface, the better for the designer. We understand "intrusive" as equivalent to attracting the attention of the designer. In other words, an intrusive interface is permanently requiring the user to do things, and tends to gain more and more control on the process of fixing geometry of a new shape or design.

Besides, our hypothesis is clearly geared to interactive sketching tools, as opposite to the avenue of lettting people sketch on paper and then capture and process the pencil-paper sketch, using a video camera, a scanner, or an instrumented marking drawing device, plus the appropriate software (e.g. [SFL*04]).

It has been extensively argued in current literature that hand-drawn sketches, i.e. traditional paper-and-pencil sketches, are almost "transparent" to the designer. Where transparent is used in the sense that the creativity flows free from the mind's eye to the paper, which neither interferes nor alters the creativity flow.

On the contrary, it is usually argued that current CAD "sketchers" are permanently asking the user to completely define all the details of every step, before proceeding to the next. This is considered to cut down the creativity flow. Hence, paper-and-pencil sketching is seen as a more usable alternative that CAD systems when conceptual design is in progress.

Besides, sketches are not only used as "creative" tools. According to Ferguson [Fer92], prescriptive sketches are also used in the design process. In this context, parametric 2D drawing is usually considered a better alternative than paper-and-pencil. The argument comes from the lack of functionality of paper-and-pencil prescriptive sketches.

If a prescriptive sketch must pay attention to geometrical details, it is argued, the expertise of the draftsman becomes crucial; because a poorly drawn sketch will not show the details, while a good sketch will require a large drawing time and a very expert hand. Following the argument, current parametric 2D CAD are seen as "intelligent tools that allow not very expert designers to generate high-quality drawings".

Our hypothesis is that the previous argument is true, although it hides a relevant advantage of hand-made sketches, and the corresponding CAD sketches disadvantage. CAD applications are permanently forcing the designer to choose what type of stroke is to be drawn next. Besides, while in automatic constraints detection mode (the default one in many applications), the applications are interactively detecting constraints (supposed to fit "design intentions") and modifying the current sketch. This means that the usability of the final "sketch" is partially extracted from a set of unconscious user action, and partially extracted from "subliminal" queries that the system is permanently asking the user. In fact, what is obtained in the output is not a true sketch, but a precise line-drawing made of "strokes" (linear entities) accompanied by an extensive set of geometrical constraints that, supposedly, retain the design intention. Hence the result is richer than a paper and pencil sketch and, besides, fully integrated in the computer flow. This means that it is more functional. But the constant access to menus to select the next "action" and the subliminal queries that the user is permanently forced to answer greatly reduces usability.

In sum, in CAD environments, prescriptive sketching functionality is achieved at the expense of usability. On the contrary, prescriptive sketches done through paper and pencil lack functionality, but do not pay any "toll" in the form of reducing their usability.

In order to validate, reject or modify this hypothesis, we elaborated a pilot questionnaire to determine the opinion of the potential users of prescriptive sketches tools. It is a pilot questionnaire because it is still too long for a real field test. However, we believed we could obtain information of capital importance to design an accurate and still precise final questionnaire.

4. Questionnaire

Our intention is to compare paper-and-pencil against parametric 2D CAD. In order to clearly separate the "intrusive" behaviour of 2D CAD from a possible "generic" intrusion of the computer, compared to paper and pencil. But, as far as we intend to determine the hypothetical usability of a future non-intrusive CAS tool, we decided to simulate this environment by asking the interviewed people to draw a sketch on a tablet PC with the least intrusive digital drawing tool we could find. We opted by Microsoft's PAINT, but reducing its set of tools to just paintbrush and rubber. 2D CAD was simulated by the sketching capabilities of UGS's SolidEdge, because of its availability and because of the familiarity that many of the interviewed had with it. In sum, the respondents were asked to compare prescriptive sketching done in three different scenarios: a) hand (H), b) Paint+tablet (P/t) and c) SolidEdge (S/E).

It was decided that just answering a set of questions related to sketching activity was not a good strategy. On the contrary, sketching should be the main task for the interviewed people. First, because in this way they would be really concerned on the subject. Second, because this should give us extra information to externally evaluate, compare and score people's ability to sketch in the different scenarios.

Our population was conceived as a mixture of experts (E's) and beginners (B's). In our case, eight teachers of engineering design and CAD, and 22 first year engineering students; who gave us the point of view of beginners. Our aim in chosing this population was to try to separate the "familiarity" issue from the underlying "usability" issue. Some of our experts are mostly used to paper and pencil and dislike current software, while other are real experts in CAD teaching. Finally our students have been taught in a computer-dominant environment, and feel less comfortable with paper and pencil.

We rated the previous experience of respondents as: null (0), poor (1), average (2), good (3) and excellent (4). Experts were asked to rate themselves, while beginners were rated according to their grades. Results are tabulated in the "previous experience" columns of table 3. Almost none of the participants had used tablet PC's beforehand. All of them received a short training session (ten minutes) about tablet PC's and Microsoft's PAINT. Some experts had never used SolidEdge beforehand, and they received a short training session (ten minutes). Those short training sessions were considered enough, because our pilot study was aimed at getting user's opinions on ease of use, rather than to objective measurements such as time taken to complete the tasks.

4.1 Templates

We selected four sketches (fig. 1 to 4), intended to be representative of the most current sketch types, while being simple enough to allow completing the test in one hour.

We asked the respondents to reproduce the four sketches as close as possible as they appear in the figures: distinguishing thin and thick lines, drawing dot-dash lines, and drawing dimensions without paying attention to the numeric value, although maintaining the general proportion of models (as usual in engineering sketching).

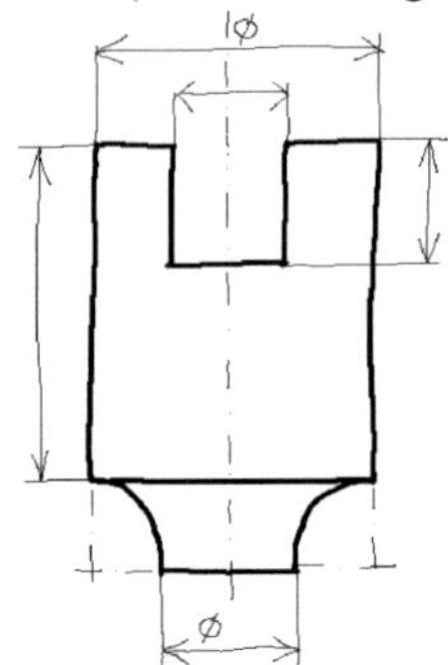

Figure 1: *Sketch A. Symmetrical shape with few rectilinear strokes and just two curves.*

Figure 2: *Sketch B. Non symmetrical shape with rectilinear strokes all of them horizontal or vertical, plus some 90° or 180° tangent arcs.*

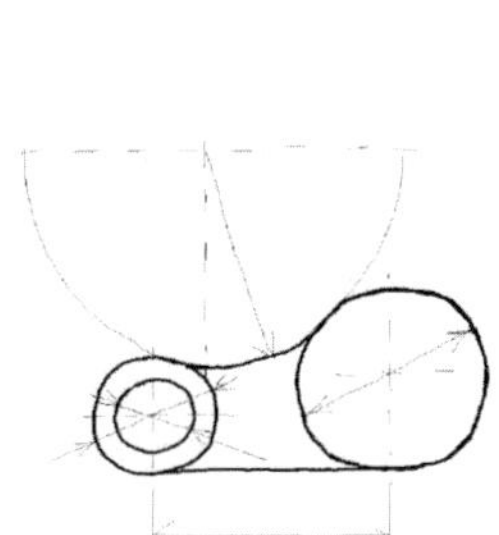

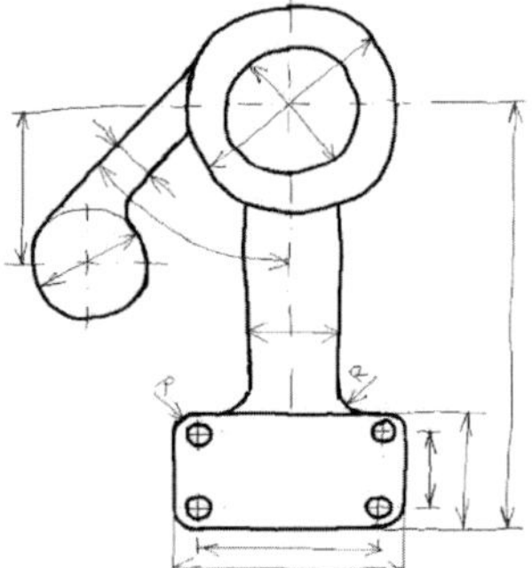

Figure 3: *Sketch C. Neither symmetric nor rectilinear shape, with concentric circles and a complex tangent arc.*

Figure 4: *Sketch D. Partially symmetric and orthogonal shape, combined with oblique and tangent arm with circle.*

Every sketch was to be reproduced in the three scenarios: a) hand, b) Paint+tablet and c) SolidEdge. The respondents were free to decide the sequence when realizing the drawings, but they had to inform us about it. We thought this information to be relevant because of the learning "effect" deduced by Bilda and Demirkan in a similar study [BD03] where they observed a significant reduction in the number of "transitions" required to solve the same problem for a second time. Our respondents also had to measure the time spent in doing every drawing. To gain some insight of the specific advantage introduced by tablet PC's we asked the respondents to draw sketch "A" using paintbrush and rubber of Microsoft's Paint in a conventional PC computer, via mouse. To prevent excessive fatigue, we demanded just sketch A; as our own experience indicated mouse to be much more tiring and frustrating than pen.

Respondent	Sequence												P/m
	Hand (H)				Paint/tablet (P/t)				SolidEdge (S/E)				
	A	B	C	D	A	B	C	D	A	B	C	D	A
B01	1	2	3	4	7	8	9	10	5	6	11	12	13
B02	3	5	7	9	10	11	12	13	2	4	6	8	1
B03	5	6	7	8	1	2	3	4	9	10	11	12	13
B04	1	11	12	13	2	3	4	5	7	8	9	10	6
B05	5	6	7	8	1	2	3	4	10	11	12	13	9
B06	5	7	8	9	13	12	10	11	1	2	3	4	6
B07	10	11	12	13	6	7	8	9	1	2	3	4	5
B08	1	2	3	4	8	9	10	11	5	6	7	13	12
B09	2	3	4	5	6	7	8	9	10	11	12	13	1
B10	10	11	12	13	1	2	3	4	5	6	7	8	9
B11	10	11	12	13	1	2	3	4	5	6	7	8	9
B12	9	10	11	12	1	2	3	4	5	6	7	8	13
B13	1	2	3	4	9	10	11	12	5	6	7	8	13
B14	10	11	12	13	5	6	7	8	2	3	4	9	1
B15	1	2	3	4	10	11	12	13	6	7	8	9	5
B16	1	2	3	4	10	11	12	13	6	7	8	9	5
B17	9	10	11	12	1	2	3	4	5	6	7	8	13
B18	10	13	12	11	6	9	7	8	2	3	4	5	1
B19	1	2	3	4	5	6	7	8	9	10	11	12	13
B20	1	2	3	4	10	11	12	13	5	6	7	8	9
B21	6	7	8	9	10	11	12	13	2	3	4	5	1
B22	1	2	3	4	5	6	7	8	9	10	11	12	13
E01	9	10	11	12	5	6	7	8	1	2	3	4	13
E02	4	7	10	13	2	6	9	12	1	5	8	11	3
E03	1	2	4	5	3	7	8	9	10	11	12	13	6
E04	6	7	8	9	1	2	3	4	10	11	12	13	5
E05	1	2	3	4	5	6	7	8	9	10	11	12	13
E06	1	2	3	4	9	10	11	12	5	6	7	8	13
E07	1	2	3	4	5	6	7	8	9	10	11	12	13
E08	3	4	6	7	10	11	12	13	1	2	5	8	9
E09	1	2	3	4	5	6	7	8	10	11	12	13	9
Average	4,2	5,7	6,8	7,8	5,6	6,8	7,6	8,7	5,5	6,7	8,0	9,4	8,2
	1	4	7	9	3	6	8	12	2	5	10	13	11

Table 1: *Drawing sequence of every respondent (where 1 stands for first drawing and 13 for last).*

In order to evaluate the results for each participant, drawing quality was rated by one of the authors of this paper, who has many years of experience in teaching engineering graphics. Finally, the respondents had to answer the following questions:

1. Arrange the four sketches (A, B, C and D) scoring them from easiest (1) to most difficult (4).
2. Arrange, from most important (1) to less important (4), the following criteria to determine which is the most difficult sketch: a) the one that contains more lines; b) the one that contains more curves; c) the one that is less symmetrical, and d) the one that contains more angles.
3. Signal the tool (H if hand, P if Paint/tablet or S if SolidEdge) with which you have obtained the best version of every sketch.
4. Arrange the tools (Hand, Paint/mouse, Paint/tablet and SolidEdge) scoring them from the easiest (1) to the most difficult (4).
5. Enumerate the main advantages of hand-made drawings.
6. Enumerate the main advantages of Paint with tablet.
7. Enumerate the main differences between Paint with tablet and Paint with mouse.
8. Enumerate the main advantages of SolidEdge.
9. Add any observation you consider to be relevant.

5. Results and analysis

First of all, some checks were made to validate the process of data collection. The ratings of students were compared to their grades and showed no significant differences. The drawing sequences were found to have so many differences (table 1) that no learning effect was considered in the aggregate data. Still, for a detailed study of the behaviour of each respondent, the particular sequences, or, at least the "average" sequence (last row in table 1) should be considered.

The numerical results linked to questions 1 to 4 have been summarized in table 3, while the main comments about questions 5 to 9 are compiled in table 2.

Query		Answers
5	a	Fast and easy
	b	Consents improvisations and imperfections
	c	Low cost
	d	Ergonomic
	e	You can move the paper
	f	It does not do what you want not.
	g	Fully accessible everywhere
6	a	Similar to hand
	b	Clean and precise erasing
	c	Fast
	d	The output is already digitized in the computer
	e	A little bit uncomfortable
	f	Easy to understand
	g	Does not consume real paper or pencil
	h	Limitless drawing space and includes zooming facilities
	i	Worse than hand for fast sketches, and worse than CAD for finished drawings
7	a	It's more complex to draw with a mouse than with pen.
	b	Pen is more precise than mouse.
	c	Pen is more synchronized with cursor than mouse.
	d	Straight lines are easier with mouse than with pen.
	e	Curved lines are easier with pen than with mouse
8	a	Lines are perfect
	b	Easy to add geometrical constraints
	c	Easy to dimension
	d	Easy to transform sketches into 3D models
	e	The drawing can be edited a posteriori.
	f	Allows dimensioning / Requires dimensioning
	g	Requires training
9	a	Tablet is a little bit uncomfortable
	b	Tablet requires more training
	c	Tablet is embarrassing for left-handed.

Table 2: *Answers to questions 5 to 9 listed from more to less frequent.*

Our initial distinction between beginners and experts seems wrong if we simply compare their average previous experiences: 3.2 vs. 2.9 in hand; 0 vs. 0.4 in Paint/tablet and 2.9 vs. 2.4 in SolidEdge environment. The explanation to this apparent contradiction can be found by comparing execution times: experts were correctly considered so, at least in sketching; because they required much less time than beginners to achieve a good solution both when drawing by hand and when drawing in a Paint/tablet environment.

Respondent	Previous experience H	Previous experience P/t	Previous experience S/E	Execution score: Hand (H) A	B	C	D	Average	Paint/tablet (P/t) A	B	C	D	Average	ABS(H-P/t)	SolidEdge (S/E) A	B	C	D	Average	P/m A
B01	3,56	0	3,4	3	3	3	3	3,0	2	3	3	3	2,8	0,3	3	3,5	3,5	3,5	3,4	2,0
B02	2	0	2,9	3	2,5	2	2,5	2,5	1	1,5	1	1	1,1	1,4	3,5	3,5	3	3	3,3	3,0
B03	3,32	0	2,9	2	2	2	2,5	2,1	3,5	2,5	2,5	2,5	2,8	0,6	3,5	3,5	4	4	3,8	3,0
B04	2,76	0	2,0	3	3	2,5	2,5	2,8	3,5	3,5	3	3	3,3	0,5	4	3,5	2,5	3,5	3,4	3,0
B05	3,96	0	3,6	3,5	3,5	3,5	4	3,6	2,5	3,5	3	3,5	3,1	0,5	3,5	4	3,5	4	3,8	3,5
B06	3,64	0	3,1	2	2,5	1,5	2	2,0	2,5	3	2,5	3	2,8	0,8	3	2,5	2,5	3	2,8	3,0
B07	2,16	0	2,5	3	3	3	2,5	2,9	2	3	1,5	2	2,1	0.8	3,5	3,5	4	3,5	3,6	3,0
B08	3,96	0	3,5	4	4	4	4	4,0	3,5	3,5	3,5	4	3,6	0,4	2,5	3,5	4	4	3,5	4,0
B09	3,44	0	3,1	3	3	3	3,5	3,1	3	3	3,5	3	3,1	0,0	3,5	3	3	4	3,4	2,0
B10	3,28	0	2,7	1,5	2	1	2,5	1,8	3	2	2	2	2,3	0,5	3	3	3,5	3,5	3,3	3,0
B11	3,12	0	1,6	2,5	2,5	2,5	3	2,6	1,5	2	2	3	2,1	0,5	3,5	2,5	4	4	3,5	2,5
B12	3,92	0	3,2	3	3	3	3	3,0	3,5	4	3,5	3,5	3,6	0,6	4	3,5	3,5	2,5	3,4	4,0
B13	3,72	0	3,3	3	3	2,5	3	2,9		3,5	3	3	3,2	0,3	3,5	2	3,5	3	3,0	3,0
B14	2,56	0	2,6	2,5	2	1	2	1,9	3	3	2	1.5	2,4	0,5	3,5	3,5	3	4	3,5	3,5
B15	1,96	0	3,4	1,5	1	2	2	1,6	2,5	1	1,5	2,5	1,9	0,3	3	4	3	3,5	3,4	3,5
B16	3,76	0	3,6	2,52	2,5	3	3	2,8	4	3	2,5	2,5	3,0	0,2	2,5	4	4	3	3,4	3,0
B17	2,52	0	2,6	3	3,5	3	3	3,1	1,5	3,5	3	3	2,8	0,4	2,5	2,5	2,5	3	2,6	3,0
B18	2,64	0	2,1	2	2,5	3	2,5	2,5	2	2,5	1,5	2	2,0	0,5	3	2	3	4	3,0	
B19	2,32	0	3,1	3	3	3,5	2,5	3,0	3,5	3,5	3,5	2,5	3,3	0,3	3	3	4	3	3,3	3,5
B20	3,72	0	3,2	2,5	2,5	2	2	2,3	1,5	3	1	2	1,9	0,4	3	2,5	1	1	1,9	3,5
B21	3,24	0	3,1	2	2	1,5	2	1,9	2,5	3,5	3,5	3,5	3,3	1,4	2	2	2,5	3,5	2,5	3,5
B22	4	0	3,7	3	3	3,5	3,5	3,3	3,5	4	3,5	4	3,8	0,5	2,5	2,5	4	3,5	3,1	4,0
E01	2,0	0	4,0	3	2,5	2	2	2,4	2	2	1,5	1,5	1,8	0,6	3	3,5	3,5	3,5	3,4	3,0
E02	4,0	0	0,0	3,5	3,5	3,5	3,5	3,5	3,5	4	3,5	3,5	3,6	0,1	3,5	3,5	2,5	3,5	3,3	2,5
E03	1,0	2	4,0	2,5	3	2	1,5	2,3	2	3	3,5	2	2,6	0,4	3,5	3,5	3,5	3,5	3,5	3,0
E04	4,0	0	0,0	4	4	3,5	3,5	3,8	4	4	4	4	4,0	0,3	3	3	3,5	4	3,4	4,0
E05	3,0	0	1,0	2,5	2,5	2	2,5	2,4	3,5	3,5	3,5	4	3,6	1,3	2,5	4	3,5	3,5	3,4	4,0
E06	4,0	0	2,0	2	3	2	3	2,5	3	3	3	3	3,0	0,5	3,5	4	2,5	3	3,3	4,0
E07	3,0	1	4,0	3	3	2,5	2	2,6	3	3,5	2,5	2,5	2,9	0,3	3	3	3	4	3,3	1,0
E08	3,0	1	4,0	4	4	3,5	4	3,9	4	3,5	4	3	3,6	0,3	3	4	3,5	4	3,6	3,5
E09	2,0	0	3,0	3,5	3,5	3,5	3,5	3,5	3,5	3,5	4	4	3,8	0,3	4	4	4	4	4,0	3,5
Ave-rage	3,1	0,1	2,8	2,8	2,8	2,6	2,8	2,8	2,8	3,1	2,8	2,8	2,9	0,5	3,2	3,2	3,3	3,5	3,3	3,2
B's	3,2	0,0	2,9	2,7	2,7	2,5	2,8	2,7	2,6	3,0	2,5	2,7	2,7	0,5	3,1	3,1	3,3	3,4	3,2	3,2
E's	2,9	0,4	2,4	3,1	3,2	2,7	2,8	3,0	3,2	3,3	3,3	3,1	3,2	0,4	3,2	3,6	3,3	3,7	3,4	3,2

Respondent	Time: Hand (H) A	B	C	D	Average	Paint/tablet (P/t) A	B	C	D	Average	SolidEdge (S/E) A	B	C	D	Average	P/m A
B01	3	4,5	6	9	5,6	9,5	12	12	14	11,9	8,5	13	4	10	8,9	9,0
B02	3	4	3	7	4,3	8	7	5	12	8,0	4	11	2	9	6,5	6,0
B03	2,5	2	2	3	2,4	5	5	4	5,5	4,9	3,5	5	4,5	6	4,8	4,0
B04	5	4	5	8	5,5	10	8	10	10	9,5	5	12	12	13	10,5	8,0
B05	4	4	8	9	6,3	8	6	5	7	6,5	4	9	4	8	6,3	7,0
B06	2,5	4	1	6,5	3,5	4	5	4,5	9	5,6	4	5	2	5	4,0	5,0
B07	5	7	5		5,7	13	10	7	8	9,5	5	10	5	10	7,5	16,0
B08	6	10	12	16	11,0	10	9	6	8	8,3	5	20	9	16	12,5	6,0
B09	3	8	6	12	7,3	5	10	8	11	8,5	4	7	5	9	6,3	5,0
B10	5	8	6	9	7,0	12	17	10	11	12,5	5	7	3	6	5,3	12,0
B11	3	5	9	9	6,5	3,5	7	8	8	6,6	4	7	4	7	5,5	4.0
B12	7	6	8	9	7,5	7	8	8	10	8,3	5	6	4	4	4,8	4,0
B13	6	8	12	15	10,3	4	5	5	5	4,8	5	6	4	5	5,0	
B14	2	3	3	5	3,3	5	10	12	9	9,0	5	10	8	7	7,5	8,0
B15	3	4	5	7	4,8	10	7	4	9	7,5	3	4	4	5	4,0	9,0
B16	6	8	8	10	8,0	7	7	3	8	6,3	4	5	3	10	5,5	12,0
B17	5	9	8	11	8,3	10	10	10	11	10,3	5	7	5	10	6,8	8,0
B18	3	7	5	7	5,5	5	7	9	10	7,8	6	10	25	5	11,5	5,0
B19	4,5	7	9	9	7,4	6	7	5	6	6,0	5,5	9	7	8	7,4	6,0
B20	5	10	15	20	12,5	10	16	3	18	11,8	5	7	2,5	10	6,1	10,0
B21	8	8	3	8	6,8	8	5	6	7	6,5	4	8	4	10	6,5	7,0
B22	5	10	13	10	9,5	10	8	8	12	9.5	7	11	5	10	8,3	15,0
E01	1,5	3	2	3,5	2,5	2,5	4,5	2,5	4	3,4	4	11	6,5	6,5	7,0	3,0
E02	1	2	2	4	2,3	3	4	2	5	3,5	14	22	14	28	19,5	5,0
E03	2	4	3	4	3,3	2,5	3,5	3	4	3,3	3,5	6	2	3	3,6	2.5
E04	2	3,5	2,5	3,5	2,9	5	10	6	7	7,0	2	5,5	2,5	6	4,0	6,0
E05	3	4	4	6	4,3	3	4	3	8	4,5	6	4	6	11	6,8	4.0
E06	1	2,5	2	2	1,9	1	1,5	0,5	1,5	1,1	5	3	6	7	5,3	2,0
E07	1,5	2	2	3,5	2,3	2	2	1,5	3	2,1	3	4	2	4,5	3,4	2,0
E08	5	5	4	7	5,3	1,5	3,5	2	5	3,0	4	7	6	10	6,8	4,5
E09	2	4	3	6	3,75	2,5	5	3	6	4,13	2	5	3,5	8,3	4,7	5
Ave-rage	3,7	5,5	5,7	8,0	5,7	6,2	7,2	5,7	8,1	6,8	4,8	8,3	5,6	8,6	6,8	6,7
B's	4,4	6,4	6,9	9,5	6,8	7,7	8,5	6,9	9,5	8,1	4,8	8,6	5,7	8,3	6,9	7,9
E's	2,1	3,3	2,7	4,4	3,1	2,6	4,2	2,6	4,8	3,6	4,8	7,5	5,4	9,4	6,8	3,8

Respondent	Easy (1) to difficult (4) A	B	C	D	Most (1) to less difficult (4) More lines	More curves	Less symmetry	More angles	Best result for every sketch A	B	C	D	Simple (1) to complex (4) H	P/m	P/t	S/E
B01	1	2	3	4	4	1	2	3	s	s	s	s	1	4	3	2
B02	4	2	3	1	3	1	2	4	p	h	h	s	1	4	3	2
B03	1	3	2	4	2	1	3	4	h	h	h	s	1	4	3	2
B04	1	2	3	4	4	1	2	3	s	s	s	s	2	4	3	1
B05	1	3	2	4	4	1	3	2	p	p	h	h	1	4	3	2
B06	1	3	2	4	1	2	4	3	s	s	p	s	2	4	3	1
B07	2	1	4	3	2	1	3	4	s	h	s	p	2	4	3	1
B08	1	4	2	3	4	1	2	3	s	p	p	h	1	3	2	4
B09	1	2	3	4	4	1	2	3	h	p	s	s	1	4	3	2
B10	1	2	4	3	2	1	3	4	p	h	s	s	2	4	3	1
B11	1	2	4	3	3	1	4	2	s	s	s	s	1	4	3	2
B12	1	2	3	4	4	1	2	3	p	s	s	s	2	4	3	1
B13	4	3	1	2	4	1	2	3	s	h	s	s	2	4	3	1
B14	1	2	3	4	4	1	3	2	s	s	s	s	2	3	4	1
B15	1	2	3	4	4	1	3	2	s	s	s	s	2	3	4	1
B16	1	2	4	3	2	1	3	4	s	s	s	s	3	4	2	1
B17	1	2	3	4	4	1	3	2	s	s	s	s	2	3	4	1
B18	3	4	1	2	4	3	1	2	h	s	p	h	2	4	3	1
B19	4	3	1	2	2	1	3	4	s	h	h	s	2	4	3	1
B20	1	2	3	4	4	1	2	3	h	s	s	s	4	2	3	1
B21	1	3	2	4	4	1	2	3	p	s	s	h	2	4	3	1
B22	1	2	3	4	4	1	2	3					3	1	2	4
E01	1	3	2	4	3	1	2	4	s	s	s	s	1	4	2	3
E02	1	2	4	3	1	2	4	3	p	h	h	h	1	4	2	3
E03	1	4	3	2	1	3	4	2	s	s	s	s	1	3	2	4
E04	1	3	2	4	3	1	4	2	h	h	h	h	1	3	4	2
E05	1	2	3	4	4	1	2	3	s	s	s	s	1	4	2	3
E06	1	3	2	4	3	1	4	2	h	h	h	h	1	3	2	4
E07	1	3	2	4	2	1	3	4	p	p	p	p	2	4	1	3
E08	1	3	2	4	4	2	3	1	s	s	s	s	1	3	2	4
E09	1	2	4	3	4	1	2	3	s	s	s	s	1	3	2	4
Ave-rage	1,6	2,9	3,1	3,9	3,6	1,4	3,1	3,3					1,9	4,1	3,1	2,4
B's	1,5	2,4	2,7	3,4	3,3	1,1	2,5	3,0					1,9	3,6	3,0	1,5
E's	1,0	2,8	2,7	3,6	2,8	1,4	3,1	2,7					1,1	3,4	2,1	3,3

Table 3: *The numerical results linked to questions 1 to 4 from the questionnaire.*

Notice that neither beginners nor experts generated excellent solutions, as they both knew excellence being out of place when sketching. But, when drawing by hand, experts required just 3.1 minutes, instead of up to 6.8 minutes required by beginners. Besides, they got better hand drawings (3.0) than beginners (2.7). A similar difference can be observed in Paint/tablet environment. Even in the Paint/mouse environment appeared similar differences. However, no significant differences were measured between beginners and experts when drawing with Solid-Edge.

From the analysis of answers to question 1, we can conclude that our attempt to obtain four examples representative of four different levels of difficulty was validated by the arrangement of the respondents: example A was considered the least difficult (average 1.6), example B was the next (2.9), example C was the third (3.1) and example D was rated to be the most difficult (3.9). However, it should be pointed out that experts rated example C to be a little easier than example B (2.7 vs. 2.8). Besides we gained an interesting insight on criteria to determining what makes sketches more difficult: more curves (1.4); less symmetry (3.1), more angles (3.3) and more lines (3.6). Again, experts disagree, as they consider more angles being less problematic than losing symmetry (2.7 vs. 3.1).

The first question addressed in this study was whether or not a paper-and-pencil prescriptive sketching environment is more or less usable than a "digital" prescriptive sketching environment. According to the results, paper-and-pencil is still considered to be easier and "handier" than our simulation of a minimalist digital prescriptive sketching tool achieved through Microsoft's Paint limited to just using paintbrush and rubber. Hand was rated 1.9; second was SolidEdge (2.4); Paint with tablet was third (3.1) and Paint with mouse was last (4.1). However, the disagreement between beginners and experts is quite significant. Beginners rated (S/E, H, P/t, P/m) while experts rated (H, P/t, S/E, P/m). In spite of beginners feeling more comfortable with SolidEdge (because "lines are perfect"…), the first conclusion is that both groups consider Paint/tablet to be more complex than hand.

However, none of the respondents had had previous experience with tablet PC's. Hence, one interesting question for a future detailed study is to determine whether or not this feeling disappears after a reasonable training time.

Actually, those feelings from respondents do no match with the objective fact that, although the execution time was a little bit greater (almost 20%, i.e. from 5.7 to 6.8 minutes), hand drawings achieved similar scores (2.8) to Paint/tablet (2.9). In fact, the differences (ABS (H-Pt)) were below the scoring minimum increment (0.5) in all but three cases. Hence, respondents achieved similar results, needing more time, but in an environment completely new to almost all of them. Besides, the time require to finish the drawings in the Paint/tablet environment (without previous experience) was similar to the time required to complete SolidEdge drawings (where most of them had had extensive training).

Certainly, this result is just an approach, mainly because our "simulation" of a digital prescriptive sketch environment may contain some hidden and unexpected significant differences with current or future digital prescriptive sketching environments. However, we can infer that currently available systems are going to still be rejected (in terms of usability) by current designers, as they are clearly less simple than our simulated environment, which was considered by the respondents not as usable as paper-and-pencil.

Some respondents included observations that can give some light about their rejection. They considered that the small uncoupling between tablet PC's pen and cursor (mainly due to bad screen calibration and the thickness of the screen that produces a physical separation between pen and cursor) distracts the draftsmen and reduces the accuracy of sketches. A future taks is exploring whether uncoupling between tablet PC's pen and cursor could be skipped by using other devices. However, the unfamiliarity of the users with Tablet PCs may have left them disliking them. According to this, the hypothesis to be validated or rejected by future studies should be that in the long run there is little *fundamental* difference between the interface provided by a tablet PC and a piece of paper.

The second question addressed in this study was measuring the validity of the belief that current "pseudo-sketchers" embedded into CAD applications can substitute hand made prescriptive sketches without loss of usability, at the time they increase functionality by semi-automatically aiding the user in creating the final model from the different views of the sketch.

As far as it is obvious that CAD environment gives users more functionality than paper-and-pencil, and because the SolidEdge output is not a sketch but a final line-drawing, we expected the respondents to massively answer question 3 by signalling SolidEdge to be the tool with which they had obtained the best version of every drawing (perhaps with the exception of those experts that rated themselves as excellent in sketching and completely null in SolidEdge). Maybe the question was not clear for the respondents, but the dispersion in the answers still seems to indicate that the belief in the strength of CAD versus hand-made sketches is not so obvious, or, at least, does not compensate its lack of usability. Indeed, comparing execution times in both environments, hand (H) times are very similar to SolidEdge (S/E) times for beginners (6.8 vs. 6.9) but much lower for experts (3.1 vs. 6.8). Besides, experts required much less time in all Paint environments (both with tablet –Pt-, and mouse –Pm-) than they required with SolidEdge. Thus, the time required to complete a drawing in this entirely new environment is a little bit greater for beginners, but clearly less for experts than the time required in the CAD environment. The Bilda and Demirkan principle of "draw and then modify" seems a plausible reason for this. Besides, some respondents observed that sometimes the system captures false design intentions, i.e. sometimes imposes constraints not desired by the user (see answer 5f in table 2). In sum, the respondents seem to put in value the increase of functionality given by SolidEdge, but still notice the loss in usability. This apparently contradictory feeling should be investigated in more detail.

Some other interesting results arose from the study. The decision to exclude handwriting from our study, assuming that text processing belongs to a relatively separate research field and is mature enough for CAS environments, was partially validated by some comments of respondents that considered easy and precise the tablet PC input panel they used simply to write the files' names.

A surprising result was the translation to the mouse movement of some "trade tricks" typical of hand sketching, like obtaining almost straight lines by moving the mouse while the hand slides on the edge of the table and so on [BWM*03]. Besides, some users confessed they used the inertia of the mouse in order to move it simulating vertical and horizontal "T-square-like" movements. This "tricky" use of mouse explains why Paint with mouse was not massively considered worse than paint with tablet. Some comments support this observation, e.g. "painting with mouse is better for straight lines, while painting with tablet is better for curves". These trade tricks were not spontaneously translated to the tablet PC environment. It remains to be determined whether or not this is due to some significant difference in the attitude of the users, or it is simply due to some ergonomic failure associated to the tablets, the tables or the optional laptop coolers we enabled as bookrests for the test.

6. Conclusions

It was argued in the first part of the paper that CAD-based design of industrial products still requires prescriptive sketches. But sketches should be "digital" so as to be linked to the rest of the New Product Development tools (CAD, PLM, etc). Digital sketches are the natural output of computer-aided sketching (CAS) tools, which should become the new paradigm. Hence, in the second part of the paper, the usability and functionality requirements that CAS tools must provide have been compared against traditional paper and pencil sketching. Our pilot study concludes that CAS tools will replace traditional paper-and-pencil design *only after* being perceived by designer as having clearly equal or superior usability, which is not the case of current CAD pseudo-sketchers. In addition to confirming this currently accepted assertion, our study detected some key issues to be addressed by a more general study aimed at separately assessing usability and functionality of different hardware and software approaches.

Acknowledgements

The authors greatly appreciate the valuable comments of the anonymous reviewers. The Fundació Caixa Castelló-Bancaixa under the Universitat Jaume I program for Research Promotion (Project P1-1B2004-02) supported this work. It was also partially supported by Spanish Ministry of Science and Education and the European Union (Project DPI2004-01373).

References

[BWM*03] BERTOLINE G., WIEBE E., MILLER C., NASMAN L.: *Fundamentals of Graphics Communication, 3rd ed.*, McGraw-Hill, (2003)

[Bar04] BARR R.E.: The current status of graphical communication in engineering education. *34th ASEE/IEEE Frontiers in Education Conference*. October 20–23, 2004, Savannah, GA. (2004) S1D8-13.

[BKA04] BARR R.E., KRUEGER T.J., AANSTOOS T.A.: Results of an EDG student outcomes survey. *Proceedings of the 2004 American Society For Engineering Education Annual Conference & Exposition*. Salt Lake City, Utah, (2004). pp. 8–13.

[BD03] BILDA Z., DEMIRKAN H.: An insight on designers' sketching activities in traditional versus digital media. *Design Studies 24*, (2003), 27–50.

[CPC*05] COMPANY P., PIQUER A., CONTERO M., NAYA F.: A survey on geometrical reconstruction as a core technology to sketch-based modeling. *Computers & Graphics 29*, 6, (2005), 892–904.

[Far02] FARIN G.: *Curves and Surfaces for CAGD*. Morgan Kaufmann Publishers, Fifth edition, (2002).

[Fer92] FERGUSON E.S.: *Engineering and the Mind's Eye*, MIT Press, (1992).

[JLA05] JUCHMES R., LECLERCQ P., AZAR S.: A freehand-sketch environment for architectural design supported by a multi-agent system. *Computers & Graphics 29*, 6 (2005), 905–915.

[LQP*04] LIM S., QIN S.F., PRIETO D., SHACKLETON J.: A study of sketching behaviour to support free-form surface modeling from on-line sketching. *Design Studies 25*, (2004), 393–413.

[OSD05] OH J.Y., STUERZLINGER W., MITANI J.: Comparing SESAME and sketching on paper for conceptual 3D Design. *Sketch-Based Interfaces and Modeling. Eurographics Symposium Proceedings. SBM'05* (2005). pp. 81–88.

[Ott98] OTTOSSON S.: Qualified product concept design needs a proper combination of pencil-aided design and model-aided design before product data management. *Journal of Engineering Design 9*, 2 (1998), 107–119.

[PA02] PLIMMER B., APPERLEY M.: Computer-aided sketching to capture preliminary design. *Third Australasian Conf. on User interfaces* (2002), vol. 7, pp. 9–12.

[Ros05] ROSE A.T.: Graphical communication using hand-drawn sketches in civil engineering. *Journal of Professional Issues in Engineering Education and Practice 131*, 4 (2005), 238–247.

[SFL*04] SAUND, E., FLEET, D., LARNER, D., AND MAHONEY, J.: Perceptually-supported image editing of text and graphics. *Proc. UIST '03*. (2003), pp. 183–192.

[Tve02] TVERSKY B.: What do sketches say about thinking? *AAAI Spring Symposium Series - Sketch Understanding*. (2002). pp. 148–152.

EUROGRAPHICS Workshop on Sketch-Based Interfaces and Modeling (2006)
Thomas Stahovich and Mario Costa Sousa (Editors)

Applying Scenarios in User-Centred Design to Develop a Sketching Interface for Human Modelling and Animation

C. Mao, S.F. Qin, D.K. Wright, Jun Peng*

School of Engineering & Design, Brunel University, Uxbridge, Middlesex UB8 3PH, UK
*Department of Environmental Art Design, School of Art Design, Tianjin Academy of Fine Arts, PR China

Abstract

This paper presents our user and usability studies for applying scenarios in user-centred design to develop a sketching interface for virtual human modelling and animation. In this approach, we utilise the User Centred System Design (UCSD) strategy and spiral lifecycles to ensure system usability and functionalities. A series of usability techniques were employed. After the initial conceptual design, a preliminary user study (including questionnaires and sketching observations) was undertaken to establish the formal interface design. Second, an informal user test was conducted on the first prototype: a "sketch-based 3D stick figure animation interface". Finally, a formal user evaluation (including performance tests, sketching observations, and interviews) was carried out on the latest version: a "sketch-based virtual human builder". During this iterative process, various paper-based and electronic-based sketching scenarios were created, which were acted-out by users to help designers evoke and verify design ideas, identify users' needs, and test the prototype interfaces in real contexts. Benefiting from applying the UCSD strategy and scenario-based design to develop a natural and supportive sketching interface, our investigation can be a useful instantiation for the design of other sketching interfaces where these techniques have not been widely acknowledged and utilised in the past.

Categories and Subject Descriptors (according to ACM CSS): H.5.2 [Information Interfaces and Presentation]: User centred design, Graphical user interfaces (GUI), Evaluation; I.3.7 [Computer Graphics]: Animation.

1. Introduction

The use of sketching in computer graphics may date back to the seminal SketchPad system [Sut63] in the 1960s. More recently, various sketch-based interfaces have been developed to combine the flexibility and ease of paper and pencil with the processing power of computers to provide an electronic sketching medium that is as natural as paper, yet considerably more interactive and smarter.

In general, a sketching interface should address an application such as user interface design [LM95], geometric modelling [KHR02][IMT99][LS02], animation [DAC*03] [HH01][TBP04], etc. During the conceptual design stage, the application needs can orientate a designer's thinking on detailed design aspects, including system pipeline, interaction routine, drawing input/output, design assumptions/questions, etc. Next, a user study needs to be conducted to verify initial design ideas and identify users' needs before formal implementation. In fact, this user-

centred system design (UCSD) approach [GGB*06] should be followed early and continuously throughout the entire development cycle. However, there have been few reports on the utilisation of UCSD strategy in sketching interface design, although it has led to the success of many other systems [KKP*04]. In reality, users were often treated as test subjects and involved only at the end of the development process. Although some research has been conducted to study users' needs and sketching behaviours [LQP*04] for interface design, there have been few reports addressing how these research outcomes have been interpreted and implemented. Moreover, the evaluation and real benefits of continuous user involvement for sketching interface design have rarely been acknowledged.

As previously mentioned, a sketching interface is meant to combine the power of paper-based sketching and computer-based automation to provide users with a more natural, functional, and supportive drawing medium. To reach this goal, sketching experimental studies and scenario-based design [Car00][Bød00] are crucial. Only when observing real users performing real tasks in real contexts, can designers verify their design ideas and achieve a deeper understanding of the natural drawing process, users' preferences and needs, and even the problems users may confront during paper-based sketching. Moreover, various scenarios can be set-up at different stages in a user-centred design process for different testing purposes to integrate usability more profoundly into system design [Bød00]. However, little work has been reported on either the application of scenario-based design or the use of scenarios in user centred design for sketching interface development.

In this paper, we present our user and usability studies for applying scenarios in user-centred design to develop a sketching interface for virtual human modelling and animation. Virtual beings play a remarkable role in today's public entertainment, while ordinary users are still treated as audiences due to the lack of appropriate expertise (i.e. mesh modelling, IK/FK), equipment (i.e. 3D body scanner, motion capture system) and computer skills. Our interface enables everyone who can draw to "sketch-out" 3D virtual humans, 2D/3D animation, crowd animation, and character intercommunication.

During the development process, we followed the UCSD strategy and spiral lifecycles to ensure system usability and functionalities. A series of usability techniques were employed. After the initial conceptual design, a preliminary user study (including questionnaires and sketching observations) [MQW06a] was undertaken to establish the formal interface design. Then, an informal user test was conducted on the first prototype: a "sketch-based 3D stick figure animation interface" [MQW05]. Finally, a formal user evaluation (including performance tests, sketching observations, and interviews) was carried-out on the latest interface: a "sketch-based virtual human builder" [MQW06b]. During this iterative process, various sketching scenarios were created, which were acted-out by users at different design stages to orient designers' reflection and action. Our approach entails paper-based scenarios to verify conceptual design ideas and identify users' needs; electronic-based scenarios to test the initial sketching interface with users for further improvements on this interactive drawing medium; and electronic-based scenarios to evaluate usability and functionalities of the fully implemented sketching interface for next iteration development. Through applying scenarios in user centred design, we have achieved a natural and supportive virtual human sketching interface, which is easy to learn and use, and entertaining for a variety of users of different ages, professions, and drawing skills.

2. Related works

Since the 1980s, sketching behaviours and the role of drawing in design [LQP*04][TP03] have been extensively researched. More recently, many sketch-based interfaces have been developed to infuse the advantages of sketching into computer aided conceptual design, such as user interface design [LM95], fast geometric modelling [KHR02][IMT99][LS02], simple animation storyboarding [DAC*03][HH01][TBP04], etc. Very little work, however, has specialised in sketch-based human modelling and animation to create and animate variational 3D virtual beings from freehand figure sketches. Moreover, the principles of UCSD and scenario-based design have not yet been widely acknowledged and practised in current sketching interface design. Although user tests [IMT99][TBP04] and user studies [LQP*04][OSD05] have been carried out, iterative user-centred design processes assisted by various testing scenarios have rarely been utilised or reported in the past.

In terms of sketch-based 3D human modelling and animation, aside from a natural and intuitive interface design, three major challenges exist. They are: 1) how to map from 2D freehand sketches into 3D posed models; 2) how to quickly and automatically animate the reconstructed key frames with little user involvement; and 3) how to generate realistic human shapes from rough figure drawings.

To address the first two challenges, some sketch-based systems [DAC*03][HH01][TBP04] have recently been developed. In Hoshino's intelligent storyboarding system [HH01], the 3D character positions and behaviours are estimated from 2D views using constraints optimization and example-based interpolation. A perspective view is required, together with a pre-built 3D character/scene database. Thorne's "motion sketching" interface [TBP04] enables overall character motions to be specified by cursive gesture drawing. The 2D-3D pose recovery, however, is not addressed by this system, since only side view figure key frames are accepted. Davis et al. [DAC*03] developed a sketching interface for 3D articulated figure animation and presumed a parallel view, which is, in principle, similar to [MQW05]. To solve the "back-front ambiguities" problem (two possible 3D poses exist for each foreshortened bone segment because of reflective ambiguity), a semi-automated method has been used for pose recovery. In this method, all possible figure poses are reconstructed and ranked for user's manual selections. Although this approach supports rapid 3D key framing, rendering information in sketches (i.e. perspective rendering) has not been effectively utilized, which is useful for interpreting the user's intended pose.

In recent years, sketch-based 3D freeform object modelling has become feasible, as demonstrated by [KHR02][IMT99]. In these systems, users draw 2D freeform strokes interactively specifying the silhouette of an object, which is automatically constructed by the system as a 3D freeform surface model represented as polygonal meshes [IMT99] or implicit surfaces [KHR02]. Incremental modelling is supported to assemble and refine the initial objects into final complicated ones through a set of editing operations including extrusion, cutting, blob merging, transformation, etc. The resulting 3D models are mostly stuffed toys, simple clothes, car/furniture models, etc. None of the above systems has embarked on the generation of human skin surface, which is irregular and complicated, thus fairly difficult to model.

3. Conceptual design of a sketch-based virtual human modelling and animation system

In this section, our initial system design is introduced through the following three aspects: 1) Figure drawing sequence, 2) 3D pose reconstruction from 2D stick figures, 3) Free-form skin modelling from figure contour sketching. Design assumptions and questions are raised, as well as the reasons and objectives for the preliminary user study.

3.1. Figure drawing sequence

As stated in [LS02], humans are accustomed to performing the reverse projection of sketched geometries from 2D back into 3D. In terms of the perception of raw figure drawings, the human brain can envision the 3D counterparts easily and even spontaneously. It is, however, mathematically indeterminate and very difficult to emulate computationally. To decompose the complexity of direct 3D modelling and animation from 'noisy' figure sketches (featured by foreshortening, contour over-tracing, body part overlapping, shading/shadow, etc.), we designed a "Stick Figure→Fleshing-out→Skin Mapping" pipeline [MQW06a]. This is inspired by the drawing sequence recommended by many sketch books [Tin92]. In principle, it echoes the animation pipeline in commercial packages (3ds Max, Maya, etc). In this design, the user first draws stick figure key frames to specify a motion. Then, they can "flesh-out" any existing stick figure to portray an imaginary character. The system can automatically reconstruct 3D figure poses and 'perceive' the intended body surface. It can then be wrapped onto stick key poses (akin to clothing wire sculptures), which can be further interpolated as 3D character animation.

Although our initial design enables multiple animation functions and outputs, we were concerned whether the "Stick Figure→Fleshing-out" drawing sequence would be natural and flexible for users. A preliminary user study was needed to evaluate conceptual design ideas, identify user's needs, and seek the optimal compromise between drawing flexibility and system functionalities.

3.2. 3D pose reconstruction from 2D stick figures

As previously stated, 3D pose recovery is one of the primary challenges for sketch-based figure modelling, because of "back-front ambiguities". In reality, humans are able to perceive figure poses from 2D drawings with little confusion. Hence, it is necessary to understand this perception process in order to replicate the effect. At the beginning, we were indebted to the understanding of human physical constraints and depth cues. Since our brain has been trained with natural and possible poses, all abnormal poses are easily excluded. Furthermore, there must be some depth cues in a sketch, which enable observers to reach a consensus without confusion. However, many questions still remained to be addressed from the user study. For example: What types of depth cues are most commonly indicated in figure drawing? What other clues are crucial for sketch understanding? Do people need interactive assistance in figure proportion maintenance, since it is a recognised challenge for not only novices, but also skilled artists?

3.3. Freeform skin modelling from figure contour sketching

As discussed earlier, humans are capable of instinctively perceiving a 'noisy' 2D figure sketch as a realistic 3D body. Thus, understanding this perception process is essential for realising computerised 2D-to-3D reconstruction. Since we see and interact with people, our brain has become familiar with various body shapes and the correlations between 2D flat features and their real 3D counterparts [LS02]. Therefore, when observing a raw figure sketch, our brain can automatically clean up the distracting 'noises', perceive the body size and shape, recall an associated body shape from memory, and then morph and fit it into the 2D drawing to obtain the final 3D image. Theoretically, if given a range of pre-stored morphable template bodies, a computer is able to perform this through performing similar 'thinking', 'recalling', and morphing routines. Moreover, when observing a sketch, our eyes tend to capture a general profile first, followed by more details to depict the surface feature. In terms of sketching, artists usually follow this "coarse-to-fine" routine too. In reality, a computer can support this incremental sketching process in a more interactive and dynamic way. In our proposed system, users can sketch figure profiles to prototype an initial 3D model and incrementally refine it through suggestive contours [DFRS03], shading/shadow, etc, in both 2D and 3D. However, there were still many questions remaining regarding the initial design, such as what degree of sketching inaccuracy and ambiguity our system should tolerate; what the real needs of various users for a natural and supportive sketching environment are; etc. These questions were to be addressed in the following user study.

4. Preliminary user survey study

After the initial system design, we conducted a preliminary user study [MQW06a] to verify design ideas, explore design questions, further identify users' needs, and obtain a true figure drawing story. This user study comprised *Questionnaires* and *Sketching Observations,* which are detailed in 4.1 and 4.2 respectively. In Section 5, an updated system design is presented according to the generalised user study results.

4.1. Questionnaire study and results

A questionnaire was designed and delivered to acquire the basic knowledge of human figure sketching, identify the requirements for developing a "sketch-based virtual human modelling and animation system", and gather users' feedback about the current system design. 60 questionnaires were collected from the research staff and students of the design department, as well as some external artists. The questionnaire consisted of three sections: S1 - General figure sketching questions, S2 - Specific figure sketching questions, S3 - Questions about system development.

In Section 1, *Proportion maintenance, Structure and tension, Balance*, and *Unifiability of the human body* were ranked by users as key principles (in descending priority) to ensure a plausible figure drawing.

Section 2 contained two parts. In Part 1, users were asked to choose one or more options from the provided methods for figure proportion maintenance in different sketching scenarios. As shown in Figure 1, the study results are:
- *Measuring devices* are most frequently utilised for proportion maintenance when sketching with models.
- *Sense of feeling* plays an important role in nearly all sketching scenarios, which raises the potential problem of imprecise proportion expression. This problem turns out to be severe when figure sketching without models.
- *Rule of thumb* plays a vital role in each scenario, especially when figure drawing without references.

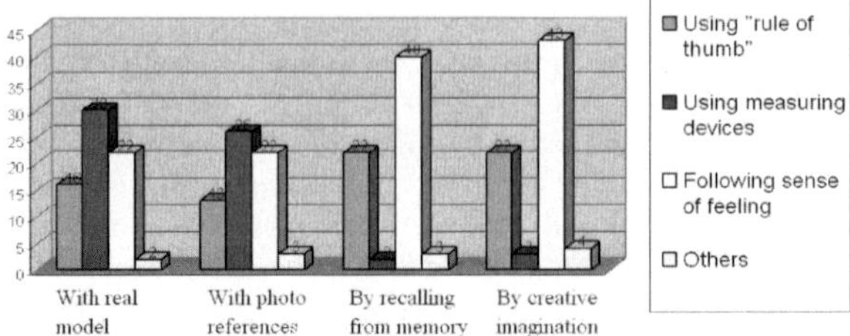

Figure 1: *Figure proportion maintenance methods in various sketching scenarios.*

In Part 2, four questions regarding stick figure drawing were asked to identify *whether* and *how* depth cues are indicated to reveal an intended figure pose. It was presumed that depth cues are often shown as forms of visual contrast (i.e. thickness/size contrast) among different body parts. For instance, artists usually render more strokes on a relatively closer body part to make it visually stronger. In addition, real-time information including stroke speed and pressure may help reveal depth information. Respondents were asked to rank the provided depth cues (or give their own options) in different circumstances. Statistical analysis showed the followings:
- 65% of respondents believe that they often convey figure pose by depth cues.
- *Joint size contrast* (bigger-closer, smaller-further) is the primary clue used to determine the relative positions between pair joints of the same type (e.g. left and right elbow). Other depth cues are ranked as: *Joint thickness contrast, Stroke pressure contrast*, and *Stroke speed contrast.*
- *Physical size* is the first priority criterion for varying the sizes of different types of joints, followed by *Joint relative positions.* Moreover, many people chose to vary the joint size randomly, which means size information is sometimes not reliable for pose understanding.
- *Line thickness contrast* (thicker-closer, lighter-further) is chosen as the principal clue to convey relative bone location. Other clues in descending order are *Stroke pressure contrast, Stroke speed contrast, others.*

From the above results, we can see that depth cues are frequently used for pose indication. Different depth cues (i.e. thickness/size contrast) are used in different circumstances. Confusion may arise when multiple factors (i.e. physical size, spatial distribution) work together to affect joint size variation. Therefore, sketching observation was needed to acquire real-time solutions for these mixed conditions.

In Section 3, users' expressed opinions regarding the initial system design:
- 85% of respondents accepted our figure drawing sequence design: "stick figure → fleshing-out".
- 95% of respondents agreed that the system should be able to provide drawing assistance for figure proportion and foreshortening maintenance.
- 90% of respondents agreed that the system should 'perceive' depth cues for pose recognition.

In Section 3, we also set an open question to enquire about users' requirements for a virtual human sketching system. The summarized answers are integrated in Table 2.

4.2 Sketching observation study and results

Apart from the questionnaire study, sketching scenarios

were designed to obtain a real-time story from users when they perform paper-based drawing tasks. Sketching observations were conducted to obtain both static (figure sketches) and dynamic (natural sketching behaviours) information in the pre-defined scenarios.

4.2.1 Participant selection

Nine participants were involved in sketching observations. The participants were from various professions including artists, designers, graduate students, and researchers. Their sketching skills varied from excellent to poor.

4.2.2 Sketching interview and sketching scenario design

The sketching interview comprised 3 stages. In Stage 1, the participants were introduced to our proposed system and the interview programs. In Stage 2, the participants were asked to sketch in three different scenarios:

Scenario 1: *Stick figure drawing with photograph references*

Participants sketch-out stick figures (3-4 expected) within 8 minutes by referring to figure photos provided.

Scenario 2: *Fleshing out with photograph references*

Participants choose one or more stick figures sketched in Scenario 1 for fleshing-out within 10 minutes. They are permitted to flesh-out details (i.e. character clothes/face, suggestive contours, shading/shadow) at their discretion.

Scenario 3*: Key frame drawing without references*

Participants draw stick figure key frames (3-4 expected) to express an imaginative motion within 4 minutes.

Scenario 1 and Scenario 2 corresponded to the *stick figure drawing* and *fleshing-out* routines in our initial design. Here, the time limit was designed to simulate a fast sketching process, which was video recorded and closely observed. A series of observation criteria were established to explore design questions and obtain a figure drawing story in real contexts. Moreover, sketching observations were aimed to investigate the nature and limitations of a paper-based drawing medium to help build a more natural, functional, and supportive electronic drawing medium. 7 indexed photo references in 3 groups were selected to represent variations of body shapes. Multiple conditions including foreshortening and body part overlapping were covered in the photo references. Stage 3 aimed to gather users' feedback/suggestions regarding the prototype system design.

4.2.3. Sketching observation criteria design

The observation criteria were designed to unfold a "real story" of figure sketching in the pre-defined scenarios. The criteria and their associated meanings are listed in Table 1. The observation results follow in the next section.

Table 1: Sketching observation criteria design

Observation criteria	Meanings
C1 Sketching tools	To analyse the use of Wooden pencils (HB-6B) and an eraser for evolving the interface tool set.
C2 Drawing modification	To determine the modification means supported by the prototype system.
C3 Proportion/Foreshortening	To gather real-time information regarding *how* people maintain proportion and foreshortening during figure sketching, and *what* problems they frequently confront.
C4 Depth cues	To reveal *whether* and *how* participants indicate depth cues to convey an intended figure pose
C5 Sketching procedures	To investigate the compatibility of the "stick drawing → fleshing out" sequence and the whole fleshing-out process.
C6 Stroke types	To identify rendering stroke types.
C7 Fleshing-out details	To examine the sketched relationships between stick lines and body contours.
C8 Reference lines	To assess whether or not reference lines are used to assist the figure sketching.
C9 Annotations	To determine if annotations are denoted and needed to be accepted as sketching inputs.

4.2.4 Sketching observation findings

Nine sets of *stick figure drawings* with associated *fleshing-outs* and 6 *key frame sketches* were recorded and analysed. Figure 2 shows some selected sketches including stick figure drawings, fleshing-outs, and key frame drawings.

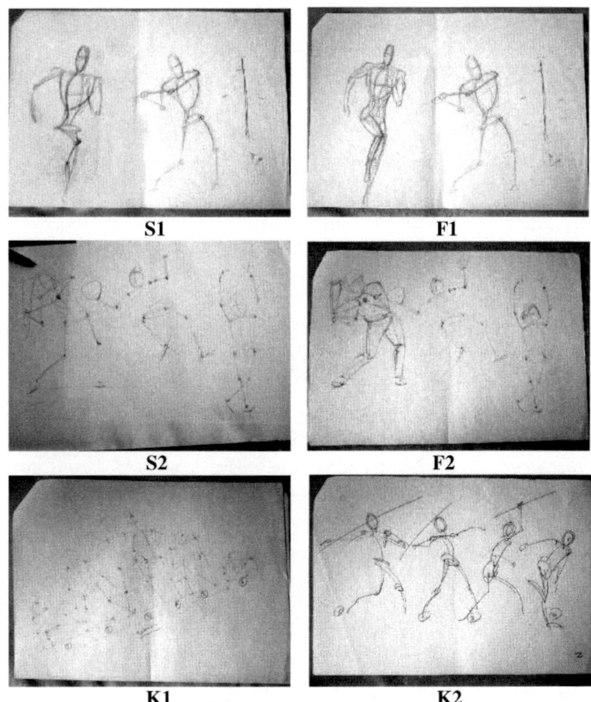

Figure 2: *Selected sketches from a designer (S1, F1), a graduate student (S2, F2, K1), and an artist (K2).*

The observation results are given below.

R1. Sketching tools: During sketching, almost all participants persisted with the same sketching tool that they had picked up at the beginning. This suggests that varying the sketching tool for certain rendering purposes is not imperative for quick sketching.

R2. Modification during sketching: Modification was made more frequently during the *fleshing-out* process. Participants sometimes performed over-tracing (see Fig 2(F2)) rather than "erasing + redrawing" to modify an existing sketch.

R3. Proportion/Foreshortening: Within a time limit, most participants sketched cursorily, even with photo references. The resultant sketches were therefore mis-proportioned (see Fig 2(S1/F1/K1/K2)), and appeared to run off the paper (see Fig 2(S1/F1)). Therefore, real-time assistance is required for supporting proper figure drawing.

R4. Depth cues: We marked the foreshortened body parts of each photo model and evaluated the usage and forms of depth cues through analysing the corresponding figure sketch. Through observation, it seemed that depth cues were frequently delineated even on a simple stick drawing, through visual contrasts of size or thickness (see Fig 2). In more detail, thickness contrasts (see Fig 2(S1/F1/S2/K1)) appeared more often than size contrasts (see Fig 2(K2)), which were varied almost randomly without following any apparent rules. This conflicted with the questionnaire study results, where size contrast was preferred. Since the latter came from real sketching, thickness contrast was adopted as the depth cue for pose identification in the prototype system. Moreover, since rendering styles varied among individuals, the depth meaning implied by a given thickness contrast was not exclusive. Hence, rendering gestures might need to be generalised. In addition, no distinctive correlations between stroke speed/pressure and depth meaning could be recognised.

R5. Sketching procedures: We observed that participants seemed to tune into the "stick drawing → fleshing out" routine smoothly, especially the professionals and intermediate users who appeared familiar with this sequence. Novices required several attempts before becoming skilled. In *Scenario 2*, participants usually fleshed-out stick figures layer-by-layer according to the degree of detail. Moreover, in *Scenario 3*, key postures were sometimes drawn first followed by supplemented in-betweens.

R6. Stroke types: Participants usually drew body contours and shading by multiple strokes instead of a single stroke. Figure contours were sometimes partially missing due to a specific view (i.e. side view), body part overlapping, etc. Every sketch had more or less imperfections depending on participants' drawing skills (see Fig 2). Thus, the system has to tolerate these types of ambiguities and imprecision to keep the sketching process natural and flexible.

R7. Fleshing-out details: When fleshing-out, the professional/intermediate (see Fig 2(F1/F2)) were normally able to treat initial stick lines as a real skeleton and incorporate body contours properly. Novices sometimes drew figure contours fused with stick lines due to limited knowledge of human anatomy. Thus, the system should provide some supportive functions.

R8. Reference lines: Some participants first drew reference curves, which they called "major dynamic lines" to show a big figure profile. Reference lines such as "proportion lines" (Fig 2 (S1/F1)) were used to help maintain figure proportion.

R9. Annotations: Annotations were frequently drawn during key frame sketching (see Fig 2(K1/K2)) to denote key frame indices, the sketch title, etc.

5. Updated system design based on user study outcomes

After the user study, our initial system design was updated (see Table2) to reflect the key points learned from the survey.

Table 2: The updated system design

Accepted design	Amended design	Newly integrated design
1) "Stick figure→Fleshing-out→skin mapping". 2) "On-line drawing assistance". 3) "Coarse to fine" drawing routine. 4) Accept various rendering forms, strokes, reference lines, and annotations. 5) Tolerate drawing imperfections. 6) Provide various modification methods. 7) Perception-based 3D skin modelling. 8) Interactive sketching in a 2D/3D mixed environment.	1) Thickness contrast is taken as a primary depth cue. 2) Generalised depth gestures are employed to correlate between 2D visual contrast and 3D depth meanings. 3) Depth cues, human body physical constraints, and key frame coherence are incorporated together for 2D-3D pose recovery	1) Sketch-based motion specification. 2) Functions to create a personalised 3D virtual world. 3) Display 3D figure models on a virtual floor. 4) 2D/3D models and animations in both PR and NPR format. 5) Functions to allow detailed character manipulation (i.e. face/clothes editing).

6. Implementation of the prototype system

Based on the validated design, we developed a "Sketch-based Virtual Human Modelling and Animation System", with two releases: 1) "Sketch-based 3D Stick Figure Animation Interface", and 2) "Sketch-based Virtual Human Builder". In this section, we present the implementation details and function highlights of these two linked systems and an informal user test on the stick figure animation system. The testing results contributed to the development of the latest virtual human sketching interface.

6.1 Implementation of a sketch-based gesture interface for 3D stick figure animation

We developed a sketch-based gesture interface [MQW05], which enables users to "draw" 3D stick figure animations. It allows users to interactively sketch stick figure key frames, graphically define motion path and timing, and finally "pop-up" 2D characters into 3D animations with a single click.

6.1.1 Sketch stick figures with on-line drawing assistance

As shown in Figure 3, users can convey imaginary motion by sketching stick figure key frames. In our system, on-line drawing assistance is provided to help maintain proper figure proportions and foreshortening. Users sketch each body part as a single stroke line, which automatically snaps to the adjacent one to ensure connectivity. Like artists refining their figure drawings by incrementally adding details, users can render extra strokes on drawings at any time to indicate depth information when posing a figure.

Figure 3: *The sketching interface with template skeleton and freehand figure sketches: Users can choose/create a template skeleton as a drawing reference. The bone segment being drawn is recognised and highlighted on the template. Its maximum length is confined by the template length. Foreshortened and non-foreshortened segments are distinguished in black and green respectively. Perspective effects are rendered incrementally by multiple strokes.*

6.1.2 Reconstruct 3D figures from 2D freehand drawings

For 2D-3D pose recovery, we developed a "multi-layered back-front ambiguity clarifier", which utilises figure perspective rendering, human joint Range of Motion (ROM), and key frame coherence to identify the user intended 3D poses. To unify the correlations between bone/joint thickness contrasts and their depth meanings, we have generalised a set of rendering gestures, which is easy to learn and efficient for pose inference by system. Generally, the thicker bone/joint is the closer (see Fig 4(Left)). Our system supports an interactive design process, through which 3D figure models can be viewed and updated in response to user's incremental sketching (see Fig. 4(Top right)). In addition, a "figure pose checking/auto-correction" routine is offered to ensure physically valid poses during a fast sketching process (see Fig. 4(Bottom right)).

6.1.3. Sketch-based 3D animation and motion control

Once a series of reconstructed figure key frames are obtained, the final 3D animation and motion control can be accomplished by interactively sketching-out the motion paths and keyframe timing (see Fig 4(Left) and 7(Bottom left)) Moreover, users can choose/add their personalised music and panorama to enhance the 3D virtual world (Fig 7(Bottom right). The resulting animation is synthesised in VRML and can be triggered by a single user click.

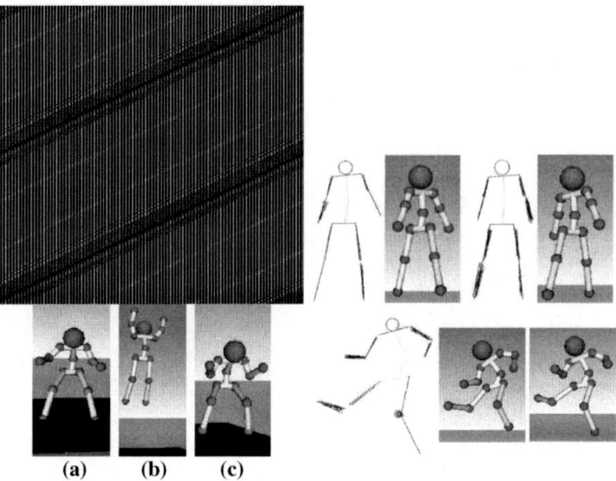

Figure 4: *(Top left) 2D key drawings and motion curves to define a jumping action; Annotations are added to denote the drawings; (Top right) After incremental sketching, the figure pose is changed according to the modified perspective rendering; (Bottom left) The sketched-out 3D jumping motion; (Bottom right) An original drawing with its ill-posed and auto-corrected 3D figure models.*

6.2 Informal user test on the first prototype interface

After the implementation of the sketch-based 3D stick figure animation interface, we conducted an informal user test to evaluate its functionalities and usability, and identify users' new needs introduced by this digital drawing medium. The participants included some internal research staff and graduate students in the design department. After a short tutorial, users were required to sketch-out simple three-framed stick figure animations using our system via a pen-based Tablet PC. Users were closely observed performing drawing/animation tasks on this digital drawing medium. During the test, users rapidly learned the modelling and animation routines, and drew-out their own 3D animations within minutes. Regarding our sketching interface, users considered it to be as natural and flexible to use as paper, yet considerably more functional and amusing to "pop-up" 2D drawings into 3D animations with minimum non-sketching interaction. Our on-line drawing assistance seemed beneficial for users during fast figure sketching. Based on sketching observations and users' feedback, further development aspects were summarised:

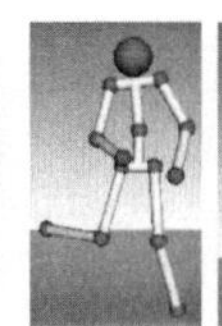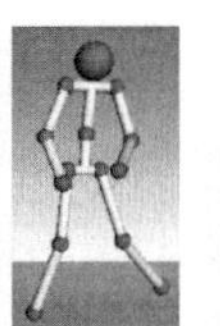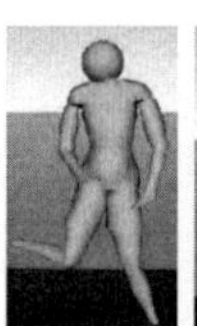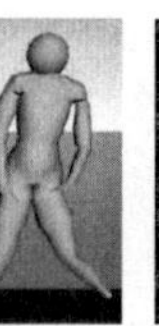

Figure 5: *Users first draw stick figure key frames to define a specific motion. Then, they can "flesh-out" any existing stick figure with body profiles. The system can automatically "perceive" the body size and shape from the sketched figure and transfer it into a plausible 3D human model. It can be mapped onto posed stick figures, which can be further interpolated as 2D and 3D animations.*

- Adopt meaningful graphical icons associated with the existing text to distinguish different function buttons.
- Produce more varieties of sketch-generated characters including 3D mesh models, 2D NPR figures models, etc.
- Integrate libraries of sketch-generated motions and characters in the system for easy saving and retrieving.
- Enable motion retargeting for reusing previous motions and characters to generate new animations.
- Enable sketch-based crowd animation and 2D storyboarding of 3D character intercommunication.

6.3 Implementation of a sketch-based virtual human builder

Through incorporating users' feedback into the initial system design, a "sketch-based virtual human builder" [MQW06b] was designed. It enables users to sketch-out and animate virtual humans of variational body sizes, shapes, and fat distributions. Its graphical pipeline is shown in Fig 5.

6.3.1 Creative model-based 3D body generation method

Users can depict the visual appearance of a virtual character through "fleshing-out" a single stick figure with body profiles. We investigated a "creative model-based method", which can perceive the body size and shape of a sketched figure and transfer it into a plausible 3D human model, through continuous graphical comparisons and generic model (The Visible Human Project®) morphing (rigid morphing→fatness morphing→surface fitting).

6.3.2 Transfer 2D freehand sketches into 3D plausible human body models

Our system can process and transfer a 'noisy' figure sketch of multiple strokes, missing contours, and asymmetry into a plausible 3D body model. An "auto-beautification" option is offered to regularise an asymmetrical human body caused by users' drawing imperfections. Moreover, users can interactively refine the resulting 3D model by over-sketching 2D figure profiles. Modifications can be made freely on any key frame sketch to obtain the updated model. Enabling 2D/3D mixed figure drawing is our next challenge.

6.3.3 Generate 2D and 3D virtual human animation

Our current virtual human builder generates various animations including articulated figure animation, 3D mesh model animation, 2D contour figure animation, and 2D NPR animation with personalised drawing styles.

6.3.4 Sketch-based crowd animation and storyboarding of 3D character intercommunication

In our system, users can build their own 3D character and motion library, and animate a population of virtual humans (Fig 6 (Bottom right)) through motion retargeting and sketch-based actor allocation in 3D space. Moreover, users are able to illustrate character intercommunication and script dialogue in each story scene, through either stick or full figure drawing. (Fig 6 (Bottom left)).

7. Formal user test on the latest sketching interface

On the completion of the current virtual human modelling and animation interface, we conducted a formal user evaluation to assess its usability and functionalities with various users through performance tests, sketching observations, and interviews. Ten users were involved in this evaluation: 5 design students, 1 engineering student, 1 social science student, 1 artist, 1 animator, and 1 twelve-year-old boy. None of them had been involved in our early user tests. Only the animator had previous experiences with 3D character modelling and animation.

7.1 User test procedures

During the test, the user was first given a briefing (5 mins) about system aims and functionalities. Then, a demo (15 mins) was provided on how to use our sketching interface to create stick and full figure animations. After that, the user was allowed to run the program for 5 minutes to become familiar with it. Then, each user was requested to sketch-out 3D animations in the following two scenarios:

Scenario 1 – Users sketch-out a 3-frame stick figure (SF) jumping animation on a Tablet PC.

Scenario 2 – Users sketch-out a 3-frame full figure (FF) Kungfu animation on a Tablet PC.

The 3D key poses (SF–jumping, FF–Kungfu) were pre-defined and shown to users, so that they could depict them through 2D sketching to achieve similar results. The evaluator timed and observed every individual task. After the performance test, user interviews were conducted.

7.2 Performance test results

After minimum training, the overall average time for creating a complete SF and FF animation was 6.27 mins and 6.75 mins respectively. Regarding animation speed and quality, the top 3 users were the animator, the artist, and a design student. This reveals that our sketching/animating routine is similar to their real practice. It was delightful to see that the young boy (12 years old) could sketch-out SF and FF animations enjoyably in just 6.5 and 8.34 minutes. From the stick figure to the full figure section, users' average time on each individual task was noticeably reduced as: *key framing* (2.54➔2.51 mins), *depth gesture indication* (1.50➔1.05 mins), *3D reconstruction* (0.93➔0.59 mins), and *motion definition* (1.30➔0.67 mins). This suggests the prominent learnability of our system to allow users to incrementally master it through previous usages. Users' average fleshing-out time was only 1.93 mins, which is even quicker than that of paper-based drawing. All created models were integrated into Fig 6 group Kungfu animations shown in Fig 6.

7.3 Sketching observation and interview results

Through observation, it was found that users drew figure key frames quickly and freely as if drawing on paper. The "on-line drawing assistance" appeared to be useful and supportive during a fast sketching process. The depth indication gestures were intuitive and logically understandable, although users sometimes needed to pay extra attention to imagine proper thickness contrasts to depict a relatively complex 3D pose. Users performed the "stick figure➔fleshing-out" routine smoothly and efficiently. The fleshing-out process was flexible and interactive assisted by auto-beautification and incremental drawing functions. Regarding 3D reconstruction and animation production, users interacted with interface toolkits fluently with the assistance of associated graphical icons. The graphical motion specification is simple and intuitive, whilst direct 3D path editing is required for more precise motion definition. During interviews, users recommended a 3D pose window to show immediate 2D depth rendering results. The artist suggested more surface depiction forms, such as shading/shadow, suggestive contours, etc. The animator recommended commercial tools to refine the sketch-generated models and motions to meet practical needs.

8. Conclusion and future work

In this paper, we have presented our user and usability studies for applying scenarios in user-centred design to develop a sketching interface for virtual human modelling and animation. User centred design and spiral lifecycles are common practice for software development. Few reports, however, have addressed their application in sketching interface development to fulfil both users' needs and system functionalities. A sketching interface is meant to combine the power, as well as minimize the disadvantages of paper-based sketching and computer-based automation to be a better drawing medium. Constant sketching experiments and scenario-based design are therefore crucial to identify the nature of drawing and users' evolving needs on paper-based and especially computerised tools to accomplish an optimal interface. In our approach, we employed various scenarios throughout the user centred design process and achieved a novel interface, which enables virtual human modelling and animation through natural and supportive 2D sketching. Benefiting from applying the UCSD strategy and scenario-based design in real practice, we hope that our investigation can be a useful instantiation to enhance the design of other sketching interfaces. In the future, we will adhere to our user-centred approaches and continuously improve our sketching interface according to users' needs.

References

[Bød00] BØDKER S.: Scenarios in user-centred design – setting the stage for reflection and action. *Interacting with Computers*, 13 (2000), 61-75.

[Car00] CARROLL, J.M.: Five reasons for scenario-based design. *Interacting with Computers*, 13 (2000), 43-60.

[DAC*03] DAVIS J., AGRAWALA M., CHUANG E., POPOVIĆ Z., and SALESIN D.: a sketching interface for articulated figure animation. In *Proc. Eurographics / SIGGRAPH Symposium on Computer Animation* (2003), 320-328.

[DFRS03] DECARLO D., FINKELSTEIN A., RUSINKIEWICS S. AND SANTELLA A.: Suggestive contours for conveying shape, *ACM Transaction on Graphics* 22, 3 (2003), 848-855.

[GBG*06] GULLIKSEN, J., BOIVIE, I , GÖRANSSON, B.: Usability professionals - current practices and future development. *Interacting with Computers* 18, 4 (2006), 568-600.

[HH01] HOSHINO J., HOSHINO Y.: Intelligent storyboard for prototyping animation. In *Proc. IEEE Int. Conf. On Multimedia and Expo* (2001), Conference CD-ROM FAI.03.

[LM95] LANDAY, J.A., MYERS, B.A.: Interactive sketching for the early stages of user interface design. *CHI'95*, (1995), 43-50.

[IMT99] IGARASHI T., MATSUOKA S., TANAKA H.: Teddy: a sketching interface for 3D freeform design. *Proc. SIGGRAPH '99* (1999), 409-416.

[KHR02] KARPENKO O., HUGHES J. F., RASKAR R: Free-form sketching with variational implicit surfaces, *Proc. Eurographics 2002* 21, 3 (2002).

[KKP*04] KULES, B., KANG, H., PLAISANT, C., ROSE, A., SHNEIDERMAN, B.: Immediate usability: a case study of public access design for a community photo library. *Interacting with Computers*, 16, 6 (2004) 1171-1193.

[LS02] LIPSON H., SHPITALNI M.: Correlation-based reconstruction of a 3D object from a single freehand sketch, *In Proc. AAAI Spring Symposium Series - Sketch Understanding* (2002).

[LSP*04] LIM, S., QIN, S.F., PRIETO, P., WRIGHT, D.K., SHACKLETON, J.A.: A study of sketching behaviour to support free-form surface modelling from on-line sketching. *Design Studies* 25, 4 (2004), 393-413.

[MQW05] MAO C, QIN SF, WRIGHT DK: A sketch-based gesture interface for rough 3D stick figure animation, *Proc. of Eurographics Workshop on Sketch Based Interfaces and Modeling* (2005), 175-183.

[MQW06a] MAO, C., QIN, S.F., WRIGHT, D.K.: Virtual human modelling and animation through a sketching interface, To appear in *Proc. HCI 06*, 2006.

[MQW06b] MAO, C., QIN, S.F., WRIGHT, D.K.: Sketching-out virtual humans: from 2D storyboarding to immediate 3D character animation. *Proc. of ACM SIGCHI Conference on Advances in Computer Entertainment Technology* (2006).

[OSD05] OH, J.Y., STUERZLINGER, W., DANAHY, J.: Comparing SESAME and sketching on paper for conceptual 3D design. *Proc. of Eurographics Workshop on Sketch Based Interfaces and Modeling* (2005), 81-88.

[Sut63] SUTHERLAND, I.E., Sketchpad: A man-machine graphical communication system. *Proc. SFIPS Spring Joint Computer Conf. IFIP* 23 (1963) 329-345.

[TBP04] THORNE M., BURKE D., VAN DE PANNE M.: Motion doodles: An interface for sketching character animation. *ACM Transactions on Graphics (TOG) 23*, 3 (2004), 424- 431.

[Tin92] TINER R.: *Figure drawing without a model*, David & Charles plc, Glasgow (1992).

[TP03] TOVEY, M., PORTER, S.: Sketching, concept development and automotive design. *Design studies*, 24 (2003), 135-153.

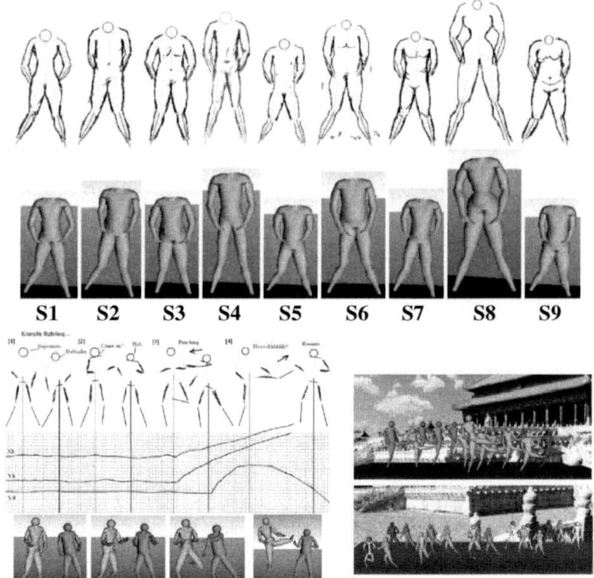

Figure 6: *(Top) A variety of 3D virtual humans and the original drawings by different users: artist (S3), design student (S4), animator (S6, S7), graduate students (S1, S2, S5, S9), and a child (S8); (Bottom left) The Kungfu storyboards with associated dialogues and motion curves, and the 3D fighting characters; (Bottom right) Kungfu group animation with music and background; A crowd of sketch-generated virtual humans and stick figures are fighting with each other in a 3D virtual world.*

EUROGRAPHICS Workshop on Sketch-Based Interfaces and Modeling (2006)
Thomas Stahovich and Mario Costa Sousa (Editors)

An Initial Evaluation of a Pen-Based Tool for Creating Dynamic Mathematical Illustrations

Joseph J. LaViola Jr.

Brown University, Department of Computer Science, USA
Email: jjl@cs.brown.edu

Abstract

MathPad^2 is a pen-based application prototype for creating mathematical sketches. Using a modeless gestural interface, it lets users make dynamic illustrations by associating handwritten mathematics with free-form drawings and provides a set of tools for graphing and evaluating mathematical expressions and solving equations. In this paper, we present the results of an initial evaluation of the MathPad^2 prototype, examining the user interface's intuitiveness and the application's perceived usefulness. Our evaluations are based on both performance and questionnaire results including first attempt gesture performance, interface recall tests, and surveys of user interface satisfaction and perceived usefulness. The results of our evaluation suggest that, although some test subjects had difficulty with our mathematical expression recognizer, they found the interface, in general, intuitive and easy to remember. More importantly, these results suggest the prototype has the potential to assist beginning physics and mathematics students in problem solving and understanding scientific concepts.

Categories and Subject Descriptors (according to ACM CCS): H.5.2 [Information Interfaces and Presentation]: User Interfaces — Interaction Styles, Evaluation/Methodology

1. Introduction

MathPad^2 (see Figure 1) is a pen-based, Tablet PC application prototype for creating dynamic illustrations used for exploring mathematics and physics concepts [LZ04]. The fundamental technology behind MathPad^2 is mathematical sketching, a pen-based gestural interaction paradigm for mathematics problem solving that derives from the familiar pencil-and-paper process of drawing supporting diagrams to facilitate the formulation of mathematical expressions; however, with mathematical sketching, users can also leverage their physical intuition by watching their hand-drawn diagrams animate in response to continuous or discrete parameter changes in their written formulas [LaV05]. Diagram animation is driven by associations that are inferred, either automatically or with gestural guidance, from handwritten mathematical expressions, diagram labels, and drawing elements.

The essential goal in developing the MathPad^2 user interface was that it be as similar and fluid as pencil and paper, since mathematics and physics problems are often solved using this medium. Thus, we did not want to use any additional hardware (e.g., a modifier key or stylus button) or

software (e.g., buttons) modes. Instead, we wanted all interaction to be derived from using digital ink. We developed a gestural user interface for invoking different operations in MathPad^2 because we wanted users able to work as fluidly as possible with the mathematics and drawings they create. We wanted to explore whether our choice of gestures, which by themselves are not part of pencil-and-paper interaction, are thought of as intuitive or at least complimentary to pencil and paper.

Given the foundations for MathPad^2, we performed an initial usability evaluation to gauge users' performances and reactions to the prototype to validate its design and potential benefit and determine if further, more in-depth studies are needed. More specifically, we are interested in how easy it is for users to use MathPad^2 with only a visual demonstration of how to invoke gestural operations, and in how many mistakes they make in performing various MathPad^2 tasks. We are also interested in how well subjects remember various gestural commands, since this is a good indicator of intuitiveness. Using interface satisfaction [CDN88] and perceived usefulness [Dav89] questionnaires, we are addition-

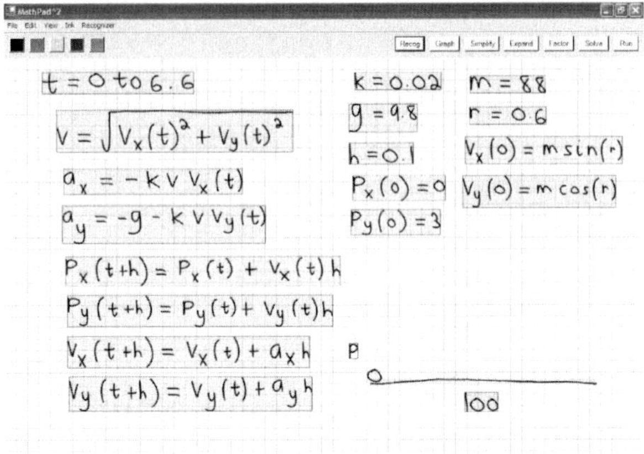

Figure 1: *A mathematical sketch, created in MathPad^2, illustrating how air drag affects a ball's 2D motion. Associations between mathematics and drawings are color-coded.*

ally interested in whether subjects would use mathematical sketching in their work and why.

2. Related Work

The idea of using computers to create dynamic illustrations of mathematical concepts has a long history. One of the earliest dynamic illustration environments was Borning's ThingLab, a simulation laboratory environment for constructing dynamic models of experiments in geometry and physics, that relied heavily on constraint solvers and inheritance classes [Bor79]. Other systems such as Interactive Physics^{TM} and The Geometer's SketchPad^{TM} also let the user create dynamic illustrations; these systems are all WIMP-based (Windows, Icons, Menus, Pointers) resulting in a significant amount of mode switching and loss of fluidity within the interface. In addition, they do not allow the user to write handwritten mathematics to create these illustrations. Because MathPad^2 uses handwritten mathematical expressions, users can leverage their knowledge of mathematical notation in order to create mathematical sketches. Java applets that provide both interactive and dynamic illustrations have also been developed for exploring various mathematics and physics principles [CT98]. However, these applets are not general, typically provide limited control over the illustration, and rarely show the user the mathematics behind the illustration.

Alvarado [Alv00] and Kara [KGS04] let the user make sketched diagrams that are recognized as drawing primitives with domain knowledge from specific disciplines and then animated. Although these systems provide powerful illustrations of physics and mathematical concepts, they are limited because of their domain knowledge and because they hide the underlying mathematical formulations from the user. Pen-based systems have also been developed for other types of dynamic illustration. For example, Pickering et al.

developed a system for sketching football plays, simulating them, and then creating a dynamic illustration of the play outcome [PBLP99] while Davis et al. developed a pen-based system for creating traditional animations [DACP04].

MathJournal, developed by xThink, Inc., is the closest in spirit to MathPad^2 because its animation controls let users write down and recognize mathematics, make drawings, and assign the mathematics to the drawings. However, a key limitation of MathJournal's animation control is that users must keyframe their animations (typically providing a starting and ending frame), making the user interface less fluid and contravening how users would make diagrams with pencil and paper. In addition, MathJournal's animation control lacks the iteration and conditional constructs, diagram rectification, and modeless gestural user interface that mathematical sketching supports.

3. The MathPad^2 User Interface

To make mathematical sketches in MathPad^2, users write down mathematics, make drawings, and make associations between the two. Additionally, users can invoke mathematical tools such as graphing, function evaluation, and equation solving to help create and manipulate their sketches. In this section, we describe how users perform these tasks with MathPad^2's modeless gestural user interface. A summary of the commands are found in Figure 2.

When designing our modeless gestural interface, we wanted the gestures not to interfere with the entry of drawings or equations and still be direct and natural enough to feel fluid. To accomplish this, we use context sensitivity to determine what operations to perform with a single gesture. We also use the notion of punctuated gestures, compound gestures with one or more strokes and terminal punctuation, to help disambiguate gestures from mathematics and drawings. We also wanted to ensure that gestures which seem logical for more than one command should be used for all of those commands. For example, if a particular gesture makes sense for two or three different operations, then we want that gesture to invoke all those operations. More details on the design of and methodology behind these gestures can be found in [LZ04, LaV05].

To write mathematical expressions, users simply write them down using the stylus as if they were using pencil-and-paper. To have the system recognize a mathematical expression, users must lasso the expression and make a tap inside the lasso. Recognized symbols are presented to users in their own handwriting since MathPad^2 has handwriting samples from individual users as a result of our writer-dependent mathematical expression recognition engine. When users move the stylus over the bounding box of the recognized mathematical expression, a green button appears in the box's lower right corner, and when pressed, shows whether the expression was parsed correctly. If a mathematical expression

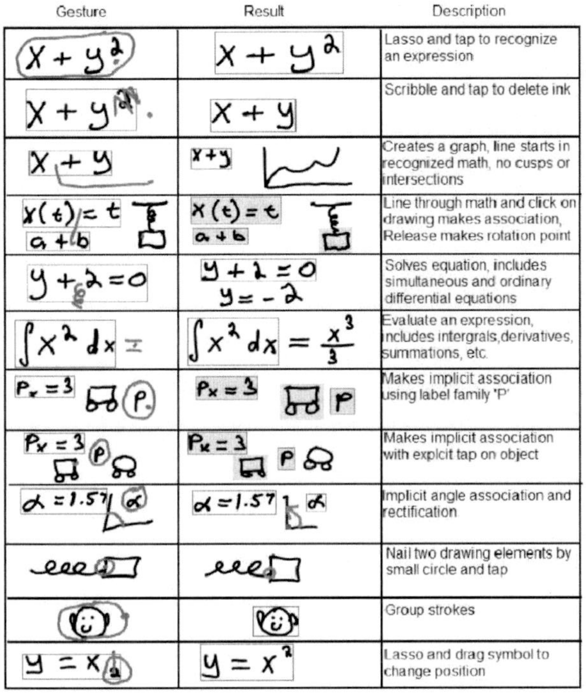

Gesture	Result	Description
$x + y^2$	$x + y^2$	Lasso and tap to recognize an expression
$x + y$	$x + y$	Scribble and tap to delete ink
$x + y$	$x+y$	Creates a graph, line starts in recognized math, no cusps or intersections
$x(t) = t$ / $a+b$	$x(t) = t$ / $a+b$	Line through math and click on drawing makes association, Release makes rotation point
$y + 2 = 0$	$y + 2 = 0$ / $y = -2$	Solves equation, includes simultaneous and ordinary differential equations
$\int x^2\,dx$	$\int x^2\,dx = \frac{x^3}{3}$	Evaluate an expression, includes intergrals, derivatives, summations, etc.
$P_x = 3$	$P_x = 3$	Makes implicit association using label family 'P'
$P_x = 3$	$P_x = 3$	Makes implicit association with explcit tap on object
$\alpha = 1.57$	$\alpha = 1.57$	Implicit angle association and rectification
		Nail two drawing elements by small circle and tap
		Group strokes
$y = x$	$y = x^2$	Lasso and drag symbol to change position

Figure 2: *MathPad^2's gestural commands. Gesture strokes in the first column are shown here in red. In the second column, cyan-highlighted strokes provide association feedback (the highlighting color changes each time a new association is made), and magenta strokes show nail and angle association/rectification feedback.*

is recognized incorrectly, users can simply erase the offending symbols using a scribble erase gesture followed by a tap and then re-recognize the expression. Users can also tap on a recognized symbol to get a list of alternates. If there is a parsing error with the mathematical expression, users can lasso the offending symbols and interactively move them to a new location where the complete expression will be reparsed.

Users make drawings in the same way they write mathematical expressions except that the ink strokes need not be recognized. We refer to these ink strokes as drawing elements and they can be grouped together to form composite drawing elements. Users lasso the drawing elements they want to composite and make a tap on the lasso line. Tapping on the lasso line distinguishes this operation from recognizing mathematical expressions. Users can also nail drawing elements together by drawing a small circle over them and making a tap inside the circle. Nailing drawing elements together lets users make stretchable objects. Note that the drawn circle must not completely contain any drawing elements in order to be recognized as a nail gesture. This constraint distinguishes it from the gesture for making composite drawing elements and recognizing mathematical expressions.

One of the most important components of MathPad^2 is the ability to associate mathematics to drawing elements so they know how to behave during an animation. Users can make associations either explicitly or implicitly. Users make explicit associations by simply drawing a line through the bounding boxes of all the necessary mathematical expressions and tapping on a particular drawing element. As the stylus hovers over drawing elements, they highlight to give users feedback about which drawing element they will select. Implicit associations are made by labeling a drawing element with a variable name or constant value and can be either point or angle associations. Point associations are made in the same way that mathematical expressions are recognized except the tap is made on the drawing element instead of inside a lasso. Angle associations are made by drawing an angle arc and label. Then users lasso the label and make a tap whose location on the arc determines the *active line* — the line attached to the arc that will move when the angle changes. The apex of the angle is then marked with a green dot, and the active line is indicated with an arrowhead on the angle arc. In either case, MathPad^2 uses the label to find all of the required mathematical expressions that should be associated to the drawing element.

Finally, MathPad^2 provides users with a mathematical toolset for graphing and evaluating functions as well as solving equations that can assist users in making mathematical sketches. Users graph functions by simply drawing a sufficiently long, smooth line with no self-intersections, starting inside the bounding box of a recognized mathematical expression, intersecting any other functions along the way, and ending outside all expression bounding boxes. This gesture creates a graph control widget where users can view plots of the functions the graph gesture has intersected and also change the domain and range of the functions by writing down the values and pressing the update button.

Users evaluate mathematical expressions such as integrals, summations, and derivatives by writing an equal sign to the right of the expression and making a tap inside the equal sign's bounding box. The results are then displayed to the right of the drawn equal sign. Users solve single, simultaneous, or ordinary differential equations, by making a squiggly gesture (see Figure 2). This gesture is identical to the graphing gesture except the line must contain two self-intersections. The results are then displayed underneath the last intersected equation.

4. MathPad^2 Evaluation

4.1. Experimental Design and Tasks

The goal of our initial usability experiment is to get users' reactions to the prototype to validate the user interface design and its potential benefit as well as determine if further, more in-depth studies are needed. More specifically, we wanted to evaluate the intuitiveness of MathPad^2's user interface and gauge the perceived usefulness of the tool. Writing down mathematical expressions and making drawings is a fairly intuitive task, and although our gestural commands need to be taught, we felt they were designed so that they should be easy to understand given simple demonstrations of their use.

In the experiment, subjects must complete six tasks representing common interactions that a student or teacher would perform with MathPad^2. Before a subject performs each task, the experimenter shows the subject how to perform the required gestures for that task via demonstration only. Tasks 1–3 were designed to test how well users were able to use the graph, equation solving, and expression evaluation gestures. First, subjects are shown how to write and recognize mathematical expressions using the lasso and tap gesture, how to erase ink using the scribble erase gesture, and how to use the correction user interface. Then, they are shown how to perform each task specific gesture or command. For task 1 (Graphing), after being shown the required gestural commands, the subjects write, recognize, and then graph $y = x$, $y = x^3$, and $y = cos(x)e^x$. Then subjects change $y = x^3$ to $y = x^2$, graph the function, and change the function's domain from $-5...5$ to $0...8$. For task 2 (Equation Solving) task, subjects write down and recognize $x^2 - 16x + 13 = 0$ and solve the equation. Next, subjects write and recognize $x^2y + 2y = 4$ and $3x + y = 2$ and solve this set of simultaneous equations. For task 3 (Expression Evaluation), subjects write down the following expressions and evaluate them:

- $\int_0^2 x^2 dx$
- $y = \int x^2 cos(x) dx$
- $\frac{dy}{dx}$
- $\frac{d^2y}{dx^2}$
- $\sum_{l=0}^5 (l-1)^2$.

In all tasks, subjects are instructed to use the correction user interface if the recognizer incorrectly recognizes symbols or expressions.

Tasks 4–6 were designed to lets users make mathematical sketches and evaluate whether they prefer to use implicit or explicit associations. Task five also was designed to evaluate how well subjects can make nails. Note that only task four required subjects to write down the necessary mathematical expressions. Tasks five and six used prewritten mathematical expressions because we felt having them write and recognize these expressions was not needed, given the many expressions they had already written in the mathematical expression recognition study (see Section 4.4). However, with task four, we wanted to see how well subjects could make a mathematical sketch from beginning to end.

The fourth task (Bouncing Ball), has subjects create a complete mathematical sketch of an object bouncing along the ground. Subjects write and recognize the four mathematical expressions shown in Figure 3, make a drawing with a horizontal line representing the ground and a composite drawing element consisting of three circles drawn near the

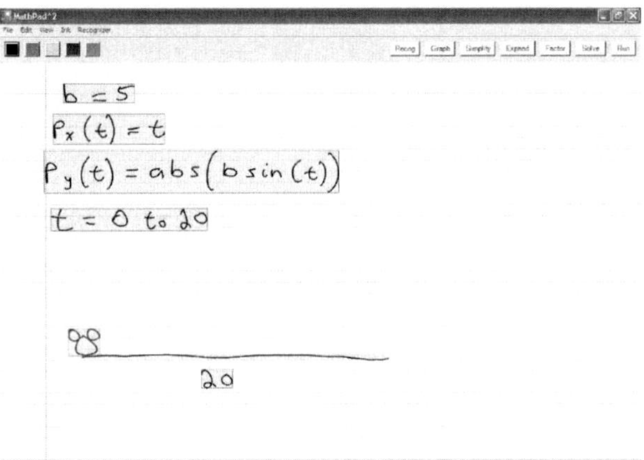

Figure 3: *The fourth task in the MathPad^2 usability test.*

start of the horizontal line. Next, subjects write the number 20 and associate it to the horizontal line. Finally, subjects associate the mathematics to the composite drawing element, either choosing an explicit association or using an implicit association with the letter "p" as a label, and run the sketch. Note that if MathPad^2 fails to recognize subjects' mathematical expressions after several attempts, we provide them with prewritten expressions. However, we do not make them aware of this when the instructions for this task are given.

The fifth task (Oscillator) has subjects create a mathematical sketch illustrating damped harmonic oscillation. The experimenter instructs subjects to first draw a line and make seven nail gestures along that line. This subtask does not have anything to do with the mathematical sketch itself, but gives us additional accuracy data on how well subjects can perform the nail gesture. Subjects make a drawing consisting of a horizontal line, a spring underneath the line, and a box underneath the spring (see Figure 4). Subjects then use two nail gestures to nail the horizontal line to the spring and the spring to the box. Next, subjects associate the mathematics to the box, using an explicit or implicit association with the letter "y" as a label, and run the sketch.

In the last task (2D Motion), subjects create a mathematical sketch illustrating 2D projectile motion subject to air resistance (see Figure 1). Subjects draw a horizontal line and a ball near the left side of the horizontal line. They then associate the number 100 to the horizontal line. Finally, subjects associate the mathematics to the ball, using an explicit or implicit association with the letter "p" as a label, and run the sketch. After all six tasks are completed, subjects answer a post-questionnaire.

4.2. Participants

Seven subjects (four men and three women), participated in the MathPad^2 usability evaluation. Subjects were recruited from the Brown University undergraduate population and

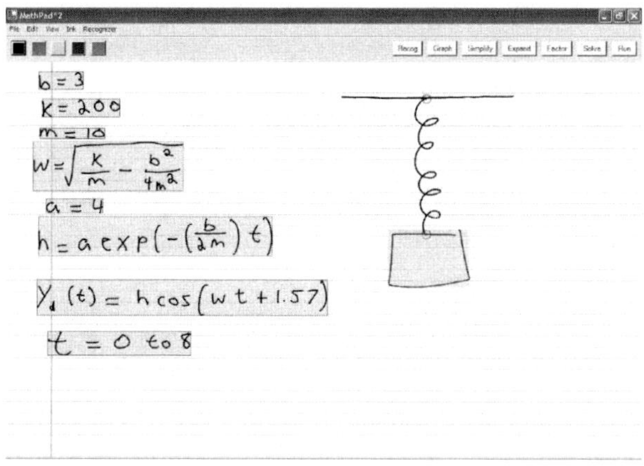

Figure 4: *Subjects create a damped harmonic oscillator in the fifth task.*

were either physics or applied mathematics majors. We chose this particular user population because MathPad^2 was designed for mathematics and physics students. Subjects' ages ranged from 19 to 23 and all were right-handed; only one had used a pen-based computer before (a PDA). All seven subjects were asked prior to the study if they had used mathematical software before and which packages: six subjects answering yes and had used a variety of different packages including Matlab, Mathematica, and Maple. All seven subjects were paid $30 for their time and effort.

4.3. Evaluation Measures

We evaluate MathPad^2's usability using quantitative and qualitative data from subjects' task performances and from a post-questionnaire. As subjects perform the six experimental tasks, the experimenter records important information about subjects' performances in completing each task, the decisions they made, and counts their mistakes. Performance is characterized by whether subjects can complete each task and how well they do on each subtask. Therefore, the experimenter records whether or not subjects make the appropriate gestures correctly and, if so, whether on the first attempt. Knowing how well subjects perform gestural operations on their first attempt is an important measure because it tells us how easy the gestures are to make and remember. The experimenter also records subjects' choices of implicit and explicit associations in tasks 4–6 so as to get a quantitative metric for their preferences.

After subjects have completed all six tasks they are given a post-questionnaire designed to get their reactions to the MathPad^2 user interface and its perceived usefulness as well as assess how well they remember certain gestures. The post-questionnaire consists of four parts. The first and second parts are adapted from Chin's Questionnaire for User Interface Satisfaction [CDN88] and asks subjects to rate MathPad^2's user interface as a whole and its individual com-

ponents. The third part of the post-questionnaire, the recall test, asks subjects to show what gestures they would use for six different operations. The fourth part of the post-questionnaire was adapted from the Perceived Usefulness portion of Davis's questionnaire for user acceptance [Dav89] and asks whether subjects would use MathPad^2 in their work. After subjects answer the post-questionnaire, the experimenter reviews it with them to make sure their answers are clear and to elaborate further on any specific parts of MathPad^2.

4.4. Mathematical Expression Recognition

An important part of MathPad^2's user interface is that users can write down mathematical expressions as if they were using pencil and paper. Thus, mathematical expression recognition accuracy is an important part of the overall user experience. MathPad^2 uses a writer-dependent mathematical expression recognizer [LaV05] that includes a mathematical symbol recognizer and a mathematical expression parsing system. Each test subject had to provide handwriting samples to train the recognizer and this task took 50 minutes per subject. Note that subjects were given rest periods to ensure they did not get tired during training. Before completing the MathPad^2 tasks, we also had subjects write down symbols and a set of mathematical expressions to test the recognizer's accuracy Overall, the recognizer recognized symbols correctly 95.1% of the time with a standard deviation of 2.65%. The parsing component of our mathematical expression recognizer made correct parsing decisions 90.8% of the time with standard deviation of 4.47%. More detailed results on the mathematical expression recognition evaluation can be found in [LaV05].

4.5. Results and Discussion

4.5.1. Task Performance Results

For the first three tasks, subjects were able to write and recognize all of the mathematical expressions fairly easily. In some cases, they had to use the correction user interface to fix recognition errors, generally getting MathPad^2 to recognize their expressions on the second or third attempt. 27 out of 28 graphing operations (four per subject) were made on the first attempt. Subjects also had to change the domain of a graph; they all completed this operation on the first attempt. 12 out of 14 equation-solving operations (two per subject) were made on the first attempt. The other two equation solves were correctly performed on the second attempt. 34 out of 35 expression evaluations (five per subject) were made on the first attempt. One subject, however, did have difficulty in getting MathPad^2 to recognize $\frac{d^2y}{dx^2}$ and even after multiple attempts was not able to evaluate the expression.

All seven subjects were able to complete tasks 4–6 making the dynamic illustrations. Subjects also had no difficulty in making the drawings for each task and only once did a subject have trouble making a composite drawing element. In the Bouncing Ball task, 12 out of 14 associations were made on the first attempt and 8 of them were done implicitly. Three subjects did have difficulty in getting MathPad^2 to recognize the required mathematical specification for the Bouncing Ball task and, after multiple attempts (about 10 minutes), were given prewritten expressions. The difficulty was not in symbol recognition, but in expression parsing. Two of these subjects had parsing decision accuracies below 90% in the mathematical expression test while the other subject's accuracy was 92%. This result provides evidence indicating that higher parsing decision accuracy is needed. In the Spring task, 56 out of 63 nails (seven per subject) were made on the first attempt. Most of the remaining nails were made on the second attempt. However, one subject required several attempts to make the necessary nails and had to recreate the drawing after inadvertently erasing part of it when erasing an incorrectly recognized nail. Subjects had to make one association in this task, and all seven were made on the first attempt explicitly. For the 2D motion task, subjects made 12 out of 14 associations on the first attempt with all of them made implicitly. One subject did had some difficulty with the implicit associations and needed several attempts to make them correctly.

Overall, subjects did well on all six tasks, considering they had no hands-on training beforehand. Their first attempt performances are summarized in Table 1. Subjects hand no difficulty in making a lasso and tap to recognize mathematical expressions or in using the scribble erase gesture. In only one case did a subject not complete part of a task and this was due to MathPad^2's inability to recognize an expression correctly. Subjects made 160 out of the 175 gestural operations correctly (91.4%) on their first attempt. This number is high considering that subjects had not practiced any of the gestural commands. One subject did have some difficulty with implicit associations due to problems with making taps. The greatest problem subjects had with the six tasks was obtaining correctly recognized expressions in certain situations. That three out of the seven subjects required prewritten mathematics for the Bouncing Ball task shows that the mathematical expression recognizer needs improvement.

4.5.2. Post-Questionnaire Results

Overall Reaction. Table 2 summarizes subject's overall reaction to MathPad^2 and shows that they had a positive reaction to the prototype. When subjects were asked why they chose their rankings, most asserted that MathPad^2 works well, is easy to use, and would be very useful for students in a classroom setting and/or doing homework problems. One subject was "amazed at the application's power". Two subjects claimed MathPad^2 was easy to use but could be frustrating when it had trouble recognizing their handwriting; this frustration explains why the second and third rankings in Table 2 are slightly below the first and fourth rankings.

Ease of Use. Subjects rated different parts of the

First Attempt Gesture Performance Summary			
	Completed	Total	Percentage
Graphing:	27	28	96%
Equation Solving:	12	14	86%
Exp. Evaluation:	34	35	97%
Nails:	56	63	88%
Associations:	31	35	89%
Total:	160	175	91.4%

Table 1: *A breakdown of test subjects' first attempt gesture performance.*

Overall Reaction to MathPad^2		
	Mean	Std. Deviation
Terrible=1, Wonderful = 7	6.42	0.54
Difficult=1, Easy=7	5.57	0.98
Frustrating=1, Satisfying=7	5.57	1.13
Dull=1, Stimulating=7	6.14	0.38

Table 2: *Subjects' average ratings of their overall reaction to MathPad^2 on a scale from 1 to 7.*

MathPad^2 user interface from 1 (easy) to 7 (hard). Table 3 summarizes these results and shows that subjects found the tasks they had to perform easy to do. Subjects gave recognizing expressions the highest average ranking, indicating the fact that some users had trouble getting MathPad^2 to recognize their handwriting. When asked about their ranking, they stated that the gesture for recognizing mathematical expressions (i.e., lasso and tap) was easy to do, but the results of the recognition operation led them to choose a higher ranking on the easy (1) to hard (7) scale.

MathPad^2 User Interface Ease of Use		
	Mean	Std. Deviation
Writing Mathematics	1.43	0.97
Recognizing Mathematics	2.57	1.81
Graphing Functions	1.0	0.0
Solving Equations	1.0	0.0
Evaluating Expressions	1.0	0.0
Grouping Drawing Elements	1.57	0.79
Making Associations	1.71	0.76
Making Nails	1.57	0.59

Table 3: *Subjects' average ratings of ease of use for different components of the MathPad^2 user interface (scale: 1=easy, 7=hard).*

Association Preference. All seven subjects preferred explicit associations, claiming they were easier to remember and simpler and faster to perform. However, they did say that when associations need to be made with a drawing element and a large set of mathematical expressions, the implicit method is more appropriate. We can thus conclude that both association methods have their place in mathematical sketching.

Correction User Interface. Five out of the seven subjects tested found the correction user interface helped them. The two subjects who said no claimed that the alternate lists gave them no help in correcting recognition errors. One subject wanted more choices to appear in the alternate lists, especially in the equation alternate list.

Positive and Negative UI Aspects. Most subjects identified the most positive aspect as its ability to quickly make drawings move as described by mathematical equations. Two subjects claimed that solving equations was one of the user interface's most positive aspect. One subject thought that the best part of MathPad^2's user interface was the scribble erase command; another subject said the user interface's simplicity was its most positive aspect. Three subjects stated that getting MathPad^2 to recognize certain symbols and equations correctly was the most negative aspect of the user interface. Two subjects stated that the lack of interactive feedback for implicit associations was a significant drawback, and one subject stated that a negative aspect was the time necessary to get used to the gestural commands. Finally, two subjects said that MathPad^2's user interface had no negative aspects.

Overall Ease of Use. On average, subjects gave MathPad^2 a 1.86 (1 equals easy and 7 equals hard) with a standard deviation of 0.69. When they were asked to explain their ratings, two dominant themes emerged. First, subjects found the interface easy to use and remember, but were in some cases frustrated by problems in mathematical expression recognition. However, the subjects who had trouble with recognition all felt it would improve with more practice. Those subjects were also asked if they would still use MathPad^2 in spite of their recognition problems; they all said they could deal with these problems because of the functionality MathPad^2 would give them. Second, subjects felt the interface was easy to use once it was explained, a result that helps to validate our demonstration-based teaching protocol.

Gesture Recall Test. Subject were asked how to invoke gestural commands for graphing, solving equations, evaluating expressions, recognizing a mathematical expression, making nails, and making implicit associations. This part of the questionnaire took place about 5 to 10 minutes after they used MathPad^2. Subjects answered 38 out of the 42 recall questions correctly (six per subject) for a recall rate of 90%. Of the four questions subjects answered incorrectly, three subjects missed the equation solving gesture (squiggle) and one missed the expression evaluation gesture (equal and tap). The 90% recall rate indicates that subjects had little difficulty remembering MathPad^2 gestures except for the equation solving gesture. Even though three out of the seven subjects forgot the equation solving gesture, they still claimed it was easy to use based on their mean ranking in Table 3.

Likely Usage. Table 4 summarizes subjects' ratings on the different "perceived usefulness" statements, on a scale of 1 (unlikely) to 7 (likely). Most would use

MathPad^2 Perceived Usefulness		
	Mean	Std. Deviation
Accomplish Tasks Faster	5.14	1.95
Improve Performance	4.71	2.36
Increase Productivity	5.0	1.91
Enhance Effectiveness	5.14	2.04
Easier To Do Work	5.57	1.90
Useful In Work	5.42	2.37

Table 4: *Subjects' average ratings of the perceived usefulness of MathPad^2 in their work (scale: 1=unlikely, 7=likely).*

MathPad^2 in their work. When asked to explain their ratings, four subjects stated that the application would help them to do their classwork and obtain a better understanding of problems and concepts. However, there was no consensus on whether MathPad^2 would speed their understanding of these problems and concepts. One subject said that the ability to quickly solve equations and make graphs would be very beneficial. Two subjects said they did not think they would use MathPad^2 in its current form in their work (explaining the high standard deviations in Table 4). Both of these subjects work in theoretical physics, one in optics and the other in modern physics. However, one of these subject stated she would have used MathPad^2 during beginning physics classes while the other stated he would use MathPad^2 if it had support for light ray and optics diagrams. Finally, all seven subjects felt the application would be a good tool for teachers of introductory mathematics and physics classes.

4.5.3. Discussion

The results of our initial MathPad^2 usability study suggest that, based on our evaluation criteria, the MathPad^2 user interface is, in general, intuitive with subjects picking up the interface with relative ease. With only minimal training, most gestures are easy to remember and use. However, if we examine the first attempt task performance results (Table 1) in conjunction with the recall test from our post-questionnaire, we see that the equation solving gesture has the lowest first attempt accuracy and was the most difficult to remember. This indicates that this gesture is not as intuitive as the others. Additionally, if we look deeper into users' preferences for making associations, we see that they preferred explicit associations and of the four associations that were not made on their first attempt, all four were implicit. Again, this result suggests that explicit associations are more intuitive than implicit ones. First attempt performance for making nails was also a bit lower than expected, but we feel this might have been an implementation issue. In terms of perceived utility, subjects think the application is a powerful tool that beginning physics and mathematics students could use to help solve problems and better understand scientific concepts.

Most subjects performed the tasks with little trouble, while a few had some difficulty, stemming primarily from problems with mathematical expression recognition. However, these subjects also said they were willing to accept these recognition problems, given what MathPad^2 can offer them. This result is somewhat contrary to our expectations about the negative impact of our mathematical expression recognizer on MathPad^2 usability. Nevertheless, we need better mathematical expression recognition that will perform robustly across a larger user population. Although these results do not tell us how much more accurate the recognizer needs to be, its clear that a mean accuracy of 90.8% for making correct parsing decisions is too low. A better correction user interface could also go a long way to helping with users' frustrations when incorrect recognitions occur. In addition, more interactive feedback is needed for implicit associations, and the equation solving gesture should be redesigned.

Although the results of our initial evaluation are positive, we recognize it can be argued that there are two limitations with our study. First, we only used seven test subjects. We could have had more subjects, but we felt that seven was appropriate for an initial evaluation of MathPad^2 and its gestural interface, given one of our main goals was to determine whether larger studies were needed. Second, we did not compare MathPad^2's user interface with any other interface metaphors. Although this could be considered a limitation, our goal in this evaluation was to determine how well users could use the MathPad^2 interface, not whether it was better than any other interface. For this work, we feel our experimental design was suited to answering our intended questions. However, as we perform future usability tests to gain a deeper understanding of the benefits of mathematical sketching, we will need more comparative experimental designs with larger subject numbers.

Given the results of our evaluation, we plan to make improvements to MathPad^2 by adding more functionality and improving the weaker points of the interface as well as improving the parsing component of our mathematical expression recognizer. Given the generally positive results of our evaluation, we are confident in pursuing further MathPad^2 experimentation. Thus, we plan to explore the pedagogical benefits of MathPad^2 in a summative evaluation where students will use MathPad^2 as part of a mathematics or introductory physics course.

5. Conclusion

We have presented an initial evaluation of MathPad^2, a prototype application for making dynamic illustrations using the mathematical sketching paradigm, to test its intuitiveness and perceived utility. Our evaluation suggests that MathPad^2's user interface is generally intuitive, although some parts of the interface need to be reevaluated. Additionally, the MathPad^2 application is perceived to be a powerful tool for exploring mathematics and physics concepts. Although some of our test subjects had some difficulty with getting the system to recognize their mathematical expressions, they still gave MathPad^2 positive feedback and would use MathPad^2 regardless of these issues because of its functionality. These results also support future MathPad^2 development and longer term evaluations.

Acknowledgements

Special thanks to Robert Zeleznik and Andries van Dam for valuable discussions. This work is sponsored in part by a gift from Microsoft.

References

[Alv00] ALVARADO C.: *A Natural Sketching Environment: Bringing the Computer into Early Stages of Mechanical Design.* Tech. rep., Master's Thesis, Department of Electrical Engineering and Computer Science, Massachusetts Institute of Technology, May 2000.

[Bor79] BORNING A.: *A Constraint-Oriented Simulation Laboratory.* PhD thesis, Stanford University, 1979.

[CDN88] CHIN J., DIEHL V. A., NORMAN K. L.: Development of an instrument measuring user satisfaction of the human-computer interface. In *Proceedings of the ACM Conference on Human Factors and Computing Systems (CHI'88)* (1988), pp. 213–218.

[CT98] CHRISTIAN W., TITUS. A.: Developing web-based curricula using java physlets. *Computers in Physics 12*, 3 (May-June 1998), 227–232.

[DACP04] DAVIS J., AGRAWALA M., CHUANG E., POPOVIC Z.: A sketching interface for articulated figure animation. In *Proceedings of the Eurographics/SIGGRAPH Symposium on Computer Animation* (2004), pp. 320–328.

[Dav89] DAVIS F. D.: Perceived usefulness, perceived ease of use, and user acceptance of information technology. *MIS Quarterly 13*, 3 (Sept. 1989), 319–340.

[KGS04] KARA L. B., GENNARI L., STAHOVICH T. F.: A sketch-based interface for the design and analysis of simple vibratory mechanical systems. In *Proceedings of ASME International Design Engineering Technical Conferences* (2004).

[LaV05] LAVIOLA J.: *Mathematical Sketching: A New Approach to Creating and Exploring Dynamic Illustrations.* PhD thesis, Brown University, 2005.

[LZ04] LAVIOLA J., ZELEZNIK R.: Mathpad^2: A system for the creation and exploration of mathematical sketches. *ACM Transactions on Graphics (Proceedings of SIGGRAPH 2004) 23*, 3 (August 2004), 432–440.

[PBLP99] PICKERING J., BHUPHAIBOOL D., LAVIOLA J., POLLARD N.: *The Coach's Playbook.* Tech. rep., Master's Thesis, Department of Computer Science, Brown University, CS-99-08, May 1999.

External Reviewers

Baxter, William
Catalano, Chiara
Ferreira, Alfredo
Kara, Burak
Monti, Marina
Santos, Pedro
Shesh, Amit

Cover Image Credits

front cover:

Dana Sharon and Michiel van de Panne:
"Constellation Models for Sketch Recognition", pp. 19–26

back cover:

Hung-Li Jason Chen, Faramarz F. Samavati, Mario Costa Sousa, and J. Ross Mitchell:
"Sketch-based Volumetric Seeded Region Growing", pp. 123–129

Color Plates

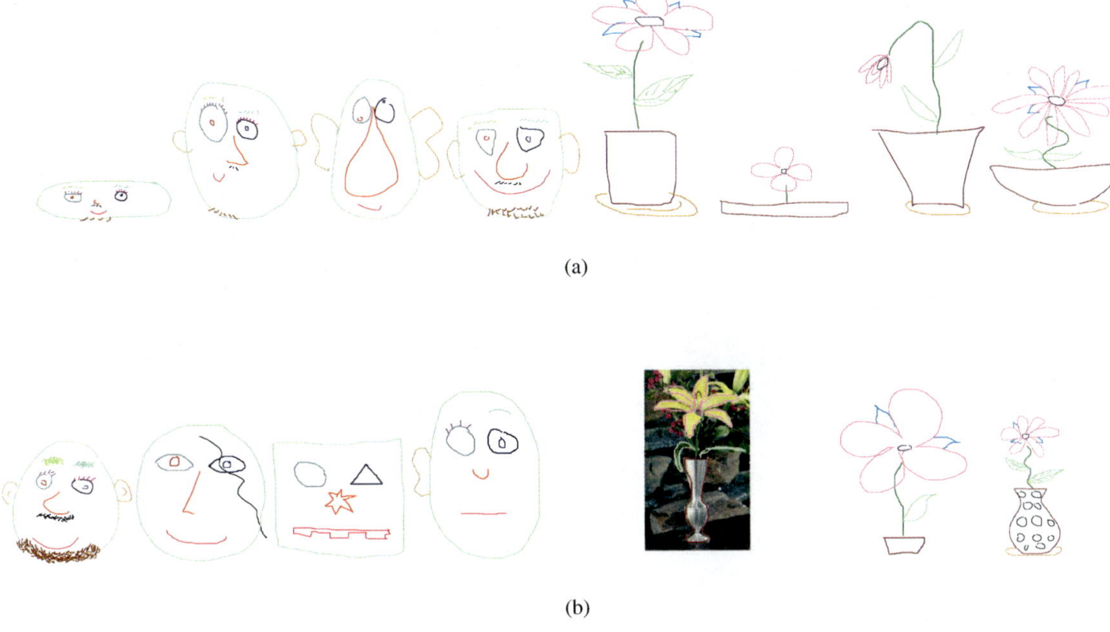

(a)

(b)

Figure 8: *Color plate. (a) Training examples. (b) Successfully-labelled test examples.*

Bartolo et al. / A Sketch Based Interface using the Co-occurrence Matrix

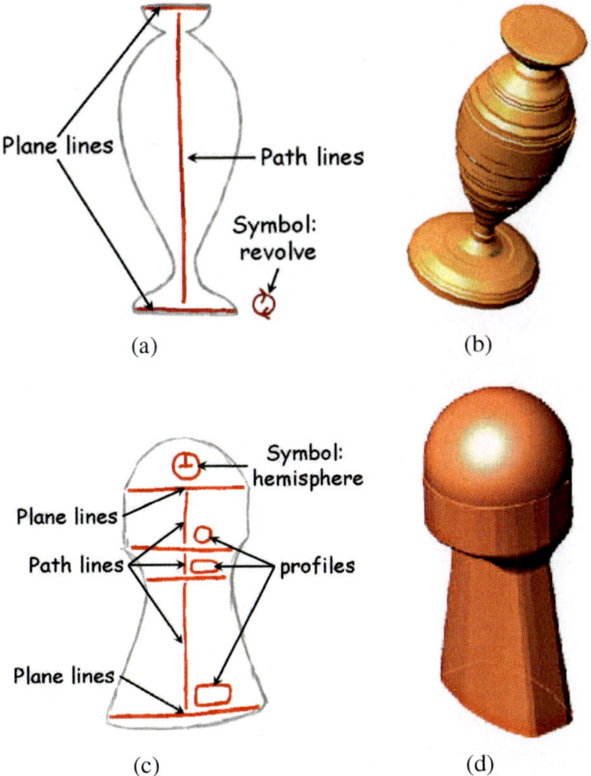

Figure 9: *An example of the sketching procedure*

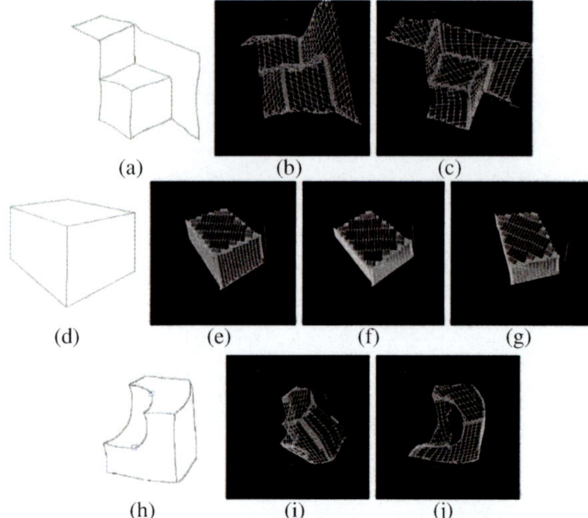

Figure 8: *Various results. Critical points in e) are outlined in blue. a,e,h) are the input drawings. b-d,f,g,i,j) are the output models.*

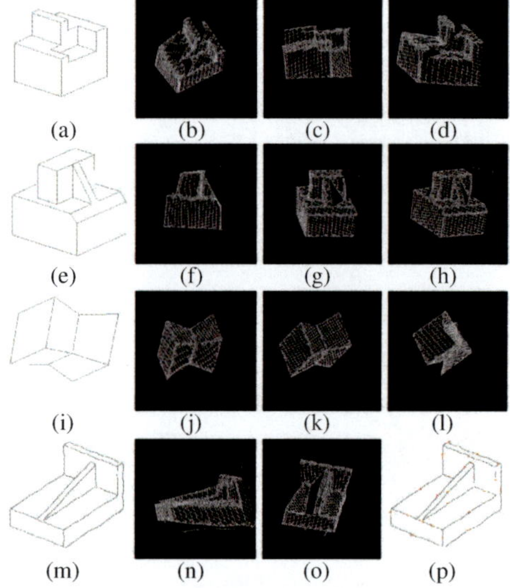

Figure 9: *Input drawings of polyhedral surfaces are shown at left. Output models are shown in the three right columns. p) Line labels can be calculated based on the constraints produced by our system.*

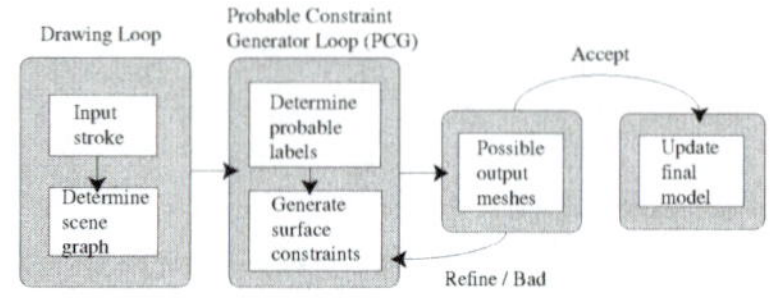

Figure 10: *This diagram illustrates the process of our system and the relationship between the principle components.*

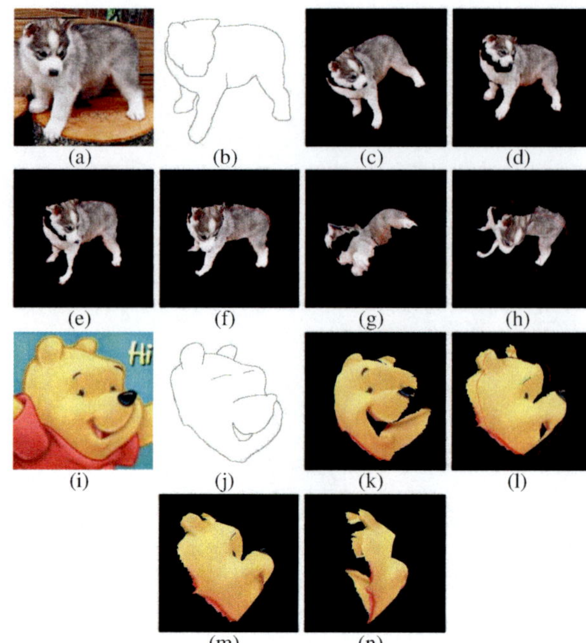

Figure 11: *a,i) source images. b,j) drawings based on the source images. c-h,k-n) output models based on the input drawings, texture mapped with the source images.*

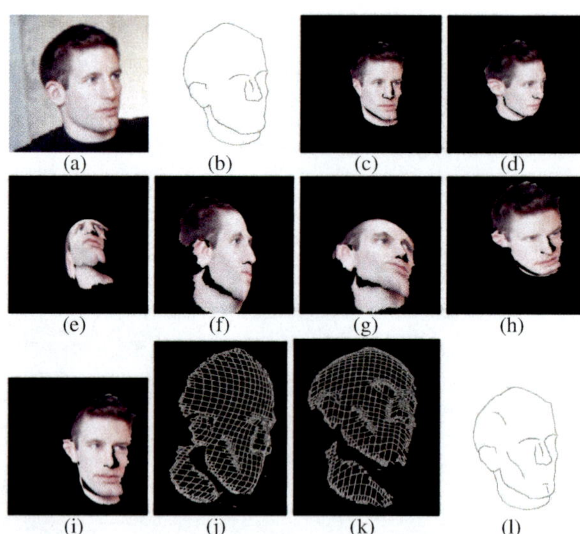

Figure 12: *a) source image. b) input drawing. c-i) output models, texture mapped with the source image. j-k) output meshes. Such models are often difficult to produce since many discontinuities present in a) are not represented in b). This occurs because some lines, such as those shown in l), are assumed by both viewer and artist when the object depicted is well understood by both.*

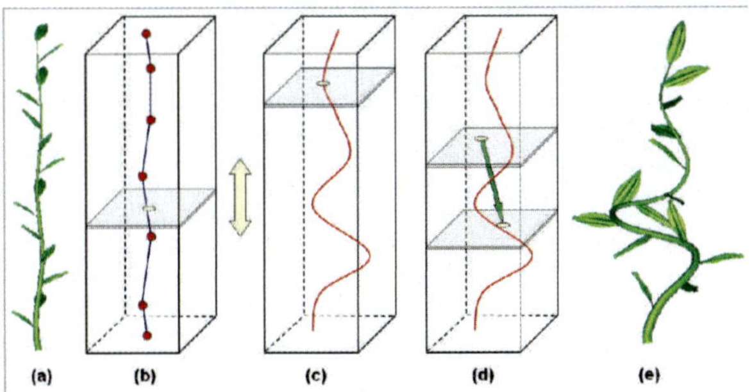

Figure 1: *Given a 3D plant model's (a) skeleton the user selects skeletal segments (b - blue) and sketches corresponding strokes (c) using the* 3D Tractus. *These strokes together with macro sketch-based motion indicators for overall growth direction (d) control growth variation (e).*

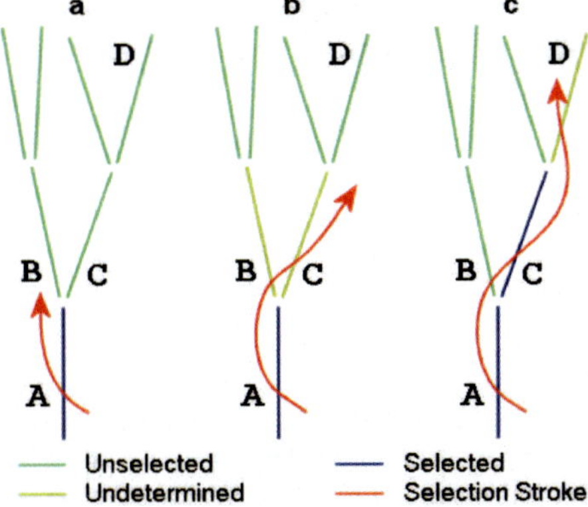

Figure 5: *Selection of branches A-D; Coloured segments show selected, unselected, and undetermined branches with progress of curved selection stroke (a–c).*

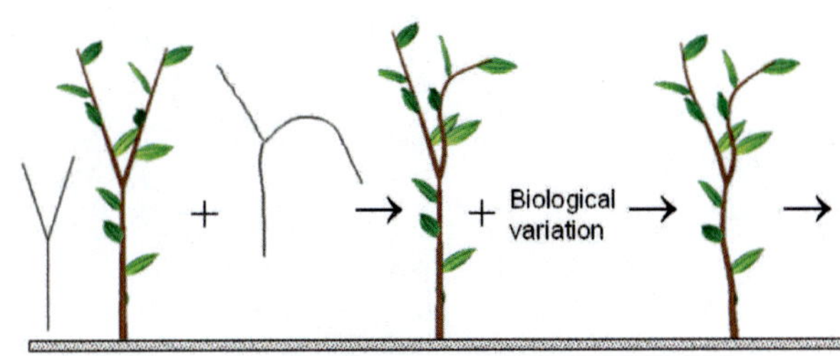

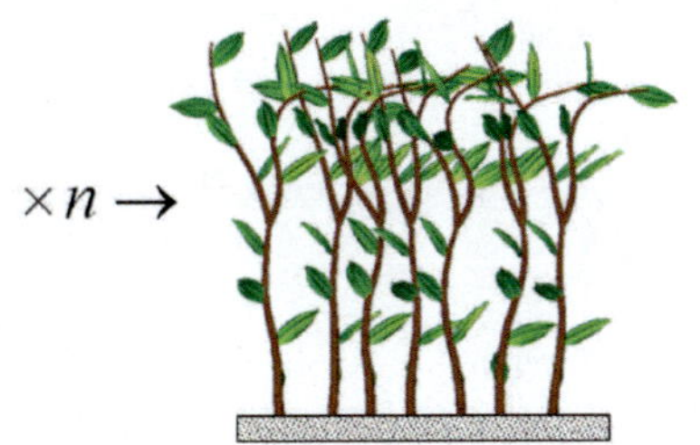

Figure 8: *Sketch-based variation of branching structures.* **Top Row:** *Original model and skeleton with stroke and biological variation* **Bottom row:** *collection of seven instances.*

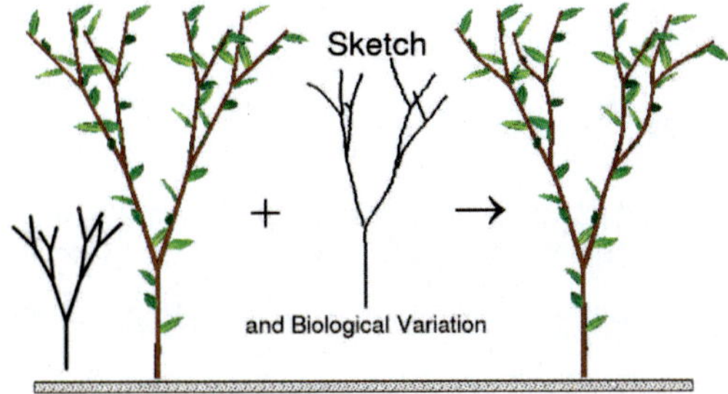

Figure 9: *Figure 8's model with more branching levels.*

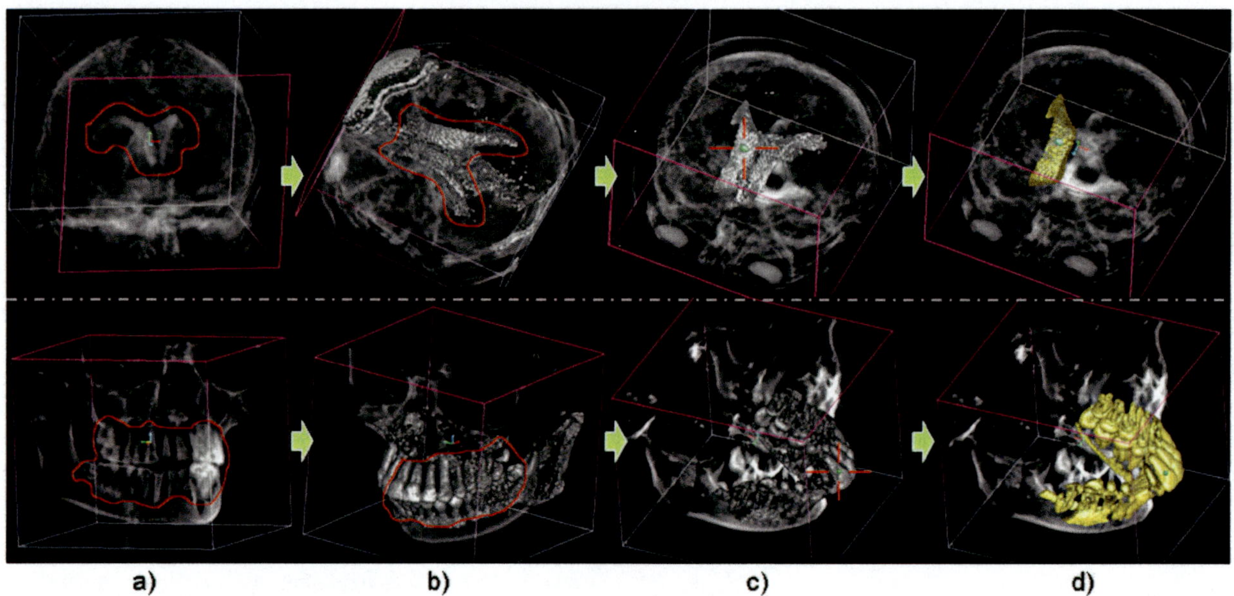

Figure 10: *Segmentation of right ventricle (top) and partial teeth (bottom). (a) Raw volume, X-ray, with sketched-region. (b) Resulting cut, rotating the view, new sketch. (c) Resulting cut, rotating the view, plating the seed. (d) Region growing contained within sketched/resulting volume from (c).*

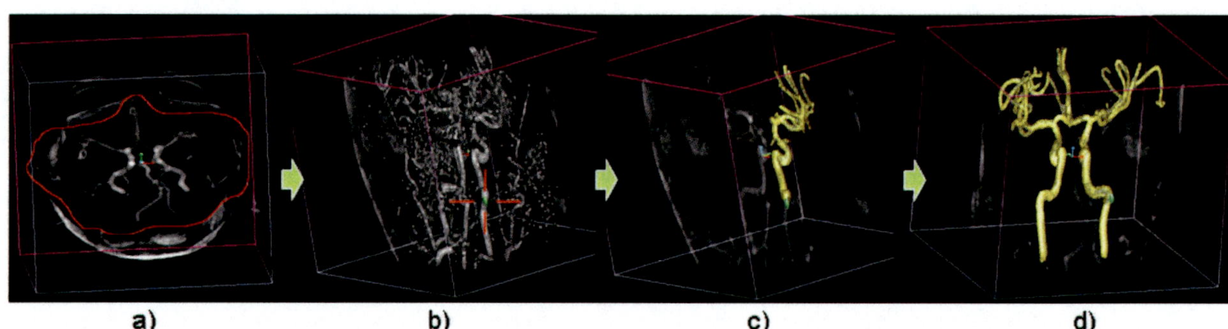

Figure 11: *Segmentation of carotid and cerebral arteries. (a) Raw volume, X-ray, with sketched-region. (b) Resulting cut, rotating the view, plating the seed on the arterial branch. (c,d) Region growing contained within sketched/resulting volume from (b).*

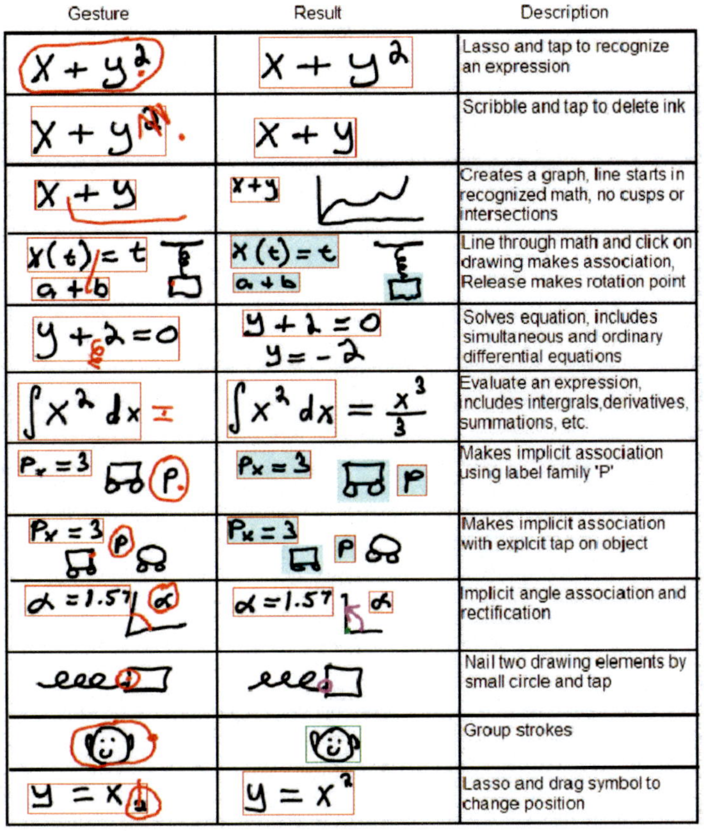

Gesture	Result	Description
$x + y^2$	$x + y^2$	Lasso and tap to recognize an expression
$x + y$	$x + y$	Scribble and tap to delete ink
$x + y$	$x+y$	Creates a graph, line starts in recognized math, no cusps or intersections
$x(t) = t$, $a + b$	$x(t) = t$, $a + b$	Line through math and click on drawing makes association, Release makes rotation point
$y + 2 = 0$	$y + 2 = 0$, $y = -2$	Solves equation, includes simultaneous and ordinary differential equations
$\int x^2 \, dx$	$\int x^2 \, dx = \frac{x^3}{3}$	Evaluate an expression, includes intergrals, derivatives, summations, etc.
$P_x = 3$	$P_x = 3$	Makes implicit association using label family 'P'
$P_x = 3$	$P_x = 3$	Makes implicit association with explcit tap on object
$\alpha = 1.57$	$\alpha = 1.57$	Implicit angle association and rectification
		Nail two drawing elements by small circle and tap
		Group strokes
$y = x^2$	$y = x^2$	Lasso and drag symbol to change position

Figure 5: *MathPad^2's gestural commands. Gesture strokes in the first column are shown here in red. In the second column, cyan-highlighted strokes provide association feedback (the highlighting color changes each time a new association is made), and magenta strokes show nail and angle association/rectification feedback.*